D0065419

THE POLITICS OF EQUALITY

New Zealand's Adventures in Democracy

THE POLITICS
OF EQUALITY

New Zealand's Adventures in Democracy

BY

LESLIE LIPSON

THE UNIVERSITY OF CHICAGO PRESS
CHICAGO · ILLINOIS

THE UNIVERSITY OF CHICAGO PRESS, CHICAGO 37
Cambridge University Press, London, N.W. 1, England
W. J. Gage & Co., Limited, Toronto 2B, Canada

TO MY MOTHER
and
TO THE MEMORY OF MY FATHER

It is possible to imagine an extreme point at which freedom and equality would meet and blend. Let us suppose that all the people take a part in the government, and that each one of them has an equal right to take a part in it. As no one is different from his fellows, none can exercise a tyrannical power; men will be perfectly free because they are all entirely equal; and they will all be perfectly equal because they are entirely free. To this ideal state democratic nations tend.

—Alexis de Tocqueville

PREFACE

IN WRITING this book, I have tried to kill three birds with one stone. Although New Zealand has been the subject of a fairly extensive literature, one major gap has hitherto existed in the available published studies. There has been no modern work which attempted a full and critical treatment of the governmental system in both its political and its administrative phases. The contributions of Bryce, Reeves, and Siegfried, brilliant though they remain, are now in certain respects out of date. More recent scholarship, like that of Morrell or J. C. Beaglehole, has illuminated the Dominion's history, or, as in the work of Condliffe and Hare, has dealt amply and ably with economic development and organization. While avoiding, so far as I could, any overlap with their writings, I have sought to offer a new and comprehensive analysis of government in a youngish state which in the course of a century has initiated a significant synthesis both of democratic politics with social economics and of liberty with equality.

I lived in the Dominion from the beginning of 1939 to the end of 1946. As the first professor of political science and director of the School of Public Administration at Victoria University College, University of New Zealand, I enjoyed an unrivaled opportunity to watch the day-by-day operations of government in the capital city and to participate in the work and vicissitudes of those grim years. So far from relegating political issues to the background, the circumstances of war served, as is customary in times of stress, to etch in bolder strokes the fundamental strengths and weaknesses of the national group and its individual citizens. The material of which the book is composed has been drawn not only from public documents and nonofficial literature but still more from current observation and from discussion with parliamentarians of all political shades, with civil servants high and low, with diplomatic representatives of other governments, with members of the press, and with people in varied pursuits and occupations.

Second, as to method, I have attempted to combine an analytical with a historical approach. Believing in the truth of Seeley's dictum about the bond between political science and history, I found that fruitful comparisons could be drawn by dividing the subject into two parts—democracy in evolution and democracy in operation—by analyzing similar topics in the earlier period and the more recent, and by studying similarities and contrasts between the nineteenth-century foundations and the twentieth-century superstructure. The momentous election of 1890 provided a convenient line of demarcation, as the following pages will show.

In the third place, because no people lives unto itself alone but receives from and gives to others, I have not confined the treatment solely to New Zealand. Wherever possible I have suggested and explored comparisons of the Dominion's problems and solutions with those of larger democracies, especially Britain and the United States. As the world attempts to strengthen a system of international organization among states thrown ever into closer contact, the study of comparative government will, I am sure, lead to a knowledge of principles and lessons upon which a workable global order may be the more securely founded.

The debt that I owe to the many good friends in New Zealand with whom I was able to discuss ideas, events, and personalities is an obligation which I gratefully acknowledge. To list them all by name would be impossible; to make a selection would be invidious. I ask each of them, therefore, to accept these collective thanks. For permission to incorporate here some material I previously published in articles my thanks are also due to the editors of the following journals: (American) *Public Administration Review*, (American) *State Government*, (Australian and New Zealand) *Historical Studies*, (British) *Journal of Public Administration*, and (New Zealand) *Journal of Public Administration*.

One supreme obligation must finally be mentioned, though it can in no wise be adequately acknowledged. In all stages of research, preparation, and writing, I have received the invaluable help of my wife. Her discerning insight has modified many a judgment, just as her literary taste has aided in polishing the style. What is more, she has steadfastly endured those lengthy silences and absent reveries which are the common lot of the wives of professors who perpetrate books.

LESLIE LIPSON

SWARTHMORE, PENNSYLVANIA
April 1947

TABLE OF CONTENTS

LIST OF TABLES

xiii

xiv LIST OF TABLES

CHAPTER I

INTRODUCTION

NEW ZEALAND has several claims on the attention of all who are concerned about the present and future of democratic government. There in two isolated islands of the South Pacific a pattern of life that combines some traditional features of a British origin with other elements drawn from the needs of a new environment has been evolved by a white population of one and three-quarter millions. Their political system was first organized just over a century ago, a lapse of time which now enables it to be viewed in perspective. Since that beginning in 1840 their institutions have been continuously modified by the New Zealanders themselves and in a democratic direction. Adapted to the attitudes of the community it serves, the system of government has thus acquired a character of its own. Both the machinery of state and the spirit in which it is used share the generic features of the democratic family tree—tinged, however, with an individualized expression.

As a setting for an experiment in democracy, New Zealand has possessed many natural advantages from the outset of its political existence. It is climatically well suited for settlement by Europeans—so well indeed that among the white population both the death rate and the infant mortality rate are the lowest of any country in the world. Climate has been equally favorable to the pastoral industry which forms the mainstay of New Zealand's economy. For every human being New Zealand contains twenty sheep, three head of cattle, and a third of a pig. The humidity of the atmosphere encourages a quick growth of the country's most valuable natural resource, its grass; animals do not even have to be housed over the winter months; and, unlike her twelve-hundred-miles distant neighbor Australia, this Dominion has no lack of water. Geography, therefore, has lent its beneficial aid to the course of economic development.

The same factor of geography has provided no less profound an

1

influence on politics. Its island character and its isolation from
the main western and oriental centers of population were, until
recent years, a guaranty of military security. It is, of course, no
accident that the principal democracies of the world have been
situated in areas that normally were relatively safe from threat of
invasion. Of European countries, Britain and Switzerland enjoy
the longest continuous tradition of democratic institutions. The
geographical reasons for that historical fact were expressed by
Wordsworth, who happened in these lines to write indifferent
poetry but good political science:

> Two Voices are there; one is of the sea,
> One of the mountains; each a mighty Voice:
> In both from age to age thou didst rejoice,
> They were thy chosen music, Liberty!

In France, on the other hand, democracy has never been so
firmly established. The weak land frontier on the east made it
necessary in peacetime to maintain a large standing army with an
accompaniment of some antidemocratic tendencies. The United
States must attribute the development in the nineteenth century
of its federal democracy partly to the absence of any comparable
power in the Western Hemisphere and partly to the spaciousness
of the adjacent oceans. The Atlantic and the Pacific were two
unseen signatories to the Constitution in 1787.

During its formative years democracy throve in New Zealand,
as also in Australia, behind the protective shields of the vast
Pacific and the British Navy, for a country of one and three-
quarter millions must needs have some protection in an international jungle where justice for the weak is usually interpreted
according to the interests of the strong. Not since the Maori wars
were concluded in the late sixties of the last century has the
Dominion required a standing army for its own domestic security. In 1899, in 1914, and in 1939 it had to improvise its army
anew, creating it from a vigorous, but not a militaristic, people.
Only in recent decades did the ambitions of Japan diminish the
distances from which an invasion of New Zealand could be
launched and make of the United States the co-guarantor of the
democracies in the Pacific region.

But the experiment in democracy depends not only on the

physical element but also on the human stock and their cultural heritage. When the whites began colonizing New Zealand, it was already partially peopled by the Maoris,[1] whose numerical superiority and fighting prowess assured them in those early days of a healthy respect. Later when the Europeans outstripped the Maori population and were rapidly purchasing their lands, tension between the races and their cultures terminated in war. Worsted and weakened after a decade of hostilities, this Polynesian people passed into a physical and cultural decline from which it took them half a century to recover. Race relations nowadays have been disposed of satisfactorily from the white point of view. If the question be viewed quantitatively, the Maoris now form about 6 per cent of the whole population; and New Zealand therefore escapes the problems that arise in South Africa, where the whites are outnumbered four to one. If it be viewed qualitatively, the Maoris are considered by anthropologists to be among the foremost native peoples of the Pacific as regards intelligence and character. There is no such gulf in the standard of personal capacity between the white and the colored New Zealander as between the white Australian and the aborigine. Race equality for the Maori people has thus become a cardinal principle in this Dominion, formalized into constitutional law and proclaimed in the perorations of political spokesmen. Miscegenation has been fairly common and has seldom carried with it a social stigma. Maoris possess equal voting rights, receive special representation in Parliament, and take cabinet office as ministers of the Crown.

From their point of view the Maoris see this question as members of a minority whose ethnological and cultural antecedents differ from that of the majority. By a remarkable feat of self-regeneration they surmounted their crisis stage and have conducted their own adjustment of a Polynesian to a European culture. Some Maoris will point out, as Negroes are known to argue in the northern part of the United States, that the equality conceded to them is at times more nominal than real. Others will refer to sporadic local symptoms of a color bar. Others again, as

1. The Maoris were mostly concentrated then, as they are now, in the northern half of the North Island.

among the Waikato tribes, still resent the mode of their treatment after the hostilities of the sixties. But on the whole they are
content with their status and co-operate, in war as in peace, with
the pakehas.[2]

While New Zealand is relatively free from race friction, it is
also strikingly devoid of contention between national groups
within its white population. The delicate and touchy issues that
plague South Africa and Canada with their dual national origins
have here no counterpart. The simple reason is that 98 per cent of
New Zealanders were drawn ultimately from the British Isles.
When that figure is analyzed, it can be found that the bulk came
from England, and the next largest section from Scotland. Irish
immigrants did not play so large a part in the settlement of New
Zealand as in that of Australia or of the United States. This same
point is reinforced by a reference to religious affiliations. At the
census of 1936, 40 per cent declared their adherence to the
Church of England; 25 per cent were Presbyterians; only 13 per
cent were Catholics. Sectarian controversy, therefore, is precluded by numerical disparities, as well as by the geographical
dispersion of the religious minorities. Hence like-mindedness,
similarity of attitudes, cultural homogeneity—these are characteristic of community life in New Zealand. Its democracy is the
political expression of the social predominance of English and
Scots Protestants. Lord Balfour once wrote of the British constitution: "Our whole political machinery presupposes a people
so fundamentally at one that they can safely afford to bicker."[3]
He could have appropriately cited New Zealand to illustrate his
text.

An additional factor which exempts this Dominion from many
of the difficulties encountered by governments elsewhere is its
size. Smallness, when viewed from some angles, may be thought a
blessing. Reducing the scale of social problems, it lessens their
complexity and intricacy. A political unit the size of New
Zealand is clearly far easier to govern and administer than
Britain or the United States or the Soviet Union. Democracy, it

2. The Maori name for the European inhabitants.
3. Introduction to Walter Bagehot's *The English Constitution* ("World's Classics,"
No. CCCXXX [London: Oxford University Press, 1928]), p. xxiv.

can be argued, began its career in smallish city-states and operates less effectively the more extensive its scope. Those intrusted with power, whether politically elected to office or appointed as civil servants, may lose touch with the population they serve if it is either too numerous or scattered over too wide an area. Increasing size demands tighter organization, which tends in turn to become unwieldy or even to inhibit democratic control.

It would, of course, be idle to deny that features which are advantageous for some purposes bring disadvantages in other respects. Isolation may have provided shelter and safety in a troubled world. But, while the volume of its international relations is diminished, New Zealand loses those that are fruitful as well as those which are dangerous. Even the radio and the telegraph cannot fully compensate for the infrequency of those direct personal contacts which spread ideas and information, for new thoughts customarily emerge in the large centers of population, where many minds can interchange their wares, and filter through more slowly to those who dwell on the periphery of things. So it is again with cultural homogeneity and with smallness of size. These may remove the occasions for conflict between social groups, but they may also rob a community of internal color and variety. Monotony can sometimes be the price of uniformity. New Zealand, in short, like every country, has the defects of its virtues. The factors which make a democracy possible also prescribe the conditions which mold its character.

Such, then, were the foundations, laid partly by nature and partly by the social heritage, on which the New Zealanders could build. In the economic sphere their efforts have resulted in a system whose prosperity is based upon the export of four products: wool, lamb, butter, and cheese. Together these amount to over 90 per cent of the value of all exports. The principal market, moreover, which consumes three-quarters of these commodities, lies twelve thousand miles away in Britain; and from that source comes more than a half of New Zealand's imports. The prosperity of the Dominion has depended on the continued good will of a mother-country at the other side of the globe. This economic tie-up is further strengthened by the New Zealand indebtedness to the British investor. Of a public debt, which in 1938 totaled

£290,000,000 no less than £157,000,000 (or 54 per cent) was domiciled in London.[4]

Although the New Zealand economy is closely linked externally with that of Britain, internally it departs widely from the British model. It is a peculiarity of this Dominion—and one much to its credit—that it lacks the great extremes of wealth and poverty which exist elsewhere. New Zealand does, of course, contain its poor and its rich, its slums and its mansions, but the gap that separates them is considerably narrower than in the big democracies. The New Zealand poor are better off than those of Britain and America, while the New Zealand well-to-do would seem penurious in comparison with the millionaire captains of modern industry and finance. Part of the reason for this lies in the difference between the resources of New Zealand and of larger countries. The economic opportunities for amassing huge fortunes simply do not exist there. Part of it, however, can be attributed to the results of governmental policies deliberately conceived and executed with the aim of leveling down and up. Steeply graduated taxation both on income and on land, comprehensive programs of social insurance, widespread extension of educational facilities and other social services—these measures have succeeded in more evenly distributing the necessities of life.

To speak of the standard of living obtaining in any country is admittedly to employ a hazy and imprecise conception. Nevertheless, those who attempt international comparisons commonly include New Zealand among the peoples whose material prosperity is highest. "Few economists," writes E. D. Simon, "would doubt that the following group as to the standards of living of the most prosperous countries in the world to-day [1939] is substantially correct. Group I: The United States, Canada, Australia, New Zealand. Group II: Norway, Sweden, Denmark, Switzerland, England, Holland. Group III: includes Finland, Germany, Italy."[5] New Zealand's ranking in that list can readily be justified if one refers to some of the familiar indices of material well-being in modern civilization. When figures for all countries

4. The recent war has resulted in an increase of the amount domiciled in New Zealand and in a slight reduction in the indebtedness to Britain.

5. *The Smaller Democracies* (London: Left Book Club [Gollancz], 1939), p. 172.

are compared, this Dominion possesses per head of population the third highest number of motorcars, of telephones, and of radio sets in the world. Incidentally, it will be noticed in Simon's classification that all the states placed in the first two groups were democracies in 1939. That raises the question whether they were prosperous because they were democratic or democratic because they were prosperous. Is prosperity the economic reward earned by those peoples which organize their governments democratically? Or is democracy a political luxury which only the richer members of the international family can afford?

In the political sphere New Zealand has developed a type of democracy which reflects its economic system and in turn reacts upon it. For purposes of study it is helpful to distinguish between the spirit of a democracy and its institutions. The spirit consists of its dominating ideals, its prevailing attitudes and community mores. It is this spirit which decides how the institutions—that is to say, the machinery of state, the governmental procedures, and the network of legal rights and duties—shall operate in practice. The distinction is needed, for, as Aristotle long ago observed, a democratic form of government can be manipulated so as to function in conformity with nondemocratic principles and vice versa.[6]

Democracies everywhere are dedicated in spirit to the twin ideals of liberty and equality. They vary, however, according to which of these two they regard as of greater importance, for liberty and equality may under some circumstances be incompatible. If individual liberty be pushed too far, it creates golden opportunities for the ruthless and the strong and tends to breed inequalities; if equality, however, be carried to the extreme, it may end in uniformity and stifle freedom. The problem of democracy, as seen from the angle of these governing ideals, is to promote a harmonious balance between them, to multiply moderate degrees of liberty and equality into each other. The United States is an example of a democracy which has traditionally emphasized liberty as its foremost principle. It is true, of course, that equality figures prominently in the opening phrases

6. *Politics*, trans. H. W. C. Davis (London: Oxford University Press, 1931), p. 158.

of the Declaration of Independence and in some of the amendments to the Constitution. But in practice both the political and
the economic systems have been arranged throughout most of
American history to produce the maximum of liberty. In consequence, equality has sometimes suffered—particularly in the
economic field. It is a statue of Liberty which greets the visitor
sailing toward Manhattan Island.

In New Zealand, if any sculptured allegory were to be placed at
the approaches of Auckland or Wellington harbor, it would assuredly be a statue of Equality. For equalitarianism is there regarded as the core of the democratic doctrine. If something good
is to be had, then, the New Zealander will argue, let it be spread
as widely as is possible. The more who can participate, the better.
Indeed it is undemocratic for any to be excluded from a share in
benefits that others enjoy. New Zealand could well subscribe to
the attitude expressed in the words of Walt Whitman:

> I speak the pass-word primeval, I give the sign of democracy.
> By God! I will accept nothing which all cannot have their
>   counterpart of on the same terms.

It was such a spirit as this which exorcised from New Zealand the
extremes of poverty and wealth, which created the high standard
of living, and which made sure that it was fairly evenly spread.
Equalitarianism governs politics and economics alike; and in
current New Zealand parlance the term "undemocratic" is
usually synonymous with "unequal." This feature of the
Dominion's life is largely understandable by the colonists' reaction in a new, young country to the privileges and inequalities
of the social system they had known in Britain.

The stress on equality has inevitably modified the interpretation of liberty. If liberty be defined in an individualistic manner
as absence of restraint, or doing what one pleases, then there is
little of it in New Zealand. If, however, it be interpreted as a
social concept, and means doing what one pleases with neither
more nor less advantages than others, then liberty in that sense
exists in New Zealand—but governed always by equalitarian
limitations. Equality, of course, often leads to leveling-down as
well as to leveling-up; and ability can sometimes be leveled down
in addition to incomes. This good principle can thus be carried

to excess with unfortunate results. Democracy itself can imitate the policy of Periander the Greek and remove the heads that stand above the crowd. There is a tendency for the idolaters of equality to sacrifice talent on the altar of their god.

The same reasons which underlie the policy of equalitarianism explain that extensiveness of its state activities for which New Zealand has acquired a reputation. It was in the nineties that the young colony, as it then was, attracted attention overseas for its program of compulsory arbitration of labor disputes and of forcing the sale of large estates accumulated by land monopolists. The habit of boldly expanding the functions of government in new directions had in fact struck its roots earlier than that and has since been steadily continued during the present century. Laissez faire died in New Zealand around the time when democracy was born, and this conjunction of events was not fortuitous. A citizenry newly enfranchised in a country which was theirs for the building sought to remedy economic abuses by the power of a state which they could command. Inaugurated in the seventies, the policy of "colonial governmentalism"[7] was intensified in the nineties, was maintained during the war of 1914–18 and afterward, and was further stimulated in the late thirties and forties. All political parties—Liberal, Reform (or Conservative), and Labor—have conformed to this propensity to wander from the conventional paths. Nor could they do otherwise in a democracy of this character. Only through the organized power of the community could social gains be widely diffused and inequalities be prevented.

The political and administrative institutions which have grown in response to such stimuli possess many features of interest. Here is an electoral system in which all adults have had the right to vote for half a century (and nine-tenths of them regularly exercise their right) and in which for nearly sixty years voting districts were so apportioned in the farmers' favor that for electoral purposes the rural population was computed by law at 28 per cent more than it was in reality. Here is a Parliament, bicameral in

7. This is the phrase of William Pember Reeves, the "brains" of the Liberal movement in the nineties (see his *State Experiments in Australia and New Zealand* [2 vols.; London: Allen & Unwin, 1902]).

form, in which the upper house is completely dominated by the lower; in which the caucus is becoming the effective body that makes the legislative decisions; and in which debates are broadcast to the public. Here is a cabinet type of government in which two men held the office of premier continuously for thirteen years. Here is a country in which the central government sells you coal or wine, insures your property or your life, rents you a house or makes your will, runs hotels and restaurants and airways and railways—to mention only a very few items of its administrative agenda; in which, in addition, nearly seven hundred separate local authorities minister to the needs of a million and three-quarter inhabitants—in short, here is a country in which the central and the local governments together employ over one-fifth of all persons gainfully occupied.

But facts such as these, significant though they may be, lose much of their meaning if they are not interpreted in the light of the Dominion's history. Much of the fascination in that history consists in disentangling the legacy bequeathed by the mother-country and the innovations that originate from local New Zealand conditions. The British influence, of course, is so obvious that it needs no laboring. It permeates the political machinery, the legal system, and the social customs of the people. In some form or other, it can be felt pervading every sphere of activity. But, as has already been stated, New Zealand democracy is not just a slavish imitation of the British model. The need of adjusting to a new environment has modified the inherited tradition. It will be noticed, moreover, that, where New Zealand has struck out on its own, it has arrived at results more analogous to those of other English-speaking democracies than of Britain. The United States, Canada, Australia—these are the countries in which some parallel features can be observed. In certain cases New Zealand has deliberately followed an American or an Australian rather than a British precedent. In others, she has independently arrived at results similar to those of America and Australia by adopting much the same solutions under parallel circumstances. Thus the liberalizing of New Zealand's electoral laws bears many traces—made explicit in parliamentary debates—of American influence. The organization of the civil service, particularly in the lack of an administrative class, was based upon the Australian system and indirectly resembles the American. The "pork barrel," moreover, with all its political consequences, was introduced to New Zealand in the seventies, when roads and railways and other governmental services were being rapidly extended through the Colony. At similar periods in the development of the United States, Australia, and Canada, the same pork barrel has been injected into politics and for the like reasons.

Hence a proper understanding of New Zealand democracy must combine a historical with an analytical treatment. The system that had grown in Britain to suit a mature culture and a complex economy was readapted to younger, simpler, and rougher modes of life. During the process New Zealand redesigned that system and has progressively forged its own democracy to fit its own purposes, for it should not be supposed that the Dominion's political habits and procedures have always been as democratic as they are now. This smallest of the parliamentary democracies acquired responsible self-government in 1856 after a decade and a half spent under the tutelage of governors appointed from London. From that time to the present, New Zealand's history divides into two periods separating at the year 1891, when the long-lived Liberal ministry came to office. The decades up to 1890 tell the story of democracy in evolution; the decades since that date represent democracy in operation.

It is the purpose of this work to survey separately both phases of New Zealand politics, the semidemocratic phase as well as the fully democratic. Only if the spirit and the institutions of government both before and after 1890 are compared can the modern democracy be properly judged. Although much of the machinery of state is the same now as sixty years ago, various parts have been greatly changed, and the whole of it operates differently. The balance of power between different branches of the government has shifted—sometimes with legal recognition, but more often without. Continuity of title has served to conceal changes in function. Dominant personalities have molded offices to their own character, and the tradition they set binds their successors. By comparing the two periods—their contrasts as well as their resemblances—one can analyze how a change in one portion of the political system has influenced the working of other portions; how the extension of the suffrage has modified the organization of parties, of Parliament, and of the cabinet; how the increase in the functions of government has affected the structure of administration; how the spread of equalitarianism has determined which persons choose politics as a career; and how the politics of democracy have been affected by the economics of socialism. Such alterations indicate the responsiveness of New Zealand to its fuller measure of democratization, and they forecast the possible lines of future development. A critical inquiry will elucidate by what steps the people of New Zealand came to fashion their present type of democracy and in what manner it now operates. Democracy, since it upholds the ideals of publicity and free discussion as essential to its political process, must consent to be assayed on its own touchstone.

PART I

DEMOCRACY IN EVOLUTION, 1840–90

CHAPTER II

THE ELECTORAL SYSTEM

Prologue to Self-government

THE early history of white settlement in New Zealand should appeal to lovers of paradox. The country was first made known to Europeans in 1642 by the Dutch sailor, Tasman, who left to posterity an incomplete and rudimentary sketch of part of its west coast. More than a hundred years elapsed before an Englishman, Captain Cook, mapped the outline of the two main islands and brought back to Europe information about their fauna and flora and about their Maori inhabitants. Toward the close of the eighteenth century and at the beginning of the nineteenth a steady trickle of ships plied to New Zealand shores. The roster of early explorers and traders is quite international in character. A trio of Frenchmen, Surville, Du Fresne, and D'Urville; an Italian named Malaspini in charge of a Spanish expedition; and an American navigator, Owen F. Smith—these are among the followers of Cook.[1]

Yet, although the adventurous spirits of many countries found their way to these isolated islands, no government was in any hurry to add New Zealand to its possessions. In the absence of organized authority chaotic conditions prevailed between the Maoris and the traders and whalers. Missionaries attempted after 1814 to introduce to the native people those Christian ethics which were conveniently ignored by most of their fellow-whites who came to the South Pacific in search of speedy gain. It is understandable that when Nassau Senior, writing his treatise on *Political Economy* in 1836, sought a contemporary example of anarchy, he took his illustration from New Zealand.[2] When

1. See J. C. Beaglehole, *The Discovery of New Zealand* (Wellington: Whitcombe & Tombs, 1940).

2. "When we read of African and Asiatic tyrannies . . . . we are inclined to suppose the evils of misgovernment to be the worst to which man can be exposed.

15

finally the British government was bestirred to appropriate New Zealand, it was only in response to two external stimuli—the unofficial colonizing ventures of Wakefield and the probability that France would annex if Britain did not.

By signing the Treaty of Waitangi in 1840, the Maori chiefs conferred upon Victoria the sovereignty over New Zealand. Even as early as 1846 the Colonial Office proposed to grant to the infant colony a federal constitution with a system of representative (though not responsible) government. But at that time the strong and capable governor, George Grey, advised the mother-country to postpone its donation. Controversies with the Maoris over land sales, as he pointed out, were still too dangerous to permit of weakening the governor's powers; also the suggested federalism was then impracticable for a population concentrated almost entirely in the North Island. Six years later, however, these arguments no longer applied with equal force. Relations with the natives had become easier, thanks largely to Grey's tact and skill; and the settlements made by the Church of Scotland in Otago (1848) and by the Church of England in Canterbury (1850) had added to the inhabitants of the South Island. Thus, in 1852, when the European population amounted to a bare 27,000, the British Parliament passed a Constitution Act conferring representative institutions. Only three years afterward the Colonial Office acquiesced in the demand that the ministers should be responsible to the elected representatives. In 1856 the first responsible ministry took office.

The rapidity with which so scanty a population received powers of self-government is astonishing. The colonists were intrusted with virtually[3] complete charge of their own political destinies a mere twenty years after Senior had uttered his judgment. But the reasons for Britain's alacrity to grant self-government readily suggest themselves. Lord Durham had submitted in 1839 his great report advocating the principle that responsible

---

But they are trifles compared to those which are felt in the absence of government. The mass of the inhabitants of Egypt, Persia, and Burma, or to go as low as perhaps it is possible, the subjects of the Kings of Dahomi and Ashantee, enjoy security, if we compare their situation with that of the ungoverned inhabitants of New Zealand.''

3. The governor still retained control over defense and relations with the Maoris, but he lost these powers in the following decade.

self-government be conferred upon Canada. The Melbourne ministry had already acted on this recommendation, and the discussion over the merits of the principle was already closed. New Zealand did not have to force its requests upon a reluctant home government. The only question that could arise was whether this particular colony was yet fit for self-government.

The answer to that was largely determined by the character of the settlers themselves. The emigrants who sought a new home in the South Pacific during the 1840's had witnessed the successful fight over the Reform Bill and the ensuing liberalization of British politics. Many belonged to the middle class; many were highly educated; many were sufficiently well-to-do to pay for a cabin passage on the long voyage out. They wished, therefore, to possess in their new country the rights and privileges to which they would have been entitled in the old. Exclaimed one of their leaders, Godley: "I would rather be governed by Nero on the spot than by a Board of Angels in London." Even though some of the earlier swashbuckling traders were nothing to be proud of, their successors were graded samples of Victorian respectability. Emigrants to Wakefield's settlements had been meticulously selected by the New Zealand Company, and the churches were no less particular about whom they exported under their aegis. A British government based on the middle-class voter could trust the same class overseas.

Equally surprising at first glance is the federalism incorporated in the early constitution. The system that Britain offered in 1846 would have established one national government and two provinces. But that was then an overelaborate superstructure for an exiguous population to support. Nevertheless, Governor Grey and the Colonial Office again approved the federal principle when the Act of 1852 was in the drafting. The United States was scanned for precedents and examples, and some American features were intentionally incorporated into the constitution of New Zealand. Thus a young colony, containing in 1856 under forty thousand white settlers, found itself saddled with six provinces side by side with its central government. Each province had its unicameral elective council and its superintendent who was chosen directly by the voters of the whole province like an Ameri-

can governor.[4] The provinces had power to legislate on all save
thirteen specified topics. These latter were reserved for the central government to handle in its General Assembly, a bicameral
body of which the lower house was filled by periodic election and
the upper by nomination for life.

It was geography which dictated this seemingly cumbersome
hierarchy of institutions. The division of New Zealand into large
islands, its mountainous and then thickly forested interior, and
the distance of a thousand miles separating northern settlements
from southern—such factors served to isolate the several communities from each other. So widely were they dispersed that
William Fox, who later became premier, published in 1851 a book
with the plural description, *The Six Colonies of New Zealand*. One
member of Parliament, after a decade and a half of self-government, retrospectively described these early conditions: "What
was the state of the country at that time? It was a condition of
absolute isolation. Every centre had been colonised [away] from
every other centre, and there was a general feeling of aversion
one toward the other."[5] According to Alfred Saunders, a pioneer
founder of Nelson, it usually took about three months in those
days for a letter to be answered between the extreme north and
the extreme south. The seat of the "central" government was
then located at Auckland in the north of the North Island. Direct
sea travel was so infrequent that colonists from Otago in the deep
south would sometimes journey to Auckland via Melbourne or
Sydney in Australia.[6] In the second Parliament Sewell, the premier, himself from the South Island, voiced the anguish of those
who love not the sea: "If the members from the South are year
after year to be summoned to this, to them, remote corner of the
colony, they will not come. At present it is almost impossible
to get fit men in the South to stand for the General Assembly.
. . . . The great misery of our progress to the place of Assembly

4. See J. Collier, *Life of Sir George Grey* (Wellington: Whitcombe & Tombs, 1909),
p. 81, for an account of the borrowing from the United States. The parallel can be
studied in my *The American Governor: From Figurehead to Leader* (Chicago: University
of Chicago Press, 1939).
5. *Parliamentary Debates* (hereinafter abbreviated as "*P.D.*"), V (1869), 547.
6. *Ibid.*, p. 516.

lies in the repeated stoppages with the consequent renewal, at each remove, of the horrors of a sea voyage."[7]

Geography, therefore, prescribed limiting conditions for the politics of a new country. Within these limits, and drawing upon her heritage of constitutional government, New Zealand was free to select the course of her own development. Since her institutions were representative, and her ministers responsible to Parliament, the electoral system should be the first to claim attention. An analysis of government by the people must commence with the part that the people play.

Qualifications of Voters

It was wealth which determined the right to vote. In a manner reminiscent of the Reform Act of 1832, the New Zealand constitution conferred the franchise upon all who owned above a certain level of property or income. A man could qualify for a vote in these various ways: he must possess a freehold estate to the value of £50 per annum or a leasehold to the value of £10, or, alternatively, he must rent a town dwelling at £10 annually or one outside the town at £5. In effect this amounted to an enfranchisement of male householders. The wealthier members of this class were further aided by the absence of any restriction on the number of electoral districts in which one person might cast a vote. A man could vote only once in the same constituency; but he could vote at the same election in any number of constituencies where he satisfied the property qualification. Hence arose a practice known as plural voting. While amassing property, the wealthy accumulated voting power; and at a closely fought election the opportunity to cast more than one vote might enable them to turn the scale in several contiguous districts.

These electoral qualifications remained virtually unchanged until 1879. Table 1 depicts the ratio of voters to population at all the elections up to that year. Notice throughout this period how low was the ratio of the electorate to the total population. The percentage for the year 1855 appears high only because more individuals had enrolled since 1853 or had acquired more property

7. *P.D.* (1856), pp. 16–17.

in different districts; and the population had not increased proportionately in the interval. Apart, however, from that exception, the population grew by leaps and bounds in between
electoral years, and the ratio of electors fluctuated consistently
between 16 and 19 per cent. It must be remembered that the gold
discoveries of the sixties attracted an influx of poorer settlers,
while the state-assisted immigration scheme of the seventies
brought many others to New Zealand who were at first financially ineligible for the vote.

TABLE 1

PERCENTAGE OF ELECTORATE TO TOTAL EUROPEAN
POPULATION, BY ELECTION YEARS, 1853-79

Date of Election	Total European Population	No. of Names on Electoral Rolls*	Percentage of Electorate to Total Population
1853.......	30,000	5,934	18
1855.......	37,192	10,324	28
1861.......	79,711	13,466	17
1866.......	190,607	33,338	17
1871.......	248,400	47,275	19
1875.......	375,856	61,755	16
1879.......	463,729	82,271	18

* Totals in this column represent more than the number of separate
individuals who could vote, since the wealthy persons would be registered
on more than one roll.

For the first quarter of a century, therefore, the political institutions of New Zealand were representative only to a very
limited degree. This was not in the proper sense a democratic or
popular government. No system could be thus described when the
right to elect members of Parliament was so narrowly restricted.
As late as 1879 less than one-fifth of the population could directly
influence the policies of the government through the electoral
machinery. Participation in politics remained a class privilege.
Such, indeed, was the intention of many among the early political leaders, and they were quite frank in revealing their fears
and their prejudices. A parliamentary debate in the year 1858
elicited some oratorical gems. Thus spoke Domett, later a premier
of the Colony: "He could not approve of the democratic tendency of the Bill. To make representation depend upon numbers

was opposed to the principles of the British Constitution, and to the principles which were developed by the progress of centuries. He believed the property qualification a good one, for it was generally found coupled with intelligence, and it was a principle maintained by the British Constitution."[8]

Equally significant was the attitude of another member named Carleton: "He need scarcely argue that the manifest tendency of representation according to numbers only was to give a preponderating control to the most numerous class—virtually to lodge the power of the State in the hands of that class—to enable the lower or operative class, in fact, to overwhelm all other classes. Now, his desire was to give fair play to all alike—to each class its own just share in the government of the country."[9] Views like these were symptomatic of the uneasiness with which the recently enfranchised middle class regarded the claims of those who were still excluded. After melting down the icy exclusiveness of the aristocracy, the new dominant group now desired to freeze the status quo in forms that suited its own interest. Democracy and the rule of the majority it considered dangers to be avoided. "The colony," said Richmond, the treasurer, "had no national Church, no aristocracy—it was all a dead-level; and he dreaded the pressure of a majority; and believed this measure was calculated to meet the evil. The Government in framing this Bill had looked forward to the future position of the colony; its present tendencies were decidedly democratic."[10]

The anxieties expressed by New Zealand politicians in the late fifties are curiously akin to the contemporary worries of the fine, if sometimes confused, mind of John Stuart Mill. His *Considerations on Representative Government*, which he published in 1861, expound the same dilemma. While conceding that the suffrage must be further extended, he was reluctant to place full power in a working-class majority. "But even in this democracy," he wrote, "absolute power, if they chose to exercise it, would rest with the numerical majority; and these would be composed exclusively of a single class, alike in biasses, prepossessions and general modes of thinking, and a class, to say no more, not the most

8. *P.D.* (1856–58), p. 15.
9. *P.D.* (1858–60), p. 8.   10. *P.D.* (1858), p. 604.

highly cultivated."[11] In similar vein argued Walter Bagehot when
in 1872 he added an introduction to the second edition of his
famous *English Constitution*. Alarmed at the potentialities of the
extension of the franchise that had occurred in Britain in 1867, he
admitted: "As a theoretical writer I can venture to say, what no
elected member of Parliament, Conservative or Liberal, can
venture to say, that I am exceedingly afraid of the ignorant
multitude of the new constituencies." Like Mill, he, too, excused
what would else have been a middle-class prejudice by referring
to the then educational level of the working class. "Their supremacy," he said, "in the state they now are, means the supremacy
of ignorance over instruction and of numbers over knowledge."[12]

But in a young country, even more than in Britain, it was inevitable that wealth would one day be forced to share its privileges. Already in the early sixties the lure of gold was drawing
to New Zealand settlers of a type likely to assert themselves. The
gold-miners were vigorous, speculative, and migrant. If discontented, they could become an antisocial and dangerous element
in the community. Hence with alacrity the General Assembly
adopted an act providing for two members to represent the Otago
gold fields and conferring upon the miners a special franchise.
Proposals to democratize the vote, already stimulated by the gold
rush, received further backing in the seventies from the newer
immigrants whose settlement in New Zealand was in many cases
assisted financially by the state. The feelings which in those years
drew more colonists to New Zealand, some from the continent
of Europe as well as from Britain, are described by Oscar Alpers,
who emigrated with his parents as a boy from Denmark in 1875,
and in later life became a judge of the Supreme Court. The family
knew little of the country for which they were bound, "except
vague stories we had heard of Maori wars, but recently concluded, of 'Hauhaus' and cannibals, and of nuggets of rich red
gold to be gathered by the wayside. It was the Land of Hope,

11. *Considerations on Representative Government* ("Everyman ed."), pp. 276–77.
Elsewhere Mill adds this proviso: "It might be highly mischievous to give them the
preponderant influence by admitting them, *in their present state of morals and intelligence*, to the full exercise of the suffrage" (*ibid.*, p. 304). (My italics.)

12. Walter Bagehot, *The English Constitution* ("World's Classics," No. CCCXXX
[London: Oxford University Press, 1928]), pp. 276 and 272.

where my father proposed to himself to repair his broken fortunes and begin life anew."[13] Since Britain had considerably extended its franchise by the Act of 1867, the pressure of the poorer settlers for equal voting rights was powerfully reinforced by the mother-country's precedent. Eventually in 1879 an important Qualification of Electors Act passed into law. The analogy with the second British Reform Act is all the closer, since the party maneuvers which surrounded the passage of the New Zealand law resembled Disraeli's feat in "dishing the Whigs." In New Zealand it was a Conservative ministry, under the premiership of John Hall, which adopted a Liberal bill and widened the suffrage. But it succeeded in so doing only through the support of four Liberals who declared their independence of party ties.[14]

The New Zealand Act of 1879 introduced a residential qualification that permitted any man of twenty-one years of age or over to vote if he had dwelt in the Colony for one year and in his electoral district for six months. The property qualification, however, was still retained, as was plural voting. Indeed, property owners were somewhat assisted, since the act reduced from £50 to £25 the value of the estate which entitled its owner to vote. The same amount of money would therefore buy double the votes if properties were purchased in different districts. That was what the premier, when he moved the second reading, described as "a moderate recognition of the rights of property."[15]

This law, it should be mentioned, was enacted only after lengthy and acrimonious debates replete with harsh words and heated tempers. Angry at seeing the Conservatives steal their own measure, the Liberals in opposition proposed more far-reaching reforms which they lacked the votes to carry. A suggestion that the property qualification be entirely abolished and only the residential one be retained met with stubborn resistance. As a Conservative expressed it: "I say that Parliament not only legislates for persons, but for property and its rights and liabilities; that property, therefore has a right to be represented, and every holder of property has a right to vote in respect of that

13. Oscar Alpers, *Cheerful Yesterdays* (Wellington: Whitcombe & Tombs, 1930), pp. 3–4.
14. See below, chap. iii, pp. 65–67.   15. *P.D.*, XXXIII (1879), 11.

property in the election of members to this House."[16] A leading Liberal who proposed to have done with the abuses of plural voting found his amendment defeated in committee, although by a narrow margin of only five votes. Yet another Liberal, the future premier, John Ballance, tried to grant the franchise to women. He carried his amendment in committee—a remarkable achievement for the year 1879—but the offending innovation was later struck out by a rallying of outraged masculine diehards.

Although this Act of 1879 did not go nearly far enough, nevertheless it achieved some success. Table 2 shows to what extent it

TABLE 2

PERCENTAGE OF ELECTORATE TO TOTAL EUROPEAN
POPULATION, BY ELECTION YEARS, 1879–87
AFTER PASSAGE OF THE ACT OF 1879

Date of Election	Total European Population	No. of Names on Electoral Rolls*	Percentage of Electorate to Total Population
1879.......	463,729	82,271	18
1881.......	500,910	120,972	24
1884.......	564,304	137,686	24
1887.......	603,361	175,410	29

*The names of wealthy voters would still be included here more than once.

broadened the base of emerging democracy. The numbers in the third column would have been higher if all who were eligible to vote had actually enrolled themselves. It appears, however, that many failed to register because of the attendant rigmarole and red tape. So many requirements had to be observed that potential electors would not bother to comply.[17] Others of the newly enfranchised failed to register because they were apathetic about exercising their rights.

Nor did all those who actually registered subsequently record their votes at the election. The election of 1879 is the first for which statistics are available to show the number of voters throughout the Colony. Consider the data in Table 3. There were four members in 1879 and eleven in 1884 who won their

16. *Ibid.*, p. 12.
17. Hall emphasized this point (*ibid.*, pp. 41–42).

seats without a contest, and this should be allowed for in interpreting the percentages for those years. In general, about three-fifths of those who registered also voted; and over the decade there was a tendency, due to adverse economic conditions, for the proportion of actual voters to increase. This was one sign that New Zealand was moving in a democratic direction.

Plural voting, however, continued to run its course for a decade more, despite frequent efforts by the Liberals to have it removed. The opportunities for repeated voting were even increased by an act of 1881 which divided the cities into separate

TABLE 3

VOTERS ENROLLED, TOTAL VOTES, AND PERCENTAGE
OF TOTAL VOTES TO ENROLLED VOTERS, BY
ELECTION YEARS, 1879–87

Date of Election	No. Enrolled*	No. of Votes	Percentage of Votes to Enrolled Voters
1879.......	82,271	43,776	53
1881.......	120,972	69,985	58
1884.......	137,686	74,672	54
1887.......	175,410	111,911	64

* The names of wealthy voters would still be included here more than once.

electoral districts. Previously each city had formed a single large constituency returning several members. As there was only one electoral roll for the entire constituency, the well-to-do could not vote more than once within the city itself. But the formation of separate districts within the cities meant separate rolls and therefore encouraged plural voting. Objections were strenuously voiced in the parliamentary debates by Liberals, who supplied instances of the existing vicious practice. Said one of them: "I know several country districts in Auckland into which large bodies of these electors are imported at elections. I know, for instance, that such is the case in respect to the district which I represent. I could take 150 electors from Auckland to vote in that district, and such a vote, in the event of a hard contest is sufficient to turn the scale."[18]

18. *P.D.*, XXXIX (1881), 505.

Another Liberal, speaking after the election of 1884, gave further confirmation: "I may say that in Hawke's Bay District during the last general election, a very large number of electors recorded four votes each. They first went to Petane, and voted for the East Coast District; then to Napier, and voted for the Napier District; then they went out by train to Hastings, and voted for the Hawke's Bay District; and then they came to Waipawa District and voted; all in the same day. By that means some fifty or sixty or even more persons recorded two, three, or even four votes."[19] However, the election of 1887 was the last in which New Zealand witnessed the spectacle of these perambulating voters. Success came to the Liberals in 1889, when Grey, their former premier, carried a motion as a private member in committee and established the principle of "one man, one vote." This seemingly small alteration had profound consequences. In the pivotal election of 1890 more than one Liberal candidate scraped home by a narrow majority in districts where, under the old system, they could have been defeated by an incursion of wealthy voters.[20]

Method of Apportionment

The ingenuity of *Homo politicus* is seldom more triumphantly displayed than in contriving methods of apportioning electoral districts. At times the cruder devices that pass under the name of "gerrymandering" may be attempted. At other times numberless opportunities present themselves for parties to intrench their own interests under the banner of high-sounding principles. Drawing electoral boundaries is the subtlest form of cartography, and New Zealand's experiments and discussions in this field amply reveal the connection between its political development and the dominant economic and regional influences.

In the Constitution Act districts were apportioned on the basis of the numbers of electors in each district, not on its total population. As early as 1858 the Stafford ministry proposed a bill to reapportion districts according to the population that each contained. The suggestion was stiffly opposed in the lower house not only because representation for numbers was dreaded but also

19. *P.D.*, XLVIII (1884), 323.   20. See below, chap. ix, p. 203.

because settlers on the land feared the power of the nascent urban centers. Indeed, the conflicting attitudes of town and country, then vehemently expressed in the parliamentary debates, have since formed an unbroken thread linking successive periods of New Zealand politics. From early times to very recent ones the country representatives consistently prevented an outright application of the principle of representation on a numerical basis. As far back as 1858 their spokesmen in the lower house urged against Stafford's bill arguments that have now been repeated decade after decade. One of them objected that "this attempt to realise a fair apportionment of the representation would give far greater influence to the towns than they ought to possess. It ought not to be forgotten that the town population could, from its powers of concentration, be more easily worked upon for good or for evil."[21] Despite such forebodings, the bill successfully passed through all its stages in the House. But, when it reached the Legislative Council, the citadel of wealth, it was unceremoniously dispatched. In a brief debate a councilor summed up his criticism: "He believed the principle on which the Bill was framed to be inherently bad, and one that had never as yet been recognised by the Legislature of New Zealand. In the apportionment of representation according to population he considered one important element to have been overlooked. He thought there were classes of superior intellectual capacity and of large stake in the country which were entitled to more than the share of representation that would fall to them under the proposed Bill."[22]

In the succeeding years it became increasingly difficult to adjust the system of representation to the development of the Colony. A "series of turbulent little Reform Bills," as one minister called them, occupied and reoccupied the attention of Parliament. In 1860, 1862, 1865, 1870, and 1875, the electoral boundaries were redrawn by new acts. Every few years the allocation of constituencies required changing. The Colony was like a young boy rapidly growing out of his clothes. Moreover, the rate of growth in different regions was disproportionate. At first, the North Island had the numerical advantage in population. But from

21. *P.D.* (1858–60), p. 10.   22. *Ibid.*, p. 26.

1860 onward a combination of factors enabled the South Island to forge quickly ahead. It was mostly in the north that the Maoris were concentrated, and their ownership of their lands had been guaranteed under the Treaty of Waitangi. European settlers could not purchase from them without running the gauntlet of protracted legal and administrative procedures. Even so, land sales were conducted on a scale which began to alarm the Maoris, who saw themselves exchanging a lasting possession for things more ephemeral. Thus disturbances broke out in the North Island in the early sixties which eventually developed into warfare.

The South Island, on the other hand, contained but few Maoris. Hence its settlement was less impeded by legal obstacles and by fears of attack. The broad level plains of Canterbury were easier to plow, to pasture, and to populate than any region of like extent in the north. Furthermore, when gold was found both in Otago and on the west coast, population rushed south, and the southern provinces began to outstrip the northern in revenues and general prosperity. By 1867 the system of representation had become quite lopsided. The South Island contributed 70 per cent of the Colony's revenue; it had 65 per cent of the total population; and it received only 58 per cent of the members of the House. Undeniably, the South Island was then underrepresented, and so it was likely to remain until the population principle was accepted for determining representation. For some years the North Island managed to maintain more than its fair share of electoral districts, even though the successive acts were slowly augmenting the South Island's representation.

Eventually, during the decade 1880–90, a number of important measures were adopted, laying down a system of apportionment which lasted without change for half a century. First of these was the Representation Act of 1881, which was adopted only after prolonged and bitter controversy. On the surface this measure wrote it into the statute-book that representation must be apportioned to population.[23] In effect, however, it established simultaneously an overriding principle. It modified

23. See the words of Premier Hall when moving the second reading: "The leading principle upon which the Bill is framed is that of representation on the basis of population. This basis, I think, has been practically accepted by the House and the country" (P.D., XXXIX [1881], 471).

the population basis by conceding to all rural electorates a far smaller number of inhabitants than was required of the urban. This "country quota," as it came to be called, was not incorporated in the main text of the law; it appeared only in an accompanying schedule that set out the proposed redistribution of constituencies. "Where a district," said Hall, "is so constituted and so situated as to possess great facilities for the exercise of political influence, that very fact in itself affects representation, and you may therefore fairly, in that case, somewhat diminish the actual proportion of representation which is accorded. . . . . We therefore propose in this Bill that the quota for the country districts shall be less than the quota for the town districts by, as nearly as possible, 25 percent."[24] The premier himself, be it noticed, and most of his ministers represented rural electorates and knew what their constituents wanted. This bonus for the rural voter was vigorously supported by the country members, all of whose arguments rested on the fear that their interests would be subordinated to the fast-growing cities.

The country quota, however, was accepted in relative calm when one compares the parliamentary discussion that fastened upon another feature. By proposing the population basis for representation, the Hall government guaranteed a predominance in political power for the South Island, so long as it could maintain its numerical superiority. In 1881 as many as 60.6 per cent of the white population resided in the south. So Hall advocated that, of the proposed ninety-one members of Parliament, the South Island should receive fifty-five (60.4 per cent). This aroused the ire of North Island representatives. Vehemently they protested against their political subordination. "I may say," lamented one northerner, "that the North Island has been kept for many years past under ground by the South Island. . . . . You are now going to give the South Island a large increase of representation, and cut down the representation in the North Island."[25]

But there were other regional groupings which cut across the division of interests between the two islands. Not all parts of the south were destined to gain from the change. The Nelson district, for instance, which lies in the north of the South Island, was going

24. *Ibid.*, pp. 471–72.   25. *Ibid.*, p. 491.

to lose some of its representation in favor of its more powerful neighbors farther south. Consequently, in a solid phalanx the Nelson members deserted their normal party allegiance to vote against the bill. As one of them exclaimed in chagrin: "The people will not submit to Otago and Canterbury having the power practically to rule the rest of the colony."[26] Some northerners, nevertheless, acquiesced in the proposal, shrewdly pointing out that the two large southern provinces would not necessarily unite to dominate others. In so far as New Zealand politics were based upon regional groupings, it had been more common for the extremes in the two islands to unite against the central areas than for one entire island to oppose the other. The powerful southern provinces of Canterbury and Otago had often fought each other in jealousy and rivalry. Similarly, in the North Island, Wellington had combatted Auckland. But Auckland and Otago—the geographical extremes—not infrequently combined against Wellington and Canterbury. This regional alignment was the natural product of New Zealand's geography. In a long and somewhat narrow country, where the four main centers of population were spaced out at great distances, it was understandable that those living on the periphery would join forces in opposition to those more centrally situated. The Representation Act was unlikely to change those relationships. Moreover, thought the more prescient of northerners, if the North Island later outstripped the population of the South Island, it would find the new principle convertible to its own advantage.[27]

The same discussion drew from other parliamentarians alternative suggestions of how to apportion electoral districts without basing them on the numbers of their inhabitants. One, for example, realistically observed: "We have been told that this House represents persons: but I say it represents, or ought to represent, interests also. If not, what are we here for? Three-quarters of our discussions are not so much in respect of the rights of persons as in respect of the interests of persons."[28] Another member, who represented the coastal town of Napier, naturally urged that the districts through which goods were exported from

26. *Ibid.*, p. 520.
27. See a striking prophecy in *ibid.*, p. 510.   28. *Ibid.*, p. 515.

the Colony should receive special parliamentary weighting because of their economic importance. "So long as we continue,"
he observed, "to be more in the nature of a large Board of Works
than a representative Chamber, I contend that the elements of
trade and export should be taken into consideration."[29] One
speaker fell back upon the rather naïve argument that acreage,
even without a present population, should be represented; while
others, by advocating the claims of agricultural wealth, provoked
the Liberal gibe that they sought to represent not men but sheep.
None of these alternatives appealed to any save those whose
regional or economic interest was immediately concerned. Consequently, New Zealand thenceforth recognized the population
principle as the basis of its electoral apportionment. But from its
inception the country quota was added as a rider.

In the following electoral law, the Representation Act of 1887,
the effects of the country quota were temporarily abridged. The
Liberal ministry of that day, under the joint leadership of
Premier Stout and Treasurer Vogel, leaned upon the urban
rather than the rural voters, and the personnel of the cabinet was
drawn from city constituencies. Already by this date certain
trends, foreseen by acute observers in 1881, were taking more
definite shape. The population of the North Island was growing
at a faster rate than that of the South Island. Whereas the north
contained only 39 per cent of all the white New Zealanders in 1881,
it had 43 per cent in 1886. Likewise the number of those concentrated in cities and boroughs was slowly catching up with the
rural population. In 1881 nearly 40 per cent, and in 1886 nearly
43 per cent, of all the colonists dwelt in areas classified as urban;
and the increase during those years was most rapid in towns of
the North Island.[30] Thus, when the question of representation came
to be debated again, northerners could be less apprehensive of
their future than they were in 1881. The country representatives,
for their part, were becoming seriously worried at the growth of
the cities and were more determined than ever to preserve a piece
of electoral jugglery that worked so much in their favor.

29. *Ibid.*, pp. 541–42.

30. Premier Stout told Parliament: "The general increase in the population
throughout the colony is about 19%, but we find that the increase . . . . in towns
. . . . in the North is about 30%" (*P.D.*, LXV [1889], 111).

A Representation Act, which reduced the country quota to 18 per cent, managed to pass through Parliament in 1887. But this partial victory for the urbanites was short lived. The succeeding ministry was a Conservative one and was dominated by farmers whose fears for their own interests were increasing at the same rate as the growth of the urban population. Hence in 1889 a measure was introduced in Parliament with the design of curtailing the representation of the four largest cities. In those cities, it was proposed, the electoral districts should contain a number of inhabitants one-third greater than in country constituencies. It soon leaked out in the debate that this suggestion had been presented to the ministry as a virtual ultimatum from the country members temporarily allied with the representatives of smaller towns. This combination of fifty-three members formed a majority in the lower house that was anxious to clip the wings of Auckland, Wellington, Christchurch, and Dunedin.[31] In response to such a threat the representatives of the four cities united to maintain a long and stubborn "stone wall." So acrimonious were the charges and countercharges that the country majority carried a resolution to clear all strangers from the galleries for a whole week.[32] Eventually, to end the obstruction, the Conservative premier, Atkinson, announced that he would fix the quota at 25 per cent, which city members were willing to accept. Later on in committee, however, a minister proposed to raise this figure to 28 per cent; and, despite the last loud protests of the urbanites, there it was fixed.

This electoral bonus for country dwellers remained for nearly sixty years as it was settled in 1889. Continuously since then up to 1945 the New Zealand law computed the rural population for electoral purposes at 28 per cent more than it actually was. By this legal fiction the farmers held their own against the city interests. The operation of the country quota has greatly influenced the modern party system and has been a characteristic feature of politics in this democracy. Its results will be fully analyzed in a later chapter.[33]

31. *Ibid.*
32. Some of the vital debates in this secret session were not reported in Hansard (*ibid.*, pp. 33–34).
33. See below, chap. viii, pp. 174–85.

Although the Act of 1889 lifted the quota by 10 per cent, it left undisturbed one other change which the Liberals had brought into their Act of 1887. The Stout ministry had wisely put an end to the old and indefensible system under which Parliament itself drew the electoral boundaries of its own members in a recurrent "series of turbulent little Reform Bills." How much gerrymandering had been practiced under that method cannot now be precisely determined. But there is no doubt that it lent itself to this abuse, and accusations were frequently bandied across the floor of the House. Thus one speaker asserted in 1881 during a bitter parliamentary controversy: "In studying this Bill it struck me that the electorates were so arranged as to give a great advantage to Ministers over their opponents. . . . . The Electoral District of Marsden returned the honourable gentleman, and most of those who voted for him were inhabitants of the northern and eastern parts of the electorate. Now what have they done? He has been a faithful friend of the Government. . . . . They have actually taken away that part of the electorate which was opposed to him, and have added it to the electorate of the honourable member for Rodney. Now, does not that look like 'gerrymandering'?"[34] As a remedy for such possibilities, Stout established the salutary principle that Parliament should settle the number of districts and members but that the actual boundaries should be drawn by a nonpolitical commission. Automatically after each quinquennial census the commission was to redraw the electoral map. Once that proposal was adopted, it has fortunately been left untouched by successive parliaments.

Numbers of Members and Districts

In deciding what number of representatives is desirable, two distinct and possibly conflicting aims must be considered. From one point of view the number of members should be so fixed that the electorate is adequately represented. The size of the population, the distances over which voters are spread, and the competition between their economic interests or racial groupings must all be borne in mind if a Parliament is to be "a reduced photograph of the whole community."[35] Seen from another angle, however,

34. *P.D.*, XXXIX (1881), 508.　　　35. *P.D.*, LVII (1887), 54.

the purpose of a general election is to select a deliberative and legislative assembly for running the country. Hence, the number must be one which will constitute an efficient working body. The "talking shop" cannot operate with too many political salesmen. Likewise the number of districts must satisfy opposite requirements. It may be better from a minority's point of view to construct large districts each returning more than one member. If smaller single-member districts be favored, minorities are likely to go unrepresented. But if electoral districts are large and are designed to return many members, a candidate must needs ingratiate himself politically with a far larger section of his fellowmen. This perennial dilemma of democratic mechanics can be well illustrated from New Zealand experience. The young colony experimented with many forms of representation and fluctuated back and forth before adhering to its present system.

As the population multiplied, ministries strove their best to fit the elective house to that growth. In the years from 1855 to 1866 the population grew fivefold, while the number of representatives almost doubled. Table 4 shows the mutations of the electoral system between 1855 and 1890. Notice the steady increase in the average number of inhabitants whom each member represented. In 1890 a parliamentarian represented almost nine times more persons than in 1855. Only once, in 1881, was an effort made to stabilize the proportion. The Hall ministry in that year raised the number of members from eighty-four to ninety-one, which temporarily kept the House in the same ratio to population as before. At the same time, however, and in the same Representation Bill, Hall advocated—what was then an innovation for New Zealand—to have only single-member constituencies. It can be seen from the table that the number of districts before 1881 had been less than the number of members. That was because each city used to comprise a single constituency returning several members.

The increase in the number of members did not provoke much discussion in 1881. An increase seldom does. Only when there is a reduction are some of the sitting members certain to lose their seats. In arguing for a larger membership, Hall contended that they should not fix an arbitrary number and then fit the electorates to it. Instead they should make the House to suit the constituencies and not the constituencies to suit the House. He objected to having too small a House on two grounds: first, because "the settlement of important questions might be often rather by private arrangements than by public discussion," and, second, because "that free and full discussion which is indispensable to the success of representative institutions is discouraged." Nevertheless, he recognized that, if the House became too big, "the greater [was] the probability of the constituencies having to take second-rate men."[36] The increase was readily accepted.[37] Thus, a

TABLE 4

NUMBER OF INHABITANTS REPRESENTED BY THE MEMBERS OF
THE NEW ZEALAND HOUSE OF REPRESENTATIVES, 1855–90

Date of Election	Total Population	No. of Members	Average Population per Member	No. of Districts
1855.........	37,192	37	1,000	....
1861.........	79,711	53	1,500	43
1866.........	190,607	72	2,600	60
1871.........	248,400	74	3,300	68
1875.........	375,856	84	4,500	68
1879.........	463,729	84	5,500	68
1881.........	500,910	91	5,500	91
1884.........	564,304	91	6,200	91
1887.........	603,361	91	6,600	91
1890.........	625,508	70	8,900	62

population of 500,000 received the rather excessive number of ninety-one representatives. For candidates this brought the advantage of smaller constituencies to canvass. The effect on the House, however, was bad. Debates became prolix, since there were more mouths to repeat a limited set of arguments. Bores harangued, while bills were held up.

But the connected proposal to increase the districts from sixty-eight to ninety-one, each returning a single member, was stoutly contested. In its favor the premier urged that it would save candidates a great deal of time and money and therefore widen the area of selection for the constituencies. Opponents raised two

36. *P.D.*, XXXIX (1881), 470.

37. An amendment to reduce the number from ninety-one to sixty was defeated by a majority of 40 to 24 (*P.D.*, XL [1881], 94).

objections. One of these was that it would diminish the representation of minorities, for, under the system prevailing in the city constituencies, where two or more members were returned, the minority could usually secure the election of at least one to voice its point of view. Throughout New Zealand there were twelve of those multimembered districts in 1881; and during the crucial parliamentary divisions on a question of confidence in the government it was usually found that in about half of these cases representatives from the same constituency were split on opposite sides. What could happen to an election in such a district was notably illustrated in the general election of 1866. Stafford, the premier, was then standing for his old constituency in the city of Nelson, which returned two members. He came top of the poll, but his opponent received the second highest number of votes and was therefore also elected. Third on the list came Stafford's own political supporter. The second objection was closely bound up with the general opposition to plural voting. The Liberals realized that, by splitting the cities into separate constituencies, the government was multiplying the opportunities for voting in neighboring districts. Until property owners lost their special electoral advantages, Liberals preferred to leave the urban districts as they were.

A few years later the whole issue was revived and was keenly disputed in a legislative controversy which shed some light on the growing pains of the cabinet system. When Stout brought in his Representation Bill in 1886, the all-important question of the number of members had still to be written into the text. The cabinet was too hopelessly divided to be able to settle on any definite figure. While the premier was moving the second reading, a member interjected: "As to the number of members?" and Stout could only reply: "I have left that blank. Members will believe that, as far as the Government is concerned, we are not unanimous on that point. I say so frankly. . . . . Personally, I am in favour of the number being slightly reduced. . . . . However, I have left that open to the House."[38] Exactly the same occurred the following year when the bill, which had failed to pass, was again introduced. The premier once more invited the House to

38. *P.D.*, LVI (1886), 568–69.

settle the vexed question, as his cabinet could not. The pros and cons were similar to those heard in the debate on Hall's bill. Fewer members, it was said, would cause a saving both of the taxpayer's money and of parliamentary time. Those of the contrary view urged that a smaller Parliament would be liable to tighter party control, that poorer candidates would be deterred by having larger districts to canvass, and that country representation would be diminished relatively to that of the towns. After innumerable divisions at the committee stage, the number of members was laid down in the act as ninety-one.

The premier and this collectively irresponsible ministry had also left blank the number of districts, although Stout's own preference was to restore the amalgamated city constituencies which existed before 1881. Amalgamation, contended its advocates, would give better representation to minorities, since in the larger cities the minority party should at least be able to elect one member out of three. Opponents retorted that amalgamation would increase the cost of fighting an election and help the wealthier side, that it would encourage the corrupt practice of personation, and that a by-election to fill one vacancy in a multi-membered district would be difficult to hold. Single-member districts, however, won the support of the majority and were retained in the law. But the law was as short lived as the majority which enacted it. When the Conservative ministry took the place of the Liberals, it upset these decisions just as it manipulated further with the country quota. At the very first session of the new Parliament, held immediately after the election of 1887, the number of members was reduced prospectively from ninety-one to seventy. A few years later the Representation Act, which raised the quota to 28 per cent, again amalgamated the city electorates. The debate was of interest if only because Hall, glowing with the distilled wisdom of an elder statesman, admitted that he had made a mistake back in 1881. Criticizing the system that he had himself initiated, he emphasized that single-member districts had failed to provide adequately for minority representation.[39]

Hence, as a result of a decade of electoral change, the franchise

39. *P.D.*, LXIV (1889), 299–300.

was extended, plural voting was abolished, the number of members was reduced to a more sensible figure, the larger cities formed single constituencies, and the country quota artificially bolstered the voting strength of the farm dwellers. Auckland, Wellington, Christchurch, and Dunedin, which housed between them one-fifth of the whole population, received one-sixth of the parliamentary representation.[40] Thus did rural Conservatives intrench themselves to resist the assaults of urban Liberals at the momentous election of 1890.

Conduct of Elections

In any clinic of political pathology the case histories of electoral corruption would assuredly fill the bulkiest of files. Glancing in retrospect at the conduct of elections in the middle of last century, one realizes what improvements have been wrought in the operation of representative institutions. The comparison of a modern with an early Victorian election, as indeed the contrast of the contemporary with the nineteenth-century civil service, shows in brighter colors the vitality of democratic machinery and its capacity for progressive development. It encourages the belief that abuses now existing—serious as some of them are—will also one day be removed.

One need not necessarily suppose that an early New Zealand election was a precise replica of that memorable contest at Eatanswill which Dickens unearthed in the papers of the Pickwick club. But there are enough parallels to indicate that the Samuel Slumkeys and the Horatio Fizkins of New Zealand were not loath to exploit the cruder possibilities of the electoral process. Through the filmy Victorian veneer the impulses of something more primitive erupted periodically to the surface. Intimidation, bribery, false counting, personation—ugly charges like these were voiced in Parliament and from time to time were substantiated. Such practices were perhaps the natural product of the confused mental climate surrounding the extension of the franchise. They reflected the insecurity of a middle class that was undecided whether to treat the vote as a right, a duty, a power,

40. These four cities contained, at the census of 1886, a population of 116,019 out of 578,482, and received twelve representatives out of seventy.

a trust, or a privilege—or simply as an enforced concession to a perilous democratic upsurge.

The first few general elections in New Zealand, besides being restricted to possessors of sufficient property, offered ample opportunity for nondemocratic influences. Since votes were recorded openly at the hustings, powerful interests could observe the behavior of those whom they had the economic means to control. One member of Parliament recorded these impressions: "It has been said that the poorer classes here were not so liable to influence as those at Home; but it was not that class which was so much affected in the colony as that respectable class of retail dealers and tradesmen who were dependent in a large measure upon merchants and wholesale firms. . . . . He knew instances himself in which voting-papers had been forwarded to parties enclosed in the business envelopes of a large firm, and when the unfortunate debtors saw them, they supposed them to contain the account, which they were not prepared to meet, but, on finding that the envelopes contained only voting-papers, these individuals were glad enough to purchase a temporary relief from the pressure of their liabilities at so cheap a rate, although very likely, entirely in opposition to their consciences."[41]

The practice of open voting was accompanied by treating, on which the early laws placed no restriction. A candidate who could provide an adequate supply of free drinks infused potency into his arguments. Bottles, therefore, brought in ballots. This was, however, a system which might recoil to the disadvantage of the more bibulous side. It was no uncommon sight under that system to find "a voter reeling about, hocussed by copious instalments of brandy and water, and holding in his hand a voting-paper which had been filled up for him, and giving it in to the polling-clerk . . . . unless, indeed, some person in the interest of the rival candidate should take the paper from him and substitute another in its place."[42] Even though the vote was publicly recorded, hard drinkers were known to follow a deliberate policy of imbibing from opposition barrels without allowing alcohol to modify their principles. "There were men," exclaimed a disgusted parliamentarian, "who would take all they could get, eat

41. *P.D.* (1856–58), pp. 600–601.   42. *Ibid.*, p. 595.

and drink at a candidate's expense, and, when they had got all they expected to obtain, would openly go up to the polling-place and vote for his opponent. This they called quartering themselves upon the enemy."[43] When there was a close election, the excitement was intensified during the final stages of the contest. The rival parties would keep a tally of each vote as it was announced, and the candidate who was trailing behind would urge more of his supporters to the poll. Consequently, many citizens found it lucrative to defer their vote until the end of the day when they might be able to turn the scale, or else might find it expedient to jump on the band wagon. One minister denounced "a large mass of electors whom he might style 'trimmers'—a set of miserable and foolish men, who waited to see how the matter was likely to be decided and then rushed to record their votes in favour of the successful candidate, caring nothing for political principles."[44]

Despite such glaring abuses, it was a long time before ingrained conservatism could be persuaded to accept reforms. In 1858 a measure to substitute the secret for the open ballot was introduced. Its proponents argued that the evils of intimidation and treating should and would be removed. Its opponents, fearing doubtless that a secret vote would be out of their control, patriotically denounced it as "un-British" and virtuously warned that it would "lead to hypocrisy and dissimulation." These fears of the standpatters overcame the faith of the innovators. By fourteen votes to eleven the bill was defeated on its second reading in the House. Nevertheless, with hopeful persistence the reformers renewed their efforts at successive parliamentary sessions. In 1858 three electoral laws were placed on the statute-book, one providing for the registration of electors, one for the regulation of elections, and a third for the prevention of corrupt practices. But the cumulative complaints heard throughout the sixties indicate that the laws either did not go far enough or else were not properly enforced. In 1869 a Conservative member questioned the government whether it intended to take more effective measures against electoral corruption. Emphatically he stated: "They had the Corrupt Practices Prevention Act, but he

43. *Ibid.*, p. 602.   44. *Ibid.*, p. 595.

might say that in all cases it had been absolutely a nullity. It was no protection whatever; it was not even a scarecrow, because it did not scare any one, from practising bribery and corruption at elections."[45]

That same year an undaunted private member, Reynolds, again introduced his Election by Ballot Bill, which in the previous year had been passed by the House and thrown out by the Council. The debate evoked many admissions of current evils. One speaker in the upper house pointed out the various influences which operated under a system of open voting. "Some are influenced," he charged, "by personal friendship, some from the nature of their business, others from their connection with trade unions and trade societies, and even in some cases I have known religion to be brought to bear in cases of election. . . . . I have heard of cases in which persons have lost their situations through not recording their votes as their employers would wish."[46] This time the secret ballot met a happier fate and passed through both House and Council. Opinion had swung round against the existing abuses and was fortified by the analogy of contemporary British efforts to clean up the electoral system of the mother-country. Although Britain had not yet actually adopted the secret ballot, there were clear signs that it was soon likely to do so—as happened in 1872.

Already were heard in New Zealand the arguments, so powerfully proclaimed in the nineties, that a young colony should be eager to experiment with novelties. As Fox expressed it: "He trusted they would not be found to be lagging behind the old country—the old conservative country—but were still prepared to go ahead as they ought to do as a young country, even though they passed the old country."[47] Already, too, the Conservatives were bewailing, as they later did in the Liberal heyday of the nineties, all this policy of experimentalism. "He would call atten-

45. *P.D.*, V (1869), 63.
46. *Ibid.*, pp. 465–66. Note some further remarks: "There was one thing which occurred in my district which was calculated to create much ill-feeling in a small community. A rather warm election took place, and the day after the poll was taken the name of every person who had voted was published in the paper with the name he had voted for. I feel that the system of vote by ballot would enable a man to give his vote without fear or undue influence."
47. *Ibid.*, p. 75.

tion to a further consideration," lamented Fitzherbert, "that if
there were one thing more than another which had been most
unfortunate for New Zealand, it was that it had always been
experimented on. . . . . Let experiments be tried in the other
countries; do not let them be considered that vile public body,
on which experiments could be made for the benefit of mankind."[48]

Even the secret ballot, however, progressive achievement
though it was, did not put a conclusion to the annals of electoral
corruption. Personation continued, treating and bribery survived, and it was darkly hinted that the party in power could
control the officials who counted the votes. The year 1879 saw
a spate of electoral acts, inherited by the Conservative ministry
of Hall as a legacy from Grey's Liberal administration. New
measures for registering electors, for regulating elections, and for
preventing corruption again passed into law—a sufficient indication that something was still rotten in the Colony. Another two
years went by, and once more the ministry sought to purify its
elections by act of Parliament. In 1881, when yet another Corrupt Practices Prevention Bill was before the House, charges
were leveled at particular districts and were indignantly denied
by their representatives. This time Fox was quite emphatic in his
belief that much corruption occurred. "I hear from rumours in
the lobbies, and in conversations with friends, of so-and-so's election having cost him from £500 to £600, and of another man's
election having cost him from £300 to £400. I have heard of one
gentleman whose election expenses are said to have been as much
as £2,000."[49] Such stories, if they were true, would suggest that
the dice were heavily loaded against a candidate of modest
means. Even Whitaker, the attorney-general, himself a person of
lax political ethics, admitted that personation was prevalent and
could be checked only by strong remedies.[50]

Over many decades, then, there were persistent efforts to
democratize the vote. The strongholds of political power were not
lightly surrendered by those whom the Constitution Act had
lodged in possession. But the reformers did not tire, and by 1890

48. Ibid., p. 77.
49. P.D., XL (1881), 563–64.   50. Ibid., p. 796.

they had achieved much. Sometimes following, sometimes anticipating, the parallel developments in the mother-country, youth-
ful New Zealand could boast after thirty-five years of self-government an electoral system more democratic than she had received
at birth. The changes had been many and for the most part along
progressive lines. But the Liberals knew, and the Conservatives
feared, that more remained to be done. Voting rights had been
extended to a wider circle of citizens; and, if to some, why not to
all? Larger numbers of the enfranchised did use their vote, but
too many still abstained. Elections were more honestly conducted,
though perfection had not been reached. One man at last had
only one vote, but a farmer's vote counted for more than that of
a city dweller. Such is the summary of the electoral balance
sheet of democracy in evolution. The surplus was on the credit
side of democracy.

CHAPTER III
POLITICAL PARTIES

THE political party in nineteenth-century New Zealand differed considerably both in organization and in function
from its contemporary descendant. The party, which nowadays
fills a central role in the governmental process, was then only
incidental to it. There is thus a risk of anachronism in talking
of parties before 1890 if this term be thought to mean the same
as in modern times. Today's party is a continuous association of
like-minded voters, organized locally and nationally with its
network of committees and secretariats. United under some
recognized leader, it seeks to carry out agreed policies through
elected representatives. Parties in that sense scarcely made their
appearance in the Dominion until very late in the Victorian era.
Yet there existed before 1890 group movements which constituted
the semideveloped stage of the modern party. These movements
were less complex and less highly organized, and their membership was more fluid, than now. They did, however, exert an
influence on the political system which deserves study, and they
did in the seventies and eighties show signs of growth and power.
Many of the newer twentieth-century features are projections of
tendencies earlier discernible.

It is convenient to distinguish the state of parties among the
general public and their emergence within the walls of Parliament. With that distinction in mind one can take the year in
which the provinces were abolished as the opening of a new
stage in party history. Earlier than 1876 no party organization
could be found among the voters on a national scale. Parliament,
as a consequence, was organized into unstable coalitions,
temporarily joined out of shifting blocs, a situation which lacked
the character of systematic party combat. After 1876, however,
the beginnings of change were apparent. National party divisions

were emerging throughout the country and were crystallizing
into nascent party groups. Correspondingly, Parliament itself
passed through two decades of slow and difficult transition from
the mobile groups of earlier sessions to the more formal modern
conflicts. Between 1876 and 1890 parliamentary strategy and
tactics still largely resembled a kind of guerrilla warfare. Political
forays were conducted in the Assembly by semi-independent
squads under lesser or local leaders. But already their skirmishes
were becoming subordinated to the steadier battle lines manned
by representatives in regular party formation. As the guerrilla
leaders and their followers were absorbed into the ranks and
placed under unified command, the national party system of
modern times took shape. The process had begun which has since
converted the backbencher from a free-lance warrior into a
disciplined private.

Parties in the Electorate, 1856–76

Up to 1876 political sentiment was regionalized to a high
degree. As one parliamentarian said: "There is really no more
national feeling amongst us than if we had been brought up in a
circle of half a yard round."[1] Provincial loyalites were paramount; people considered themselves Aucklanders or Wellingtonians rather than New Zealanders. This was only to be expected when the functions of provincial governments—education,
police, immigration, road-building, and land sales—touched the
daily lives of the people more nearly than those of the central authority. Provincial politics were close at hand; their effects were
omnipresent. "Central" politics were geographically distant
from most of the colonists, and their effects did not so readily
obtrude.[2] Internal communications were developed only slowly,
especially in the poorer provinces; and travel was consequently
arduous and exhausting. The newspapers, numerous and flourish-

---

1. *P.D.*, V (1869), 482.

2. "For years the Government of the Colony had been established chiefly at
Auckland. They had a ship in those days called the Government brig, which cruised
about, collecting the revenue from the various settlements . . . . and carrying it off
to Auckland, to the great annoyance and jealousy of the people, where it was supposed to be spent on public works . . . . from which they received no benefit"
(*ibid.*, p. 516).

ing as they were, catered to local audiences and could not reach a wider market.

Political activity was thus mainly confined to the compartments within which pioneer life was segmented. Opinions were localized because life was localized. The franchise, moreover, was restricted; the number of those eligible to vote was small; and party organization was scarcely needed in a diminutive electorate. Under such conditions national party divisions were not to be expected. After nearly nine years' experience as premier, Stafford pronounced his view: "We have ventilated our opinions, and the condition of what is called 'public opinion' in this Colony, which is indeed very raw and unformed, is nothing more than an aggregate of opinions ventilated in different places."[3] The influence of political leaders was for many years mostly local in character. Stafford, for example, was a dominant figure in Nelson; Macandrew had his bailiwick in Otago; and Featherston, his in Wellington.

Yet it remains true that even in these early days issues did arise which cut horizontally across the vertical lines of provincial politics. Throughout the Colony broader cleavages of opinion emerged which served to bring together on a common plane both regional interests and regional leaders. The first of these issues to come to the forefront concerned the grant of self-government.[4] The demand for representative institutions culminated in the passage of the Constitution Act in 1852 and in the permission to institute a responsible ministry. The new constitution embodied a second issue which was to permeate New Zealand politics until 1876. This was the conflict between the provinces and the central government. As inevitably happens under a federal system, New Zealand politicians soon resolved themselves into those who favored the provinces at the expense of the central government and those who preferred central to provincial authority. From 1856 to 1860 the provincial question vexed the public affairs of the Colony. A new and serious problem presented itself in 1860, as friction in the North Island between Maoris and white settlers

3. *P.D.*, XIII (1872), 680.
4. See J. B. Condliffe, *New Zealand in the Making* (London: Allen & Unwin, 1930), pp. 171–72.

flared up into acts of physical violence. For nearly a decade the normal political currents were confused by cross-eddies of groups advocating conciliation and others eager for war. The troubles of the Maori wars brought to a close the arguments over the first political issue. After controversies between the ministers and the governor, and between the governor and an incompetent general from Britain named Cameron, the Colonial Office agreed to hand over to the ministers control over native affairs and defense which hitherto had been vested in the governor.

The war issue also had pronounced effects on the concurrent question of provincialism. Driven to numerous expedients for financing the war, the central government naturally looked with avid eyes at the provincial revenues; and the hands of harassed treasurers soon followed the direction of their gaze. The war upset any possibility of a financial equilibrium between central and provincial governments, and the provinces did not long survive its termination. But it was the fourth issue which finally settled the problem of federalism. Commencing in 1870, successive New Zealand ministries under the ambitious leadership of Julius Vogel, launched upon a vigorous policy of state-assisted immigration and of building roads, bridges, and railways. The provinces speeded their own doom when they offered resistance to certain of Vogel's proposals. In 1876 they were abolished, and the central authority garnered up their governmental functions. New Zealand henceforth became a unitary state. Self-government, the provinces versus the center, war against the Maoris— these were now closed questions. Only the public works program remained as a live subject for further political controversy.

At the general elections held during this period, the issues mentioned above were placed one by one before the few citizens who possessed the right to vote. In 1853, when only representative institutions had been granted, the cry for responsible government in addition was raised in some of the constituencies. In another two years, after responsible government had been attained, the provincial issue was debated in many electorates. By the time of the 1861 election, the paramount question of peace or war with the Maoris occupied the political arena. At the next election in 1866, the conduct of the war still supplied a live campaign topic, although it was no longer as important as five years before. In 1871 the electorate was clearly asked to decide whether it approved of Vogel's borrowing for immigration and public works. Four years later, Vogel again provided material for discussion through his bill to abolish the provinces. Since this was to take effect only after the newly elected Parliament assembled, the decision was left to the voters. At most of these general elections, problems of broad colonial interest were mooted in the newspapers and the public meetings within the different provinces. In separate parts of the Colony candidates and voters, individually unknown to each other, were taking sides and ranging themselves into party alignments as their similar interests and attitudes happened to coincide. The seeds of the modern party were already sown, and the seedlings were pushing up through a fertile soil.

It is instructive to observe the political forces opposing each other on the various issues. One source of political conflict lay in the ever recurrent feeling of outlying areas against a central jurisdiction. During the first decade of responsible government much of the strongest provincial sentiment came from Otago far down in the south. This was only to be expected when the central government was located at Auckland, almost one thousand miles away in the far north. Macandrew, who had been elected in 1855 to represent Dunedin, did not even trouble to come to Auckland for the parliamentary session of 1858 and consequently forfeited his seat. Nevertheless, when a by-election was held in 1859, the errant Macandrew was re-elected with the enormous total of forty-four votes! This will indicate the importance then attached in the deep south to the government located in Auckland. After the discovery of gold in 1861, the self-contained provincialism of Otago was built upon a secure basis of plentiful financial resources. With its well-filled treasury, Otago could now afford the best roads and the best schools. It could even exhibit in 1869 the luxury of possessing the first university in New Zealand.

At the extreme north of the Colony similar motives influenced the politics of Auckland Province. In its early days Auckland did not regard the central government with disfavor, and this for very good reasons. Since its finances were none too opulent, the province had to court the good will of colonial treasurers, and, too, the seat of the central administration was then located at Auckland itself and was not a distant object of suspicion. But two events combined to alter the Aucklander's point of view. One was the finding of gold at Coromandel in the early sixties, with its consequent enrichment of the provincial revenues; the other was the removal of the central government to Wellington in 1865. Aucklanders who thus became equidistant with Otago from the seat of colonial authority now viewed it with the same distaste. During the final decade of New Zealand federalism, Auckland and Otago—the geographical extremes—joined hands in their last-ditch defense of the provincial system.

The opposite change occurred in the attitude of Wellingtonians. This province early manifested strong regional loyalty. Its internal politics were led by the great superintendent, Featherston, who was re-elected many times and held office continuously from 1853 until 1870. An outstanding exponent of provincial views, Featherston frequently collaborated with Fox, the leading provincialist in New Zealand. His dominance in Wellington for many years fostered opposition to centralism. Nevertheless, the outlook of the province changed when Wellington became the capital city of the colony. Rivalry in the North Island between Wellington and Auckland had contributed to Wellington's provincialism when the capital lay in Auckland Province. Now that the position was reversed, feelings were reversed also. Wellington grew more friendly toward centralism, while Auckland was encouraged to champion provincial autonomy. Add to this the important circumstance that Featherston, at Fox's invitation, resigned the superintendency in 1870 to accept the post of agent-general for the Colony in London. With this stalwart removed, the government of Wellington Province and the colonial government in Wellington city were less likely to remain distinct entities. Moreover—one more factor not to be forgotten—Wellington Province contained practically no gold.

Through the course of arguments over centralism the Maori war injected a new irritant. The merits of war or conciliation provided a debate on matters other than the federal controversy.

It involved the racial question of relations between white and colored, as well as a constitutional question, less momentous but not less heatedly debated, of whether a governor sent from Britain or locally elected ministers should determine native policy and defense. But the war issue, though separable from that of federalism, impinged upon it. Successful conduct of any war always results in an accretion of power to the central government. Hence it is not surprising to find that the leaders of provincial thought in New Zealand were also leaders of the peace policy. Fox and Featherston, together with Sir George Grey, the governor who had originally helped to create the provinces, at first urged conciliatory methods. Centralists such as Stafford and Domett favored the strong hand.

The war, however, put a new twist into regional antagonisms. Because nearly all the Maoris and their lands happened to be in the North Island, it was there that the fighting took place. Only the North Island settlers were physically endangered by the hostilities. While Auckland and Taranaki endured the hardships of military operations, Otago, tucked away in the south, was basking in peace and prosperity. North Islanders claimed to control the handling of native affairs, because they were directly touched by the results, but the expenses, mounting as the troubles continued, fell principally upon the inhabitants of the South Island. This was natural enough, since the wealthier region contributed more to the colonial exchequer. Thus, signs developed of an interisland conflict. Ominous talk of separating the two islands into distinct jurisdictions was heard within the provinces and in the General Assembly itself. The North Islanders, being closer to the theater of war, and knowing the fighting qualities of the Maoris, preferred conciliation with the natives; but southerners, removed from the fields of combat and less conversant with the Maoris, favored war and swift suppression.[5]

As hostilities dragged on without any conclusive results, the South Island became impatient of expenditure which produced such small returns. Interisland bickering was larded with acrimony and recrimination. "I would ask," said a Colonel Kenny in the upper house, "who were the persons who were practically

5. *P.D.*, V (1869), 410.

carrying on the war at present? Who have been the sufferers? Who the persons who have been murdered? On whom have the massacres fallen? The inhabitants of the North Island. As I said before, the settlers of the North are the best judges of their own affairs, and it is to be regretted that they have been thwarted by the action of the Southern Island. I think a defensive and not an aggressive policy should now be followed." Contrast with this the attitude of a South Islander: "There is a strong feeling growing up in the South Island against spending more money for war purposes. I do not mean to say that such a measure would not be repudiation on their part—I have heard that ugly word often used—but it behoves us to think well of the matter, for I believe that the people of the South Island would come forward willingly if they could see anything like an end to their at present undefined liability, and heartily unite with the North Island in putting down this war."[6] The idea of separation seems to have been first propounded by the northerners to extricate themselves from the policy advocated in the south. Later, as the financial liabilities of the south increased, it was there that separation became popular. Fortunately for New Zealand, the war came to an end around 1870, and with it died the thought of secession.

In 1870 the *raison d'être* for a peace party and a war party ceased to exist. But in that same year Vogel, the colonial treasurer, tossed a new and juicy apple of discord into the political picnic by proposing that the Colony should borrow £10,000,000 for assisting immigration and developing public works. It is ironical that this plan, which speeded the downfall of the provinces, was introduced by arch-provincialists. Fox was premier of the ministry, and Vogel, representing Dunedin in Otago, had consistently stood forward as defender of the provinces. Featherston, too, was a member of the same ministry until he went to London in 1871. Vogel's scheme was warmly approved throughout the Colony, except in Otago, which was Scots, canny, and contented. Most of the provincial governments had by this time become "pensioners on the colonial chest," and they welcomed the opportunity to batten on it farther. The public works policy, nevertheless, killed the provinces because the latter would not sur-

6. *Ibid.*, p. 364.

render to the central government a portion of their lands through which the new roads and railways were to run. These public lands had been reserved to the provinces in an agreement of the year 1856, and the revenues derived from land sales were vital to them. Centralists, when they sought to cripple the provinces, naturally aimed first at their lands. Vogel wanted to defray part of the cost of his plan by reserving to the central government the lands whose value would be enhanced under his scheme. But the provinces, convinced that to receive was better than to give, would sacrifice not an acre. In 1876 they were abolished, after a brief, sharp conflict in which their financial dependence on the central government for public works grants laid them at Vogel's mercy. Vogel, the former provincialist leader, supported by Stafford, the centralist, legislated them out of existence.

On the whole, then, provincialists tended to support peace, and it was they who introduced the public works program. But such divisions were not hard and fast. There were provincialists who argued for war, just as there were centralists urging conciliation. Among those eager for public works were centralists, while some of the provincialists stood opposed. Since the various issues were essentially disconnected, party groupings could hardly be clear cut and precise. Political conflicts in the electorate were consequently based upon coalitions as transient as international alliances in an era of power politics.

Parliamentary Parties, 1856–76

Inevitably the same pattern was reflected in the internal organization of the General Assembly. When the electorate itself was crisscrossed by divergent lines of cleavage, a picture of similar confusion was bound to reproduce itself inside Parliament. Hence the party system functioned there with all the futility that arises when ministries are unstable and governments cannot lead. The weaknesses that have beset the French Republic and other continental European democracies could be paralleled from mid-nineteenth-century New Zealand.

The events of the parliamentary session in 1856 illustrate the task of forming a ministry responsible to a House that was in a state of flux. The first ministry was organized by Sewell, a lawyer from Canterbury and a confirmed centralist. It fell within three weeks by seventeen votes to fifteen. There followed an interval of a few more weeks in which three persons (two provincialists and one centralist) tried to establish a ministry and failed. Stafford, who was one of these three, explained the cause of the difficulty.[7] Parliament contained three parties, of which the two smaller, if combined, had a majority of one vote over the largest. No ministry, therefore, could last which was not based upon a two-party coalition. During the ministerial interregnum Fox, representing provincial opinion, proposed a series of resolutions guaranteeing to the provinces all revenues from land sales and a generous share of the customs duties. These were carried by the same majority of seventeen to fifteen which had defeated Sewell, and Fox felt emboldened to take office as premier. But in less than two weeks his majority proved inadequate, and he was defeated by eighteen votes to seventeen. Once again the ministerial bench went begging for occupants, until Stafford, who had cleverly played a waiting game, was able to fill it. Stafford was a centralist who had voted for Sewell and against Fox in all those three divisions. But he placated the provincialists because he was himself superintendent of Nelson Province, and he agreed to accept Fox's resolutions. To his support now swung a large number of moderates, and he won his first division by twenty-four to ten. One of those, for example, who had voted for Fox in the earlier divisions, thus explained his reasons for backing Stafford: "I have done with party, for the rest of the session at all events. I am tired of Ministry-making, and am desirous of proceeding with the practical business of the country."[8] Considering that it had taken the House six weeks to find a stable government, such a reaction was hardly surprising. It indicated the fluidity of early parliamentary organization at a time when the opposite sides of the House were not demarcated by fixed frontiers.

Stafford maintained himself in power through two more sessions. His majority weakened, however, as the personnel of the House changed and the war supervened to blur the previous lines of demarcation. An election held in 1861 brought together a vastly altered collection of representatives, whose record proved

7. *P.D.* (1856–58), p. 85.   8. *Ibid.*, p. 212.

one of the most unsatisfactory in the history of the New Zealand
Parliament. During five turbulent years they produced an unedifying sequence of wrangles, upheavals, and confusion. In fairness let it be admitted that this Parliament had to decide upon
the grievous question of war or peace with the Maoris; that during its first three years the governor still possessed a control over
native affairs which resulted in dividing responsibility; that, in
addition, once the war started, New Zealand was unlucky to receive from England so poor a general as Cameron (nicknamed by
the scornful Maoris "the lame sea-gull"). Nevertheless, the fact
remains that Parliament vacillated between conciliation and the
mailed fist and suffered the consequences of drift. This Parliament assembled annually for five sessions between 1861 and 1865.
At every session the ministry either was defeated or resigned
without awaiting defeat, and a new ministry was chosen which
lasted only until the next session. In 1861, at its first meeting,
Parliament opened with Stafford as premier and defeated him.
Then, after trying four other premiers in the next four years,
Parliament reverted to Stafford in 1865. All this was due to the
confusion of issues, the conflict of personalities, and the absence
of party organization.

When Stafford lost power in 1861, his supporters numbered
twenty-three and his opponents twenty-four. Since the speaker,
however, was one of his followers, the House was in reality equally divided. The Fox ministry, which came next, was backed by
the peace party. It fell in 1862 when twenty-two voted on each
side, and the speaker gave his casting vote against the government. Fox, the provincialist and conciliator, was followed by
Domett, a centralist and war advocate. After an inglorious year
this ministry resigned in 1863 without even waiting a division.
Since the peace party and the war party had both failed separately, they now tried to succeed by a coalition. Whitaker, who
believed in war, became premier and led the Legislative Council,
while Fox, who believed in peace, became colonial secretary and
leader of the House. This union was dissolved in thirteen months'
time and, as in Domett's case, anticipated the verdict of the
House by resigning before a vote. Weld became the next premier
with a policy of war and self-reliance. As New Zealand intended

to fight without British troops or generals, the ministry took over from the governor the control of defense and native affairs which he had hitherto retained. In one year, observing the same monotonous regularity, Weld resigned; and the despairing House, which by this time had literally left no ministry unturned and no premier unexplored, again sought refuge in Stafford.

It was, of course, the confusion of party groupings which caused such ministerial instability. On each of the two major issues confronting Parliament there were roughly three blocs of opinion. There were, for instance, extreme provincialists, extreme centralists, and a band of moderates occupying a midway position. Each ministry was insecurely based upon a transient alliance between groups. If the groups separated from below, down toppled the ministry that was erected upon their coalescence. Or the disunity might first appear in the cabinet itself and work downward. The rival leaders often distrusted each other, and their coalitions were never fruitful. As late as 1869 the same party formation which had persisted for a decade still continued. "Looking at either side of the House," said Richmond, "I observe it to be divided into three sections. . . . . You have men on either side who, if they spoke their minds, you would find are united only by Provincialism or anti-Provincialism, but who would arrange themselves in totally different parties—some who would support some extreme war policy, some who would take the view of . . . . the Government, thinking £150,000 worth of war is as much as we should allow ourselves; and some who would . . . . have no war at all, or have it represented by a moderate aggressive army, ready to commit aggressions whenever the occasion might arise."[9]

This trifurcation on the war question ran parallel to a similar division on the provincial issue. After regaining power in 1865, Stafford held it until 1869. During those years he was backed, as any premier at that time had to be, by a multiplicity of groups. His fall occurred when different groups had, one by one, withdrawn their support. Among those, for instance, who had combined to restore him to office in 1865 were provincialists as well as centralists. But within a few years the inevitable happened.

9. *P.D.*, V (1869), 540–41.

By attempting to appease both wings, the premier satisfied neither. Provincialists came more and more to oppose him because of centralist tendencies, and centralists became disgruntled because their objectives were not being pursued vigorously enough. Ultimately both wings of Stafford's following broke away —the provincialists to coalesce into an opposition united under Fox, and some of the centralists into an independent opposition known as "the Cave." One old parliamentarian explained in frank terms the reasons which had motivated his own maneuvers: "Now, there are many who have come to this House, like myself, partisans of no Ministry whatever. . . . . Sir, we all know that there is a section of this House, which I shall denominate for courtesy's sake, borrowing a phrase from the French Chamber of Deputies, 'the extreme left.' . . . . I myself, in common with others, stood in terror of a section whose advent to office I believe, on my conscience would have brought the Colony to ruin before the Assembly could have met again to have called them to account for it. I did that last session [1868], in common with others, for I did not act alone, which I never did before and hope never to do again. For the last fortnight of the session I did place my vote at the unreserved disposal of the Government, upon the understanding that they should remain in office in order to keep others out. . . . . The peril is not so great now, and therefore not only myself but those honourable members who acted with me, return to our previous position of perfect independence."[10]

This significant self-justification reveals the weakness of party ties in the early days of New Zealand politics. The conflict of political issues and the lack of party cohesiveness produced parliaments that were littered with blocs and cluttered with independents. It is true that, even in its most disorganized period, the House was always more than a mere collection of unconnected units. Community of interest and outlook did bind various members together in the same team at successive sessions. At stages in their meandering parliamentary course the many tributaries and currents of political opinion merged awhile into broad-flowing rivers. But the rivers were ever terminating in deltas. When Vogel, adventurous in ideas and action, cut across the older

10. *Ibid.*, p. 266.

party divisions, he found that his program could no longer reconcile the claims of an expanding central government with those of
"a number of miserable little federal republics." Abolition set
the stage for a new conflict with deeper social implications.

Parties in the Electorate, 1876–90

Besides the antipathy between center and periphery and the
squabble over the distribution of public works, a more profound
cause contributed in placing the provinces on the lumber heap.
This was the politicoeconomic conflict of the wealthy landowners
against the small holders and the landless. At a time when land
and sheep comprised the dominant interest in the New Zealand
economy, around their ownership developed the keenest political
battles. Because the tenure and sale of land was a governmental
function reserved since 1856 to the provinces, it was mostly in the
provincial arena that the battle raged. Over some years various
provincial councils had been divided between parties of large
"runholders" and their opponents, and in certain provinces the
challenge of the landless and the small owners was already proving too much for the land aggregators. The "Radicals" or "Liberals"—meaning those who sought to prevent the accumulation
of land in few hands—hoped to achieve their aim by controlling
the provincial institutions. They had less hope of immediate
success in the central government because of the electoral obstacles which prevented their dominating Parliament. In the
lower house they could hardly obtain a majority until the
franchise was extended; and the upper chamber, filled by the
method of nomination, had for years been packed with representatives of the big runholders. Liberal legislation was unlikely
to be approved in a Parliament so constituted.

While Liberals wanted to preserve the provinces, their opponents viewed them as a menace. Hence the result of Vogel's action was not only to remove the old political controversy of centralists versus provincialists but also to introduce at the national
level a new lineup of Liberals against Conservatives. The latter
thought that they were acting cleverly when they voted to abolish
the provinces; in reality they merely took a shortsighted view exemplifying on that occasion Mill's dictum that Conservatives are

"by the law of their existence the stupidest party."[11] They succeeded in sweeping the provinces away, but they did not sweep
away the Liberal movements those provinces contained. Instead,
by centralizing the control of land sales, they centralized the
scattered opposition to the landowners and brought a new
Liberal party into being in the General Assembly. The most
prominent Liberal leaders of the eighties—Stout, Seddon, Montgomery, and McKenzie—were men who started their political
careers in the provincial councils and entered Parliament between 1874 and 1881. The carry-over of party divisions from
provincial to central politics was well illustrated by these statements of a Liberal representative who first joined the House in
1879: "I came into the House," said this parliamentarian, "the
day of the division on the want of confidence motion. There were
eight gentlemen beside myself present who had held seats in the
Provincial Council. Seeing those gentlemen, I knew, without inquiry which side it was right to vote upon, and, like an old
cavalry horse, I took my place in the ranks of my own party,
and went with them into the lobby."[12] This was the direct result
of the Conservatives' own action toward the provinces. In the
short run it was true that the Conservatives triumphed. Save for
two brief and unsatisfactory Liberal ministries, Conservatives
dominated New Zealand for the next decade and a half. But in
the long run they failed dismally. The Liberals struck an emphatic counterblow in 1890–93, when they crushed their old
adversary.

Controversy over the tenure of land served to unite on the
same plane of ideas and interests the scattered farms and town-
ships of which New Zealand was composed. In the South Island,
where settlement had proceeded at a rate faster than in the north,
were exhibited the worst evils of land accumulation. Here, for
over a decade before the provinces were abolished, Liberal politicians had inveighed against "dummying," "spotting," and
other favorite devices of land monopolists.[13] Consequently, the

11. *Considerations on Representative Government* ("Everyman ed."), p. 261, n. 1.
12. *P.D.*, XXXII (1879), 614.
13. A man who wished to conceal the extent of his acquisitions could take out a
title in another person's name, using him as a "dummy" owner. Or, if he wished to
gain control over a large area without purchasing all of it, he could pick out or

south, particularly Otago and Canterbury, provided a strong
bloc of support for the emerging Liberal party. In the north, land
aggregation had been somewhat retarded by the Maori troubles.
But Auckland could parallel some of the abuses practiced in the
south, and Liberalism found here another stronghold. When
Otago and Auckland voted in the main against abolition, theirs
were the votes not only of extremes against the center but of
provincial Liberals against Conservative centralists. After 1876,
therefore, public opinion was slowly passing from a provincial
into a national phase. This development in feelings and attitudes
was made possible by the roads and the railways of the public
works policy; and Vogel, who originated the policy, foresaw
what its result would be: "New Zealand," he said, "is a peculiar
country. You cannot get over its geographical configuration.
. . . . There will always be a certain amount of isolation in different parts until the iron horse runs through the two islands."[14]
Steadily up to 1890 the isolationism of the several regions was
breaking down. Although in the middle eighties a member of
Parliament from the deep south could state that he, in Otago,
was not going to be taxed to complete even a productive railway
in the North Island,[15] by that date this species of parish-pump
politics was becoming a declining force.

Accompanying the land controversy were articulate demands
for the revision of constitutional machinery. Balked in their
efforts to achieve reform speedily, Liberals sought first to alter the
institutions of government which impeded them. Hence arose a
mixed campaign with numerous cries and criers. Extension of
the franchise, removal of plural voting, redistribution of electoral
districts, proportional representation, triennial parliaments, a
reformed Legislative Council, an elective governor—these were
suggestions freely mooted after 1876. All of them, except proportional representation and the elective governor, had been
achieved by 1893. Henceforth, there was to be no constitutional
check on the expression of the popular will and no political
institution designed to conserve the economic interest of one

---

"spot" the best sections, buying only these and leaving the inferior portions which
were valueless without the adjacent good land.

14. *P. D.*, V (1869), 522.   15. *P.D.*, LVI (1886), 63.

social group in the state. The emergence of such issues involved a thoroughgoing change from the politics of the preceding twenty years. Henceforth the provincial problem ceased to worry New Zealand. Only occasionally might the ghosts of the old provinces flit across a public meeting or a parliamentary lobby. Relations with the Maoris likewise became a matter of secondary importance to the white politicians. That burning issue of the sixties was extinguished to smoldering point in the seventies and eighties. Although trouble flared up again in Taranaki around 1880, and the repressive policy of the native minister, Bryce, was severely criticized, thereafter native policy ceased to be a major parliamentary issue. In fact, of the problems dominant before abolition, only the public works question continued to provoke party alignments in the succeeding years. Whether to borrow more or not to borrow, whether to construct new railways in this district or in that—here was the ammunition for many a wordy war. When the slump of the eighties followed on the boom of the seventies, Conservative opinion clamored for retrenchment, for economy, for cutting expenses to the bone. Actually, the politicians of all parties preached parsimony when in opposition and when in power practiced largess for the benefit of their own supporters. The pressure for further borrowing and public works was too strong to be resisted. Only a few lone and unpopular souls, such as Alfred Saunders, consistently denounced the public works program.

One other line of cleavage separated political partisans in these years. This was the growing rivalry between town and country. Although it was intensified after 1876 by the increase in the size of the towns, it had existed before that date. But during the provincial period the urban-rural conflict was mostly staged on the scene of provincial, not of national, politics. For this there was a very good reason. The opposition of town and country centered principally around the competitive quest for roads and bridges and other utilities. Until the seventies the central government had left it to the provinces to provide these, and town had fought country in an effort to secure larger shares of the provincial expenditure. A representative from Nelson explained this very clearly in words that were not applicable to his region alone;

"In the Nelson Province, the present arrangement gave the whole power to the city of Nelson and the immediate vicinity. . . . . The people in the goldfields districts and the outlying districts called upon the Provincial government to make roads and bridges for them, but they never got them. . . . . The people in the town naturally looked to their own interests first, and it would be more to their advantage to increase the value of their property by making roads there, than spending the money in distant places."[16]

"Pork-barrel" procedure, which was a recognized feature of provincial politics, developed the character of a city-country feud. But the result of Vogel's public works program, combined with abolition of the provinces, was to centralize the pressures hitherto diffused. The clamor for roads and bridges still persisted, and the rival suitors were still town and country. Their antagonism, however, was now translated to the sphere of central politics. It is this which accounts in large part for the bitterness accompanying the debates over the successive representation acts from 1881 to 1889. Each of these gave rise to an urban-rural conflict.[17] Vogel launched the public works policy in 1870; the provinces were wiped out in 1876; in 1881 town and country members were fighting in Parliament over their quota of representation. Between these events was an intimate causal connection. The pork barrel had become nationalized. Thus the state of public opinion and parties between 1876 and 1890 represented a transition. Political attitudes were crystallizing on either side around the one outstanding issue: ownership of the land. It is true that other important problems cut across the picture and blurred the symmetry of the design. When town was opposing country, both Liberals and Conservatives might split to form new and temporary alliances; when funds were being doled out for public works, interregional scrambles might produce *mariages de convenance* which broke up after the desired items had been appropriated. But the recurring land issue led to more permanent groupings that always reasserted themselves. Party politics outside Parliament were by no means organized in the fashion observable since 1890. They were, however, more cohesive than

16. *P.D.*, XI (1871), 298.   17. See above, chap. ii, pp. 28–32.

in the years before 1876. Despite relapses and recessions, there was a persistent trend toward a more stable system.

Parliamentary Parties, 1876–90

The same transition can be observed inside Parliament itself. Reflecting the crystallization of public opinion among the electors, parliamentary politics now manifested more fixity of purpose. At every session between 1876 and 1890 one could pick out groups of Liberals and Conservatives. The same representatives stayed continuously in a team and between them developed the understandings and the loyalties which go to make up a political party. However, the degree of party solidarity must not be overstated. While party divisions were becoming clarified, many independents remained who owed allegiance to neither side. "Independent," of course, was the euphemistic description which they accorded to themselves. Their more cynical colleagues dubbed them "rail-sitters," insinuating that they waited to bargain with any ministry in difficulty and to offer their vote at a price. The pernicious aspect of the public works policy could be traced in the internal working of Parliament. Throughout this transition period the pork barrel served as bait to entice many a representative into the appropriate lobby. At every session the presence of these floating votes introduced an element of instability and marred a party division based upon principles. More than one cabinet was turned out of office by the aggrieved representatives of "neglected" districts.

Apart from the land issue, other factors in these years encouraged the growth of the party system. Strong leaders were emerging with personalities that could attract the electorate and dominate its representatives. In the earlier decades New Zealand had found at least two capable leaders in Stafford and Fox. But sheer difficulties of internal communication prevented their gaining a truly national following. When Vogel became premier, however, the political stage was occupied with the restless motions of his adventurous spirit. His bold program, with its far-reaching effects on all regions of New Zealand, made his name almost a household word. Political drama was intensified when the chief actor was challenged by an equally eminent rival. This was Sir George Grey, the man who had twice been New Zealand's governor, had helped to draft the Constitution Act, and had later quarreled with a stiff and stuffy Colonial Office and retired from its service. For some years he had lived in embittered retirement on a small island to the north of Auckland. But at the threat to the provincial system, of which he had been joint architect, he rose to the defense. Entering the House of Representatives in 1875 as a private member, he fought, debated, and obstructed, employing every tactical maneuver to defeat the abolition bill. In the following election he stumped the country, haranguing public meetings with fiery eloquence. It was as a Liberal that he re-entered the political arena. Autocrat and aristocrat, he came forward as the champion of democracy and the underprivileged. In this clash between Vogel and Grey, party politics were dramatized by personal rivalry. As in the contemporary British conflicts between Gladstone and Disraeli, the minor characters were less noticed when prima donnas were competing. No other figure up to 1890 acquired a prestige comparable to that of either Grey or Vogel. Other leaders of the period—Hall and Whitaker, Stout and Atkinson—were able, but less colorful, men. Even they, however, felt the need to appeal directly to the public. The Conservative leader, Atkinson, toured the electorates in 1883 in a manner imitative of, but less successful than, his rivals. It was a significant omen that a party leader must now appeal directly to the voters and on a national scale.

The direct appeal to the voter was stimulated by another factor which encouraged the growth of regular party organization. As the legislation of 1881 had extended the franchise, a larger electorate had to be canvassed, which made party organization all the more necessary. The newly enfranchised had votes to cast, and it was imperative for rival politicians to win their allegiance. Moreover, the independent voter could be more easily swayed if a party had an outstanding leader to attract him with a personal loyalty. It was the improvement in communications which first offered the opportunity for a stronger form of national party organization; the growth of the electorate provided the occasion; together these produced the recognized party leader. Frequently from 1876 onward members of the House applied to themselves and their opponents the labels of British party politics. One side named itself "Liberal" and was dubbed "Radical" by its adversaries. The latter in turn were self-styled as "Conservatives" but received the derogatory title of "Tories." It was the Conservatives who ruled Parliament during most of the period from 1876 to 1890. For two short intervals the Liberal group gained the ascendancy, under Grey's leadership from 1877 to 1879, and under Vogel and Stout from 1884 to 1887. Party and ministerial history was made up of successive Liberal assaults and the final breakup of the Conservatives.

When Vogel resigned the premiership in 1876 to represent New Zealand in London, his treasurer, Atkinson, succeeded to the chief post in the cabinet. Atkinson's party support was composed of the erstwhile centralists and of the Conservatives who looked with a benign eye on large landholdings. Arrayed against them were the survivors of the provincialist party together with the Liberals. The Conservatives held power for only one year after Vogel left them. In his financial statement of 1877 Atkinson said that the need of the country was political rest. Such a policy, which received the soubriquet of "rest and be thankful," was scarcely likely to satisfy Grey and his Liberals. Their attacks on Atkinson were aided by the difficulties which the premier encountered over his education bill of the same year. Since the provinces, which had formerly been responsible for education, were now no more, the central government had to provide its own legislation. Inevitably the question of educational policy stirred up a sectarian controversy in which Protestants fought Catholics on the lines of a religious rather than a political cleavage. The confused divisions over the education bill weakened the ministry and lowered its prestige. Consequently, Grey was able to defeat them on a motion of no confidence by the narrow margin of forty-five to forty-one. He then formed a Liberal ministry, which held office for two years but without much success. Indeed, the Liberal party of this time was later aptly described by Reeves as "rather a party of attempts than of achievements."[18]

18. William P. Reeves, *State Experiments in Australia and New Zealand* (2 vols.; London: Allen & Unwin, 1902), I, 105.

Grey's ineffectiveness as premier was partly due to his precarious hold over the House. In the session of 1877, parties were so nearly equipoised that Grey requested a dissolution. The governor, however, refused. Not to be outdone, the premier took into his ministry two new and able Liberals (Stout and Ballance) and decided to appeal directly to the people. Touring the country, he visited all four main centers and addressed large audiences. His reward came in some by-elections, which strengthened his parliamentary majority. Throughout the session of 1878 Grey's position was temporarily more secure. But the defects of his character now came to the fore and undermined his gains. The autocratic tendencies, foreshadowed in his younger days, became more prominent as he grew older. Unwilling to compromise, irritable, and tactless, he lost the good will even of his own supporters. Ballance, a man of mild disposition, resigned from the ministry after an argument in which Grey lost his temper. Stout also left him in order to resume his law practice. It was not surprising, therefore, that in the first session of 1879 Grey suffered a defeat of forty-eight votes to thirty-four. Again he requested a dissolution, which this time was granted. A general election increased Grey's parliamentary support but not sufficiently to save him. Defeated by two votes in the new Parliament, he resigned.

These circumstances led up to one of the most striking situations in the parliamentary history of New Zealand. In the events that followed Grey's resignation the state of the party system, as it had so far evolved, was clearly revealed. John Hall, the leader of the opposition, had beaten Grey by two votes and proceeded to form a ministry of Conservatives. Including such men as Atkinson and Whitaker, it was devoted to the interests of the large landholders. But, as soon as Hall's ministry was announced, two of the representatives who had voted for him switched over to Grey. Consequently, Hall and his party found themselves in office but in a minority of two. A Gilbertian tangle ensued. Hall proposed to introduce the bills of the former Liberal ministry, and Liberal backbenchers were loftily exhorted by Conservative ministers to vote for their measures irrespective of the men who sponsored them. The Liberals, on the other hand, were infuriated

at seeing a minority government audaciously steal their own beloved program. With overanxious haste, they obstructed the
debates, seeking to place on the order paper a motion of no confidence in which they were sure that Hall would be defeated. The
premier countered this obstruction by refusing an opportunity to
debate their motion. The Liberal opposition, on their part, were
weakened through disputes over the leadership, for, when his
ministry was beaten, Grey resigned from leading the party, and
no one else had prestige comparable to his. Thus for two weeks
the deadlock was protracted, while Hall avoided divisions as best
he could. At long last the impasse was broken by four Auckland
Liberals who had been supporters of Grey. These agreed to vote
for Hall on certain conditions: (1) he must enact the representation bill proposed by the Liberals; (2) he must leave undisturbed
the principles of free, compulsory, and secular education in the
Act of 1877; (3) he must take into the ministry an Auckland member but not one of themselves; and (4) he must allot to Auckland
its appropriate share of public expenditure.

Over this agreement arose a virulent, rancorous controversy
whose echoes reverberated through the debates for many sessions.
From the Conservative side of the House the four Aucklanders
who changed over were greeted as patriotic men who placed
principles above persons and country above party. The Liberals,
however, assailed their erstwhile colleagues with every known
parliamentary epithet and with many that were unparliamentary, the most common designation being "the Auckland rats."
The gravamen of the charge lay in the act of "desertion." The
Liberal party had held various caucus meetings, at one of which
Grey resigned the leadership. Unable to unite on a leader to
succeed him (no fewer than four were proposed), the party
nevertheless agreed to act together as a body until the division of
no confidence. In Grey's own words: "Forty-two gentlemen
entered into an agreement that they would form no coalition until the vote which had been so long pending was taken."[19] One of
the four Aucklanders, named Reader Wood, had himself supported this agreement in the caucus. Later he justified himself to
an angry Parliament by admitting that he was "not a model

19. *P.D.*, XXXII (1879), 526.

party man."[20] The House, in his view, had reached an impasse in which the Liberal measures now sponsored by a minority Conservative government were being obstructed by a Liberal opposition, while the ministry in turn blocked the debate on the no-confidence motion. He thought the Liberals so disunited that, even were they to carry their motion, they could not form a ministry. It was therefore better to support Hall provided that he enacted Liberal measures. Another one of the four, named Colbeck, stated that his support of liberalism was a personal allegiance to Grey which lapsed when Grey ceased to be leader. He was therefore free to act as he chose.[21]

The whole situation was realistically summed up by a Conservative in this way: "The Opposition hoped that some members would go over from our side, and we hoped that some members would come over from their side. Sooner or later it was bound to come about."[22] It did come about, also, because the party system was passing through its transitional stage. The Liberals were making the effort to constitute themselves an organized body which would formulate a concerted plan of action. The importance to the party of their leader was proved by the chaos which followed his resignation. Loyalties of individual members were based on their devotion partly to a set of principles, partly to a particular man. Caucuses were held to determine party policy, and decisions were reached which the majority considered morally binding on the minority. Some members, on the other hand, still claimed their right of independent action, denying that the party could bind them, especially when it was internally split.

The Conservative party, which thus scraped into office in 1879, remained there until 1884. It survived a general election in 1881 and emerged unscathed from various ministerial metamorphoses. It served under three different premiers—Hall, the laborious and unimaginative; Whitaker, a cunning lawyer-financier devoted to his dividends; and Atkinson, a farmer and tough former major from the Maori wars. These Conservatives were confronted with

20. *Ibid.*, p. 525.
21. Grey himself vindicated Colbeck on this ground (*ibid.*, p. 530).
22. *Ibid.*, p. 538.

the economic aftermath of the Vogel boom. Their task was to grapple with the slump and the urban unemployment that persisted through the eighties. Inevitably their remedies consisted in economy and retrenchment. For instance, a civil service commission, appointed in 1880 under the chairmanship of Alfred Saunders, secured drastic slashings of departmental staffs and salaries. The ministry leaned strongly upon the rural representatives, whom it courted with its Electoral Act of 1881. It was solicitous for the vested interests of large landowners. Hall himself represented the Selwyn electorate in the Canterbury plains, a citadel of the "squattocracy"; and Atkinson, the Egmont district in the rich Taranaki farmlands. The Liberals, meanwhile, were disorganized and disconsolate, despite their early flowering under Grey. Freed from the responsibility of office and leadership, Grey himself kept liberalism in ferment by introducing proposals as controversial as he could devise.[23] Among these were suggestions to abolish the Legislative Council, to stop plural voting, and to prevent a premier from holding directorates, all thoroughly sound ideas and calculated to cause the maximum of annoyance to the Conservatives. Apart from Grey and a few still faithful supporters, the main body of Liberals was led by a Canterbury representative, Montgomery, who lacked both dynamism and popular appeal. Powerless, because they were disunited, the nascent Liberal party straggled through five lean years.

Eventually in 1884 the Conservatives were defeated in the House, and the causes of their defeat were again symptomatic of the condition of parties. A motion of no confidence was proposed by a Liberal who had to admit that his own party was then divided under two leaders. The two wings, however, combined for this occasion against their common opponents, since their differences were largely personal and since on fundamentals of social philosophy they were in agreement. The future premier, Seddon, already a vociferous Liberal, stated clearly his opinion on the gulf that separated Conservatives from the Liberal groups: "It is all

23. See his statement: "Whilst in office, I was hampered by my colleagues and by my party, but, out of office, I can bring in Bills which I entirely believe in" (quoted by Alfred Saunders, *History of New Zealand* [2 vols.; Wellington: Whitcombe & Tombs, 1896], II, 470, from an election speech).

nonsense to talk of Liberalism and Conservatism in New Zealand. It is the rich and the poor; it is the wealthy and the landowners against the middle and labouring classes. That, Sir, shows the real political position of New Zealand."[24] But the Liberals could not have carried their motion by themselves. They were aided by an all-important defection from the Conservative ranks. For several sessions many South Island members, particularly those from Canterbury and the west coast, had been urging the government to build a railway line across their island from east to west. The government had dallied with them, making gestures and promises and doing nothing. Consequently, a number of Conservatives from Canterbury, disappointed in their hopes of securing the line from Atkinson, decided to join the Liberals and turn the ministry out of power. As the price of their desertion, they would require a Liberal ministry to give them their railway. Thus the downfall of the Conservative party was due quite as much to regional groupings as to a conflict over social issues. Across the economic division ran a railway line, leading to a temporary junction of incompatibles.

When his government was defeated, Atkinson requested a dissolution which the governor granted. In the following general elections, the Liberals attacked the Conservative administration of the preceding five years. But the campaign was complicated by the re-entry into New Zealand politics of Vogel, whose borrowing policies again became a subject of bitter dispute. The Conservatives under Atkinson's leadership found their support more in the North Island than in the South Island and more in the rural than in the urban electorates. The Liberals conducted the election under four distinct leaders, each with his different sphere of influence. In Dunedin, Vogel and Stout were popular; Christchurch was a stronghold both of Vogel and of Montgomery; and Auckland was devoted to Grey. When the new Parliament assembled in the same year (1884), the process of ministry-making was as confused as in 1879. The relative strength of the opposing groups made some form of coalition necessary. Roughly a third of the members supported Atkinson. But the Liberals, who together constituted more than a half of the House, were split into

24. *P.D.*, XLVII (1884), 171.

three groups under Vogel, Grey, and Montgomery, of which Vogel's following equaled that of Atkinson. It was, therefore, impossible for Atkinson to form a ministry without aid from at least one section of the Liberals. Similarly, if the ministry was to be Liberal, more than one group and their leaders would have to sink their differences.

Personal animosities, however, between the leaders also contributed to the parliamentary tangle. Grey disliked Atkinson, his old Conservative foe, and almost hated Vogel, the destroyer of his beloved provinces. He had also estranged Stout, who had resigned from Grey's ministry in 1879. Nevertheless, Grey was anxious to regain the premiership and sought to maneuver himself into it. Vogel was similarly inimical to Grey and was now opposed to his former colleague, Atkinson, who had laid on him the political blame for the slump. With Stout and Montgomery, on the other hand, Vogel was prepared to co-operate, even though his liberalism had a far more Conservative tinge than theirs.[25] Atkinson, too, was always eager for office and would combine even with Grey to keep out Vogel. And while the gods quarreled on Olympus, the demigods found it seasonable for bargain-hunting. Canterbury members, still determined to get their railway, supported Vogel en bloc and opposed any ministry from which he was excluded.

The stage was thus set for a tragicomedy in four acts. As the curtain rose on the new Parliament, the first act opened with Atkinson's resignation. Vogel was then requested to form a ministry. With the collaboration of Stout, Ballance, and Montgomery, he did so and, because of his own ill-health, made Stout the premier. This did not please Sir George Grey, who saw a Liberal ministry of his own former colleagues allied to the semi-Conservative Vogel.[26] Hence, in the first scene of the second act Grey switched to the opposition, taking with him his small band of Liberals and some non-Liberal Aucklanders who felt that the new ministry should contain more Auckland representatives. Combining his votes with Atkinson's, he was able to defeat Stout

25. While Vogel was in England, he had stood for the Falmouth constituency in the 1880 election as a Conservative supporter of Disraeli.

26. Although invited to join this ministry, Grey declined if Vogel was also to be a member (*P.D.*, XLVIII [1884], 58).

and Vogel on the first division. But Grey himself could not form a ministry, though he tried desperately to weld a coalition between Atkinson's group and the Liberals, minus Vogel. Failing in this, and still envenomed against Vogel, he advised the governor to send for Atkinson.

The third act ensued when Atkinson, glorying in the disunity of the Liberals, resumed the treasury benches, doubtless expecting that he would hold them, as Hall had done in 1879, through more defections from the Liberal ranks. Sir George, however, soon grew disgruntled with his new alliance, since he found Atkinson unwilling to institute a land tax. Switching his support once again, he took his group of supporters across the House to rejoin the Liberals. Thus Atkinson was speedily defeated in a division where thirteen members, including Grey, who had formerly voted against the Stout-Vogel combination now sided with it. In the final act of the drama, the Stout-Vogel ministry returned to power, dropping Montgomery (whose support was in any case assured) and taking in another Aucklander in his place. From this welter of intrigues it was Grey who emerged with lowered reputation. The Liberals were rightly incensed at his tactics. It need not be supposed, however, that the ministry which finally survived the mêlée contained harmonious exponents of the quintessence of liberalism. Between Premier Stout and Treasurer Vogel were cleavages of view upon which the opposition delighted to expatiate. For three years the Stout-Vogel ministry awkwardly maintained itself in office, but it gained little luster for liberalism. At the next general election in 1887 it was so badly beaten that even Stout lost his seat. Grey, who had contributed to Stout's downfall, enjoyed grim satisfaction in seeing Atkinson victorious.

The Conservative party now returned to another three years of power, its last and mournful swan song. To face the problems of urban unemployment and industrial depression, Atkinson had contested the election on the slogans "Retrenchment" and "No More Vogelism and Extravagance." Soon, however the pressure of events drove him into policies which split his own party. In 1888 he introduced a protective tariff designed to encourage local industries and raise revenue through customs duties. Protection was accepted by thirty-four of his party, who became known as the "government swallowers." But there were another twenty, the "government malcontents," who preferred to break away. It was only with the aid of Ballance and a number of Liberals that Atkinson carried his proposal. At long last, the Conservatives were broken by an economic issue that cut through their common interest to conserve their property. Professor Condliffe has compared Atkinson, who split the Conservatives by introducing protection, with Peel, who split the British Conservatives when he brought in free trade.

The Liberals, who had suffered a setback in their electoral defeat of 1887, now seized their opportunity. In 1889 they organized into a compact body under Ballance. Throughout the country the situation grew daily more encouraging for their political prospects. The working class and the middle class in the towns, as well as the landless and the small farmers, were all uniting in protest against the plutocracy which dominated both economics and politics. They were ready for new and more drastic solutions to the economic malaise, and they supported new men to carry the task through. The Conservatives had been tried in office for many years and had now nothing to offer. Their one hope lay in the prestige of their leader, Atkinson, who had been in office almost continuously since 1874. But Atkinson was now gravely ill, and his energies were inadequate to confront and master a reinvigorated Liberal opposition. With the breakdown of the old Conservative oligarchy, and the emergence of a powerful Liberal party, the country was ready for the commencement of a new era in its political history. From 1891 onward New Zealand was to experience alike the benefits and defects of a modern party system.

CHAPTER IV

THE CABINET

IT IS over seventy years since Walter Bagehot first explained that the British system of politics meant government by the cabinet. Any scientific analysis of the cabinet's internal structure and operation was long precluded, partly by a skilfully woven veil of official reticence and partly by that attitude of awe with which so many Englishmen have regarded their *arcana imperii*. In place of such analysis writers have often sought refuge in literary metaphors. Bagehot himself initiated a long series of attempts at descriptive imagery when he pictured the cabinet as "a hyphen that joins, a buckle that fastens the legislative part of the Constitution to the executive part." Later the Haldane report named it "the mainspring of all the mechanism of government"; while Mr. Ramsay Muir has termed it "the steering-wheel of the ship of State." Only in recent years has Professor Jennings garnered together the material which depicts the cabinet as it functions from inside.[1] The obscurity traditionally enshrouding the British cabinet has been transmitted to the Antipodes, where it has cloaked the New Zealand counterpart. But enough information can be picked out of the parliamentary debates and biographies to throw light on this vital institution. The cabinet, of course, is an outgrowth of the party system and is unintelligible except in the context of the functions and organization of parties. When, therefore, the electorate was small, when issues were confused, when rival politicians contested for leadership, and when organization among the voters was a novelty, inevitably the cabinet reflected the character of its environment.

Duration in Office

An outstanding feature of New Zealand politics in the nineteenth century was the frequency with which ministries were

1. W. Ivor Jennings, *Cabinet Government* (London: Cambridge University Press, 1938), *passim*.

made and unmade. Ministerial crises were continually recurring; motions of no confidence were an ever present threat; and resignations, shakeups, and coalitions constituted the party history of more than three decades. For the thirty-five years from 1856 to 1890 the official record of the New Zealand Parliament lists no less than twenty-five separate ministries. On an average, therefore, each remained in office under a year and a half. Such brief tenures form an instructive contrast to the duration of British cabinets in the same period. In the mother-country, from Palmerston's ministry, which commenced in 1855, up to the Salisbury ministry, which fell in 1892, there were only twelve governments in just over thirty-six years. That makes an average tenure of three years for each ministry, or twice as long as the New Zealand average. The reasons for the difference are not hard to seek. The economic impact upon Britain of the Industrial Revolution, combined with the political influence of the French Revolution, had led to a cleavage within the social framework of so old a country, translating itself into a struggle on parliamentary lines. Great principles were debated and profound issues were at stake, and both principles and issues were dramatized by conflict between strong leaders. The party battle in Britain was, therefore, drawn along clear-cut lines at an earlier date than in newly settled New Zealand, and parliamentary groupings were somewhat more stable; in consequence, British ministries enjoyed a longer term. Only in the eighties did New Zealand politics assume the character of a class conflict, and even then it took some years before disciplined parties emerged.

How short lived were the New Zealand ministries may be seen from Table 5, which classifies them according to the length of their terms. Twelve ministries (almost half the total) were in office for less than a year. Only five in the whole period survived for over three years. The Stafford ministries (1856–61 and 1865–69) were the two most long lived. But the first of these lasted for as long as five years chiefly because Parliament then met biennially;[2] and the second clung precariously to life because after the political chaos of the preceding years no one else wished to assume the thankless task of government. The Fox

2. Parliament did not meet in 1857 or 1859.

ministry (1869–72) owed its three-year term to the success of McLean's native policy and to Vogel's financial proposals. The Stout-Vogel (1884–87) and the Atkinson ministries (1887–90) held power between them for the last six years of the period, and their lengthier tenures marked the growing cohesiveness of party groupings. Of the seven which expired within two months, two were strangled in infancy during the early attempts to set up responsible government in 1856. Two more were the victims of Grey's parliamentary maneuvering in 1884. Another was an unsuccessful ministry under Stafford which slipped into power for a month in 1872 and was speedily dispatched. All of these, therefore, represented newly born ministries which failed in the strug-

TABLE 5

LENGTH OF TERM OF NEW ZEALAND MINISTRIES, 1856–90

Length of Term	No. of Ministries
Under two months	7
Two months to one year	5
One year to two years	6
Two to three years	2
Over three years	5
Total	25

gle for survival. The remaining two in this group of seven were not in the strict sense new ministries, although they were so recorded officially, but rather ministerial reshuffles. Even if allowance be made for these two, there was certainly a high mortality rate among early New Zealand cabinets.

Continuity of Personnel

But the cold, bare statistics of cabinet changes conceal as much as they reveal. They do not, for example, convey an accurate picture of the continuity of personnel which underlay many ministerial mutations. The statistics would be considerably modified if one picked out only those changes of ministry which involved a substantial difference in personnel and in policy. Thus the two inaugural cabinets of Sewell and Fox, each an abortive attempt lasting only a few weeks, could reasonably be neglected, and Stafford's long and stable ministry could be selected as the starting-point. The first real change of government occurred in the year 1861, when Fox displaced Stafford. The next four years witnessed four alterations which deserve to be counted as separate ministries, and these were followed by another long spell of power for Stafford. The sixth change occurred in 1869, when Fox again ousted Stafford and sponsored Vogel's plans for borrowing. Except for a month's interlude under Stafford in 1872, all the ministries from 1869 to 1876 were really the one same ministry dominated by Vogel. When Vogel resigned the premiership in 1876, Atkinson merely took over a cabinet which remained virtually the same. Not until Grey rode into power in 1877 could another radical change of men and measures be detected. There was an eighth change two years later when the Conservatives under Hall wriggled deviously into office. Despite two reconstructions, it was the same government which lasted up to 1884. The advent of the Stout-Vogel combination marked the ninth change, and Atkinson's return in 1887 constituted the tenth. Hence, if one looks beneath the official records to the political actualities, it appears that New Zealand had roughly eleven different governments during these thirty-five years. Viewed in this light, the cabinet system manifests somewhat greater stability than would otherwise appear.

In fact, a case can be presented for an even higher degree of continuity. Dividing the ministerial history of the period at the year 1869, one can argue that before that date a group headed by Stafford held office for almost ten years. Their ten-year term was, however, interrupted by a series of short-lived wartime governments. After 1869, one and the same ministry stayed in power right up to 1890. Its tenure was broken only by the two Liberal cabinets of Grey and of Stout. So persistently did one group of politicians dominate New Zealand politics during the seventies and eighties that they actually received the title of the "Continuous Ministry" and were so described in parliamentary debates. A minister, speaking in 1884, ascribed the parenthood of the "Continuous Ministry" to Vogel and said that it had originated in 1869.[3] In the course of its long history, this ministry naturally underwent much internal modification. At its outset it was headed by Fox, Vogel, and McLean. Fox went out of it in

3. *P.D.*, XLVIII (1884), 74.

1872, and Vogel became its mainstay. When the latter quit in 1876, he left it in Atkinson's hands. During the eighties it was under the control of Atkinson, Whitaker, and Hall. It had begun in 1869 as a liberal-minded group but developed in a more conservative direction. Its membership was subject to the same subtle metamorphosis as its policies. Vogel, who was instrumental in founding it in 1869, was opposed to it in 1884; and Atkinson, a free-trader of liberal instincts in his early career, ended up as a conservatively minded protectionist. Reeves, who helped to deliver its death blow in 1891, described it in these words: "The Continuous Ministry was a name given to a shifting combination, or rather series of combinations, amongst public men, by which the Cabinet was from time to time modified without being completely changed at any one moment. . . . . The Continuous Ministry might be likened to the pearly nautilus, which passes by gradual growth and movement from cell to cell in slow succession; or, more prosaically, to that oft-repaired garment, which at last consisted entirely of patches.[4]

There is evidence, therefore, of the continuity as well as the mutability of cabinets. "New" ministries were seldom composed entirely of new men. It was indeed the exception, not the rule, when an incoming government included no members from the outgoing. The looseness of party ties permitted coalitions between erstwhile opponents and compromises of their principles. In this phase of its political development New Zealand closely resembles the parliamentary system of democratic France. Despite incessant changes of government and ministerial crises in France, the cabinet personnel often continued to be substantially unchanged. A similar parallel can be found in the politics of democratic Italy, whose technique of *trasformismo* finds its analogue in New Zealand.[5] It was thus a common practice in New Zealand before 1890 for leading politicians to participate in numerous ministries under different premiers. Even men who had themselves been premier accepted office under the premiership of another. In the whole period from 1856 to 1890 the total per-

4. W. P. Reeves, *The Long White Cloud* (3d ed.; London: Allen & Unwin, 1924), p. 245.
5. See M. Hentze, *Pre-Fascist Italy* (London: Allen & Unwin, 1939), *passim*.

sonnel of the twenty-five ministries amounted to eighty-five individuals, many of whom were members of an astonishing number
of cabinets. Fox, for instance, participated in five ministries, in
four of which he was premier. Whitaker held office eight times,
occupying the premiership twice. Vogel's name also appeared in
eight ministries, and Sewell's in seven. But Atkinson holds the
record, if that be an enviable distinction. He belonged to eleven
cabinets and was premier five times.

It will be seen in the next chapter how the premiership,
though frequently swapped around, remained in few hands.[6]
Two other important portfolios were similarly treated. The
colonial treasurer (nowadays known as the minister of finance)
held the second highest office in the cabinet. New Zealand witnessed fourteen different persons in that position while its democracy was in evolution. But half of those fourteen graced the
office only once, whereas Vogel and Atkinson each filled it seven
times. Certain politicians, such as the flexible Wood, managed
to remain treasurer continuously under successive ministries of
quite different character. Actually between 1856 and 1869 three
men (Richmond, Fitzherbert, and Wood) held this post among
them for over eleven years; and between 1869 and 1890 Vogel
and Atkinson monopolized it for nearly twenty years. The other
portfolio of crucial character was that of native affairs, and for
four-fifths of this period a member of the cabinet was specially
designated as native minister. Although this portfolio was allocated to thirteen different persons, the combined terms in
office of four of these amounted to nineteen years. The most remarkable achievement in this office was that of Donald McLean,
who was native minister continuously for almost eight years
(1869–76). His long tenure of a thorny assignment constituted an
imperium in imperio from which no premier dared or desired to
oust him.

So frequent were the exchanges of office among a relatively
small group of men that much sarcastic comment was evoked.
Fox, whose witty tongue could flicker like a fencer's rapier, once
spoke in these terms of a notorious office-seeker: "Of course, I am
extremely glad to hear that my old colleague Mr. Sewell, the

6. Chap. v, p. 98.

friend and the colleague, under varying circumstances, of so many honourable members, in so many Ministries of so many opinions, has become a member of the Ministry."[7] Similarly Saunders, writing in the nineties from the vantage heights of retrospective omniscience, commented thus about Wood, who was continuously treasurer under the peace ministry of Fox, the war ministry of Domett, and the coalition ministry of Fox and Whitaker: "Mr. Wood had become the useful standing Treasurer to both parties. He could talk figures well, and was a pleasant, lively, racy speaker upon general subjects; but he was easy-going as a politician, and would, at any time, be more likely to give weight to the strong than to throw himself away upon a weakly supported cause."[8] Fox himself recognized that it was unwise for a limited clique to swap the portfolios among themselves, and he had the honesty and strength of character to apply this conviction to his own case. In 1872 when the Stafford ministry was defeated on Vogel's motion, Fox could have been premier again had he wished. Instead he left it to Vogel to form the ministry, announcing that it was now someone else's turn: "There has been in this Assembly too much interchange of office, between certain old members of the political world."[9]

This remark was well substantiated by the facts. It was perfectly true that up to 1869 New Zealand ministries had resembled a group of interlocking directorates with the bulk of the shares held by Stafford, Fox, Whitaker, Sewell, and Wood. In 1869 Fox introduced to the charmed circle two extremely able men— Vogel and McLean—who succeeded to his power and were indispensable to the ministries of the next seven years. Not until 1877 did there occur a really drastic change in personnel. When Grey and his Liberals came into office, the impetuous premier made a clean sweep of all the old ministers. With one minor exception, none of Grey's ministers had ever before held such rank. The first Liberal premier of New Zealand infused new blood with a vengeance! Possibly this may have contributed to

7. *P.D.*, XIII (1872), 164. Fox was referring to the personnel of the third Stafford ministry.

8. Alfred Saunders, *History of New Zealand* (2 vols.; Wellington: Whitcombe & Tombs, 1896), II, 102.

9. *P.D.*, XIII (1872), 751.

the ineffectiveness of Grey's ministry, which broke up in 1879 from its own internal weakness. After Grey's interlude the "old gang" returned to power headed by the shrewd and conservative trio, Hall, Atkinson, and Whitaker. To assist them, they brought in one very able new man, William Rolleston, who had sensible proposals for land reform, and another new man of less ability, named Bryce, who failed to equal McLean's success in handling native affairs. The ministry established in 1884 by Stout and Vogel represented a queer admixture of the conservative Vogel (who could no longer be regarded as "new blood") with a team of Liberals who had graduated under Grey. One of these, John Ballance, was later destined to launch on its career the great Liberal ministry of the nineties. After Stout and Vogel were defeated in the election of 1887, the last ministry of the period marked positively the final appearance of the aging conservative leaders, Atkinson, Whitaker, and Hall,[10] around whom pirouetted a number of less competent satellites. When Atkinson was beaten at the polls in 1890, the electoral verdict spelled the political death sentence on the measures, as well as the men, of the old triumvirate.

Cabinet history up to 1890, therefore, exhibits two seemingly inconsistent tendencies. To all outward appearances ministries were unstable and impermanent. Yet beneath the ripples and eddies of the surface the political current flowed, on the whole, steadily and strongly. Sudden and erratic changes in its course were relatively few. The inconsistency, if such it be, requires an explanation. Why was it that ministries changed, whereas some of the ministers did not? The answer is that Parliament contained in those days many influential leaders; but their influence was either circumscribed within a limited region of the colony or was confined to a particular field of governmental activity. There were many politicians who could be useful members of a ministry, and there were a few whose local power or experience in some special branch of administration made them almost indispensable. Featherston, for instance, could bring to a ministry the backing of his followers in Wellington Province, and Mac-

10. Hall, who was old and ill, did not join the ministry but remained as an adviser in the background.

andrew was a popular vote-getter in Otago, while McLean could contribute to the government his unrivalled ability in conducting relations with the Maoris, or Rolleston his skill and wisdom in the reform of land tenures. Scarcely ever was there any one man whose general influence throughout the entire country accorded him a pre-eminent position above all other members of Parliament. Vogel was perhaps the clearest exception to this generalization. From 1870 onward when he was in Parliament, no ministry could be formed without him. Though pre-eminent in finance, his genius was not limited to the fiscal aspect of general policies, and his vision broadened from that of a provincial partisan to a nation-builder. Usually, however, political power was parceled out among a number of independent leaders who did not necessarily acknowledge a common allegiance to a single party generalissimo. For this reason, when the leaders quarreled, ministries were unmade and then refashioned. Some of the leaders merely entered into new alliances and remained in power. Otherwise no new ministry could be formed.

The Cabinet's Relation to the House

The same causes account for another notable trait of cabinet government during this period. In general, the survival of ministries depended only indirectly on their support in the electorate. In the fifties and sixties particularly the subordination of the ministry to the House of Representatives was so marked that it was the House, and not the voters, who decided what kind of government should take office. Not before 1884 was any cabinet unseated as an immediate result of a general election. This contention can be proved by a survey of ministries and elections before 1890. The ministries at the very beginning, which rose and fell in the session of 1856, were dependent on the shifts of parliamentary blocs over which they had no control. Premier Fox, insecurely perched on a parliamentary quicksand, expressed the true position at that date with characteristic candor: "The Ministry was quite willing to stand or fall on the deliberate voice of the House being expressed."[11] Stafford kept his power for the

11. *P.D.* (1856–58), p. 109.

next five years largely because the blocs were temporarily tired of shifting and because Parliament met too infrequently to dislodge him. In 1861 a general election was held; but, although Stafford lost power soon after the new Parliament assembled, his defeat could not be ascribed to the election. The old Parliament, at its last session, had been almost equally divided on the war issue, and so was the new one.[12] It was not the electorate who settled that Stafford should go, but the House.

The kaleidoscopic ministerial changes of the next four years were decided by the same body. In this quinquennium (1861-65) the nadir of cabinet influence in Parliament was reached. When a general election occurred in 1866, Stafford remained premier. Yet the newly elected House forced him to reconstitute his cabinet. Again it was the House, rather than the electorate, which determined the composition of the ministry. Three years later the representatives decided that Stafford had held office long enough and superseded him with Fox. The result of the election in 1871 was to indorse the policies of the Fox-Vogel-McLean combination. Despite this electoral victory, the ministry was temporarily defeated by Stafford in 1872 for the plain reason that some of the private members who had been supporting Fox were disappointed with the helpings allotted from the pork barrel to their particular districts. Although the audacious Stafford was turned off the treasury benches within a month, his exit from office was marked by a significant novelty. He requested the governor for a dissolution which the latter refused to grant.[13] This was the first occasion in New Zealand history when a ministry, lacking a majority in the House, was unwilling to accept its verdict and sought to appeal beyond the House to the people.

Of the ministerial changes between 1872 and 1877, none was due to an electoral setback. The 1875 election was held on the specific issue whether the provinces should be abolished and again confirmed the Vogel ministry in power. Before long Grey and his nascent Liberal party managed to depose Atkinson. But once more the government's defeat was due to a switching of

12. In 1860 Stafford had a majority of 19 votes to 17. Saunders, who participated in the 1861 election, said that its "net result was to leave the House as it had been before" (op. cit., I, 423). In 1861 Stafford was beaten by 24 votes to 23.

13. On the subject of parliamentary dissolutions see below, chap. v, pp. 109-14.

parliamentary votes rather than to the clearly declared wish of the people. An identical experience befell Grey himself in 1879. Beaten in the House and obtaining a dissolution, he fought an election in which the voters failed to indicate clearly which ministry they preferred. The decision was left to Parliament, and, when it assembled, Grey and the Liberals fell from power under the circumstances already described.[14] Again the defeat of the cabinet was ascribable, not so much to the electoral results, as to the maneuvers of parliamentarians. Thereafter Conservative ministries maintained themselves in office for five years, their parliamentary position being unaltered by an election in 1881, which Saunders, who took part in it, called "uninteresting." The cabinet changes of 1881 and 1883 were mere reshuffles due to the premier's retirement, Hall resigning through illness, and Whitaker because embarrassing publicity was given to his private financial speculations.

After the general election of 1884 New Zealand witnessed so hasty a succession of ministerial changes[15] that it provoked much discussion about the relation of the cabinet both to the House and to the electorate. Stout argued that the elections results were evidence of public dissatisfaction with Atkinson. "The question," he stated, "put to the various electorates throughout this colony was 'shall we have the Continuous Ministry or not?' "[16] Atkinson's supporters replied that the elections had not pronounced a clear verdict for either side; and, in any case, they challenged the doctrine that it was for the voters to select the ministry. "To say that the constituencies," retorted Wakefield, "shall dictate to this House as to the men who shall be on these benches and the policy they should pursue is simply to turn representative institutions upside down."[17] But the final outcome of the ministerial turmoil in 1884 was to place in office a new government which undeniably represented public opinion better than that which it displaced. Decidedly the election contributed to the change. Yet it should not be forgotten that Atkinson had actually been defeated at the last session of the old Parliament, and the voters' verdict at the election merely instructed the new Parlia-

14. See above, chap. iii, pp. 65–67.
15. See above, pp. 69–71.

16. *P.D.*, XLVIII (1884), 69.
17. *Ibid.*, p. 78.

ment to confirm its predecessor's action. In 1887 the last ministerial change during this period followed a somewhat similar
pattern. Defeated in the House, the Stout-Vogel ministry decided to hold as soon as possible the election which was legally
due for that year. The voters turned against the Liberals, thus
bringing Atkinson back to power. Again, be it noticed, the general election indorsed the defeat which the outgoing Parliament
had already inflicted on the ministry.

A clearly defined trend emerges from this survey of ministerial
changes. For the first two decades it was emphatically the House
which made and unmade cabinets. Such elections as were held
either confirmed the existing ministry without change or led to a
few substitutions in personnel. The House was supreme over the
ministry, not the ministry over the House. Reasons for this relationship may be found in the limitations upon the franchise, the
weakness of party organization, and the somewhat lengthy five-
year term enjoyed by members of the lower house. After 1876
ministries still continued to be the servants of the House, but
slowly they are forging the weapons to dominate it. Premiers and
their cabinets were less inclined to accept the decision of the representatives and were beginning to appeal over their heads to
their sovereign master, the electorate. When the representatives'
term was reduced from five years to three, their independence of
their constituents and the cabinet was somewhat diminished.
More than before, the ministerial weapon of a dissolution was
brandished over recalcitrant backbenchers. Dissolutions were
even secured on three occasions by ministries which no longer
had a parliamentary majority. It so happened in each case that
the voters ratified the decision already taken by Parliament. But
the appeal for an electoral decision was a significant innovation.
The way was at last clear for the crucial election of 1890, in which
for the first time a ministry, weakening but not yet defeated in
the House, was ejected at the polling booths.

The tendency after 1876 for the cabinet to emancipate itself
from parliamentary control and grow more dependent on the
electorate arose from the same factors which were responsible for
the development of the party system. An additional influence
upon New Zealand was the example of the mother-country. In

Victoria's Britain during the middle decades of the nineteenth century it was Parliament primarily which determined the choice of a ministry. Party organization, however, received a tremendous impetus when the franchise was extended by the second Reform Act of 1867 and later by the third Reform Act in 1884. Thenceforth the ministry gained predominance over the House of Commons. Disraeli and Gladstone, each in his own way, made the cabinet and Parliament more responsive to the voters. Disraeli gave proof of this after his defeat in the election of 1880, when he immediately resigned without waiting for the formality of a vote in the new Parliament. The precedents of Britain, and of the neighboring Australian colonies, were repeatedly cited by parliamentarians in New Zealand. Eventually the ministry succeeded in establishing its control over the House because it was only the ministry, not the House as a whole, which could give a political lead to the country at large. The member of Parliament, notwithstanding some of the opinions quoted above, could no longer wisely ignore the wishes of his constituents or of a government which had helped him to get elected. "Representative" democracy, in short, was at last beginning to deserve its name. Ministers had once been quite literally the servants of the king. For some decades past they had been servants of Parliament. Now they were developing into servants of the people.

Collective Responsibility

The causes, which at first subordinated the ministry to the House, also retarded the development of collective responsibility. The political history of Britain has shown that a ministry divided against itself cannot stand. To continue in office, it must remain united. Originally the cabinet had instituted the practice of collective responsibility as a policy of mutual security in its relations with the monarch. Ministers became colleagues and defended each other by a common bond of loyalty. If the king wished to oust any single individual, he would be obliged to replace the entire team. Essentially this is the principle on which trade-unions are organized. It is ironical that it was first introduced into British politics by conservative aristocrats. Collective

responsibility was their version of the "closed shop," and collective resignation was a ministerial general strike. Elevating this
expedient device into a constitutional convention, the cabinet
successfully maintained its independence of the Crown. By a
later corollary of the same principle it was able to assert its
mastery over Parliament. If Parliament were dissatisfied with
any one minister, it must substitute an entirely new cabinet.
Such was the general theory, even though exceptions might occur
at times. In New Zealand during those decades when the House
dominated the ministry, the latter's weakness was partly due to
the absence of collective responsibility among its members. The
cabinet became more cohesive as party organization grew
stronger. Thereby it became the master of the House.

To form a ministry in any of the early parliaments, it was
usually necessary to achieve a coalition between groups temporarily willing to work together. Leading members in each bloc
had to be offered a seat in the cabinet, and the choicest portfolios
were bestowed upon those who controlled the greatest voting
strength in the House. For the time being the group leaders
would agree to sink some of their political differences and co-
operate for limited purposes. The composition of a ministry was
thus federal rather than unitary, and its federalism was more
akin to confederacy than to federal union. Those who teamed together within the cabinet retained their residuary rights of independent action, and in the last resort they could employ without
challenge the ultimate weapon of secession.

Various parliamentary incidents will illustrate these generalizations. In 1866 the Stafford ministry found itself confronted
with a bill to limit the number of members of the Legislative
Council. Already approved in the Council, the bill was sponsored
in the House by a private member. During the debate on the
second reading the premier announced that, as the proposal
was not a government one, each member of the ministry would
vote according to his own opinions. Later, in a committee discussion, he expressed his own preference for an elective instead of
a nominated upper chamber. Almost immediately he was followed by his own postmaster-general, John Hall, who defended
the principle of nomination. He justified his disagreement with

Stafford by explaining that "on this occasion the individual members of the Government were not called upon to express a similar opinion and to give a like vote; because before the Government was formed they had expressed opinions differing from each other."[18] When the House eventually divided in committee on this bill, the cabinet members voted on opposite sides. A few years afterward ministers again agreed overtly to differ about a major principle. The bill to provide for the secret ballot in parliamentary elections was introduced by a private member and was carried on the second reading by thirty-seven to eighteen votes. In that division Stafford and other ministers voted for the "Ayes" along with the leader of the opposition, while three members of the cabinet sided with the "Noes." Admittedly, in both these instances it was a backbencher, not a member of the ministry, who introduced the measure in question. Plausibly, therefore, the ministry could waive the principle of collective responsibility. It happened, however, in these early decades that private members frequently exercised their legislative initiative and did not confine themselves to petty issues. The cabinet had not yet acquired its present-day monopoly over all legislation that matters. The activity of the nineteenth-century representative multiplied the occasions on which ministers voted in opposite lobbies.

As late as the eighties occurred a more remarkable cabinet split over a government measure. When Stout proposed his Representation Bill in 1886 and again in 1887, the ministry could not agree over the two vital issues of the number of members or the number of districts.[19] At the committee stage ministers distributed themselves between the lobbies with delightful impartiality. Leading the opposition in 1886, Atkinson could not forego such an opportunity to taunt the government. In his ex-major tones he proclaimed: "When I was in office my colleagues voted with me or they left me. They did not remain on those benches and vote against me. When one of my whips disagreed with me, he ceased to act."[20] Next year when the same bill was reintroduced, the cabinet surpassed even its previous

18. *P.D.*, (1864–66), p. 904.
19. See above, chap. ii, pp. 36–37.   20. *P.D.*, XLVI (1886), 731.

exhibition of split-voting, and a series of extraordinary committee divisions occurred. On a motion that the number of members of Parliament should be sixty, Stout and two ministers voted "No" with the minority, while two ministers joined the "Ayes." When it was proposed to have seventy-one members, one minister voted "Aye," while on the minority side were Stout and another colleague. When ninety-one members were proposed, Stout and three other cabinet members were among the "Ayes," and two of their colleagues sided with the "Noes." Such a hopeless spectacle of a disunited cabinet elicited afterward from an opposition backbencher the sarcastic comment: "We were tripping over Ministers whichever lobby we went into. The Ministers divided with the Whips the task of keeping both sides of the House in good humour."[21] In the ensuing Parliament Atkinson's own government could not conceal its internal dissension when a private member proposed that the term of elected representatives should be lengthened from three years to five. One of the ministers, Russell, uttered this revealing comment during the debate: "I rise to oppose the second reading of the Bill, although I do not disagree with it. 'Our life is two-fold,' and on this occasion I speak as a Minister and not as a private member. Were I in the position of a private member, I should be found supporting the honourable gentleman in the second reading of the Bill."[22] Afterward in the division Russell and one other minister voted "No," and two others voted "Aye."

Although the enforcement of the collective responsibility of the cabinet was a slow process, there were nevertheless some clear instances in which the principle was successfully invoked either by the majority in the cabinet or by one minister who disagreed with his colleagues. In the Fox ministry that held office from 1869 to 1872 Henry Sewell was at first a member. From statements made subsequently by Vogel and corroborated by Fox[23] it appears that, before Sewell joined the cabinet, Vogel read to him at the premier's request all the particulars of the proposed financial and public works policies. On Sewell's agreement to these proposals he joined the government; and it was distinctly

21. *P.D.*, XLVII (1887), 566.
22. *P.D.*, LXVIII (1890), 289.   23. *P.D.*, XIII (1872), 929–32.

understood that, if he were unable to agree, he was not to join. Subsequently Sewell fell out of step with the rest of the cabinet because of his attitude toward two bills dealing with the harbor docks and military reserves at Auckland. Prepared by Vogel, these measures were brought before the cabinet, where they were discussed clause by clause. Sewell objected to certain features but was unable to convince his colleagues. The bills were introduced as government measures, were passed by the lower house, and were sent to the Council. There Sewell, who represented the ministry in the upper house, refused to take charge of them. Vogel then offered Fox his resignation, stating that he could not work with a colleague who flouted cabinet decisions. When other ministers joined Vogel, the premier found himself compelled to dismiss Sewell. It became a question whether the rest of the government should resign or whether a one-man minority should do so.

It was Vogel also who precipitated a second incident in which the principle of collective responsibility was explicitly invoked. A somewhat theatrical scene took place in the House in 1874 when he moved the resolution that paved the way for abolition of the provinces. One of his ministers, O'Rorke, an arch-provincialist, immediately resigned from the cabinet and acted on his word by walking straight over to the opposition benches. Again, ministerial solidarity was asserted in 1881 during the controversy over the actions of John Bryce, the native minister. He had arrested an eminent Maori leader, Te Whiti, after a dispute in which many felt that right was on the Maori's side. In face of criticism Bryce preferred to leave the cabinet than to alter his policy. He returned to the cabinet only when a majority switched round to his view. Manifestly, Vogel in 1871, O'Rorke in 1874, and Bryce in 1881 all acted on the view that the ministry is a collegiate body which can speak with only one voice. Collective responsibility had gained some ground, but it awaited the firmer discipline of party organization to assert its full power.

Representation of Interests

If the cabinet was to be collectively responsible for all measures, it should be formed of like-minded men. Like-mindedness, however, was an elusive quality, but no prime minister had a completely free hand in selecting his ministry. He must offer a place to the prominent members of all the coalescing groups. He must concede to the wishes of leading politicians, who would enter the cabinet only if their closest associates were also invited. Ministry-making was further complicated by the need to include a representative of every major interest. Each of the principal regions, for instance, had to be represented in the cabinet by at least one member. Fox criticized the ministry newly formed by Domett in 1862 on the score that it contained only one person from the North Island. When Stafford announced the composition of his cabinet in 1865, he explicitly stated his belief that all large interests and population centers should be represented among its personnel. He confessed that at that moment he did not yet have any colleague who resided in Wellington Province but that he hoped soon to remedy that deficiency. Vogel likewise paid homage to the principle of allocating portfolios on a territorial basis. Informing the House of the personnel of the Waterhouse-Vogel ministry, he explained that there would be an equal number of ministers for each island, so that jealousy between the islands could be avoided.

The ministerial upheavals in the newly elected Parliament of 1884 were due to some extent to regional rivalries. When Stout and Vogel first formed their ministry, it contained three members from Canterbury (representing the railway pressure group) and only one from Auckland. This disproportionate treatment of Auckland was one of the factors which enabled Grey (whose own political strength lay in that area) to place himself at the head of the malcontents and turn out the ministry. When Stout and Vogel, after laying Atkinson low, reorganized their ministry, they dropped one of the Canterbury members. To conciliate the far north, they took in another Aucklander, Larnach by name, who had hitherto voted against them. Such concessions to regional competitiveness were a political consequence of New Zealand's geography and the dispersion of her main population centers. The four principal regions haggled for their share of public offices as well as of public works. The plums had to be distributed along with the pork.

A sagacious premier also needed to exercise care in the distribution of portfolios between town and country. Particularly in the eighties, when the growth of the cities was frightening the rural interests, cabinet-making required political acumen to fit the urban tenon into the rural mortise. The rising Liberal party represented in large part the protest of the urban working class against the dominant landowning oligarchy. It was chiefly from the cities that Liberal members were returned to Parliament. The landowners correspondingly sent to the legislature representatives of their own class and further fortified their electoral position by the device of the country quota. In consequence, the Liberal ministries of Grey and Stout were dominated by city members, while the Conservative cabinets were mostly filled with country representatives. Party divisions, however, did not follow with exactitude the line of the city-country cleavage. Certain urban constituencies normally elected Conservative members, and some country districts which contained mining centers would return such a Liberal as Seddon. If well constructed, the ministry contrived to avoid the appearance of sectional bias. Conservative cabinets usually included at least one city member as a sop to the urban voters, while the Liberals would give proof of their attention to rural problems by finding room for a country representative.

Ministers in the Legislative Council

Another consideration influencing the choice of ministers was the need to placate the Legislative Council. Since the New Zealand legislature was, as it still is, bicameral, bills had to be indorsed by both houses before becoming laws. Every government required its representative in the upper house to explain its policy and to pilot its measures through the various stages. A premier forming a new ministry was faced with the alternatives either of taking into the cabinet someone who was already in the Council or, if none of its members was suitable, of introducing a new appointee from outside. At a time when the upper house claimed authority almost co-ordinate with the lower, it was a political necessity to include a competent councilor in the ministry. A premier might be thought to offer a slight to the

Council if he selected as its leader one who did not enjoy its respect and confidence, and during that period most premiers carefully avoided any offense to the easily wounded vanities of the nominated chamber. Moreover, since the volume of legislative business was sometimes very great, it was unreasonable to place on one man the entire burden of guiding ministerial bills through the Council. Consequently, most ministries contained two members from the upper chamber who shared between them the responsibility for government measures.

In retrospect it is amusing to note that the first New Zealand ministry contained exactly four members divided equally between the two houses. Never since then has any cabinet been composed of the same number of members from the upper house as from the lower. Some ministries, indeed, in the decades up to 1890 had only one representative in the Council. In 1884, for example, the first and abortive Stout-Vogel ministry contained one lone councilor. As a result, the aggrieved upper house staged a debate in which many urged that the government ought always to include at least two from their body. Mindful that they were the New Zealand equivalent of the peers of the realm, some appealed to British precedent. The House of Lords, as they pointed out, supplied several members to every British cabinet; and by analogy so should the Legislative Council. The protest succeeded in its object, for, when Stout and Vogel formed their second cabinet a few weeks later, two ministers were duly allotted to the upper house.

After determining the number of ministers he would post in the Council, a premier was faced with the equally delicate question: What portfolios should they receive? A minister selected from the upper house might simply be included as a member of the cabinet but have no department assigned to his charge. It seemed stupid, however, to place an individual in the ministry and then give him no administrative duties. Usually some departmental activity would be intrusted to the government representative in the Council, if only in order to lighten the burden of his colleagues. Councilors themselves resented the practice of denying a portfolio to the government representative in the upper house, feeling that it was derogatory to the dignity of the minister and of themselves. Waterhouse thus persuaded the upper house to pass a resolution in 1884 that the government of the day should be represented in the Council by a minister holding a portfolio. Experience had proved that a minister who lacked this crowning glory was sometimes not invited to cabinet meetings; and, if summoned, he could not always speak with the requisite authority. While his colleagues in the cabinet were all wedded to their departments, he, like a spinster among married women, could only voice opinions and proffer suggestions lacking in equal prestige. Nor could the Council's special point of view, it was argued, be put to the cabinet with adequate force by one in a position of responsibility without power.

If prudence advised that the pride of the Council be satisfied, what were the best portfolios to confer on their ministerial representative? It could not be a portfolio of outstanding importance, or the lower house in turn would feel affronted. The customary solution was to assign to the minister in the Council one of two portfolios: the attorney-generalship or the post of colonial secretary. Each carried with it a certain amount of dignity; neither was of paramount political significance. Occasionally other departments might be intrusted to a councilor, such as the office of postmaster-general or even the ministry of native affairs. At times, moreover, the premier himself was a member of the upper house.[24]

The nominative character of the Council might sometimes prove a blessing and sometimes a curse to a prime minister constructing his cabinet. If he remained in office long enough, it was possible for a premier to pack the Council with his own supporters. His successor might then find that there was no one in that body whom he could take into his ministry. Indeed, this was exactly what Fox experienced on the two occasions (1861 and 1869) when he gained power after the lengthy Stafford ministries. In 1861 Fox put his own nominee, a doctor named Pollen, into the Council and made him a member of the cabinet without portfolio. Soon after, he also named Sewell a councilor, giving him the post of attorney-general. But to create a vacancy for this second appointment he had to induce a councilor to resign, which

24. See below, chap. v, p. 100.

was embarrassing. In 1869, when Fox was once again confronted with a Council filled with Staffordites, he went outside its membership and selected a competent civil servant, William Gisborne, whom Fox introduced to the upper chamber as the government representative. The Council could further be used as a back-door entrance into the ministry for someone who had not been elected to the lower house. This questionable practice was indulged in by Hall in a manner which aroused criticism. Anxious to secure a colleague who was shrewd and experienced, he invited Whitaker in 1879 to join his precarious cabinet. The only obstacle was that Whitaker had been a member of the lower house for the preceding three years and had recently lost his seat at the general election. That did not deter the Conservative premier from putting a defeated candidate into the upper house and making him attorney-general. Hall's action was strongly condemned by Grey, who protested that the voters' wishes were being disregarded. Grey even tried to persuade the governor not to appoint Whitaker but without avail. In principle Grey was right. Abuses of this nature were always possible as long as the constitution contained an element as utterly undemocratic as a legislative chamber filled by nomination.

Size of the Ministry

The administrative efficiency of any cabinet depended in part upon its size. Its size in turn was the result of converging political forces, one of which was the relationship between Parliament's two houses. At times the number of ministers allotted to the Legislative Council was determined by the total size of the ministry and by its voting strength in the lower house. If the ministry was small, say, six or under, there was not more than one councilor among its personnel. When it was larger, a premier might afford to be more generous to the upper chamber in his assignments. But he could only give a place in the cabinet to a councilor at the expense of a member of the lower house. If his majority were insecure, he might be pressed to invite into the inner sanctum an extra representative whose support, if he were denied office, would otherwise go to the opposition. If the premier had a strong party backing and a secure parliamentary margin of votes, he would find that the claims on the small number of ministerial positions were correspondingly multiplied. The claims of the lower house inevitably took priority over those of the upper. Hence, to produce the maximum satisfaction among his supporters, he might be induced to appoint another representative in a councilor's place.

Surveying the various ministries which guided New Zealand in its years of growth, one is struck by their disparity in size. They ranged from four members to ten. These variations did not follow any definite pattern, nor do they depict the steady enlargement of the cabinet to meet an ever growing volume of work. It appears impossible to detect any rationale in the successive expansions and contractions of the cabinet—apart from the one constant factor of political expediency. The ministries up to 1860 numbered only four or five persons, but, during the parliamentary topsy-turviness of the early sixties, the size jumped rapidly to seven or eight or, under Domett, to ten. Later in the same decade it varied between six and eight. Then, as a result of Vogel's vigorous policies, it was increased to nine. Abolition of the provinces, however, did not produce the further enlargement that might have been expected. The size either remained stationary after 1876 or contracted to six or seven. Throughout the eighties the number fluctuated from six to eight, and the last two ministries of the period were both manned with a complement of seven. On the whole, the tendency toward expansion, which manifested itself first in the early sixties and then in the early seventies, received in each case a subsequent check. The economizing measures, undertaken in the late sixties as a consequence of the Maori wars and again in the eighties as an aftermath of public works expansion, were applied by cabinets to their own personnel. More ministers meant more high salaries.

New Zealand derived some advantages from keeping the size of its cabinet within manageable limits. Already during those same years the British cabinet was swelling into the unwieldy and amorphous body that it has become in the twentieth century. The New Zealand ministry remained small. It was of a size which could operate effectively as a unit. But, while it avoided one defect, the Dominion steered full tilt into another. The functions of the central government had expanded in the early seventies under Vogel's touch, and they were further enlarged when the provinces were abolished. Though the cabinet continued to be generally the same size as before, the number of departments under its control grew steadily. Premiers were confronted with the task of distributing ever more portfolios among their colleagues. In the seventies and eighties on abundant occasions one minister was in charge of several portfolios. This was a practice which requires a mention here, for in modern times it has been perpetuated with unhappy administrative consequences. Nowadays it is all the more difficult to change, since its roots go far back in New Zealand history.

When a growing number of portfolios was distributed among a few men, the result was to throw upon ministers the heavy managerial responsibility of co-ordination and to overload them with administrative routine. The pressure of work upon cabinet ministers was not continuously heavy in the Victorian era, yet it rose to a peak in the two months before the parliamentary session and during the session itself. In one of the rare glimpses that Hansard offers of the cabinet in its day-to-day operation, Fox described the machinery of his ministry: "There was no time when the Government did the work of administration so badly as during the sitting of the Assembly. There was at present a huge accumulation of Cabinet papers on his table, which urgently required the attention of the Government, and he had not been able, during the whole session, to bring one of those papers under the attention of the Cabinet. The attention of the Cabinet had been wholly engrossed with the large questions referred to, and the other business brought before the House."[25] Subsequently, when out of office, he added this item of information: "The Cabinet met to prepare measures for the ensuing legislative action of the Assembly, and from day to day they held meetings of the Cabinet. He believed there was scarcely a day on which the Cabinet did not meet and deliberate for hours together."[26]

Such was the system in the days when the government undertook a tenth of what it does now. Hyphen, buckle, mainspring, steering-wheel—call the cabinet what you will—even in the seventies it was manifestly operating under strain.

25. *P.D.*, XI (1871), 1007.   26. *P.D.*, XIII (1872), 931–32.

CHAPTER V

THE PREMIERSHIP

THE statesman who said that even a society of angels would need its executive committee omitted to add that the committee would also require an archangel for its chairman. Athenian democracy flourished most successfully when it had a Themistocles or a Pericles for its first citizen. Modern democracies likewise put forth their best fruits when the people discover an eminent man whom they can trust to exercise his power in their interest. A Lincoln or a Wilson, a Gladstone or a Masaryk—men like these have impressed their characters on the offices they filled. Operating over an area as wide as the nation-state, democracy needs its premiers and presidents to focus popular attention, to organize public demand, and to infuse abstract principles with flesh-and-blood personality. Nor should democratic leadership be decried by confusion with the *Führerprinzip*. There is every difference between a leadership that is based on popular consent and is constitutionally controllable and one that is arbitrary, authoritarian, and despotic. Even in the smallest democracy the premiership is all-important to the functioning of the political system. Merely to describe this office, in Morley's phrase, as "the keystone of the Cabinet arch" is to understate its broader national significance.

It took time, however, before the modern implications of the premiership were fully realized and developed. Before the inauguration of responsible self-government the Colony was ruled by the governor, who was assisted by an executive council and a legislative council, the embryos, respectively, of cabinet and Parliament. Subsequent constitutional development, extending over four decades, resulted in a bodily transfer of the governor's powers to the premier. The transition commenced in 1856, when the governor was first required to select his ministers from

97

among the members on the majority side of Parliament. The head of the ministry and leader in Parliament was at first known as the colonial secretary. In the early sixties, however, the highest position was designated by the title and office of premier; and the colonial secretaryship (which has since developed into the Ministry of Internal Affairs) was allotted to a different member of the cabinet. The governor's authority was further weakened when the control of defense and native affairs was taken from him and handed over to ministers. His remaining discretionary powers, derived from the royal prerogative, were successively surrendered in favor of the premier. Attaining his office through party leadership, the latter found himself able (provided he maintained a hold on his party) to control governor, Parliament, and ministry alike. When the transition was completed in the early nineties, the premier could normally gain his will in Parliament, since only on his advice would the governor exercise his powers of dissolving the lower house or appointing new members to the upper. Similarly, through his commanding position in the party and his prestige in the country, an able premier could dominate his cabinet. To analyze how and why these institutional changes occurred is to record New Zealand's adaptation to the needs of evolving democracy.

A preliminary glance at the facts and figures shows that the tenure of office by early premiers corresponded with the vicissitudes of their cabinets. During the twenty-five ministries from 1856 to 1890, the premiership was filled by thirteen different persons. Some held it only once, but Whitaker, Vogel, and Stout all served as premier on two occasions; Stafford on three; Fox on four; and Atkinson, a man covetous of power, on five. On an average each of the thirteen individuals spent two and three-quarter years in the chief political office. That the average should be so high was due to the records of the few more eminent premiers whose combined occupancy covered many years. Fox, for example, was premier for four and a half years all told; Atkinson, for over five; and Stafford, for nearly nine. Among them these three men shared the post for eighteen and a half years, that is, for longer than the other ten premiers combined.

Although there were periods when the premiership was kicked around like a political football, at least on five occasions the premier retained his office continuously for over three years.

Previous Careers

New Zealand's early premiers were on the whole well-educated men with considerable experience of public affairs. Ten of them had studied at a university; while the other three—Waterhouse, Atkinson, and Hall—had been educated up to the secondary-school level. The occupations in which they had gained their livelihood represented a fairly wide range of callings: farming, law, journalism, medicine, and government service. The legal profession had the distinction of contributing four premiers in the Dominion's formative stage, namely, Sewell, Fox, Whitaker, and Stout. But farming predominated with its five representatives—Stafford, Weld, Waterhouse, Atkinson, and Hall.[1] Vogel and Domett found in journalism both a career and a medium for making their political opinions known; Pollen was a doctor; and Grey had served the Colonial Office illustriously as governor of three British colonies.

Except for Weld, Waterhouse, and Grey, all the premiers had gained their first experience of politics and administration in the sphere of local government.[2] Vogel, Pollen, Domett, Atkinson, Hall, and Stout could all point to over four years' practice on local bodies. When these future premiers graduated from local to national politics, they served in Parliament for varying lengths of time before they became its principal figure. Prior to their elevation to the premiership, Vogel, Atkinson, and Hall had each belonged to the House of Representatives for more than nine years and had thereby acquired a thorough knowledge of legislative tactics and psychology. The value of such experience to a political leader under the cabinet system of government can be illustrated by two clear cases of men whose failure as premier was due in part to their unfamiliarity with Parliament. These were the two early Liberal premiers, Grey and Stout. Although the former had

1. Hall had been an official in the British post office before he emigrated.
2. The provinces are included under this description.

been a brilliant governor in the days when the governor had monarchical powers, he could not adapt himself to the position of leader in an elected legislative chamber. He had in fact spent only two and a half years as an ordinary representative before catapulting himself into the premiership. Stout had less than four years' knowledge of Parliament at the time when Vogel made him premier. A lawyer who tended to cross-examine the opposition and an intellectual who could not descend from his pedestal, he irritated the legislature instead of conciliating it.

It would, however, be quite fallacious to argue that any member with adequate parliamentary experience would made a good premier or that no newcomer to Parliament could ever lead it satisfactorily. There were, for example, two such undistinguished incumbents as Domett and Weld, each of whom, before he bungled the premiership, had acted as a representative for more than six years. Stafford, on the other hand, was an adroit and capable leader who "climbed to the top of the greasy pole" in the very first session at which responsible government was introduced and effectively maintained his power. There were other premiers who had long parliamentary experience, but in the Legislative Council. In four ministries before 1890 the premier was seated in the upper house, Whitaker filling this role twice and Waterhouse and Pollen once each. Prior to their premierships Whitaker and Pollen had been in the Council for more than ten years. Waterhouse had belonged to it for only two years, but he had arrived in New Zealand somewhat late in life from the colony of South Australia, in which he had already been premier.

Besides their service in the Council or the House, eight premiers had previously held office in another premier's ministry. Those with the longest ministerial experience were Vogel, Whitaker, Atkinson, Pollen, and Hall, of whom each received more than three years' training inside the cabinet room. Again it is significant that, of the Liberal premiers, Stout had been a minister for only one year, and Grey, to whom collegiality was an art unknown, had never at all filled such a position. Yet Stafford, without ever having occupied a subordinate post in any other cabinet, was immediately successful at leading one.

The Premier's Leadership

To estimate the types and methods of governmental leadership is to enter upon a subject where statistical data have little to contribute. This is a problem of evaluation, not of enumeration. Duration in office, age, previous experience—these and other numerically definable factors are only faint indices of the qualities that enable a man to lead or to dominate his fellow-politicians and fellow-citizens. In New Zealand as elsewhere prime ministers fall into two broad classes: the titular heads and the effective leaders. That is a necessary distinction, since the power actually wielded by the different holders of the same office has varied enormously.

If it is the realities and not the appearances of leadership that matter, certain premiers can straightaway be placed on the discard. In many of the early cabinets the dominating force, the direction, and the drive emanated from some minister who was nominally subordinate to his chief. An example was the Domett ministry, whose real head was Thomas Russell, the minister of colonial defense and, in his private capacity, director of the Bank of New Zealand. Another premier who acted at the prompting of a mastermind was Hall. In his cabinet much of the policy was determined by the attorney-general, the subtle, shrewd, and skilful Whitaker. Hall himself admitted his dependence on Whitaker in a statement to the House two days after his ministry was formed. Invited to declare his policies, he replied: "There are some subjects upon which obviously we cannot speak as yet, because our colleague, the Attorney-General, has not yet arrived in Wellington. . . . . It would be improper for us to commit the Government on subjects upon which we do not precisely know the sentiments of that honourable gentleman."[3]

Another political leader who more than once exercised supreme power from a supposedly inferior position was Vogel. When he was sent for by the governor after defeating Stafford in 1872, he presented Parliament with a ministry in which he was the treasurer and Waterhouse the premier. It was well known

3. *P.D.*, XXXII (1879), 180.

that the government was Vogel's creation, and Stafford was quick to point out the embarrassing position of the figurehead. "I would very much have preferred," he said, "to have seen the Colonial Treasurer Premier in name as well as in fact; I like realities and not shams."[4] Before long Waterhouse evidently came to feel the same. Not finding the role of a political Pinocchio to his liking, he resigned and left it to Vogel to assume the premiership which was his due. Again it was Vogel in 1884 who constructed the cabinet in which he assigned the first place to Stout and took the post of treasurer for himself. Only his own ill-health, Vogel explained, induced him to confer on a younger man the more onerous burden, but more distinguished office, of the premiership. None of these premiers—Domett, Hall, Waterhouse, or Stout—could properly be described as keystone of the cabinet arch. To employ the same metaphor, they merely served as a sculptured relief to ornament the keystone.

The premiers of the other group, whose leadership could not be called in question, diverged markedly in personalities and in techniques. Stafford was an able parliamentarian who could promote co-operation between groups which would combine under no other leadership. His tactical cleverness was manifested in 1856, when he watched the rival group leaders exhaust themselves in creating fruitless and ephemeral ministries, and then, capitalizing on the general desire for a strong government, he attracted and welded together a large and mixed following. His second ministry also owed its longevity to the weariness of the House, which had reconstituted the ministry five times in five years. Stafford stayed in power from 1865 to 1869 because "he knew—and the country knew—that he was the only New Zealand Premier who had ever held that office long enough to have learned his work."[5]

Yet Stafford's leadership was marred by two defects. First, his adroitness in managing a legislature was not balanced by any broad popular appeal. His power rested primarily on Parliament and secondarily on the voters. Perhaps this was inevitable in a

4. *P.D.*, XIII (1872), 749.
5. Alfred Saunders, *History of New Zealand* (2 vols.; Wellington: Whitcombe & Tombs, 1896), I, 168.

period when the electorate was small, when settlements were dispersed, and when national opinion was unformed. It meant, however, that Stafford's usefulness was limited to the early stage of New Zealand's development. Significantly enough, after representing the politically vigorous city-constituency of Nelson continuously from 1855, he found it expedient in 1868 to become the member for the quieter rural district of Timaru. Finally after 1875, though only fifty-six years old, he abandoned New Zealand and its politics just at the time when the transition to a more democratic system, based on a wider electorate, was commencing.

Stafford's second weakness lay in the administrative rather than in the political sphere. He might justly be considered the founder of that long line of overworked New Zealand premiers who have concentrated too many functions in their own hands and whose microscopic eye for detail has blurred their broader vision. During his first ministry it was Stafford who bore the brunt of administrative work. This was equally true in the opening year of his second ministry, for his team of colleagues was quite inferior to him in ability. When Stafford first announced to the House the personnel of the cabinet, a critic described it as "one honourable gentleman, without officers of state, without a Treasurer, without an Attorney-General, without anyone."[6] This opinion that the ministry was a one-man show was confirmed by another representative who wrote these contemporary impressions in a letter to his constituents: "Even on questions of mere detail, in whatever department, Mr. Stafford was almost the sole spokesman. If a member asked why an occasional tide-waiter at some unknown port in Auckland had been dismissed, or why an extra deputy-assistant letter carrier in a gold fields village in Otago had had his salary raised, Mr. Stafford was the man to answer, and showed himself to be acquainted, not only with the circumstances of the case, but with the whole history of the individuals referred to from the day of their entering the service."[7] Such incidents, though they were impressive evidence of the premier's thoroughness and versatility, failed to satisfy the House, which rightly considered that it needed more than a Pooh-Bah to make up a cabinet. In 1866 a majority of represent-

6. *P.D.* (1865), p. 685.   7. Quoted in Saunders, *op. cit.*, II, 189.

atives voted for an unusual no-confidence motion in which the mover expressly stated that he wished to change the premier's colleagues but not the premier. The cabinet was accordingly reconstituted, and Stafford distributed some of the powers he had accumulated. Even so, in three years' time, just before Stafford's final downfall, Vogel found enough causes for complaint to describe him as being "practically king of New Zealand."[8]

It is ironical that such a criticism should have emanated from Vogel, who was soon destined to be the target for the same accusation. Vogel's leadership, while no less pronounced than Stafford's, rested on different foundations and was exercised by different methods. To accumulate administrative cares had little attraction for Vogel, who gladly left them to his colleagues. The broader aspects of policy, and these alone, were to his taste. Nor did Vogel resemble Stafford in using lesser men to assist him. It is noteworthy that Stafford was one of the few premiers in this period who never served under another's leadership.[9] He had to be captain, or he would not play. Vogel, however, was not only willing to perform a captain's duties while holding the post of first mate, but almost seems to have courted the second rank. For three years he served loyally under Fox, though it was his borrowing policy, even more than McLean's native administration, which dominated the ministry. When Fox's retirement gave Vogel his turn to establish a ministry, the latter elected to donate the premiership to Waterhouse. Similarly in the eighties he was content to take office as treasurer, while for prime minister he chose Robert Stout, his junior in political status, age, and popular prestige. That he sought out the most eminent men he could find for his associates was a mark of Vogel's greatness. This is stressed even by Saunders, who has practically nothing else good to say for him. Unlike some men of outstanding qualities, Vogel never feared having other able men about him. Atkinson, McLean, Hall, and Stout—all these were members of his cabinets.

In yet another respect Vogel differed from Stafford. He cultivated the art of appealing to the electorate on a national basis.

8. *P.D.*, V (1869), 168.

9. The only other cases are those of Domett and Grey.

He was the first leader whose policies and personality became the subject of hot debate and sharp divisions of opinion. To his followers—and they were many—he was the incarnation of New Zealand's future. On the public platform and at the polling booth his was a name to sway people. In his enemies' eyes he was a visionary or adventurer, reckless, unscrupulous, and unprincipled. Personal ambition seemed his guiding instinct and autocracy his aim. Opinions so remarkably variant could only accrete around a remarkable man. Vogel possessed, in short, many of the qualities of his great British contemporary, Disraeli. Among New Zealand's politicians he suggests the closest parallel to the Conservative statesman of the mother-country.

Sir George Grey, who could match Vogel's capacity for far-sightedness, was otherwise entirely unlike his opponent. The spokesman for the ordinary man, he heralded the movement that was destined to remold New Zealand society in the days of Ballance and Seddon. As a leader he sought his strength directly among the people. Beyond an obstructive Parliament, beyond a recalcitrant governor, he would appeal to the voters, and the unfranchised, moving public opinion as he in his eloquence knew how. Grey, like Vogel, made his name and his views a byword throughout New Zealand. But, however effective in his popular leadership, he must be classed a failure in managing Parliament and his cabinet. Grey belongs to that type of reformers—Karl Marx is the famous example—who love humanity in the abstract but cannot co-operate with individual human beings. Estranged and separated from his wife, an outcast from the Colonial Service despite brilliant accomplishments, alienating the sympathy of moderates and forfeiting the good will of his cabinet colleagues, he became a soured and lonely devotee of principles and lost his attachments to persons. His handling of Parliament was marred by a tendency to flood the debate with platform rhetoric. He did not know that the declamations of a people's tribune may fire the people but chill their representatives. Grey founded the Liberal movement; he was never able to organize and control a Liberal party.

Premier of five cabinets and minister in six more, Atkinson won his spurs largely by default. His first premiership was conferred upon him in 1876 as the successor of Vogel. Again in 1883 he emerged as premier after both Hall and Whitaker had relinquished the lead. Atkinson was a capable but not an outstanding man carried to the top by those copybook virtues of zeal, hard work, and tenacity. Intellectually inferior to men like Vogel, Whitaker, Stout, or Grey, he nevertheless attained a political eminence equal to theirs. Toughness of fiber enabled him to outlast, outargue, and outmaneuver most of his rivals. In the elections of 1884 and 1887 it was his name pitted against Vogel's, and from 1887 to 1890 he was the backbone and last support of the old Conservative clique. Yet Atkinson was never a popular leader in the same sense as Vogel or Grey. Somewhat heavy and prosaic, he lacked the touch which could fire the imagination of men. Atkinson, in fact, represents a type of leadership akin to that of Stafford. A shrewd and seasoned parliamentarian, a forceful if ungraceful debater, and voracious for administrative responsibilities, he was a useful member in any ministry but not best fitted to be premier.

A leader of unusual methods was Whitaker. In him were combined legal talent, political influence, and financial power. But it was the last of these which guided his ambitions. Whitaker represented in politics the wealthy landowners and the big financial institutions of the country such as the Bank of New Zealand. With his partner, Thomas Russell, who was also a politico-financier, he was involved in much of the land speculation that characterized New Zealand's early development. When participating in ministries, as he frequently did, he was sedulous to protect the interests of the land-finance oligarchy against Liberal encroachment. His legal acumen made him a valuable member of a ministry, so that, when he was not premier, he usually held the attorney-generalship. By his subtle, indirect methods Whitaker usually succeeded in dominating any ministry to which he belonged. His cleverness is well indicated by his habit of securing some colleague, less suspect than he, to bear the main burden of cabinet work. After serving his ministerial apprenticeship under Stafford, in 1863 Whitaker formed a ministry in coalition with Fox and gained his first experience as premier. It was a strange alliance, because Fox was in most things the antithesis of Whitaker. Honest, direct, and trusting in character, of democratic sympathies, a provincialist, a supporter of prohibition, and pro-Maori in policy, Fox entered a coalition in which Whitaker secured most of the advantages. Stationed in the Legislative Council and serving as premier, Whitaker saw to it that Fox, as leader of the House, was fully occupied with routine duties.

Once more, when he entered Hall's ministry in 1879, Whitaker was perfectly content to serve under a hard-working premier whose political scruples were somewhat higher than his own. The wily lawyer-financier found in the erstwhile civil servant, now turned farmer, a convenient factotum for executing his ideas. After Hall resigned from overwork, Whitaker became premier, again ruling the country from the Legislative Council, while he used the indefatigable Atkinson, whom he made treasurer, to face the Liberal opposition in the House. But even in the upper chamber Whitaker was not beyond the reach of the vigorous and vociferous Liberals. Inimical to him, because he was the spearhead of the plutocracy, Liberals also resented the fact that the premier was not a member of the elected chamber.[10] At the session of 1883 a series of concerted attacks were launched by Liberal representatives of whom a capable Auckland lawyer, Dargaville by name, opened the offensive. Dargaville broadly asserted that Whitaker and Atkinson had subordinated the interests of the Colony to the financial speculations of the Bank of New Zealand. Supplying specific cases where companies of which Whitaker was a director had profited through his political connections, he forced the ministry to set up a committee to investigate his charges.[11] Grey then swept into the attack, contributing to Whitaker's embarrassment with a motion to prohibit any premier from holding a post as director or manager of any bank or trading company.

This motion, designed rather for its nuisance value than because it was likely to be carried, provoked a most interesting

10. The criticisms against Whitaker on this score in *P.D.*, XLIV (1883), 17, are similar to those previously leveled against Waterhouse for the same reason in *P.D.*, XIII (1872), 612.

11. See Dargaville's striking speech in *P.D.*, XLIV (1883), 195–96.

debate on the premier's status in the cabinet. Grey and his supporters argued that a premier was so predominant in the ministry that his influence determined the direction of policy. Dargaville said that he was the "very embodiment of the Government." Another Liberal rightly refuted the silly dictum that the premier is *primus inter pares*. The head of the ministry, he pointed out, can rid himself of any obnoxious colleague; and the life of the ministry as a whole depends on its head, since, if he resigns, all must resign. These generalities were illustrated by a concrete instance, which another member described. The government had been recently negotiating to establish a direct steam service to Britain, and it was revealed that, while the minister of immigration was corresponding with the Shaw-Savill and Albion Company, the premier was dealing with the New Zealand Shipping Company quite independently of his minister. As the Liberals contended, to the discomfort of the minister in question, there was nothing to prevent an all-powerful premier from overriding the authority of his associates in the departments nominally allotted to them. Their positions were held on sufferance through his grace. The answer to such arguments, all of which accurately portrayed the practices of many a ministry, was supplied by William Rolleston, the minister of lands. Unfortunately, Rolleston merely replied to the political realism of his opponents with the legalistic formulas of traditional constitutional principles. According to this line of reasoning, no premier was in any sense an autocrat. Although he was the first member of the ministry, that was only because the Constitution Act made him the channel of communication between the cabinet and the governor. The ministry was a corporate body which acted in unison. Such a theory did not fit all the facts. Granted that in many ministries the premier was not necessarily the outstanding personage, there were nevertheless some premiers who outshone and overshadowed their colleagues. Like the mother-country in the decades which yielded a Palmerston, a Gladstone, and a Disraeli, this small young and distant colony felt the same political need for clear direction of the government, and the need was producing the men. Stafford, Grey, and Vogel, each in his different way, left an ineradicable impress on the political habits and institutions of New Zealand.

The Power To Dissolve Parliament

The tendencies which were making party organizations more cohesive and which were elevating party leaders to national prominence caused tension and at times conflict between premiers and governors. The powers wielded by the governor were of two kinds. In the capacity of colonial representative of the British government, he exercised an authority which was whittled down in successive decades as the emigrants acquired fuller control over their own affairs. Through this process his powers were transferred to the government which the New Zealanders selected. In this other capacity as representative of the Crown the governor performed those functions which the queen herself carried out in Britain by virtue of the royal prerogative. Even Victoria, tenacious though she was, could not stem the democratic tendency to set ever new limits on the range of the monarch's discretion. A fortiori, in a young colonial democracy the queen's emissary was still less likely to retain unchallenged all the authority that the prerogative conferred. Alike in Britain and in New Zealand, the curb upon the monarch's discretionary power redounded to the advantage not of the ministry as a whole but of its leader. Leaving the ancient forms and procedures unchanged for the most part, evolving democracy saw to it that effective authority passed from the head of the state to the prime minister. The prerogative, which derived its legal source from the century-old custom of the constitution, could be modified either by the explicit enactments of statute law or by the subtle incursion of new usages that finally crystallized into conventions. Basing their political strength on the emergence of parties within Parliament and outside, the premiers dared successfully to encroach on the field hitherto reserved to the Crown. What Palmerston, Gladstone, and Disraeli achieved for Britain was secured for New Zealand by Stafford, Grey, and Atkinson. Their demands upon governors—rejected at first, then repeated, and finally conceded—culminated in reformulating the unwritten portion of the constitution.

A case in point, exemplifying this de facto transference of authority, is the royal power to order a dissolution of Parliament.

If it lay at the discretion of a hereditary monarch to grant or to withhold a dissolution, in any parliamentary crisis the political system would be at the mercy of a dignitary not amenable to democratic control. If, however, it was for the premier to decide when Parliament should be dissolved and for the monarch automatically to rubber-stamp that decision, the premier, though ultimately responsible to the people at the elections, would hold the whip hand over Parliament. All rested on the question of discretion. Did the Crown's representative have any choice when a premier requested a dissolution? Could the premier, whether possessing a majority in Parliament or not, force a general election whenever he thought expedient? New Zealand's answer to these queries was given in the following stages. The first hints of a dissolution earlier than the prescribed date were heard in the late sixties. In 1872 a ministry defeated in Parliament made the first formal request for an immediate appeal to the voters. Such a request, refused on that occasion and again in 1877, was first granted in 1879. By the end of the eighties the wishes of a premier were normally accepted by the governor as conclusive. The governor's discretion, broad before 1870 and narrowing during the seventies, was fading to nothingness by 1890.

Toward the end of Stafford's second ministry, the possibility of an early dissolution was much discussed in the lobbies. The government's majority so dwindled in 1868 that in one critical division only the speaker's casting vote saved them from defeat. Fox, leading the opposition, boldly invited the premier to face the country, but his challenge was not accepted. In the following year Stafford himself, now tottering to his fall, employed the threat of dissolution as a last device to rally his wavering supporters. It was a delaying maneuver which may have helped him in the rear-guard action that accompanied his withdrawal from office. One parliamentarian commented: "The threat of dissolution has been used with some effect by the Honourable the Premier. There are some rank jibbers in his ranks, and that whip of dissolution is a very good whip to keep them straight."[12] But, unable to stave off ultimate defeat, Stafford was at last ejected. Either the whip lacked sting or else the premier's grasp on the

12. *P.D.*, V (1869), 226.

whip handle was not yet firm. Stafford accepted Parliament's decision and resigned without requesting a dissolution. Certainly in 1869 it was highly improbable that any dissolution would have been granted to the defeated premier, especially when the leader of the opposition had a majority adequate to support a ministry. A stickler for the constitutional status quo, Carleton dogmatized in terms which Victoria herself could not have bettered about the broad discretion belonging to the sovereign's representative. "This [question of dissolution]," he asserted, "is a matter reserved entirely for the consideration of the Governor and the Ministry cannot give advice on the subject."[13] To that proposition the events of the next twenty years provided a complete refutation.

It was in 1872 that Stafford took the plunge of requesting a dissolution of a Parliament elected only eighteen months before. The circumstances were peculiar. Although Fox had triumphed in the elections of 1871, Stafford was able in 1872 to defeat him by forty votes to thirty-seven on a motion which condemned not the policies but the administration of the public works and immigration program. In a month's time, himself defeated on a motion of no confidence by thirty-seven votes to thirty-five, Stafford risked that from which he shrank in 1869. The reasons with which he supported his request to Governor Bowen were these: No party in the House was strong enough to command a reliable working majority, and a great change had come over the feeling of the country since the general election. Before replying to these points, the governor inquired whether the premier was sure that Parliament, if its dissolution was ordered, would grant the necessary supplies to carry on the government until a new Parliament could meet. To this Stafford answered that by constitutional usage it was Parliament's recognized duty to grant supplies and that he had no doubt this would be done. The governor then stated his objections to Stafford's request. Since an election had been held so recently, only the gravest necessity could justify the expense and inconvenience of another one at such a short interval; the country was probably just as divided as the legislature; and there was no question of magnitude to put to the con-

13. *Ibid.*, p. 272.

stituencies. If the House, moreover, was split almost equally, the premier was rather sanguine in expecting that it would grant supplies. However, suggested the governor, if Stafford cared to test the opinion of Parliament on that matter, he could do so. This was a challenge which Stafford dared not accept. Knowing that the majority who had voted against him would not indorse their own dissolution, Stafford handed in his resignation.[14]

What Stafford had begun, Grey continued. The situation when Grey became premier in 1877 ran parallel to the events in 1872. The ministry, which Vogel had led to victory in the election of 1875, lost ground in the second session of the new Parliament, and Grey snatched enough stray votes to depose Atkinson. Without waiting, as Stafford had done for his precarious majority to revert to a minority, Grey asked the Marquis of Normanby for an immediate dissolution. Although he asked twice—first during the session and again after it was prorogued—each time the governor refused. The persevering Liberal premier was forced to wait until 1879, when his third effort met with success. Although by this time he had lost his majority, there was now a new governor in office, and Parliament was nearly four years old. To his grant of a dissolution, the governor attached these conditions: Parliament must be dissolved without delay, no measure could be introduced in the meantime except what was imperatively required, and the new Parliament must be summoned at the earliest possible date. Notwithstanding such conditions, Grey had won a victory both for himself, for all the premiers who followed, and for democracy. The right to appeal to the people was conceded for the first time in New Zealand history to a premier lacking the confidence of the House.

All that remained was to build upon the precedent which Grey had established. Atkinson was the next premier to request and receive a dissolution. Defeated in the House in 1884 through the defection of the South Island railway-seekers, he decided to call an immediate election instead of resigning. His justification rested on three very cogent arguments. The Liberal who had proposed the motion on which the ministry was outvoted had himself de-

14. The correspondence between Premier Stafford and Governor Bowen is recorded in *P.D.*, XIII (1872), 580–82.

clared that he wanted to see the House dissolved at once. In any case an election was due by law to be held in that year, and the dissolution merely advanced it to a date several months earlier. Moreover, Atkinson could and did point out to the opposition that he was following on the trail blazed by their own former premier. Many Liberals, nevertheless, took the Conservative leader to task. Having obtained a parliamentary victory which apparently they did not anticipate, they asserted that Atkinson should have resigned and allowed a Liberal ministry to be formed after which the election could have been held at the normal time. The real motive that underlay their desire to take office before the dissolution was their belief that in fighting the election the "ins" had an advantage over the "outs." But the constitutional maxim with which they urged their case was the time-worn one that a governor must exhaust the opposition side of the House before consenting to dissolve it. In the mouths of Liberals such an argument was foolish in the extreme. Under the pretext of "exhausting the House" many a governor in New Zealand, and elsewhere, had refused to grant dissolutions.[15] It was a maxim which broadened the discretion of the Crown's representative almost without limits. Grey had been far wiser when he argued in the late seventies that a governor was bound to follow the premier's advice and had no discretionary power. While some Liberals took this long-sighted view and approved of Atkinson's action, others voted for a resolution which condemned him for not resigning.[16] Condemnation, however, was inadequate unless accompanied by a stoppage of supplies, and to this length the majority were not prepared to go.

It suited the Conservative prime minister to defend himself against the Liberals by appealing to the authority of their own former leader. Such a situation was implicit in the nature of a democratic constitution, since a precedent, no matter by whom it was established, could be turned to the advantage of any party. But consistency was not one of Atkinson's virtues. In 1887 constitutional principles were flexibly adapted by politicians to suit

15. See the remarks of a parliamentarian in *P.D.*, XLVII (1884), 172.

16. In the division on this resolution thirty-seven voted on each side, and the speaker's casting vote went to the "Noes" (*ibid.*, p. 193).

their supposed interests. Party positions this time were reversed, for Stout's ministry was defeated on a Customs Amendment Bill by forty-two votes to thirty-eight. This occurred in the month of May in a year when an election was legally due. Following Atkinson's example, Stout asked the governor for an immediate dissolution, and the latter agreed. Loud were the criticisms that emanated from the opposition. Atkinson protested with vigor that, if Parliament were dissolved then and there, the new Parliament would have to assemble later that same year and that the country would pay for two sessions in one year. The prime minister, he asserted, should have resigned and allowed the leader of the opposition to form a ministry.[17] To this contention issuing from such a source there was only one possible answer, and it was flung back contemptuously by the never daunted Dargaville. Referring acidly to Atkinson's own action in 1884, which had also resulted in two sessions within the same year, he snapped: "This to my mind sounds very much like Satan reproving sin."[18]

Up to 1877, in short, a premier three times sought and failed to obtain a dissolution. In the next decade the same request was three times granted, and to premiers whom the House no longer supported. The successive precedents constituted a usage which now placed almost entirely in the premier's hands the decision whether a Parliament should be dissolved. Momentous political consequences flowed from this transfer of power. Possessing such a weapon, any prime minister gained an effective instrument to control the House, provided that he himself dared to put the issue to the people. Did the House have any means of self-defense against a premier who wished to make every representative contest his seat? All that it could do was to stop supplies. The possibility of this drastic step was hinted in 1872, in 1884, and in 1887; but the House never applied its ultimate economic sanction. Thereby it hastened its own subordination to the cabinet and prime minister.

17. *P.D.*, LVII (1887), 541.
18. *Ibid.*

Choosing a Premier

Further limitations were placed upon the royal prerogative in the selection of a premier. Constitutional theory permitted the Crown to send for any "trusty and well-beloved" subject and confer on him the task of forming a government. Constitutional practice narrowed the field of choice to this extent that the monarch must pick somebody whom a majority in the lower house would support. If the House were so organized that a clearly defined majority followed a recognized leader, the monarch had no alternative but to make that individual prime minister. If, however, there was a multiplicity of groups none of whose leaders commanded a majority, the Crown or its representative had ample opportunity to pick and choose. As in the discussions over the question of dissolution, everything resolved itself into the issue of discretion. It mattered greatly whether the leader of this group or of that received the invitation to form a ministry. Gubernatorial influence on the course of colonial politics and on the careers of politicians was necessarily considerable in an era when parties were unformed or in process of formation. In general practice the governor's discretion in selecting a premier varied inversely with the cohesiveness of parliamentary parties. Parliamentarians debated whether there were any rules to govern the governor, and two schools of thought conflicted in their points of view—one justified the Crown in exercising a broad discretion; the other sought to restrain it by fixed and precise rules. The pundits differed over various procedural niceties. Points that were seemingly trivial possessed a deeper import, since on them depended the occupancy of democracy's most powerful office.

The effort to mark out a fixed line of procedure which a governor must follow was wrapped up with controversies over constitutional metaphysics. It was a well-recognized principle that the Crown must act only on the advice of its responsible ministers. How was this principle to be applied in the interregnum between the exit of a defeated ministry and the incoming of its successor? Whose advice was the governor to seek during these transitional phases? It could be argued that, when a defeated premier tendered his resignation, the governor was no longer bound by his advice. In that case, until a new premier was chosen, a governor's discretion was unfettered; he could look for advice wherever he wanted and invite whomsoever he thought fit to form a ministry. Against this it was contended that a resigning premier still remained the responsible adviser of the Crown up to the actual appointment of his successor, and for a governor to request advice elsewhere was to commit the constitutional error of consulting a private citizen. Each of these views might produce undesirable results in practice. Governors who used their own discretion could be partial to one side at the expense of the other, or, to be more explicit, since most governors were conservatively minded aristocrats, they might employ their power to the disadvantage of the Liberals. Correspondingly, an outgoing premier, whose advice was sought, could act unfairly toward his rivals if he was politically unscrupulous.

So many were the ministerial changes in three and a half decades that practices of all kinds were cited as precedents in recurring disputes. Sometimes the governors asked the advice of an outgoing premier; sometimes they did not. Fox, for example, was requested after his defeats in 1856 and 1862 to suggest who should form the next cabinet. So were Sewell in 1856 and Weld in 1865. Stafford, on the other hand, resigned in 1872 without giving any advice to the governor, who had refused to grant a dissolution. Fox protested in the House that it was usual for a resigning premier to nominate his successor to the governor; but Stafford disagreed that this was either usual or necessary. Grey was not asked for his advice in 1879 and thereupon criticized the governor, who had acted on his own initiative in sending for Hall. Of course, if the governor did ask for advice, then the responsibility was placed upon the defeated premier to be strictly just toward the opposition. Sewell after his defeat in 1856 made the mistake of not nominating Fox, who had obtained a majority in the House for his resolutions on provincial finances. The latter accordingly delivered to his errant rival a sermon on constitutional ethics, embroidering the text that a retiring premier must advise the Crown to send for either the leader or a prominent member of the victorious party.

Custom required a premier beaten in a division of the House to advise that the mover of the victorious motion or amendment be sent for. At times, however, the mover might be only a subordinate figure in the opposition ranks put up as a "front." In that case the proper procedure was to invite the real leader to build the new cabinet. Thus, when Atkinson was defeated in 1877 on a motion proposed by Larnach, the governor rightly sent for Grey, the outstanding figure of the Liberal party. But in 1884, when the Stout-Vogel ministry was crushed at its first division, the governor wrongly sent first for the insignificant politician who had proposed the successful amendment and not for Grey or Atkinson, who had backed him. A further difficulty might arise if the individual who was first summoned failed to scrape a ministry together. To whose advice should the governor then turn? It happened in 1862 that the governor after Fox's defeat acted on his advice in calling upon Stafford. The latter declined to form a ministry but was himself asked to suggest a new premier and mentioned a certain Fitzgerald. This candidate in turn was invited and failed to form a cabinet. He, however, proposed Domett, who managed to succeed. With his usual correct judgment, Fox castigated the procedure of the governor, of Stafford, and of Fitzgerald. As the retiring premier, he contended that his advice should again have been requested after Stafford's refusal. Only he was entitled to advise the Crown until a new premier had actually taken office. On this view the governor had no choice but to follow the premier's suggestions. The argument was repeated in 1884, when the governor behaved in the very way which Fox had complained of twenty years earlier. Grey himself was then one of the offending parties. After failing to form a ministry, he gave advice to the governor, who should by rights have had recourse again to Stout, the retiring premier.

The precedents, in short, which surrounded the choice of a premier were somewhat chaotic and confused. Incidents and usages could be quoted which would justify the most widely divergent procedures. Undeniably on many occasions the gover-

nors used very broad discretion in their search for a prime
minister. Nor can they be altogether blamed. Whenever Parliament contained an organized majority, the governor as a matter
of course invited its leader to head the government. But while
parties were undeveloped or semideveloped, the choice of a
premier lay with the governor by default. Where Parliament
failed to indicate its wishes, the representative of the Crown was
forced to act. As parties became systematized, the premier was
clearly designated, and all the governor could do was automatically to register the decision of a victorious majority. Always
about a decade ahead of his time, Grey, who had served New
Zealand both as governor and as premier, summed up his obser-
vations: "You may alter the terms as you please, but the Governor is in this country a mere machine who signs the edicts the
Premier prepares. Necessarily, so long as the Premier has a
majority in this House, the Governor must adopt his advice,
and must follow every command he issues."[19] Spoken in 1883,
those words exaggerated the position at that date, but in another
fifteen years events had caught up with his statement. In the
early nineties a sharp struggle between the ministry and the
governor put the latter once and for all in a subordinate place.
An emerging democracy was producing its own political instruments with which the status of a hereditary monarch and the
powers of the prerogative were incompatible. Residuary legatee
of the Crown, the premier at last emerged as a people's leader.

19. *P.D.*, XLV (1883), 537.

CHAPTER VI

PARLIAMENT

THE early Victorian Parliament had three historic functions: to enact laws, to authorize public expenditure, and to make ministries. In the later decades of the nineteenth century Parliament's active participation in these functions was steadily reduced. By gradual stages the cabinet cornered the legislative field and tightened its control on finance. At the same time the choice of the ministry passed to the parties then being organized among the electorate. The internal structure of Parliament was modified to accord with its altering role. But innovations in the machinery of so ancient an institution could not be introduced without considerable stress and strain. While the mother of parliaments was having to adjust to the implications of modern industrialism and the social service state, its colonial daughter-assembly was required in addition to take root in new soil. Transplanted to the Antipodes, Parliament grew acclimatized to a community not only more democratic but also more exacting in its pressures upon the government. The working of the legislature during this transitional phase and its responsiveness to the pull and tug of antagonistic tendencies form the theme of the present chapter.

Turnover of Personnel

One of the signposts indicating the progress of these adjustments is the turnover of personnel in the elected lower house. Representative government insists upon recurrent general elections in order to establish two democratic principles: the responsibility of the rulers and the consent of the governed. The results of elections determine the composition of the House of Representatives, on which depends the stability of the ministry and the effectiveness of the legislative body. Fluctuations in public opinion, extensions of the franchise, the rise and fall of parties—these are the causes of turnover in parliamentary membership. The rate of changes in personnel may vary between the opposite extremes of "rump" or "lame-duck" parliaments and of landslides. If a large proportion of members retain their seats through successive parliaments, the continuity of their experience may be invaluable. If the continuity is excessive, lack of new blood may conduce to intellectual staleness and may perpetuate an oligarchical clique. The happy mean consists of regular and moderate infusions of new legislative personnel into the old—an ideal hard to attain while legislative institutions were being adapted to fit the New Zealand environment.

When the New Zealand cabinet was subordinate to the House, the frequency of ministerial crises was connected with the rate of turnover among the elected personnel. An analysis of electoral returns over thirty-five years reveals that this turnover was exceptionally high. At nine consecutive general elections, on an average, 49 per cent of the successful candidates were not members of the preceding Parliament. Furthermore, there were so many resignations and by-elections in between the general elections that the composition of a Parliament was often considerably changed during its lifetime. Even the balance of power between government and opposition might be altered through the recurrence of by-elections, for the average rate of turnover during the term of each Parliament amounted to 26 per cent of its membership. At the opening of every new Parliament, therefore, half the personnel were different; and, by the time the dissolution came, one-quarter of its members had again altered. Table 6 contains the detailed figures. When these are interpreted in conjunction with the development of parties and the cabinet system, they help to explain further why parliamentary groupings were fluid and government majorities insecure. Before party discipline was enforced, a ministry's survival frequently depended upon bargains which it negotiated with individual members. Sometimes these bargains were of a private or personal nature. A railway line for his constituents or a land grant for himself or his friends might be the member's price for a vote on a no-confidence motion. If half the representatives changed after a general election, many such agreements lapsed. A cabinet which had contracted for the firm support of a particular member might have to bargain anew when his place in the House was filled by someone else. In a Parliament as unorganized as a world of independent nation-states, backbenchers claimed the privileges of sovereignty. Laboriously the ministry pieced together its majority by dynastic marriages between blocs and by a network of bilateral treaties with independents. Not until party organizations were strongly established could the ministry count on a new member to vote in accordance with his known party affiliation.

TABLE 6

TURNOVER OF PERSONNEL IN THE NEW ZEALAND HOUSE
OF REPRESENTATIVES, 1855–90

GENERAL ELECTION	SIZE OF HOUSE		No. of REPRESENT-ATIVES NOT IN THE HOUSE IN THE PRE-CEDING PAR-LIAMENT	No. ELECT-ED AT BY-ELECTIONS BETWEEN GENERAL ELECTIONS	PERCENTAGE OF NEW MEMBERS	
	At opening of Parlia-ment	At close of Parlia-ment			At opening of Parlia-ment*	During Lifetime of Parlia-ment†
1855........	38	42	25	15	66	36
1860........	56	56	36	23	64	41
1866........	68	76	31	47	46	62
1871........	78	78	39	23	50	29
1876........	86	88	42	28	49	32
1879.... ..	88	88	33	7	38	8
1881........	95	95	46	7	48	7
1884........	95	95	40	15	42	16
1887........	95	95	33	6	36	6

* Average turnover at each general election, 49 per cent.
† Average turnover during each Parliament's lifetime, 26 per cent.

Although over the whole period the high average turnover is significant, still more striking is the contrast between the earlier and the later parliaments. The general election which indorsed the extinction of the provinces was a turning-point in the evolution of New Zealand democracy. Consider separately the average rates of turnover of personnel at the elections up to 1876 and at those held after this date:

AVERAGE TURNOVER AT ALL
GENERAL ELECTIONS

	Per Cent
1855–87............................	49
1855–76............................	55
1879–87............................	41

Thus the proportion of newcomers was 14 per cent lower after 1876, evidence that the composition of the House of Representatives became relatively less fluid in the eighties than it had been in previous decades. This conclusion is confirmed by a comparison of the rates of turnover at the by-elections held during each Parliament's lifetime. The Parliament elected in 1876 and dissolved in 1879 again serves as a dividing-line. The contrast between the early group of five parliaments and the later group of four is as follows:

AVERAGE TURNOVER DURING EACH
PARLIAMENT'S LIFETIME

	Per Cent
1855–90.........................	26
1855–79.........................	40
1879–90.........................	9

Up to the end of the seventies, two-fifths of the membership of the lower house changed in between the general elections; while in the eighties one-tenth changed. The increase in the continuity of legislative personnel could not be more convincingly demonstrated.

These data conform with the Colony's advance beyond its early struggling conditions when settlements were scattered and communications were undeveloped and when an immigrant had first to insure his livelihood before he could leave his farm or business for an annual session of three months' duration.[1] It is plain that such factors were not offset by the greater frequency of general elections in the eighties. The Constitution Act had prescribed five years as the upper limit of each Parliament's duration, and the first twenty-five years of self-government witnessed five elections. The three-year term approved by the legislature in 1879 was a Liberal device for making Parliament more responsive to the people. Four elections took place in the decade 1879–89. Shorter parliaments undoubtedly contributed to lower the proportion of by-elections in between the general elections. Yet the voters, though they were granted more opportunities in the eighties to select new representatives, tended on the whole to

---

1. There were thirteen sessions of Parliament between 1856 and 1870. The average duration of ten of these was 103 days. The three sessions held in 1862, 1863, and 1864 during the Maori wars lasted, on an average, for 48 days each.

change them less. It should be noticed that the continuity of legislative membership increased even despite the electoral fluctuations of the rising party organizations. After the election of 1881,
which strengthened the pre-existing Conservative majority, almost half the lower house was changed. But at the election of
1884, which bolstered the Liberals and the Vogelites, the turnover dropped by 6 per cent; and in 1887, when the Conservatives
regained power, it again dropped by the same amount. The in-
ference from these facts is that on each side of the House a large
number of members in both parties were sure of re-election if they
offered themselves as candidates for another term. So far the
emergence of better-defined party groupings was tending to
greater continuity in the composition of Parliament.

The Rise of the Caucus

The internal machinery of Parliament was similarly modified
when the growth of parties produced their characteristic institution, the caucus. Nowadays the caucus is the well-established
medium for arranging a concerted strategy for all party members
within the legislature. Critics of the caucus system in its present-
day operation are likely to regard it as a peculiarly modern innovation designed extralegally to detract from the powers of the
legally constituted Parliament. Such opinions overlook the nineteenth-century antecedents of the caucus which passed through
the stages of birth, baptism, and boyhood over sixty years ago.
Although it is true that this institution has attained special importance in twentieth-century democracy, the gradual building
of its current position should not be ignored. The caucus is in
reality part and parcel of the party system, and the life-history
of the one is integrally related to that of the other. The origins of
the caucus can be traced as far back as the beginning of responsible government. Sporadically for two decades parliamentary
party meetings were held as occasion required, though not until
1876 was the term "caucus" introduced to describe them. Thereafter, as parties grew more cohesive, the caucus became regularized.

The first meeting of this nature was held in 1856 during the interregnum between Sewell's fall and Fox's accession to office. Ex-

cusing his own inability at that stage to form a stable ministry, Stafford explained that two blocs which together composed a majority of the House had decided for the time being to work in unison on Fox's side. The members of this majority had met and agreed to "a resolution which bound them individually as well as a party."[2] Stafford had therefore to wait his chance until the temporary coalition broke, which it did after a few weeks. This was an incident which contained the rudiments of a caucus system. A would-be premier consulted his potential supporters, while his opponents settled on a common policy among themselves. The majority meeting was similar to that which foreshadowed Stafford's loss of power when the next Parliament was newly convened in 1861. Stafford had proposed unqualified military support for the governor in coping with hostile Maoris, but the opposition headed by Fox demanded only conditional assistance, desiring in particular that regular troops be employed as far as possible in place of the militia. A number of parliamentary conferences were held, at which a majority of the representatives attended. Various amendments to the government's policy declaration were suggested, and finally a compromise statement was adopted which had been drafted by Saunders. Many details in this procedure anticipated the current practice of the caucus system. Rival motions were introduced and debated, and finally a resolution which committed all persons present was accepted as the view of the meeting. Even the secrecy of this prototype caucus was upheld, for, when its activities were subsequently mentioned in the House, Saunders stated that he did not feel at liberty to describe what had taken place. Here may be observed the germ cell of that inner legislature which the caucus of today has become.[3]

Other instances of these embryonic caucus meetings can be quoted. When Stafford, after Weld's downfall, formed his second ministry, the premiership was offered to him at a meeting of parliamentarians who promised their support. Likewise his decision

2. *P.D.* (1856–58), p. 85.
3. *P.D.* (1861–63), pp. 98–100. By a significant anachronism, when Saunders in the nineties described this incident in his *History*, he actually used the name "caucus" to describe this meeting in 1861 (Alfred Saunders, *History of New Zealand* [2 vols.; Wellington: Whitcombe & Tombs, 1896], I, 446).

to request a dissolution after he was beaten in 1872 was based upon the wishes expressed at a conference with his followers. Thus on several occasions in these early parliaments legislative procedure and tactics were settled upon at gatherings of temporarily like-minded members. The votes on the floor of the House were more than once prearranged at conferences in the committee rooms. The instances cited above were taken from the years 1856, 1861, 1865, and 1872; but that list is not necessarily exhaustive. It is sufficient to prove that, however inchoate the parties then were, representatives of kindred political views did assemble together when special circumstances arose.

The earliest instance known to me when such a meeting was actually referred to in the House itself as a caucus is dated to that crucial year 1876. In the opening days of the first session of the new Parliament, Grey and his "greyhounds" (as his Liberal followers were called) found a weak spot to attack Vogel's ministry. Asserting that the proposed conditions of sale of crown lands in the Piako Swamp to two former ministers (Whitaker and Russell) were illegal, Grey obtained a majority of nine votes against Vogel in the first division he was able to force. Consequently, the premier held a meeting of his party, compelled their approval of the government's action by a threat of resignation, and then explained in the House what he had done. It was left to Robert Stout, then a young Liberal lawyer siding with Grey, to rebuke the almighty Vogel. "I am not aware," he said, "that Ministers of the Crown have been in the habit of bringing before Parliament what took place at a meeting of their supporters. It is supposed that these things are done secretly; and if it is parliamentary to refer to such a thing as a caucus meeting, I can only assume we are getting sort of Americanized in some of our proceedings, and this serves as the first step in making us acquainted with what are called caucuses and rings."[4] Stout's linguistic innovation, for which he seemed to expect a caution from the speaker, had crept into regular parliamentary usage by 1879. In the contentious debates over the action of the four "Auckland rats,"[5] the machinery and the discussions of the Liberal caucus were publicly aired to the delight of Conservatives. Charges and countercharges re-

4. *P.D.*, XX (1876), 8.   5. See above, chap. iii, pp. 65–67.

vealed the confusion that reigned among Liberal counsels and the powerlessness of the majority in the party to control its own minority. The growing-pains of the caucus were those of the developing party system.

Throughout the eighties the caucus was firmly installed in the legislative machinery; nor was its use confined to any one side. When Parliament was cutting the salaries of civil servants in 1880, the House dilly-dallied in choosing among the innumerable economy proposals that were suggested by various of the taxpayers' representatives. Eventually a majority of members took the initiative in their own hands, met in an improvised caucus, and settled upon a compromise which was adopted in the House on the following day. On this occasion the decision passed out of the premier's control, and Hall himself protested, in terms that have a very modern ring, against "the reprehensible and unconstitutional practice of settling the affairs of this House outside its walls, and against the highly objectionable practice of resorting to caucuses."[6] So regularly was the caucus convened in this decade that some backbenchers before long assumed the view that they were entitled to be consulted by party leaders in planning every item of parliamentary strategy. In 1883, for instance, when Dargaville's castigation of Whitaker and Atkinson compelled the ministry to appoint a committee of inquiry, rival partisans disputed over its composition. Seddon, the autocrat of future days, complained that the arrangements had been made by consultation between the party whips negotiating on behalf of the party leaders, while he, a loyal Liberal, was kept in the dark. To which Montgomery replied in elementary terms that caucuses could not be held on all questions and that no party could exist without some trust being placed in the discretion of its chief.

It is clear from this incident that, once the system was introduced, members came to expect it as right and proper that regular caucuses should be held. In the early days a party meeting was something of a rarity which occurred, if at all, when a ministry was in danger of defeat or when a new government was in construction. But accumulating precedents created an expecta-

6. *P.D.*, XXXVI (1880), 77.

tion that the practice would continue. Thus usage grew into custom, and custom into convention. There is an important difference between irregular meetings of partisans, assembled merely
to assure a ministry of their general support, and periodic conferences for mapping strategy and discussing policy. When the
latter type of caucus occurred, the possibility was open for the
party's rank and file to challenge the dominance of their own
leaders. Vogel, for instance, found it necessary to cow the caucus
in 1876 by threatening to resign. Hall saw in 1880 that a majority
of representatives could on occasion take the bit between their
teeth. Seddon in 1883 laid upon Montgomery the onus of explaining why a caucus had not been called. Already in the
eighties many of the familiar modern traits of the caucus were
sketched in outline. Its discussions were supposed to be secret; its
procedure was relatively formalized; and its decisions were at
least morally binding on all participants. The very word "caucus," which was first used by Stout in 1876 as opprobriously as
Disraeli employed it in England in 1878, soon lost its early unsavory connotation. The institution became familiar and normal
alike to Conservatives and Liberals, and its name ceased to convey an insinuation of the sinister. The caucus, which in this century has so modified the traditional concepts of cabinet government, had come to stay.[7]

Private Members

The rise of the caucus was not the only symptom of the impact
of party organization on the legislative machinery. As the tight-
ening of party discipline diminished the private members' liberty
of action, so the ministry's growing ascendancy over the House
reduced its prestige and power. The shift in the balance of power
within Parliament was accompanied by restrictions on the representative's freedom to vote as he pleased and to introduce what
bills he chose. The cabinet became a holding company controlling a network of subsidiary members and making their actions
conform to a central will. In the earlier parliaments the cabinet

7. See below, chap. xii, pp. 334–40, and also my article, "The Origins of the
Caucus in New Zealand," *Australia and New Zealand Historical Studies*, II, No. 5
(1942), 1–10.

had been suitably deferential to the private member whom as yet it lacked the means to coerce. Thus Stafford in 1858, when introducing a bill on so important a subject as electoral apportionment, admitted that he was ignorant of the views entertained by the majority and invited any suggestions of which the House approved. The metamorphosis of the ministry from pristine deference to its subsequent dominance was slow, but it was sure. When Stafford took the reins again in 1865, he commented somewhat grimly on the "most disorganized Houses" of the four preceding sessions.[8] Promising that he would try to maintain discipline among his own supporters, he asked the opposition to follow suit. In this, if one judges from the criticisms expressed in the late sixties against the activity and energy of the whips, he must have been at least partially successful. But he was bettered by Vogel, who had a capacity for learning his rivals' methods and excelling them. Vogel was the first premier really to control backbenchers under a rigid direction. "Last year," said Stout in 1876, "he had a very pliant majority at his back . . . . , he had nothing to do but send round his Whips; and when told to remain silent his supporters remained silent, when told to vote they voted, and when told to walk out they walked out."[9]

With gathered force this trend persisted through the eighties. Unless a party was irreconcilably split—as were the Liberals after Grey's resignation—its members normally voted together in all divisions on paramount issues. Many a stalwart stood dutifully by his party, like one who confessed that he had repeatedly voted for ministerial measures which, if free, he would have opposed.[10] Periodically, of course, the party ranks would break. Some question would temporarily intervene to weaken the cabinet's control and enable the private members to reassert their fading independence. Religious controversy, for example, was set ablaze when Bowen, the minister of justice, introduced his Education Bill in 1877. Sectarian cleavage between Protestants and Catholics assumed for the time being the place of political conflict. Unable to find a formula for compromise, the majority agreed only to disagree and struck out all the religious clauses

8. *P.D.* (1864–66), p. 690.
9. *P.D.*, XX (1876), 31.   10. *P.D.*, XLIV (1883), 381.

while the government helplessly acquiesced. So in the stone-wall fight over the Representation Bill of 1889 members divided not as Liberals against Conservatives but as town versus country representatives. Conservatives from city constituencies declared that they were forced by the government's own action to vote against those whom they were pledged to support. But party discipline surmounted such lapses and gradually brought the members to heel. Even Seddon was compelled to toe the line in 1890, when Ballance reached an agreement with Atkinson to curtail debates, wind up the session, and hold an early election. Notorious for his intractability and powers of obstruction, Seddon painted his self-portrait as "the wreck of what was originally the independent member for Kumara."[11]

The need for some measure of party discipline was proportionately greater when independents still abounded and, like neutrals in a warring world, were courted by both belligerents. These were numerous enough, at times when the parties were nearly equally divided, to hold the balance. Each additional vote acquired a scarcity value, and the independents, men of no fixed affiliation, found their bargaining power enhanced. In the frantic episodes which Grey successfully contrived in 1884, stray votes were at a premium. After the House had been canvassed by Vogel, Stout, Atkinson, and Grey, one member thus released his pent-up feelings: "I have never before in my whole life experienced so much worry, nor have I been subjected to so much solicitation, to so much entreaty, to so much temptation, as I have been during the last three weeks or month."[12]

In the eyes of party leaders, seeking by concerted action to convert a political program into legislative enactments, the independent was a nuisance and a menace. In the independent's view party discipline appeared a clamp on his freedom and a clog upon his principles. Stoutly but unavailingly, the back-benchers fought their losing fight. Each passing decade saw them squeezed into ever smaller focus on the background of the parliamentary picture. A debate that was held in 1890 summarized from the private member's standpoint the causes and effects of his

11. *P.D.*, LXIX (1890), 80.   12. *P.D.*, XLVIII (1884), 113.

lowered status.[13] The discussion was stimulated by a motion to devise a new method of selecting the cabinet whereby this body would once more become the servant of the House. The system of government through parties, with their organization and their disciplinary controls, was the principal target of attack. Enlarging upon their single theme, speakers complained that, when Parliament had convened in 1887, the ordinary representatives were as helpless as a flock of sheep. They could choose only between following one of two men. If a member newly entering the House sought to accomplish anything, he must belong to a party. Yet if he did so, he must support measures he disliked; he must renounce his conscience and his individuality. There was one who related that, when asked by a prominent politician how he intended to vote, he replied that he would give a discriminating support to the government. Explosively came the rejoinder: "Who ever heard of a soldier in an army giving his general a discriminating support? . . . . We want our party to vote for us when we are in difficulties—when we are in the wrong, in fact."

Irked by the obligations of partisan adherence, independents sought a method of escape from ministerial domination. Some advocated an imitation of the American system, which excludes the chief executive from a seat in the legislature. Others preferred the Swiss model of a bipartisan or multipartisan cabinet which the legislature elects and controls. The debate terminated in the appointment of a committee which reported in favor of adopting the Swiss practice in New Zealand. Nothing was done to follow up this recommendation, although in subsequent parliaments the same suggestion has often reappeared. The proposal to have an "elective executive" has been in modern times a hardy quinquennial of New Zealand politics—but it has never yet borne fruit.

Not only did private members chafe at the restrictions on their freedom to vote but they resented also the curbs on their legislating initiative. As the ministry increasingly occupied the time of Parliament with its own proposals, it advanced the claim that all topics of major political consequence were its own reserve. Atkinson and the Liberal opposition dueled over this very principle in 1883. The Conservative ministry had announced in the speech

13. *P.D.*, LXIX (1890), 35–45.

from the throne that it would suggest some reforms in the Legislative Council. When the session dragged on and no proposal was
in sight, Grey typically decided to force their hand by introducing a measure of his own. Atkinson thereupon argued that it was
quite unparliamentary for Grey to bring in a bill on a subject
with which the government was going to deal. In response a Liberal contended that any member had the right to initiate any
bill he pleased—a view which in strict constitutional theory was
correct but which was ceasing to be politically realistic. The private member's bill was being relegated to the subordinate places
on the legislative agenda; ministerial measures had right of way.
After he had served three years in Parliament, Reeves sardoni-
cally wrote a "Lay of Legislation" which contains this stanza:

> Yea, of objects deserving of pity,
> Meet subjects for sorrowful ditty,
>   Who wrangle or yawn,
>   From noon until dawn
> In caucus, debate or committee;
> Of all chosen victims of ill,
> All targets for spite and ill-will,
>   The sorriest sight,
>   The unluckiest wight,
> Is the member who fathers a Bill.[14]

The representatives who could be so portrayed had suffered a
sharp descent. The process of their subordination to the ministry
was not unlike the fate of the chorus in Greek tragedy. Originally
the protagonist and center of the drama, the chorus was later el-
bowed to the side until it was reduced by Euripides to a mere on-
looker interposing sententious banalities or lyrical relief. Such
was the evolution of the private members' role. From leading ac-
tors they became in four decades a chorus of applauding or helpless spectators of the cabinet.

The Pork Barrel

The pork barrel, whose origins and connection with the party
system were described in chapter iii, was one of the instruments
responsible for the decline of the private member. Once they were
inaugurated, pork-barrel practices acquired an irresistible hold

14. W. P. Reeves, *The Passing of the Bush and Other Poems.*

and wrought upon the parliamentary machine a design which it
has never since lost. Many of the consequences, both political and
economic, were deplorable. The routing of railway lines and
roads and the erection of bridges conformed to the demands of
those districts or interests which the ministry thought it expedient to satisfy. Thus the New Zealand Government Railways have
been overcapitalized from the outset because they were politically constructed. While localities vied with each other in claiming
their "fair share" of national expenditure, the members of Parliament were converted into brokers. The people judged the merits
of their representative by the appropriations he secured on their
behalf; the ministry angled for his vote, and a barter deal was arranged.

Let it be said to the credit of Vogel, initiator of the centralized
public works program, that he tried to avert these abuses which
he foresaw. The safeguard he proposed in 1871 was to create a
Board of Works, composed of one minister, two civil servants,
and six representatives. This body would authorize the various
projects and dole out the items of expenditure. But Parliament rejected this idea, arguing perhaps correctly that a board so constituted would itself be susceptible to political pressure. No alternative or stronger safeguard was suggested, and, as a result, politics gravitated inevitably in the direction where the authority for
allocating public works resided. The cabinet and backbenchers
were left face to face without an intervening buffer. Nor were
cabinets slow to realize the possibilities that lay in their grasp.
The House of Representatives degenerated in a few years into a
body whose prevailing atmosphere was thus described in 1880:
"It is current talk in the lobbies at the present time, 'Has So-and-
so got his railway?' 'I cannot tell.' 'How does he vote?' 'Against
the Government.' 'Then he has not got his line.' Then again.
'Has So-and-so got his line?' 'I do not know.' 'Does he vote with
the Government?' 'Yes.' 'Then his line is in the schedule.' " So
common did this system become that the parliamentarian added
a descriptive phrase to his vocabulary. The ministry which used
this method to win support was said to "consolidate votes." Every
railway, road, or bridge that was sanctioned meant another vote
consolidated.

The effect on the parliaments of the eighties was disastrous. Every opposition as a matter of course charged the ministry with political favoritism in its administration of public works. Frequently this charge was too well substantiated to admit of denial or evasion. In 1883 Montgomery made it the kernel of his criticism of Whitaker and Atkinson: "It was the numerous and very large votes to favoured districts which gave them their support throughout the session. The estimates were loaded with votes for roads and bridges."[15] Debates became preoccupied with squabbles between the representatives of the more favored districts and the less favored. Disappointed members enviously compared the sums granted to their own constituencies with what others had been allotted; fortunate members, if they were tactful, glossed over their successes by explaining how urgently their own locality needed attention and how poorly it had been treated in the past. Others boasted with pride of the appropriations which they had negotiated. "I glory in my share of the transactions," announced one exultant member, "and if I had the same opportunity at my disposal again I would do the same thing."[16]

How much of the expenditure on public works was politically dictated cannot now be precisely ascertained. Vogel once said that he had been obliged to spend a million and a half in railways to purchase political support. At the end of the eighties a representative summed up the whole system as "a channel of corruption," alleging that two-thirds of the money devoted to roads was simply a means of conciliating political support.[17] Repeatedly the members from more thinly populated regions argued that the bulk of the outlay went to the most populous areas because of their electoral strength. Undeveloped districts, which needed the roads and railways if they were to attract settlers, were neglected. Thus a vicious circle was established. Areas relatively well developed gained more inhabitants and became still more attractive. The local districts applied to Wellington for money, voted for the ministry which granted it, and then received more funds. "The constituencies corrupt the House," commented a representative. "They look for these works, and regard the members

15. *P.D.*, XLIV (1883), 15.
16. *P.D.*, LVI (1886), 271.
17. *P.D.*, LXIV (1889), 6.

of this House very much as fishermen regard bait."[18] Viewing the same relationship from the opposite standpoint, others held that it was the central government which bribed the local bodies. In abolishing the provinces, they had destroyed nine beggars, but in their place they had created ninety.

There were times, moreover, when this type of politics assumed the uglier form of personal corruption. Graft was always a possible ingredient of the pork barrel, and on occasion the ministry might enter into bargains for the direct financial benefit of the member in his private capacity. Again, the extent of this cannot nowadays be judged, but one instance is so well authenticated and so succinctly described in Hansard that it deserves to be quoted in full: "I recollect, myself, one of the most scandalous scenes that ever occurred in this House. In 1882 a member began a speech against the Government, and began speaking against them most bitterly. Then the half past five adjournment took place. He went out of the chamber, and then he was sent for to the Cabinet room. I saw him sent for. The honourable member for Egmont [Atkinson] was there, and the honourable member for Waitotara [Bryce] was there. The honourable member sent for had been trafficking in Native lands, but could not get his title. The honourable member for Waitotara had lodged a caveat against his dealing with the land, and he could not get his land until the caveat was removed. The Government was engaged in a life-and-death struggle. Something happened in that room: then the honourable member came out. At half-past seven he resumed his speech. This is as true as Gospel, and can be vouched for by many members in this House. He continued his speech, and after he had got a little further he said that, although he had no confidence in the Government, he did not see how a Government could be formed from the other side, and he should feel it to be his duty to support the Government. Soon after the caveat was removed, and he got his title."[19]

Though incidents such as this were quite indefensible, the general indictment against the pork barrel and its consequences can be somewhat softened. As Atkinson once replied to his accusers, if a public works project was to be constructed at all, it had to be

18. *P.D.*, XLIV (1883), 32.   19. *P.D.*, LVII (1887), 550.

in someone's electoral district. If the district was one which a government supporter represented, then the ministry was *ipso facto* charged with political favoritism. If it was in a district represented by an opposition member, the government was said to be buying his support. In neither case could such accusations be avoided. Moreover, there were some opposition representatives in various parliaments who acknowledged that their districts had been well treated by a cabinet which they did not support.[20] Apart from cases of individual graft, whatever corruption there was embraced all political elements without distinction. The Liberals, when they were in office, followed the practice of the Conservatives. The locality which sought a grant, the representative who negotiated it, the ministry which authorized it—all were at least tarred with one brush. Who was to blame whom? Finally, if these issues be viewed on a broader screen, let it be remembered that other democracies have acted no differently at similar stages of their economic development. In the westward expansion of the United States, in the history of the land grants and of railway construction, Congress and the state legislatures were subjected to these very same pressures. The term "pork barrel" itself was taken from the southern plantations to describe a system which became a national abuse in America. When Canada and Australia were developing their hinterlands and spreading their communications, the same lobbies of landowners, municipalities, and corporate interests infused the cash nexus into politics. So, too, in democratic Italy, the chamber of deputies earned some of its unsavory reputation from the deals and jobs and intrigues that vitiated the construction of the railways. Many countries have fared badly in handling this problem. New Zealand can only say that its record has not been the worst.

The Tone of the House

The House of Representatives took its tone from its personnel and from the practices in which they indulged. The Hansard reports of the early parliaments yield the impression of a stiffly correct Victorian assembly, consciously aping the mannerisms of the

20. *P.D.*, XLVII (1884), 179.

mother of parliaments. The language was usually stilted or
florid, the style of speaking was a trifle pompous, and political
criticism was either larded with sarcasm or suffused with virtuous
indignation. Among the members were men educated in the
classical tradition, and their oratory was sprinkled with quota-
tions in the original from Vergil or Horace. The intellectual
standard of debate was reasonably good, although the prejudices
of a limited outlook and narrow sympathies marred the judgment
of many representatives. The spokesmen of a sectional interest
dominated the House, and their common class affiliations pre-
ponderated over their political disagreements. But a change of atmosphere was already discernible by the middle of the sixties.
The long-drawn-out insecurities of the Maori wars made tempers
prickly and discussion embittered. Provincial jealousies and interisland rivalries provoked ill feeling which occasionally lapsed into
personal bickering. Speeches might still be eloquently phrased,
but their mood was often rancorous. Sarcasm was twisted into
insinuation; moral indignation into recrimination. Continuously
a member until 1870, the old-time Victorian Carleton listed the
faults of Parliament as "acrimony in debate, mistrust of each
other, the frequency of imputations of paltry and even dirty motives, frequent reflections cast upon veracity . . . . and the creep-
ing in of miserable party feeling amongst us."[21]

As two more decades slipped by, these tendencies were confirmed rather than checked. The destruction of the provinces
aroused an animosity that bit deep and left with the defeated side
a sullen resentment. Grey's fiery invective resuscitated the memories of Featherston's oratory in an earlier decade. But the new
eloquence was more polemical than the old, and its barbs were
fashioned to stay in the flesh of the victim. The Liberal onslaught
on conservatism and the latter's resistance occasioned debates
whose ripostes were the sharper and fiercer, since more fundamental issues were at stake. Property was on the defensive, and an
economic hegemony was under challenge. In 1890 "the bitterness of party strife" was singled out as one of Parliament's worst
features.[22] Leading men of both sides were set on edge by this bitterness of criticism and retaliated in kind. Vogel was savagely as-

21. *P.D.,* V (1869), 5.   22. *P.D.*, LXIX (1890), 43.

sailed by the provincialists; Grey was ready to fence with any adversary, but he was the easy victim of his own vanity; Atkinson became notorious for trampling on his critics "with hobnailed boots." In the pork-barrel era leaders and backbenchers alike were implicated in a system which further lowered the tone of Parliament. Any volume of the debates in the eighties reveals a legislative climate of squalls and murk.

The quality and methods of discussion deteriorated as an inevitable consequence. Leaders who could not carry their measures by the merits of argument sought success through tactical advantage. The government could manipulate the order paper and could exhaust its opponents by protracting debates over trivialities. The opposition could obstruct and stone-wall; it could pester the ministry with motions of no confidence; it could call for information and returns which consumed departmental time. In the ninety-five-membered parliaments of the eighties speeches became repetitious, wearisome, and inartistic. Seddon first received notice through his powers of obstruction. He held up the Representation Bill of 1881 for forty-eight hours; he delivered in 1883 a harangue occupying seven and a half pages in Hansard; in 1890 he had to be gagged by Ballance so that the session could be finished in time for the general election. Hall understated the situation when he referred to "the awful waste of time which takes place in the House."[23]

Parliament, therefore, lost greatly in dignity and esteem. Many of its own members, able to watch from inside how the Colony's affairs were managed, were cynical or disgusted. Some used the debates not to discuss controversial issues on their merits but to seize opportunities for self-advertisement. The divisions were less affected by arguments heard on the floor than by caucus agreements and corridor cabals. "I have had nine sessions' experience in the House," said a member, "and have never yet known a speech affect a single vote. Votes depend upon other considerations than arguments, unfortunately."[24] As its membership grew and the Colony reached its social and economic adolescence, the House became ill equipped to perform its functions. Even in 1871 Macandrew complained about "the annual stand-

23. *Ibid.*, p. 48.   24. *P.D.*, LVI (1886), 277.

ing dish of one hundred to one hundred and fifty Bills" which could not be properly considered. For a partial remedy he sensibly suggested that one session periodically should be devoted only to the Appropriation Act and to bills dealing with public works. Parliament found that the details of finance were beyond its power of review and instituted a Public Accounts Committee to study the annual estimates. But already in 1883 this committee was considered a failure.[25] The shortening of Parliament's duration to three years made it difficult for the new member to use his power with effect. It took him two sessions to learn the ways of the House, and at the third session an election was already imminent, and he could accomplish nothing. The public watched and wondered why their representatives wasted six or seven weeks in wrangling recriminations and then rushed through a mass of legislation so hastily that it would later require amendment and correction.

Not all the changes, however, were for the worse. The House could justly claim that it was becoming more truly representative. It contained in 1890 a fairer cross-section of the community than in 1856. If there was bitterness in the legislative combats, that was unavoidable when economic fundamentals were at issue. The eighties were a decade of slump, depression, and unemployment. Labor was making its initial attempts at trade-union organization and groped for alleviation of its economic ills. The House merely mirrored the widespread insecurity among the populace. If members competed and disputed for public works, they could argue that a flow of central funds to their localities was desperately needed. The stiffer etiquette and more formal phrasing of an earlier time were no longer relevant, and the acrimony that penetrated into parliamentary debates echoed the suffering in many a poverty-stricken home of disillusioned immigrants. The House was evolving from a middle-class club to a popular assembly. The underprivileged groups were finding their voice; and, if their accents sounded strident, that was because they had been so long stifled.

25, *P.D.*, XLV (1883), 549.

The Legislative Council

Whatever its faults, the lower house compared favorably with the upper. The familiar dictum, that a second chamber is superfluous if it agrees with the first and obnoxious if it disagrees could be well illustrated from the case of New Zealand. Before the culminating crisis of 1892[26] the Council frequently disagreed with the House and was therefore obnoxious. Since 1892 it has never been able to disagree and has become quite superfluous. The history of the Council—and of New Zealand—might have been very different had the Colonial Office adhered to its original plan[27] of modeling the upper house upon the American Senate. If the Council had been established as a federal chamber with equal representation for each province, possibly the provinces might have avoided abolition. But the view which prevailed in Britain of the early fifties was that the Colony should develop an aristocracy whose interests would be politically safeguarded in a nominated upper house. Once this principle was accepted, appointment for life appeared the nearest approximation to hereditary membership. It followed also that the Council should receive sufficient powers to curb any "dangerous" tendency emanating from the elected chamber. The Constitution Act itself was discreetly silent concerning the relations between the two houses. Since that relation was governed in the mother-country by conventions and understandings unknown to the law, it was taken for granted that the same usages would operate in New Zealand without formal legislative prescription. The child would not only speak the parental language but would do so with the parental accent.

As early as 1854 the Council raised the issue in general terms. It sought an opinion from the Colonial Office whether it could alter any measure of supply which the lower house had approved. The answer briefly stated that the analogy of the English constitution ought to prevail. Money bills, in short, were not to be amended by the Council; other bills it could amend. In 1862 the problem was again raised, but this time over a concrete case. A

26. The Liberal ministry then overcame the Council's obstruction (see below, chap. xii, pp. 356–57).
27. Also supported by Gladstone.

native lands bill had come up to the Council, which changed a clause containing a financial provision that was merely incidental to the general policy. Though acquiescing in the merits of the particular alteration, the House challenged the Council's right to amend any clause involving the element of finance. The law officers of the Crown of England, whose opinion was asked, pronounced it in the Council's favor. In ten years' time, however, when another disagreement was referred to the same authority, they found for the House of Representatives. The Council on this occasion had amended the Payments to Provinces Bill, which the law officers considered to be strictly a money measure and, as such, beyond the Council's jurisdiction. Controversy recurred in the early eighties over a pensions bill; but Sir Erskine May, whose opinion was sought, judged this a money bill and warned the Council to keep its hands off. In all these incidents, it may be noticed, the Council was claiming a position and a power coordinate with the lower house. Nor did it even abstain from encroaching on the exclusive control of the elected members over finance.

There was another way in which the Council aimed at making itself independent of the lower chamber. In England the convention was already established that if the Lords would not agree to a measure on which the Commons insisted, the monarch would create enough new peers to override the majority. It was understood in New Zealand that a governor would likewise consent to swamp the Council with new nominees if it obstructed the ministry and their supporters in the House of Representatives. As the Constitution Act failed to state how large the Council should be, there was nothing in the law to preclude indiscriminate swamping. To be freed from this threat, the Council tried to impose a legal limit on the size of its membership. Measures with this objective were frequently proposed in the upper house, but the lower chamber wisely refused to surrender the ministry's ultimate sanction.

Although the Council many a time rejected bills which the other house had passed, no major crisis occurred to disrupt legislative relations before 1876. Dominated by the well-to-do landowners and sheep farmers, both bodies saw eye to eye over questions of their economic interests. After 1876, however, this was no longer so. Grey and his Liberals burned to avenge their beloved provinces, and they could not forget that the Council voted for abolition by a far greater majority than had the lower house. As the citadel of the land monopolists, the Council must first be reduced before any bill to redistribute the large estates could pass through Parliament. Hence in the eighties the Council was placed upon the defensive. In session after session Liberal representatives inveighed against the upper house and urged that it must be ended or mended.

Their indictment was presented in two debates, one held in 1881 on a motion that the Council should be elective and a second in 1883 over Grey's proposal to abolish it. It was anomalous, so the Liberals argued, for one house of Parliament to be elected every three years and for the members of the other to be appointed for life. Not only did the method of nomination enable a ministry to offer bribes to subservient partisans, but life-membership set the Council apart from the rest of the people. The Council was, therefore, unresponsive to public opinion, and its character was unduly conservative or even reactionary. Representing a privileged social group, it took care to legislate for their interest, Moreover, its undemocratic influence extended to the lower house. Councilors were invariably wealthy men wielding authority in agricultural and financial circles, on whose good will various of the elected representatives depended for gaining their livelihood. Nor did bicameralism promote legislative efficiency. Hasty legislation was not prevented, as long as the dominant economic interests were left untouched. In fact, the existence of two chambers divided the responsibility and encouraged each to be careless in the hope that mistakes would be revised by the other. To these criticisms the reply was unconvincing. Unable to deny that the Council was a stronghold of the landed oligarchy, Hall could only plead that there must be "some check, some drag, some conservative element in the Constitution."[28] Nevertheless, to blunt the edge of the Liberal attack, even the Conservatives of-

28. *P.D.*, XXXIX (1881), 221–22.

fered suggestions of their own for reforming the Council, but they were very careful not to press any of these to a conclusion.

Restively tied in double harness, Parliament's two houses skirmished for a decade until in the early nineties the battle was joined. After a sharp conflict, twenty years before Asquith's great fight against the Lords, New Zealand at last reduced its upper chamber to impotence.

CHAPTER VII

PUBLIC ADMINISTRATION

ALL aspects of government reduce in the final analysis to public administration. When the froth of election campaigns has evaporated and parliamentary speechifying has subsided, it is the administration that creates or confounds the policy. For, as Dewey has remarked, the state is as its officials are. Even in an era when the state supplied but a tithe of the services which it performs today, the well-being of individual citizens and the prosperity of the whole community were affected for good or ill by the departmental machinery and the organization of the civil service. Founding a colony was itself an experiment in social planning. The settlement of New Zealand particularly was inspired by men like Wakefield who were anxious to avoid the dangers of haphazard and unsystematic colonization which they had studied elsewhere. From 1840 onward the young country was treated to a higher degree of controlled management than many other overseas enterprises. Thus its modern characteristic of governmentalism was part of its natal endowment. Several features in the administrative structure of today have continued unbroken from the middle of last century. A tradition so formed and so perpetuated is difficult to shake even in a Dominion which celebrated its hundredth anniversary of organized government as recently as 1940. Administration in this twentieth-century democracy is that of Stafford, Vogel, Atkinson, and Stout—writ large.

State Functions and Departments

The portfolios held by Stafford and his ministers record the principal state activities of the new self-governing Colony. As colonial secretary, the premier himself headed a department which, besides conducting official relations with the British government and the governor, acted as a general maid-of-all-work.

Since money is the sinews of administration, a Treasury was an integral part of this original establishment. A Customs Department was instituted to manage one of the main sources of the Colony's revenue, for a tariff (with preference for Britain in certain commodities) had been introduced as early as 1841. The Attorney-General's Office stood as a reminder that the rule of law in English-speaking countries implies the rule of lawyers. A postal system organized under a postmaster-general betokened the willingness of the central government to provide a service to its citizens. Finally, because the vital need in the forties and the fifties was to maintain cordial relations with the Maoris while much of their land was purchased from them, a Native Department and a Lands Department were both indispensable. Such was the skeletal administration which sufficed at the center when the provinces could take care of the rest.

In the early sixties under the stress of the Maori wars a Defense Department was called into being and for a time remained the pivot of state activities. But, as the military prospects of the European settlers improved, some constructive and forward-looking developmental schemes were initiated. A pair of projects, both undertaken in the same year 1865, ushered in that lengthy series of experiments in public enterprise for which New Zealand has become famous. Military operations in an undeveloped country had been hampered by inadequate communications. Consequently, the central government provided a system of electric telegraphs which it intrusted to a new department separate from the post office although supervised by the same minister. Simultaneously, because the facilities of the private banks were available only in the few main centers, the state decided to adopt the public savings bank which Britain had inaugurated at Gladstone's instigation in 1861. For the administration of this new function the post office was wisely made responsible, since its branches extended through the Colony more widely than those of any other agency.

Further instances of this tendency for the state to provide social services were multiplied aplenty in the dynamic decade that commenced in 1869. Vogel's was the brain, and his the driving power, which designed and directed most of this expansion. As colonial treasurer in Fox's ministry, Vogel brought in a bill, which he had earlier sponsored as a private member, for a system of government annuities and life insurance. Gladstone was again the great exemplar, since he, as Vogel explained to Parliament, had secured in Britain in 1864 the enactment of a measure along similar lines.[1] New Zealand needed state insurance all the more imperatively because it contained no local life insurance companies. For the same reason it was easy for Vogel to carry his proposal. Gladstone had met and defeated the powerful opposition of the private companies, but in the Colony there were no vested interests to bring pressure upon the legislature. Since Hall, who was prominent on the opposition side, supported Vogel's measure, it passed through the House unanimously. In 1869 the Government Life Insurance Department opened its doors for business. It was constituted at its foundation, as it remains today, under the aegis of a commissioner whose statutory powers and obligations make him semi-independent of political control by any minister. Another extension of governmental activity, whose adoption in New Zealand was due to Vogel, improved on the traditional British method of land registration. A civil servant named Torrens in an Australian colony had devised a system under which the ownership and the transfer of land were registered in an office of the central government. The title to land rested not on a cumbrous series of deeds but on the simple fact of registration. A valid title was thus guaranteed by a method which was simple to administer and which reduced the private lawyers' fees. The motive behind Torrens' plan was the pragmatic one of assuring a secure title in a young colony where most of the territory was still unsurveyed, where land speculation was rife, and where transfers were frequent.

Pragmatism once more led to the founding of the Public Trust Office—another of Vogel's creations, although he did not claim originality for this idea. Under pioneer conditions in a young colony far distant from lands of ancient settlement it was hard to find satisfactory trustees for property. Trusts had been undertaken by men who subsequently left the Colony or who mismanaged their estates. It was a novel remedy and a salutary principle

1. *P.D.*, V (1869), 91.

to institute a public official performing the duties of a trustee with the state as his guarantor. More opposition was encountered by this proposal than by the Government Life Insurance Bill. The Public Trust Office would inevitably take away business from private lawyers, and there were many members of this profession in Parliament. So after passing the House in 1870, the bill was thrown out by the Council, which wanted further evidence of its desirability. When this evidence was secured by a select committee, the bill was enacted into law in 1872. Like the insurance commissioner, the public trustee was accorded a status semi-independent of political control. His primary obligation was not to the cabinet but to his clients. There was yet this further parallel between the two agencies. Although each was organized as a state department conducting a business enterprise, neither was granted a monopoly in its own field. Each competes to this day with private firms.

The expansionist policy lubricated by Vogel's ten-million-pound loan of 1870 resulted in the creation of two more departments. Their functions were new ones for the central government to undertake, but both were constituted in orthodox fashion under the immediate charge of ministers. One was an Immigration Department, designed to add to the human resources of the Colony. Thanks to its activities, in the single year 1874 as many as 32,000 state-assisted immigrants landed in New Zealand; while in the whole decade 1871–80 there were 136,000 more persons who came to the Colony than left it. Its twin agency had the task of developing the material resources of the Colony. This Public Works Department, as it was named, built roads and bridges and constructed and operated the railways. For some years thereafter the portfolio of public works ranked with those of finance and of land administration as one of the three most important which any premier could bestow.

When the provinces were abolished, the central government received a great accretion of administrative power. Functions formerly exercised by the provinces were either taken over at the center or were distributed to various of the existing or newly created local bodies. Of the activities transferred to central administration, most were allocated to the departments already established. This presented few difficulties, since in the preceding five years under Vogel's lead the central government had successively encroached upon provincial spheres. Thus the Lands, the Immigration, and the Public Works departments could easily absorb all activities of that character which the provinces had undertaken. But in the case of certain former provincial functions no central counterpart existed. Education was the outstanding instance, and one of Parliament's first duties in 1877 was to pass a national Education Act which set up a new department under a minister of the Crown. Besides all these already mentioned, New Zealand possessed by 1890 four other departments of significance: Marine, Justice, Mines, and Agriculture. In Atkinson's last ministry there were some seventeen portfolios distributed among seven ministers. But the figure seventeen by no means represented the total number of separate government agencies. It does not include such a small and politically unimportant concern as the Printing Department, or the independent Audit Department, or those like the Public Trust Office and the Government Life Insurance Department, which were semi-independent. Nor did the list of portfolios in 1890 include the railways, whose administration was separated from the Public Works Department in the early eighties and was intrusted in 1889 to a three-membered commission.

This sketch of the central government's growth over half a century reveals some well-marked tendencies. New Zealand had already displayed its readiness to utilize the machinery of state for providing needed social services. There was a creditable boldness in experimentation, particularly during the years 1865–72; and, even though many of the enterprises commenced at that time had been originated elsewhere, the settlers in the Colony were quick to welcome a novelty and give it a trial. The record is the more striking because, if the immigrants had any social philosophy at all, it was one which ran counter to the activities on which they embarked. Most of the New Zealanders who participated in politics accepted without question the principles of laissez faire which had dominated the circles to which they belonged in the mother-country. This typical opinion was expressed in 1869: "The real desire of all true Englishmen must be not to reduce the powers of the people, not to monopolize them in the hands of a few, but really to minimize the operations of the Government to the greatest degree. . . . . For once the word government is mentioned by the public at large in England it is mentioned a hundred times in New Zealand. I should like to forget the name of government as much as possible."[2] Similarly, when the Public Trustee Bill was rejected by the Council in 1870, it was criticized on the score that the government should not undertake private business.[3] Most of the theories that were then articulate were derived from doctrines of anti-governmentalism. But much of the practice of successive ministries was based upon a policy of active state enterprise. Why this paradox?

Along with their material possessions the emigrants who embarked for the long sea voyage to the Antipodes brought with them the ingrained attitudes of their British home. But the ideas which were relevant to a land long inhabited and rich in historical memory became preconceived dogmas when transported to a pair of lonely South Pacific islands. It was, in the phrase of Grover Cleveland, a condition which confronted the colonists, not a theory. In the British Isles the manifold institutions of society bulked larger in the life of the community than those of the state. There the modern state is a manufactured framework superimposed upon other social relationships. But New Zealand, as it appeared to Europeans in 1840, possessed neither the institutions of society nor those of the state. Both kinds of social structures, the political and the nonpolitical, had to be imported and constructed simultaneously. Inevitably it was the state—that is to say, the community organized for political purposes—which took the lead. Society in New Zealand has been supplementary and subordinate to the state. Private interests in the mother-country could build the railway lines and provide life insurances. In the Colony, at least during its early developmental phase, only the state could or would carry out these ventures from which profitable returns were a distant and dubious dream. Said one parliamentarian, reflecting on the process of colonization: "There was a fortuitous concourse of atoms, and they found themselves in New Zealand."[4] Only through the extension of state activity into

2. *Ibid.*, p. 542.
3. *P.D.*, IX (1870), 399.   4. *P.D.*, XXXVI (1880), 70.

new fields could these human atoms be combined together. Such must be the sociological explanation. The contrast between the theories of colonial politicians and their actions were due not so much to time lag as to space lag. Geographically removed to the South Pacific, they remained psychologically in the English Channel.

There is a politico-economic explanation as well, and it is ably put by Reeves, who himself contributed to the trend of governmentalism in the early nineties. "The State," writes this authority, "has always been the great colonial landlord, and, like other landlords, has been called upon to do its duty by its estates. When, in addition, the State took up the work of providing transport and of borrowing great sums to build railways, roads, and bridges, the die was cast. Government, with a partial grip of the soil and a complete grip of land-transport, held a position too commanding for any private capitalists to challenge."[5] The series of state experiments, as Reeves points out, was initiated by members of the middle class. It was not the fruit of pressure from organized labor; nor did it result from any deliberate endeavor to apply principles of socialism. It was an empirical response to the newness of the environment.

While adding to the functions of the state, New Zealand also multiplied the departments responsible for their administration. Normally each new governmental activity was assigned to a newly created agency. But there were some exceptions to this general rule. The savings bank was assigned from the start to the post office, where it has rested ever since. The railways were at first managed by the same department which constructed them. For a while there was much friction between the engineers of the different branches, and later the operation of the railways was transferred to an entirely separate agency. On the other hand, the telegraph system, which for some years formed a department on its own, was eventually amalgamated with the post office. The usual tendency of administrative fragmentation appealed to many of the leading civil servants (since separate departments meant more headships) and to ministers (since more portfolios

5. W. P. Reeves, *State Experiments in Australia and New Zealand* (2 vols.; London: Allen & Unwin, 1902), I, 60.

fostered the appearance of greater power). Once a department had enjoyed independent existence for a decade or more, it was unlikely to be consolidated with any other. Every established agency nourished its own vested interest to survive as an autonomous unit.

The financial effects of the growth of the government were set out in a parliamentary document prepared in 1887 (see Table 7). This showed at quinquennial intervals the cost of maintaining the governor, the ministry, the legislature, and the respective departments. The expenses incurred for the governor, cabinet, and Parliament together rose from £17,000 in 1860–61 to only £70,-000 in 1886–87—a negligible proportion of the total. But the details of departmental expenditure, covering both salaries and general costs, contain valuable information. They vividly portray the consequences of abolishing the provinces. Before 1876 the most costly department was the Post Office, necessarily so because its branches were flung the farthest afield. After 1876 the expenses for this agency ranked the third highest on the list. The two departments which cost most to operate after 1876 were Public Works and Education. The expense of administering the former rose in five years by nearly half a million pounds; that of the latter, by a quarter of a million. Between them these two functions consumed half of the total appropriations.

The Public Service

The continued extension of state activities called for a larger civil service whose salary bill formed a prominent item of expenditure. Hence in periods when the colonial finances were under strain, the expanding civil service was a regular target for political criticism. Greatly as they suffered from the lack of any classification plan or personnel system, public servants suffered still more from changes inspired solely by the belief that economy equaled efficiency. Salary cuts, staff reductions, consolidation of agencies—these were always proposed on occasions of economic stress. From the main road of constructive reform ministries were diverted by financial stringency to the by-ways of cheese-paring.

In the middle sixties when the Maori wars were proving burdensome to the exchequer, Stafford appointed the first of New

TABLE 7

Effects of Growth of Government on Departmental Costs of Salaries and General Expenses for Selected Financial Years

Departments under the Control of the—	Cost of Salaries and General Expenses for the Financial Year						
	1860–61	1865–66	1870–71	1875–76	1880–81	1885–86	1886–87
Colonial Secretary	£ 9,920	£ 33,630	£ 70,701	£ 76,678	£ 208,837	£ 237,304	£ 162,727
Colonial Treasurer	3,553	5,576	12,011	10,795	103,759	59,735	54,691
Minister of Justice	15,541	45,248	49,449	52,618	119,382	113,666	118,571
Postmaster-General and Commissioner of Telegraphs	33,574	146,891	138,997	223,970	256,152	287,524	290,046
Commissioner of Stamps	2,717	7,814	17,542	23,416	23,786	28,212	30,120
Commissioner of Customs	17,006	43,573	57,062	65,724	86,666	77,623	80,751
Minister of Education				11,520	271,165	357,806	371,603
Minister of Native Affairs	1,117	28,508	30,038	29,454	33,968	22,243	26,836
Minister of Mines					11,001	19,056	32,093
Minister of Public Works	851	931	32,347	126,767	603,498	726,576	723,946
Minister of Defense	6,880	27,470	83,773	131,995	141,465	161,108	182,569
Total	£91,159	£339,641	£491,920	£752,037	£1,860,279	£2,090,853	£2,074,553

Zealand's three civil service commissions. Its terms of reference authorized it "to inquire generally into the clerical strength and efficiency of the several departments in the Public Service" and to report improvements in the existing organization. The commission was composed of three civil servants from New Zealand and one from the Australian colony of Victoria, where a similar investigation had been recently made. Anxious to secure legislative action at the parliamentary session of 1866, the commission worked with excessive speed. Within one month of its appointment it had submitted a preliminary report together with the draft of a bill. These were followed by a second report two months later and by a final report after another month. Although these surveys were too hurried to be thorough, they provide the most reliable material about the civil service at this stage of its history.

To speak, however, of the civil service in 1866 is a misnomer. The Colony really contained, as the commission pointed out, ten separate services—one central and nine provincial—all entirely independent of each other. In none of these had any plan of organization been established. Thus, "the total absence of any general rules" was the root cause of many defects.[6] There was no rule concerning promotion, dismissals, or leave of absence. Few degrees of rank were defined, and the remuneration for similar types of work varied greatly. Only for superannuation had the central government introduced any uniform provisions. The isolation and separatism of the different departments, "each of which regards itself as distinct from even kindred offices,"[7] were responsible for numerous irregularities. A clear case existed for systematizing the conditions of employment among the 1,602 servants of the central government. The relative inadequacy of their salaries formed one of their chief grievances. The salaries and fees paid to these 1,602 persons amounted to £193,404 in the year 1865. But the nine provincial governments together employed 599 officials at a cost of £136,000; that is, the staffs of the provinces, who numbered only 37 per cent of the central staff, were paid 70 per cent of what the latter received. There were thirty-five

6. "First Report of the Civil Service Commission, 1866" (appendix to the *Journal of the House of Representatives*, D. No. 7), p. 1.

7. *Ibid.*, p. 2.

chief clerks of central agencies, and the average rate of their annual salaries was £280. Other clerks subordinate to these numbered 308 and were paid, on an average, £175. Rates of pay in the central government contrasted unfavorably with those prevailing not only in the provinces but also in private business firms. A poorly rewarded service was a discontented service.

The commission rounded off its diagnosis with a prescription of remedies whose ultimate aims were to counteract excessive departmentalism and to enhance the prestige and attractiveness of public employment. The principles which should underlie a sound organization were defined to include "classification, promotion from class to class, salaries with minimum and maximum limits and with annual increments for each class, rules of discipline, retirement and other allowances in certain cases."[8] The bill prepared by the commission provided for a classification of the central service into five classes. Salaries of members of the first (or highest) class were to be determined individually by parliamentary appropriation. For each of the other four classes a minimum and a maximum were laid down in the law, and the general level of pay was to be raised. Recruits would enter the lowest class (the fifth) between the ages of seventeen and twenty-two. They would qualify for admission by passing a noncompetitive examination, and for six months after appointment they would be on probation. When a vacancy occurred in any class except the first, the official to be promoted was the one standing next in rotation on the classified list, as long as he was qualified to occupy the higher position. It was possible, however, to enter the service by another method, which later came to be known as "the back door," for the bill granted the power to admit to a class above the lowest "some person of known ability" drawn from outside the established personnel.

The machinery of administration was divided between the governor in council (in effect, the ministry) and the civil servants in the first class, the latter acting together as a board. It was for the ministry to settle the number of offices in each class and then to classify existing offices so as to conform to the new system. The ministry, too, filled any vacancy in the first class, but on the rec-

8. *Ibid.*, p. 3.

ommendation of those who were already members of it. The
board of first-class officers served as a tribunal to hear appeals for
a higher classification or salary and also conducted inquiries into
matters referred to it by the ministry. Disciplinary provisions and
a generous superannuation scheme made up the rest of the measure. Such was the bill which received the approval of the cabinet
and of Parliament and became the Civil Service Act of 1866.

This act marked an improvement and an advance if only for
the simple reason that to have any system at all was better than
having none. Some of the principles embodied in the law, e.g.,
the insistence upon a basic classification plan, were those which
are nowadays regarded as indispensable to personnel administration. Judged, indeed, by the standards of its time, the measure
was a progressive one and went as far as could then be expected.
Viewed by modern standards, however, it contained some obvious defects. The examination, for instance, that was required of
entrants to the service was merely a qualifying one, and open
competition was expressly rejected. New Zealand thus imitated
the practice which Britain had introduced in 1854 but was soon
to abandon in 1870. Moreover, while the methods of promotion
paid lip service to the principles of efficiency and merit, the main
emphasis in fact was laid upon seniority. Civil servants were to
climb the rungs of the official ladder in rotation. A further weakness lay in the administrative machinery for operating the act.
For supervising the details of staff management it was senseless to
rely upon the cabinet and a standing committee of department
heads. What was intrusted to everybody became nobody's concern. But the day had not yet come—nor did it arrive in New
Zealand until 1912—when the need for a specially constituted
personnel agency was realized.

Some persons, like Alfred Saunders, criticized the commission's
proposals as furthering the interests of the civil service and not of
the public. Those who looked at all social problems only from the
taxpayers' point of view considered state officials to be inescapably tainted with the original sin of bureaucratic tyranny. To
many an English mind, recalling the memories of Pym and
Hampden and Locke, or intoning the shibboleths of laissez faire,
the whole executive branch and all its component departments

were naturally suspect. Any addition to the salaries of officialdom, any betterment of their status, was construed as a potential
menace to the inalienable rights and the natural liberties of the
private citizen. There was a workhouse theory of the civil service
which held that public employment should be made less congen-
ial than private. Thus could the best talent in the community be
diverted from a government career.

The Act of 1866 was more impressive on paper than in practice.
Salaries were raised, superannuation was made more generous,
the civil service board met at intervals, and examinations were
held for would-be entrants. But no system of classification was
introduced, possibly because the act had failed to set up the
proper administrative machinery. Anomalies, therefore, remained uncorrected, promotions could not be regularized, and
grievances continued unallayed. The civil servants in the first
class, who depended on ministerial and parliamentary favor
for any increase in their pay, exerted competitive pressure on the
legislature. Although Stafford remarked that department heads
in New Zealand were underpaid as compared with those in other
colonies,[9] many a representative consistently attacked the higher-
salaried officials. One member of Parliament was shocked to find
in an official statement that there were 131 individuals paid over
£400 per annum by the central government. Others asserted
that salaries were largely fixed by favoritism. Nor could this
charge be disproved. It was widely known and freely admitted
that civil servants used whatever influence they could muster in
the cabinet or in Parliament to better their other positions.
Representatives who had an anti-civil-servant bias argued that it
was difficult to resist this influence. The ministry had to ingratiate itself with its "servants" on whose loyalty and efficiency its
own policies depended; and in the legislature each civil servant
could usually find some eloquent and friendly champion. But
this sort of pressure by the civil service upon Parliament was only
a recoil of the pressure by Parliament itself upon the service. In
the speculative environment of the Colony, many persons sought
for themselves or their kinsfolk the relative security of a government job. Thus arose what one member called an "immense

9. *P.D.*, XI (1871), 87.

pressure . . . . to make appointments and provide for those who otherwise would be comparatively destitute." The method of recruitment by examination which the law prescribed was easily circumvented. Candidates who qualified in the examination were not always given appointments, while in many cases relatives of members of Parliament were recruited who had never qualified.

All the faults that sprang from the lack of a classification plan were aggravated in the seventies, first, when the departments expanded with the boom, and, second, when the central government absorbed the staffs of the provincial services. When the bubble burst at the end of the decade, public spending was drastically curtailed. The salary bill of the civil service became a favorite hunting ground for economy-minded, tax-paying representatives. A Colony not yet half-developed was confronted with unemployment; the remedy for this was to dismiss more men. The purchasing power of the community was declining; the solution adopted was to reduce salaries and wages still more. Legislative attacks on public officials were approaching their climax in 1879, and Hall had to come to the defense of his own former profession. To those who said that the civil service was very costly, he replied that many valuable officials were still inadequately paid and that the expenses of government were ultimately due to popular demands and to New Zealand demography. "They lived in scattered communities," said Hall, "and each community required that there should be placed in its midst advantages which were not required by the larger communities of older countries." An example was the Telegraph Department, with its widespread network of branches, only one-third of which operated at a profit. There were some telegraph offices costing £100 a year which brought in only £25. The New Zealand government was expected to give a high standard of service to a small population scattered over an extensive area. Hence the comparatively large civil service.

But Hall's apologies could not stave off the renewed assaults. In 1880 he was forced to arrange for a Royal Commission with a personnel dominated by the taxpayers' viewpoint. Its chairman was Alfred Saunders (a colonial Herbert Spencer), whose conceptions of governmental economy confused the distinction be-

tween surgery and butchery. This second civil service commission
went to work with a zest and a relish. Appointed on March 10,
1880, it presented its report on June 18 of the same year. "We
are conscious," stated the commissioners, "of having left some
large and important branches of the Service altogether unin-
vestigated, of having inquired very superficially into others, and
of having gone exhaustively into none."[10] This admission did
not deter them from stringently criticizing a number of agencies
or from making general recommendations which they anticipated would be considered illiberal. Only one department received any detailed attention, namely, the South Island railways
which were then managed by a commission responsible for that
island alone. If one can rely on the hastily gathered indictment in
this report, these railways were beset with almost every sin in the
administrative decalogue. Responsibility was divided; lines of authority were confused; sinecure posts were held at high salaries;
men without expert qualifications were placed in technical positions; stores were mismanaged and allowed to deteriorate; and
contracts were improperly allocated to the pecuniary gain of the
railway commissioner. The departments of Public Works, Survey, and Justice also came in for their share of criticism; and in
each case it was about the cost of their administration that the
commission complained.

Consistently with these attitudes the commission opposed the
principle of superannuation, since it interfered with the "free
choice of service" which the state should exercise as an employer
of labor.[11] They urged the abandonment of all ideas that a
government should treat its employees in any way different from
those working for private businesses. Already the civil service
contained so large a proportion of the Colony's wage-earners that
its standards necessarily influenced the rest of the community.
In 1875 the central and the nine provincial governments employed 4,500 persons, their salaries amounting to over £750,000.
In 1880 the civil service comprised 10,853 individuals at a cost of
over £1,000,000. One-thirteenth of all adult males were in the

10. "Report of the Civil Service Commission, 1880" (appendix to the *Journa
of the House of Representatives*, H.–2), p. 3.
11. *Ibid.*, p. 15.

employ of the government. Aware of these facts, private employers—such as were the members of this commission—viewed
the state as a strong and dangerous competitor in the labor
market. To make public employment less attractive suited their
economic interests.

When it was presented to Parliament and made public, the
report aroused a furore. Although some of the criticisms were too
severe and others were derived from prejudice, undoubtedly in-
efficiencies did exist which deserved to be laid bare. In many departments the quality of administration was not high enough.
Even defenders of the civil service admitted that there were too
many officials on the government's pay roll. But much of this
had resulted from the ever growing pressure of job-seekers on
ministers and parliamentarians. "Patronage is the curse of
ministerial life," said a representative who was both a former
minister and a former civil servant. "A Ministry is continually
pestered to put in this person and that person, and for the last
twenty years Ministry after Ministry has succumbed to those
influences."[12] Parliamentary critics of the service were merely
exposing aspects of a vicious system to which they had themselves
contributed. Every member of the House, stated one representative, had a relative or friend in a government job.[13] For this
reason it had always been difficult to persuade Parliament to
legislate against the service en bloc.

Saunder's own opponents quite rightly argued that whatever
items of truth the report contained were marred by its universally
hostile and unsympathetic point of view. One Liberal leader
even charged the commissioners with gross partisanship and
mentioned that Saunders himself was "concerned, or nearly
connected, with a firm which was at daggers-drawn with one of
the departments against which this report is chiefly aimed [the
South Island Railways]."[14] Nevertheless, despite the shortcomings of the commission and the influence of the civil service, the
report found in 1880 a Parliament bewildered at the slump and
desperate for remedies. Antagonism to the service collectively
overcame any friendly feelings that representatives might have

12. *P.D.*, XXXVI (1880), 167.
13. *P.D.*, XXXIII (1879), 509.   14. *P.D.*, XXXVI (1880), 161.

for civil servants individually. So when Saunders moved his resolution, previously agreed upon at a caucus meeting, to reduce all salaries by 10 per cent, it was carried without difficulty. "If a man does not like the salary he receives," was one typical comment, "let him leave; there will be a hundred applicants for the appointment. They come to me by the score and ask if I can get them into the Government employ by hook or by crook."[15] With equal candor leading councilors upheld the 10 per cent cut because of the effect it would have upon the price of labor. In this spirit did the representatives of the public treat the servants of the public.

The next legislative effort to remold the conditions of employment in the civil service was made by the Liberal administration of Stout and Vogel. Stout's liberalism was of John Stuart Mill's variety, which, even when it condoned state activity, ascribed higher ethical quality and greater social benefit to private enterprise. Whatever civil service existed must not endanger the rights of the individual; nor must public employment offer advantages not available in employment outside. Impressed with the achievements of American democracy, Stout considered that "we can gather more lessons from the United States than we can gather from any other nation in the world, both in regard to our government and to social affairs."[16] Deliberately he chose the United States as the example which the civil service of New Zealand must imitate. Unfortunately, though, the model to which he looked was the spoils system based upon the pseudo-democratic principle of rotation of public office. Although legislating in 1886, Stout completely ignored the Pendleton Act of 1883, which had set up the United States Civil Service Commission and established the principle of recruitment by open competition.

In the view of the Liberal premier, New Zealand needed a new act of Parliament, since the recruitment of its civil servants was still utterly haphazard. Although examinations were held for admission to the service, many were appointed without ever passing it. The back door stood so wide open that anyone with influence could find his way into a departmental job. As a corrective for these weaknesses Stout proposed reorganizing the service on the

15. *Ibid.*, p. 30.   16. *P.D.*, LV (1886), 382.

basis of two principles. First, candidates for public employment must be nominated by members of the House of Representatives. Those nominated would qualify by passing a junior civil service examination, which was of low standard, after which they would be appointed. Stout opposed the system of open competition with an examination of high standard. His reasons were significant. The merit he claimed for his own proposal was that it placed all districts on an equal footing. If open competition were adopted, town dwellers with their better educational opportunities would have an advantage over country dwellers, for in 1886 the national system of free primary education had existed for less than ten years. Educational facilities were not yet evenly spread through the Colony. Stout professed, therefore, to be upholding the excellent democratic notion that opportunities must be equalized. In reality, however, he was abusing a sound doctrine by carrying it to an absurd extreme. If the service was to recruit the talented, it needed to have open competition in a stiff examination. But since this method would have excluded all those of limited education, Stout chose to push the standard down to the point where all stood equal on the same low educational level. Thus was the principle of equal opportunity preserved at the expense of the caliber of public personnel. His was an attitude fraught with future significance, since it has become a dogma of the New Zealand conception of democracy.

Stout's second proposal was that all civil servants should be liable to three months' notice. Tenure was to be insecure in the interests of efficient and democratic government. It was presumed efficient, because unsatisfactory servants of the state could be easily dismissed; and democratic, because the public could thus control its officials. Entrants to the service should not view it as a permanent career. State employment was like a limited national dividend to be shared round at different times to different stockholders. This was a pleasing idea to many parliamentarians, one of whom, for instance, referred ominously to the "growing tendency towards the establishment of . . . . a civil service caste."[17] The bill, therefore, passed the lower house with a big majority. But in the Council something surprising happened.

17. *Ibid.*, p. 373.

pened, and for once a measure was improved by the upper chamber's amendments. The Council struck out the method of nomination by members of the lower house, partly because they feared an aggravation of spoils practices, partly because the right to nominate was conferred only on representatives and not on councilors. Wisely they substituted the principle of an open competitive examination. When this amended bill returned to the lower house, the premier and many other Liberals disliked the changes but decided to let them pass as the session was nearly at an end. As a parting shot, however, Stout remarked: "If I have to do with drawing up the syllabus for the examinations, I shall take care that it is so drawn that the pupils of the town secondary schools shall not have all the advantage."[18] In other words, the entrance standard would be a low one. Next year Stout secured the passage of an amending bill which gave the government a broad latitude to make "temporary" appointments. Thus the intellectually fitted could enter the service through competitive examination; while the others would be appointed temporarily in name but permanently in fact. Patronage received another lease of life, which lasted precisely twenty-five years more.

As economic conditions grew worse from 1887 to 1890, a panicky Parliament renewed its onslaughts upon the civil service. Job-holders were dismissed; general wage reductions on a percentage basis were again imposed; and the salaries of department heads, which were separately appropriated, were slashed in the Committee of Supply. So drastic was the treatment that a representative alluded in 1890 to "the way in which our own civil service has been torn piecemeal limb from limb."[19] Behind all these attacks lay the widely held belief that the service was gaining in power and numbers to an alarming extent and must be controlled. In 1887 the central government employed 7,200 persons,[20] their salaries amounting to just over one million pounds. From these figures some inferred that the service cost too much; others, that New Zealand was overgoverned. But even Whitaker, who certainly spoke with the taxpayer's voice, said in 1890 that

18. *P.D.*, LVI (1886), 551.   19. *P.D.*, LXIX (1890), 304.
20. This figure excludes the police, the military, and the part-time country postmasters.

this civil service was the worst paid and the worst treated in the British dominions.[21] By this date, at the culmination of a decade of economy-minded parliaments, the effect on the service of repeated dismissals and wage reductions was demoralizing in the extreme. Uncertain of his promotion, insecure in his job, and liable to find his salary cut at any minute, the civil servant's lot was not a happy one. As a remedy for their own mutual protection, some of them began in the year 1890 to band together into a civil service association—a movement inspired by the contemporary growth of trade-unionism.

Only one constructive act stands out from the record of legislative policy toward the service in the ninth decade. In 1890 Parliament passed an act for the classification of the Post and Telegraph Department. Unable or unwilling to classify the service in its entirety, the legislature at any rate provided an organization plan for one of the state's largest departments. The debate on this measure showed a far more sympathetic attitude for this agency than for most other branches of the government. Being the most widely spread of all departments, the post office had a broader political support. It undertook an indispensable service, and, as Hall and others had organized it on the lines of the British post office, it was run with a certain amount of efficiency. Many a representative who habitually condemned the civil service spoke in a more friendly tone on the Post and Telegraph Regulation and Classification Bill of 1890. There were glimmerings of the idea that the public would receive good service from its officials if it was a good employer. But the new light did not fully dawn until 1912.

It is noticeable that throughout the incessant attacks on the civil service the more virulent parliamentary critics were usually men who had not held ministerial rank. Although ministers and former ministers sometimes joined in the criticisms, it was mostly the backbenchers who led the assault. Men like Saunders and Seddon (the latter being a severe opponent of the service until he attained power) had never been in charge of state departments or depended on the knowledge and co-operation of their officials. Various cabinet members, on the other hand, paid some striking

21. *P.D.*, LXIX (1890), 666.

tributes to the value of the service. When, for example, a suggestion was discussed in 1871 to convene Parliament periodically in the South Island, Waterhouse stressed the inconvenience of having a legislature in one place while the departments were elsewhere. During the legislative session, no less than during the recess, ministers relied upon their civil servants to help them through. A leading official from the department would regularly accompany a minister to supply him with information on the floor of the House or to prompt him when answering questions.[22] Hall, too, was a politician who knew how important it was to have a competent permanent staff. He once told the House that it was better to have a good undersecretary than a good minister.[23] Yet a third premier, Pollen, admitted that the government of the Colony was practically carried on by the civil servants and would function quite steadily if they "shut up this talking shop for two or three years." Ministers, in his experience, "did no more than represent what are called the walking assistants in the draper's shop, their business being to look pleasant, and make themselves agreeable to customers who have votes, and see that the shop is closed at the proper time."[24]

Those who complain in the twentieth century about the evils of bureaucracy—and New Zealand has no lack of these complainants—pretend to have uncloaked a "new despotism." Cabinet ministers nowadays are often likened to puppets whose words and motions are controlled by their official subordinates. The real truth is that ministers and civil servants are mutually dependent, each group relying on the other for different purposes. It is historically significant that the nineteenth-century civil service was charged by backbenchers with wielding excessive powers, while it was vindicated by premiers and other ministers. What Lord Hewart has called the "new despotism" is not so despotic, nor are some of its features new.

22. *P.D.*, XI (1871), 579.
23. *P.D.*, XXXVI (1880), 31.   24. *P.D.*, LV (1886), 568.

PART II

Democracy in Operation, 1891–1947

CHAPTER VIII

THE ELECTORAL SYSTEM

THE general result of the changes before 1890 was to annul various of the principles embodied in the Constitution Act of 1852. In the early institutions of New Zealand were to be found, along with many British elements, two characteristics of government in the United States: federalism and a separation of powers. Four decades of social development and political adaptation had stimulated new tendencies. One of these was centralization, or the transfer of effective power from subordinate units of government to the central jurisdiction. This culminated in the abolition of the provinces, converting the Colony from a federal to a unitary state. The other was integration, meaning the consolidation of power within the central government and a removal of the checks and balances between its component branches.[1] The political system became integrated as the premier and his cabinet absorbed the governor's powers and the lower House grew ascendant over the upper. Both these trends reached a decisive climax in the early nineties. The Liberals' philosophy of state enterprise was centralist of necessity, and their leader, Seddon, favored integration by temperament.

A third feature of the original constitution was the narrow restriction of the right to participate in politics. If democracy implies, among other things, government *by* the people, during most of the nineteenth century the Colony could be called only semidemocratic. It was to a small segment of the adult population that the electoral and parliamentary machinery conceded the means of making their wishes known and of translating them into action. Politics was at first a preserve of the privileged, but in the seventies and eighties privilege was slowly forced to enlarge

1. For this distinction between centralization and integration see Leonard D. White, *Introduction to the Study of Public Administration* (2d ed.; New York: Macmillan Co., 1939), p. 45.

its boundaries. In the nineties, by the formal grant of equal voting rights to all adults regardless of sex, one major requirement of a modern democracy was satisfied in full. The overthrow of political privilege was accompanied by a successful assault on some of the social and economic inequalities which sheltered behind it. For the last half-century, therefore, New Zealand's politics have rested on the electoral foundations of a matured democracy. Through the ballot box the majority of the people periodically enjoy unfettered legal power to select the government they wish. "Squattocracy" has evolved into popular sovereignty. Simultaneously this shift in the balance between social groups within the community at large has reacted upon the relations of the separate governmental branches. Each of the principal parts of the political system—the electorate, parties, cabinet, premiership, Parliament, and the administration—has been remodeled for new tasks. Some branches have lost influence; others have gained. How the powers, structure, and personnel of each institution have altered is the subject of the discussion that follows.

Voting Qualifications

If the political system be studied as a whole, all changes over the last fifty years are ultimately explicable in relation to the franchise. The sheer increase in the number of voters can be considered the root cause from which all other developments have sprung in sequence. Two of the critical battles in the campaign to extend the suffrage were won when the residential was added to the property qualification (1879) and the principle of "one man, one vote" was adopted (1889). During the nineties these reforms began to take their effect. They were reinforced in 1893 by two further measures which completed the process of democratizing the franchise. In that year the advantages of property were again abridged by the provision that a voter could be registered on the roll of only one electoral district. At the election of 1890 a man who owned sufficient property in several districts was still permitted to register in each one of them. He could then wait for election day and choose in which particular constituency he would cast his single vote. The party of the well-to-do might thereby still swing an election by directing their votes to any district in which their candidate faced a close contest. In addition, those registered on several rolls could vote at more than one by-election if any occurred in between the general elections. Such an element of choice, a relic of the former plural voting, was removed by the new principle of "one person, one roll." Henceforth a voter was allowed to register in only one district; and, what is more, this was required to be done some months before the election.

More momentous was the accompanying innovation of the same year. In 1893 New Zealand granted its women citizens the right to vote, thus proclaiming itself the first British country to regard the sexes as equal in the presence of the ballot box. How did Parliament bring itself so early to adopt what was then considered a radical experiment? For over a decade progressive-minded men of both parties had championed the cause of women. Among the Liberals, Stout and Ballance were leading proponents; so were Hall, the Conservative, and Vogel who straddled both sides. Outside Parliament a feminist movement was urging women's rights in the eighties, but it did not make much headway until it became connected with the vigorous activities of the anti-liquor crusaders. Reeves, a contemporary observer and the outstanding intellect in the then Liberal cabinet, has commented: "Whether their [the Prohibitionists] hot advocacy helped the suffrage cause amongst men more than it hindered it, is a moot point; but it is fair to say that such active desire for the franchise as there was amongst the women was mainly aroused by them. Outside their lodges and their Women's Christian Temperance Union, the attitude of the sex was one of passive interest."[2] When the proposal for woman's suffrage was introduced in the House, all the temperance forces rallied behind it, while the liquor interests stood opposed. Victorian traditionalists, already horrified at Darwin's announcement of their monkey ancestry, were further outraged by this invasion of their masculine monopoly of politics. Yet the loyal subjects of a queen who accorded to a woman their greatest political deference were hopelessly torn by a conflict between their sentimentality and

2. W. P. Reeves, *State Experiments in Australia and New Zealand* (2 vols.; London: Allen & Unwin, 1902), I, 104.

their prejudices. Seddon, newly chosen in 1893 as the Liberal premier, was both antiprohibition and antifeminist. But he had not yet acquired the mastery over Parliament which in a later session would have enabled him to block the measure. Approved by the House, the bill barely slipped through the Council by a majority of two votes. Thus did the women of New Zealand receive equality of political status.

It took only a decade and a half (1879–93) of legislation to establish fully democratic qualifications for the franchise. Apart from such obvious exceptions as minors, criminals, and lunatics, the entire population, both European and Maori, has possessed voting equality for some fifty years. Not until 1928 did the electoral laws of the mother-country advance to this point, and even the present decade has still witnessed plural voting in Britain. There is no poll tax in New Zealand to debar the poor. Nor is the number of otherwise eligible voters reduced by illiteracy, since the percentage of illiterates in New Zealand is quite negligible.[3] As far as constitutional machinery can provide, the government of the Dominion really rests on a broad basis of popular consent. To express the same point differently, the entire adult population has had for five decades every opportunity to see that parliaments and ministries are responsive to its needs.[4] Statistics will confirm this generalization. Table 8 shows at various years in which a general election was held the numbers of voters registered on the electoral rolls. The big increase in the percentage for 1893 shows the effect of enfranchising the women. Since then, over one-half of the population (i.e., nearly all the adult population) have regularly enrolled themselves as voters. This forms a high proportion of all those eligible for the franchise. It is noteworthy when one remembers that up to the middle of the twenties registration was purely voluntary. Only in 1925 did the duty to register on an electoral roll become a compulsory obligation of the citizen. In 1938 and 1946 two-thirds of the whole population—in other words, virtually the entire adult population—were duly enrolled.

3. There are a diminishing number of Maori illiterates, mostly elderly and remotely situated.
4. Normally a general election is held in New Zealand every three years.

Although New Zealand has made it compulsory to register, voting has never been made so. A citizen must enrol, but he need not subsequently vote. The example of Australia and of Belgium, both of which countries have compelled people to vote, has not been followed in this Dominion. Why New Zeland has not needed to take this further step is explained in Table 9, which contains for the same election years as the preceding table the proportions of actual to registered voters in the seventy-six European con-

TABLE 8*

NUMBER OF VOTERS REGISTERED ON ELECTORAL ROLLS
BY ELECTION YEARS, 1890–1946

Election Year	European Population	Registered Voters	Percentage of Registered Voters to Population
1890	625,508	183,171	29
1893	672,265	302,997	45
1902	807,929	415,789	51
1908	888,376	537,003	60
1919	1,142,081	683,420	60
1928	1,344,469	844,633	63
1935	1,487,905	919,798	62
1938	1,491,484	995,173	67
1943	1,602,000†	1,000,197	64
1946	1,603,554‡	1,061,445	66

* The figures in this table do not include the Maoris.
† Approximate figure only, incluing an estimate for the armed forces overseas.
‡ Figure for the census of September, 1945.

stituencies. These figures, it will be readily granted, make an extremely good showing. That such a high percentage of its citizens should actually use their votes is one of the most commendable features of this small democracy. New Zealand can regularly expect more than four-fifths of its adult population to visit the polls on election day.[5] The number of actual voters rose in 1938 to 93 per cent, and in 1946 to the all-time record height of 95 per cent. That is a striking proof of political vitality on the part of the electorate. In any comparisons with other democracies New Zealand on this score rates very favorably. Elsewhere, even

5. The percentage of actual voters is usually lower at by-elections than at general elections. But this exception is not very serious.

since the suffrage has been liberalized, large sections of the electorate have often been all too apathetic about exercising their great democratic right. The prevalence of nonvoting has given much concern to political scientists.[6] In Britain, where the whole adult population, both male and female, did not receive equal voting rights until 1928, the proportion of actual to registered voters fluctuated between 74 and 81 per cent in the twenties and thirties. In the United States at the presidential elections of 1920

TABLE 9

PERCENTAGE OF VOTES CAST TO TOTAL REGISTERED VOTERS
BY ELECTION YEARS, 1890–1946

Election Year	Registered Voters	Actual Votes Cast	Percentage of Votes Cast to Registered Voters
1890.................	183,171	136,337	74
1893.................	302,997	220,082	74
1902.................	415,789	313,885	75
1908.................	537,003	428,648	80
1919.................	683,420	550,327	81
1928.................	844,633	743,691	88
1935.................	919,798	834,682	91
1938.................	995,173	924,057	93
1943.................	1,000,197*	911,370*	91
1946.................	1,061,445	1,010,778	95

* The number of registered voters is that of the civilian roll. The actual votes cast include those of the armed forces.

and 1924 only 50 per cent of those eligible recorded their votes. At the subsequent elections of 1928 and 1932, 60 per cent came to the polls, a symptom of protest against the depression; and in 1936 and 1940 the percentage again rose. But neither of the two largest English-speaking democracies can match the consistently good voting record of New Zealand.

If the problem of nonvoting scarcely exists in New Zealand, what are the reasons for so fortunate a state of affairs? Part of the answer lies in the volume of functions undertaken by the state. There is no group in the community whose economic interests and social welfare are not positively controlled or else closely

6. See Charles E. Merriam and Harold F. Gosnell, *Non-voting: Causes and Methods of Control* (Chicago: University of Chicago Press, 1924).

affected by what the state does. To a far greater extent than in most democracies the individual New Zealander is a recipient of state-provided services, a subject of state regulation, a competitor against state enterprises, or an administrator of a state activity. Everyone in the Dominion falls into one or more of these categories. The omnipresence and omnipotence of the state explain the keenness to vote. It is partly a sense of public duty, but more the awareness of individual self-interest, that draws the New Zealander to the ballot box.

Yet that is not the whole explanation. The temperance movement, which helped women gain the vote, has also contributed to the large turnout of voters at general elections. In the year 1894 for the first time licensing polls (or referenda) on the liquor question were held under the principle of local option, and for convenience the same boundaries were used for licensing as for electoral districts. Since 1896 these local licensing polls have regularly been conducted on the very day of the general election— and in the same polling booth. In addition, since 1911 at every general election (except that of 1931), a national referendum on the prohibition issue has also been held simultaneously. At a modern general election the New Zealander votes on three matters. First, he selects a party candidate to represent the constituency in Parliament. Second, in a national referendum he ballots for one of three choices: prohibition, state purchase and control of the liquor trade, or continuance of the existing system of licensing and regulation. Third, there is a local poll to determine whether or not alcoholic drinks shall be sold in his particular district. The keen public interest aroused by the prohibition controversy has often attracted to the polls a class of citizens who were less concerned with party warfare than with social and ethical issues.[7]

Conducted with uncompromising zeal and with much organizing ability, the temperance campaign has provided for four militant decades an outlet for that Anglo-Saxon propensity to attempt the reform of one's neighbors' morals. It has enlisted in its ranks many Protestant clergymen, some prominent political leaders, and various women's organizations. It has sought the

7. See, e.g., *P.D.*, CXLIV (1908), 594.

election to Parliament of members pledged to ban alcohol from New Zealand. It is nonpartisan, does not contribute to party funds, and never puts forward candidates of its own. But it has advertised widely and at election time canvasses all candidates and publishes statements of their views on the liquor question. So powerful a movement has conjured up against itself the concerted strength of the liquor trade. Brewers and hotel-owners have become a political force, fighting to make New Zealand safe for beer-drinkers. It is generally asserted that they contribute to party funds and help those candidates who prefer a system of licensing and regulation to outright prohibition. On many occasions the fight between "the trade" and "the Alliance" has been so vigorous that the votes on the liquor referendum have almost equaled the number cast in the political contest. In 1922, for instance, 620,650 persons votes for parliamentary candidates and 619,187 in the national referendum. The arrangement by which people record their preference in the same place and on the same day for and against legislators and liquor undeniably increases the proportion of voters.[8]

The Country Quota

Jeremy Bentham, the founder of nineteenth-century utilitarianism, laid it down that everybody was to count for one, that nobody should count for more than one, and that electoral districts should be equal. Up to 1945 the electoral laws of New Zealand only partly conformed to those principles. This Dominion deviated from pure Benthamism in the method of apportioning its parliamentary districts. For sixty-four years the basic electoral law itself prescribed that, as between city and country, districts were to be unequal; and it even specified the exact percentage of their inequality. This was achieved by means of the "country quota," which, after various vicissitudes, was fixed in 1889 at the figure of 28 per cent and remained the same until 1945. At every election for more than six decades the farmers

8. In 1931 only 83 per cent of the registered voters actually voted (a drop of 5 per cent on the figure for the preceding election). This was due to two reasons: two of the three contending parties had formed a coalition and Parliament had decided not to hold the liquor referendum that year.

have received a free electoral gift in the form of this fictitious
increment to their voting strength. The way in which the quota
used to operate was simple. After the periodic censuses, normally
held every five years, a representation commission (composed
partly of civil servants, partly of government nominees) was called
together to draw the boundaries of the constituencies. The commission ascertained the total European population at the last
census and the respective numbers of urban and rural inhabitants.[9] It then increased the actual figure for the rural population
by 28 per cent, which determined the nominal rural population.
The nominal rural population was added to the actual urban
population, and the sum gave the nominal total of the electorate.
This nominal total was then divided by 76 (the number of European seats in the House of Representatives) in order to arrive at
the quota of population for an electoral district. Every district,
as delimited by the commission, had to contain a nominal
electoral population approximating very closely to this quota.
Again using the census figures, the commission worked out separately the nominal population of the two islands and assigned to
each the proportion of the 76 seats to which it was entitled. Then,
once the number of seats per island was determined, the commission split into two subcommissions which mapped the
electoral boundaries within each island. The provisional boundaries were publicly advertised, and anyone interested had the
opportunity to appeal for alteration. Complaints were lodged
sometimes by individual citizens, by private organizations, by
local authorities, or by local branches of the political parties. All
requested changes were considered by the commission, which
subsequently presented a public report to Parliament of its
decision on each case. In practice the majority of objections were
usually disallowed, but some received approval. Finally, the
commission published the definitive boundaries beyond which
there was no further appeal.

The whole procedure can be specifically illustrated by the most
recent reapportionment under the old system—that which took

9. For electoral purposes the "rural" population was defined to include all who
lived in communities of less than two thousand inhabitants and were more than five
miles distant from the central post office of the four principal cities. The remainder
comprised the "urban" population.

place in 1937. At the census of 1936 the population, excluding
Maoris, came to 1,491,484. Of this total, the urban population
was 864,194; the rural, 627,290. The latter figure was increased
by 28 per cent (175,641) to a nominal rural population of
802,931; and, when this was added to the urban population, it
produced a nominal electoral total of 1,667,125. Dividing this
total by 76, the commission reached a quota of 21,936 per district. The North Island had an actual population of 938,939 and
a nominal one of 1,046,204; the South Island, an actual population of 552,545 and a nominal one of 620,921. The north was
entitled to 47.7 of the 76 seats and was granted 48. The south,
being entitled to 28.3, received 28. Previously the north had had
47 seats and the south 29. So the commission proceeded to rear-
range electoral boundaries in both islands. It took one district
away from the part of the south in which the relative decrease of
population was greatest and added it to the north. Furthermore,
as the urban population had increased in the North Island faster
than the rural, one of the northern rural electorates was abolished. As a result, the metropolitan areas of Auckland and
Wellington each gained a new constituency, while Dunedin in
the South Island lost one. When the provisional boundaries were
published, seventy-four objections were submitted. Fifty-two of
these were refused by the commission; four were partly granted;
eighteen were wholly approved. In Table 10 are given a few
samples of electoral districts, as finally determined, with figures
taken from the commission's report to Parliament. By this means
the electorate was apportioned into geographical districts whose
actual populations differed considerably but whose nominal
populations were equalized. In 1890 each of the districts whose
population was solely urban contained in round figures 9,700 persons, while each of the districts with only a rural population
contained actually 7,500. In 1937 the corresponding averages for
actual inhabitants were 22,000 in the entirely urban constituencies and 17,000 in the entirely rural.

Using the reports of the ten representation commissions which
sat between 1890 and 1937, I have analyzed the results of
this system of apportionment. Electoral districts can be conveniently classified if the nominal population figures are disre-

garded and only the actual population is taken into account. Districts whose actual population was over 95 per cent urban can reasonably be called "entirely urban"; those whose population was over 95 per cent rural, "entirely rural." "Mainly urban" are those whose actual population was between 67 and 95 per cent urban; while "mainly rural" districts contained between 67 and 95 per cent rural. "Mixed" districts had over 33 per cent rural and over 33 per cent urban. This classification is my own, but it is based on the commission's statistics. The unbracketed figures in Table 11 show how many constituencies fell into each

TABLE 10

ACTUAL POPULATION AND NOMINAL POPULATION AS DETERMINED BY
THE REPRESENTATION COMMISSION FOR SELECTED
ELECTORAL DISTRICTS, 1937

| ELECTORAL DISTRICT | ACTUAL POPULATION | | ACTUAL TOTAL | NOMINAL POPULATION |
	Urban	Rural		
Bay of Islands.............	....	16,763	16,763	21,457
Waitemata................	13,533	6,597	20,130	21,977
Auckland West............	22,018	....	22,018	22,018
Roskill..................	20,540	905	21,445	21,698
Waikato.................	4,392	14,408	18,800	22,834

of these five groups. Some comparison, however, is needed if the effect of the country quota is to be gauged in full. It is plain that, by the addition of a fictitious 28 per cent to the actual rural population, some parliamentary seats, which would otherwise have gone to city dwellers, were transferred to the farmers. Is it possible to estimate how the country quota modified the number of districts that are classified into each of the five groups just mentioned? I have attempted to do this by ignoring the 28 per cent increase. I have worked out a revised quota of the actual population for each electoral district by dividing the figure 76, not into the nominal total population (as the commission did), but into the actual total. If this "true" quota is then divided into the totals of the actual population in the five groups, the results show how many seats of each type might have been allotted if there were no 28 per cent donated to the countryside. These results are merely approximations and cannot be regarded as precise. Nevertheless, they do serve as a check on the old method of apportionment. In Table 11 the bracketed figures in every column represent my estimate of a reallocation based upon the "true" quota.

This analysis illustrates clearly the effect on the electoral system of the gradual urbanization of New Zealand. The trend has been for the entirely rural districts to decrease in number and move over into the mainly rural group. Entirely rural districts in

TABLE 11*

ANALYSIS OF ELECTORAL DISTRICTS, 1890–1937, SHOWING THE INFLUENCE OF THE COUNTRY QUOTA

Date of Representation Commission	Entirely Urban Districts	Mainly Urban Districts	Mixed Districts	Mainly Rural Districts	Entirely Rural Districts	Total No. of Districts
1890........	9 [11]	6 [7]	14 [14]	8 [8]	33 [30]	70
1892........	12 [14]	4 [4]	13 [14]	7 [7]	34 [31]	70
1896........	12 [14]	3 [3]	12 [12]	12 [12]	31 [29]	70
1902........	13 [15]	2 [2]	19 [20]	10 [10]	32 [29]	76
1907........	17 [19]	8 [8]	15 [15]	12 [12]	24 [22]	76
1911........	17 [19]	12 [13]	10 [10]	13 [12]	24 [22]	76
1918........	19 [22]	10 [11]	10 [10]	15 [14]	22 [19]	76
1922........	19 [22]	12 [13]	10 [10]	21 [19]	14 [12]	76
1927........	22 [24]	11 [12]	10 [10]	22 [21]	11 [9]	76
1937........	23 [26]	12 [12]	8 [8]	23 [21]	10 [9]	76

* Figures inclosed in brackets are an approximate estimate of the numbers which there would have been in each group without the country quota. Note that the table does not include the four Maori constituencies.

1937 numbered less than one-third of what they were in 1890. Mixed districts likewise have passed into the mainly urban class and the latter into the entirely urban. In 1890 there were fifteen entirely and mainly urban districts as against forty-one entirely and mainly rural. The two former groups in 1937 included thirty-five constituencies; the two latter, thirty-three. An electoral tendency due to this urbanizing process has been an increase in the number of members returned to Parliament by the four largest cities. Each of these elected exactly three members in 1890.[10] But in 1937 Auckland comprised eight entirely urban districts; Wellington, five; Christchurch, four; and Dunedin,

10. In 1890, however, slightly more than 5 per cent of the population of Wellington City, as defined electorally, was rural. Wellington's three members are therefore included in the mainly urban group for that year.

three. New Zealand exhibits the demographic paradox of a primarily agricultural country, a large proportion of whose population is congregated in a few metropolitan centers.[11]

The increase of the entirely urban districts is further explained by the recent growth of various secondary cities which have now become just big enough to form a constituency by themselves. In earlier years the electoral map-makers had to add to these smaller urban communities a portion of the adjacent rural population (weighted, of course, by 28 per cent) in order to create a nominally equal constituency. Nowadays there are some secondary cities whose population reaches or surpasses the quota required for an electoral district. Nevertheless, these electorates are not urbanized to quite the same degree in their interests and outlook as the four principal centers. An instance is Palmerston North, situated at a junction on the main railway line ninety miles north of Wellington in the midst of an important farming area called the Manawatu. Its inhabitants are engaged in such urban pursuits as retail trade or the provision of professional services; but they partly share the rural outlook, since their own prosperity depends very directly on the farmers' purchasing power. Wanganui, another city of this class, is located at a river mouth on the west coast of the North Island. It, too, provides urban services for an agricultural hinterland and also possesses a small harbor which is used principally for coastal shipping. A different case, however, is the city of Lower Hutt, which, together with the contiguous borough of Petone, spreads across the flat surface of a river valley within a few miles of Wellington. Related to the capital as a "satellite industrial town"[12] it contains over six thousand residents who daily commute to Wellington for their work and also a number of manufacturing plants. Its interests, therefore, are more fully urban than those of the other lesser cities. All the electorates classed as mainly urban included some borough with a population between ten and twenty thousand which could not constitute a separate electoral district without

11. In 1938 the four chief urban areas of New Zealand contained 37 per cent of the population.

12. For this description see the report by J. W. Mawson, *The Hutt Valley Development Scheme* (Wellington: Government Printing Office, 1940), p. 9.

the admixture of some rural neighbors. Napier, Hamilton, New Plymouth, Invercargill, and others belonged to this group.

The effect of the country quota can now be judged by comparing the bracketed and unbracketed figures in all columns of Table 11. If the apportionment had been made without the country quota, at every election there would have been two or three more districts in the urban groups and correspondingly less in the rural. Thus, in 1937 after the commission had finished its allocation, the entirely and mainly urban districts numbered thirty-five; the entirely and mainly rural, thirty-three. Had the country quoted not intervened, there would probably have been thirty-eight constituencies of the two urban types and only thirty of the rural. Expressed in terms of practical politics this meant that, but for the country quota, the urban representatives would have had a majority of eight, instead of two, over the rural members. If, therefore, the interests of town dwellers and farmers diverged, the existence of the quota had a direct bearing on the political balance of power. Any political party which predominated in the rural areas was virtually presented with two or three extra seats in Parliament. Up to 1945 a New Zealander's vote counted for one, if he lived in a city, and for one and twenty-eight hundredths, if he lived on a farm.

Until the apportionment of 1922, with the aid of the country quota the number of districts in the two rural classes exceeded that of the two urban groups. At the apportionment of 1927 the numbers were equalized. In 1937 for the first time the urban representatives took the lead. Hence even with the weighting of 28 per cent the farm population could no longer maintain voting parity with the city dwellers. That likelihood, or certainty, left three possible alternatives: (1) the country quota would remain fixed at 28 per cent, in which case the farmers would become a subordinate minority in Parliament; (2) the farmers would seek an increase to some higher percentage in order to restore their parliamentary strength to parity; or (3) the city representatives would use their growing parliamentary votes to reduce or abolish the quota and would give themselves the larger representation to which they were entitled on the basis of population.

For a number of years (1912–28) the political effect of the

country quota was to aid the conservative Reform party, which predominated in rural areas, in keeping control of Parliament. Obedient to the farmers' voice, this party gave less heed to city businessmen and its other urban supporters. Consequently, during the Reform ascendancy the cities more than once complained of governmental neglect. The opposition parties—and especially Labor—concentrated on the town constituencies and of necessity designed their programs with an urban bias. Had there been no country quota, the Reform party, in order to win a parliamentary majority, would have been forced to join to its farm program policies which satisfied urban requirements. But, as it was, the political parties tended to divide along the alignment of a city-country schism. Thereby they accentuated the friction arising from economic rivalries that were possibly more apparent than real.

The rise to power of the Labor party has confirmed this trend. Basically Labor has always been an urban movement supported by industrial workers. Around this central nucleus are attached other low-income groups, which included, in the depression, a number of North Island farmers. Originally Labor advocated the abolition of the quota. But, on acceding to office, they received enough rural support to be reluctant to offend their backers in the countryside. When the farmers, however, returned a profoundly anti-Labor vote in 1943, the ministry decided to cut their losses. Accordingly in 1945 they used their parliamentary majority so as to abolish the quota outright.

The arguments advanced in the debate offer an interesting comparison with those brought forward in the 1880's.[13] It was then argued that in a colony which was only partly settled farmers in outlying districts (the "backblocks") were placed under greater political handicaps than city dwellers. Country electorates of wide extent, forested and mountainous and inadequately roaded, were harder to canvass than urban constituencies. Farmers could not so easily attend meetings or record their votes. The country quota was designed, not unreasonably, to offset such disabilities, and so it did. Until the turn of the century those disabilities were genuine ones; yet they were mitigated by

13. See above, chap. ii.

the addition of 28 per cent to the farmers' voting power. But in the middle of the twentieth century this method of justifying the quota had to be discarded. The Dominion's railway lines and road system are now much more extensively developed. Rural isolation has been lessened by the advent of broadcasting, by the spread in the ownership of automobiles, and by the centrally operated Country Library Service. New Zealand still has its "backblocks." But they are no longer sufficiently numerous or so remote as to justify a wholesale electoral weighting of the entire rural population. As far as polling facilities go, country dwellers appear to be as well off as town people if one is to judge from the electoral results. To test this, I have worked out the percentages of actual to eligible voters in the entirely rural and entirely urban districts, respectively. At the election of 1935 the average percentage of persons actually voting in all the entirely rural constituencies was 91; in all the entirely urban ones, it was 90. The corresponding figures for 1938 revealed a rural average of 94 per cent as against an urban one of 91 per cent. Thus the size of country electorates did not diminish political interest or prevent a large turnout at the polls.

When Parliament debated the case in 1945, among all the points pro and con only one on each side had any substantial merit. Defending the status quo, the National party argued that the economic importance of the rural minority warranted an electoral adjustment in their favor. Besides feeding the Dominion's urban centers, which consume but a small proportion of the total farm produce—the farmers contribute practically all the country's export wealth. Only with the money obtained overseas by the sale of wool, butter, cheese, and meat can New Zealand import manufactured articles and the raw materials for its nascent industries or pay off the interest and capital on its debt. Thus a mere count of heads does not accurately represent the full significance of the farmers to the Dominion's economy. Farmers have complained that city dwellers do not properly understand the problems of agriculture. They resent the well-known tendency of an urban drift with its implications of rural decline and point out that they cannot offer wages or amenities as attractive as those obtaining in the towns. They are aware that many a city dweller adds to his ignorance of the countryside a contempt for the tiller of the soil and the tender of sheep and cows. Farmers consider themselves, rightly or wrongly, the best judges of their own welfare and, consequently, since New Zealand's economy is still so largely agrarian, of the national interest. Fearing to be governed by a Parliament in which urban representatives unduly predominate, they claim that the balance of political power must be adjusted to conform with their economic primacy.

To this viewpoint Labor retorted that the country quota was akin to a gigantic national gerrymander. It was unfair that a farmer's vote should count for more than a city dweller's. One vote, wherever cast, should have one value. Otherwise, the basic democratic principle of equality at the voting booth was violated. Farmers were often so engrossed in questions of crops and cattle, of fences and fertilizers, of sheep and shearing, that their outlook became narrow and parochial. The value of the towns in the economic life of the community was insufficiently acknowledged by those who live on farms, for, besides providing a market for farm produce and a gateway for imports and exports, the towns supply all those goods and services which add to the comforts and raise the living standards of the rural areas. Although in the past New Zealand's prosperity has been based chiefly on its agriculture, this need not necessarily hold true of the future. So striking has been the growth of urban secondary industries since 1936 that the economy of tomorrow may be more evenly blended than that of yesterday. The farmers were a minority of the nation. Let the majority rule.

Such were the principles advanced for and against the abolition of the quota. In choosing between them each party, needless to say, judged the merits of the case from the standpoint of its own political advantage. Being predominant in the cities, Labor supported a change which meant an increase in the urban constituencies. The Nationalists, backed by the farmers, opposed a lowering of their parliamentary representation. For similar reasons the parties took different stands on another alteration that was made simultaneously. Up to 1945 the total population was counted in for electoral purposes, including those under the age of twenty-one who lack the vote. The Electoral Amendment Act of 1945 now requires that constituencies be apportioned on the basis of only the adult population. On an average there are more persons under the age of twenty-one residing in the country than in the towns. So this further change—sponsored by Labor and resisted by National—marked a further drop in the representation of rural areas.

After the passage of this act a census was held in September, 1945—the first for nine years—and in 1946 the Representation Commission[14] proceeded to redraw the electoral map. The census disclosed some considerable changes in the distribution of population. Earlier trends were continued in two important respects. The North Island, which in 1936 contained 64.3 per cent of the population, was inhabited in 1945 by 67.3 per cent. As a consequence, two electorates were taken from the south and transferred to the north. Furthermore, the cities and boroughs, whose total population amounted to 59.3 per cent of the total in 1936, had grown at a faster rate and now possessed 63.1 per cent. Adults constituted 65 per cent of the population in the cities and boroughs, as against 60 per cent of the farm dwellers. For these reasons, together with the abolition of the country quota, the principal gainers were the two big cities of the north. Unfortunately, however, it is no longer possible to classify the new and greatly altered constituencies with the same exactitude as before. Since the distinction between those who live in boroughs of over 2,000 inhabitants and those who do not has no longer any legal relevance, the report of the Representation Commission for 1946 merely gives the total number of adults[15] in each electorate without, as before, subdividing them into urban and rural. No one, therefore, can precisely tabulate the constituencies into entirely urban, predominantly urban, and so on. But this much can be safely said. The metropolitan areas of Auckland and Wellington received two new seats each, and in the South Island four rural

14. The legislation of 1945 also altered the personnel of the Commission. It now contains three civil servants who belong ex officio (including the chairman) and four members appointed by the government who may not be members of Parliament.

15. The average number of adults in each constituency is now 14,067.

seats were eliminated.[16] Thus the abolition of the country quota has confirmed the urban preponderance in the new House of Representatives.

Disproportional Representation

From the country quota alone it could be correctly inferred that the proportion of seats obtained by the parties in Parliament has not corresponded with the proportion of votes cast for their candidates. There are other electoral features, however, which have served, even more than the country quota, to increase the disproportion between the seats received and the votes. Modern New Zealand has not yet experimented with the numerous devices covered by the generic name of "proportional representation." Although in the nineties the four main cities were amalgamated to form single constituencies each returning three members, since the election of 1902 every district without exception has been represented by one member only. At two elections (1908 and 1911) the "second ballot" was tried in districts where no candidate had won 50 per cent of the votes. Otherwise a seat in Parliament has always gone to the person who receives the highest number of votes, even if that be less than half the total. For the last thirty years the electoral system has combined two principles: single-member districts and victory by a bare plurality.

In these respects New Zealand conducts its elections in the same way as the mother-country. Modern Britain, with few exceptions, has used single-member districts, and the winner is "the first past the post." The defects of the British method of representation have been well described by Ramsay Muir.[17] The most serious are these. The system does not produce a really representative Parliament, because the number of seats a party gains sometimes bears little relation to its votes. Since the majority party acquires more strength and the minority party becomes still weaker, landslides are encouraged. Also a large number of votes are wasted in every district, and people are discouraged

16. This result tallies with my estimate in Table 11, since the urban drift has accelerated since 1937.

17. *How Britain Is Governed* (3d ed.; London: Constable & Co., 1933), pp. 155–70.

from going to the polls in constituencies in which one party
overwhelmingly dominates. Muir has illustrated all these disadvantages from the figures of British election returns. New Zealand elections could provide equally cogent examples. Each of the
criticisms just cited, except one, applies with the same force to
this Dominion's electoral machinery. The exception is that New
Zealand voters have not been deterred from recording their votes,
even though many a vote cannot affect the result. Britain has
many safe constituencies, some Conservative and some Labor,
where it really is quite useless to vote for the minority candidate—
a fact which lowers the total number of actual voters in the country as a whole. In New Zealand, however, there are relatively
fewer safe constituencies, as the population is still fairly mobile,
and electoral boundaries are often changed.

Table 12 supplies the detailed figures of the operation of the
representative system at every election held since 1890. A comparison of the two right-hand columns shows the divergence between the seats a party actually obtains and those to which it
would be entitled if seats were allocated proportionately to votes.
The present-day machinery does not produce a Parliament which
is proportionately representative of public opinion. If allowance
be made for victories in uncontested electorates, the votes a party
receives offer a fairly sure sign of its popular strength. But the
number of seats won in the House provides a very fallible guide.
This can be proved from the history of each of the major parties.
The Liberals in 1890 won 38 seats with 56 per cent of the votes,
and in 1893 took 51 seats on 58 per cent of the votes. In 1905 the
same party, with 54 per cent of the votes, secured 55 seats; yet at
the next election, with an increase of 5 per cent in their votes, they
took 8 seats less. In 1911 the Liberals, having 41 per cent of all
the votes, won 30 seats. But their rivals, the Reform party, with
6 per cent less of the votes, gained 6 more seats. Reform won 43
seats with 36 per cent of the votes in 1919, and in 1922 took 35
seats on 40 per cent of the votes. Labor, with 47 per cent of the
votes in 1935, gained 53 seats and, with 56 per cent of the votes
in 1938, captured 50 seats. There is something queer and freak-
ish about an electoral system whose results jump about in this
incalculable way.

TABLE 12*

ELECTORAL AND PARLIAMENTARY STRENGTH OF PARTIES, 1890–1946

Date of Election	Party	Votes Obtained in European Districts	Percentage of Votes Obtained to Total Valid Votes	Seats Actually Obtained	Seats Proportional to Percentage of Votes
1890.......	Liberal	76,548†	56	38	37
	Conservative	39,338‡	29	25	23
	Miscellaneous	20,451†	15	7	10
1893.......	Liberal	175,814§	58	51	41
	Conservative	74,482†	24	13	17
	Miscellaneous	53,880	18	6	12
1896.......	Liberal	165,259	46	39	32
	Conservative	134,397	37	25	26
	Miscellaneous	59,748	17	6	12
1899.......	Liberal	204,331§	53	49	37
	Conservative	141,758†	36	19	26
	Miscellaneous	41,540	11	2	7
1902.......	Liberal	215,845	52	47	39
	Opposition	85,769	21	19	16
	Labor and Socialist	10,501	2	....	2
	Miscellaneous	104,847	25	10	19
1905.......	Liberal	209,731	54	55	41
	Opposition	117,118	30	15	22
	Labor and Socialist	3,623	1	....	1
	Miscellaneous	60,717	15	6	12
1908‖.......	Liberal	242,261	59	47	45
	Opposition	114,245	28	25	21
	Labor and Socialist	17,492	4	1	3
	Miscellaneous	36,508	9	3	7
1911‖.......	Liberal	191,323†	41	30	32
	Reform	164,627	35	36	26
	Labor and Socialist	40,759	9	4	7
	Miscellaneous	68,859	15	6	11
1914.......	Liberal	222,299	43	31	33
	Reform	243,122	47	39	36
	Labor and Social Democrat	49,482	10	6	7
	Miscellaneous	1,004	0	....	....
1919.......	Liberal	155,708	29	17	22
	Reform	193,676	36	43	27
	Labor	131,402	24	8	18
	Miscellaneous	61,954	11	8	9

* The table does not include the four Maori constituencies.
† One seat also won without a contest.　　　　§ Two seats also won without a contest.
‡ Four seats also won without a contest.　　　‖ Second ballot.

TABLE 12—*Continued*

Date of Election	Party	Votes Obtained in European Districts	Percentage of Votes Obtained to Total Valid Votes	Seats Actually Obtained	Seats Proportional to Percentage of Votes
1922........	Liberal-Labor	162,149	26	21	20
	Reform	245,281†	40	35	31
	Labor	150,448	25	17	18
	Miscellaneous	56,192	9	3	7
1925........	National (Liberal)	135,419	20	9	15
	Reform	312,932†	47	51	36
	Labor	184,616	27	12	21
	Miscellaneous	39,004	6	4	4
1928........	United (Liberal)	219,648	30	25	23
	Reform	256,014	35	25	27
	Labor	197,759	27	19	20
	Miscellaneous	61,970	8	7	6
1931........	Coalition (United-Reform)	304,750‡	44	42	36
	Labor	242,301	35	24	25
	Miscellaneous	146,021	21	10	15
1935........	National (Coalition)	258,270	31	17	24
	Labor	392,321	47	53	36
	Democrat	65,217	8	....	6
	Miscellaneous	111,987	14	6	10
1938........	National	368,809	40	24	31
	Labor	513,397	56	50	42
	Miscellaneous	35,478	4	2	3
1943........	National	390,343§	43	34	34
	Labor	439,207	48	41	36
	Democratic Soldier Labor	40,423	4	....	3
	Miscellaneous	41,397	5	1	3
1946........	National	495,128	49	38	37
	Labor	513,718	51	38	39
	Miscellaneous	1,932	0	....	....

New Zealand proves as clearly as Britain that the system tends to help the more powerful party. All through the period of Liberal supremacy from 1893 to 1908, the dominant party won more seats than it was entitled to receive on a proportional basis. Reform was similarly aided during its heyday from 1911 to 1925. The Labor victories in the late thirties repeat the same pattern. Conversely, the weaker parties, or the smaller groups whose votes are classed together as "miscellaneous," are normally underrepresented. Glancing down the columns, one finds that, except in 1925 and 1928, wherever a party has received under 20 per cent of the total vote, it has always won less seats than its due proportion. Most New Zealand parliaments have not constituted an accurate sample of electoral opinion.

On the figures, then, proportional representation seems to have a strong case. But, as with most panaceas, its advocates emphasize one element to the exclusion of others. Politics require something more than an exercise of mathematical ingenuity, and parliaments need putting-together with more materials than an arbitrary percentage. The skeptic who distrusts a proportional legislative paradise can point out that even under the present imperfect methods in six of these eighteen elections the number of seats actually won did not differ so very widely from the correct proportions. Those were the elections of 1890, 1908, 1914, 1922, 1928, and 1946. What the believers in "P.R." usually overlook is the effect of their schemes on the working of the legislature. Ideally from the electoral point of view it is desirable to have a legislature which is truly representative. To be so, Parliament must embody the various shades of opinion and must reproduce each in its precise quantitative strength. Yet never was political truth more evident than that a legislature so constituted could not legislate effectively, could not reach decisions without wrecking its principles by halfhearted compromise, and could not be organized to maintain a stable government. "P.R." holds out hypothetical electoral salvation with one hand and positive legislative damnation with the other.

New Zealand experience bears out this argument even though proportional representation has not actually been tried there. At six elections, as was just stated, Parliament has approximated very nearly to a proportionately correct miniature of the electorate. But the parliaments established by two of the three most recent of those elections (1922 and 1928) were hardly of the kind that bring glory to democratic institutions. The elections of those years were confused, exactly as in Britain, by the co-existence of three major parties. The New Zealand Liberals, their historic mission finished, were being crushed between Reform and Labor.

In the parliaments lasting from 1923 to 1925 and from 1929 to 1931 no single party had a majority over both the others. Ministries in those periods were weak and tottering, and their legislation was necessarily shot through with bargaining and logrolling. The parliamentary futility of that time, to which many representatives and ministers have testified in Hansard and in their memoirs, would probably only be perpetuated if proportional representation were introduced. "P.R." encourages a multiparty Parliament, and that is often the parent of weak government.

The Second Ballot

There is, however, one electoral device to which New Zealand has given a brief trial during the present century. This is the second ballot, familiar to students of French politics. It was used in the Dominion at the elections of 1908 and 1911, after which it was abolished. The political motive for its introduction was the desire of the then Liberal government to stave off its own decline. The Liberals at the time were being weakened by the breakaway of Labor groups on the left and by the rise of a consolidated Reform party on the right. At successive elections there had been a great increase in the number of seats won by a candidate who received not a majority of the votes but a bare plurality. Seven minority winners represented their constituencies in 1899; thirteen in 1902; and sixteen in 1905. The second ballot was consequently brought in by the Liberals prior to the election of 1908. In any district where no candidate secured a majority of all valid votes cast, a second election was to be held soon afterward between the two candidates who came out highest at the first poll. At the election of 1908 a second ballot was needed in twenty-three of the seventy-six European constituencies, and in fifteen of these the candidate who led at the first poll was victorious at the second. In 1911 second ballots were held in thirty districts, in twenty-one of which the winner at the first poll kept his lead the second time.

The results of the experiment can be thus summarized. The number of citizens who voted always decreased somewhat at the second poll. In 1908 the average percentages of actual to registered voters in the districts which required two ballots were 78.5 per cent at the first poll and 74.4 per cent at the second. In 1911 the corresponding figures were 82 and 78.7 per cent. It was unfortunate for the Liberals that they were not helped by the change they had initiated. They lost at the second ballot in 1908 three constituencies where they led on the first poll; in 1911 they lost one such district. The system did little to check the growing support for Reform and Labor. The latter won a seat at the second ballot in 1908, although nowhere had they topped the first poll, while in 1911 they led in only one district at the first ballot and then secured four seats on the second. The positive advantages of the experiment were negligible, for it neither altered significantly the percentages of votes obtained by the major parties nor did it materially rectify the proportions of seats which they won. What the system did do, however, was to encourage political deals and bargaining in the interval between ballots. The parties whose candidates ran third or fourth at the first poll were able to offer their conditional support to the surviving contestants. This was precisely what occurred in France under the second ballot, and in that country the political huckstering between the two polls did much to discredit the parties and the electoral machinery. Nor can it reasonably be said that the second ballot in New Zealand provided a truer indication of the voters' wishes. To confine the second poll only to those who came in the two top places at the first poll was itself an arbitrary limitation. It sometimes happened that the third highest candidate at the first poll came very close to the second highest, yet he was excluded from the run-off election. For instance, at the Christchurch East district in 1911 the votes cast at the first ballot were Thacker, 2,392; Davey, 2,360; Hunter, 2,356; Cooke, 418. The third candidate, with only four votes less than the second, was eliminated from the final round, and his supporters had to redistribute their votes. The second ballot system was scarcely any improvement on that which it temporarily replaced.

One purpose of the experiment, however, was to prevent anyone sitting in Parliament who did not represent a majority of voters in his constituency. At many elections since 1914 there have been numerous instances of representatives elected by less than half the votes. In 1922 there were twenty-two seats held by a minority candidate, in 1935 there were thirty-three, and in 1928 there were thirty-eight. The last figure, constituting exactly one-half of the European seats, is the highest yet recorded. In this particular election so evenly were the parties balanced that the votes obtained by all the successful candidates of all parties formed only 49.6 per cent of the total votes cast. Literally the legislature elected in that year was a minority Parliament. When the party situation created triangular contests, the number of seats won on a plurality was always high. Britain shared the same lot during the twenties, when the Liberals were on the downgrade and Labor was rising to challenge conservatism. It should be noticed, though, that in 1938 New Zealand reverted completely to a two-party system. Consequently, in that year's election every one of the seventy-six European seats was won by a straight-out majority vote.

Number of Members and Districts

Until 1899 Parliament's lower house consisted of seventy European members and four Maoris. In the four principal cities districts were amalgamated, each city forming a single electorate and returning three members. In the twentieth century there have been seventy-six European members, all of whom are now elected in single-member districts. Each member represented on an average 11,000 persons in 1902 and 20,700 in 1946. Although after four decades a member now represents a constituency twice as large as before, there is adequate, or even abundant, representation in New Zealand. In Britain a member of the House of Commons represents on an average some 70,000 persons. In the United States a representative in the lower house of Congress serves about 300,000. In Australia a member of the lower house of the Commonwealth Parliament represents 98,000 people, while in the lower house of the State of Victoria, whose population is a little larger than New Zealand's, 31,000 persons have one representative. When compared with other English-speaking countries, New Zealand appears, if anything, to be overrepresented.

The Maori people are equitably represented on a numerical basis. The provision in the Act of 1867, which added to Parliament four members representing the Polynesian race, has remained unchanged. The Maori population, on the other hand, has fluctuated considerably. It dropped to under 40,000 in 1896, but then it picked up by a remarkable effort of self-regeneration and rose to nearly 99,000 in 1945. Each Maori member now represents on an average about 15,000 adults, a figure slightly higher than that for European members. Four special districts— three in the North Island and one in the South Island[18]—are constituted for Maori citizens. Maoris vote only in one of these four constituencies,[19] and only Maoris are candidates therein. The percentage of actual voters is usually lower in the Maori electorates than elsewhere. Thus in 1946 an average of 9,000 votes was recorded in the four Maori districts. In the seventy-six European districts the average was 13,300. Normally the Maori elections are fought along party lines analogous to those prevailing in the rest of the country. But the special problems which concern Maori welfare naturally form the dominant electoral issue, and, in selecting between rival candidates, the Maori voter may be influenced as much by his own tribal loyalties as by European political labels or programs.[20] An opinion prevails in New Zealand that the Maoris always vote for whatever party is in power (from 1944 to 1947, for example, all four Maori representatives were Labor). That is not, however, by any means universally correct. The truth seems to be that the majority of the Maoris vote for whoever is prepared to do most for them. If the party in power is well disposed, it can count on the Maoris' vote. But in this respect the Maoris as a group by no means stand alone! Much the same would apply to most of the European voters, who do not ignore their own interests on election day.

18. The southern Maori electorate is the one constituency in New Zealand which could fairly be called a "rotten borough." Its parliamentary representative was returned in 1946 with a bare 862 votes.

19. Half-castes may be placed on the roll of either a European or a Maori district.

20. More than once, distinguished Maori leaders have held Cabinet office as ministers of the Crown.

The Conduct of Elections

Happy the country where there is little to say about the administration of the elections, and practically all of that little is good! Some instances of corruption have occurred, for no system devised for fallible mortals can ever be absolutely foolproof all the time. At different elections there have been authenticated cases of impersonation, of double-voting, and of inaccurate electoral rolls. Such corruption, however, has been only local and sporadic. It was not committed on a wide scale, nor was it systematically organized so as to cheat the people. Quite recently, however, a dispute did arise concerning the results of the election of 1943. The opposition alleged that there were serious irregularities in connection with the recording and counting of the votes of the armed forces. Suspicion was heightened by the facts that the soldiers' votes determined the result in some closely contested electorates[21] and that the ballot papers in the Middle East theater were burned before they could be recounted. A bipartisan parliamentary committee of inquiry was appointed to investigate these circumstances. After examination of the available evidence, the committee divided on purely party lines, and the majority and the minority presented separate reports. In the nature of the case, as the ballot papers had been burned, no charges could be substantiated. The best that can be said is that the verdict was "not guilty"; the worst that it was "not proved."

In general, over the last fifty years New Zealand's elections have been clean and honest. Parties fight hard in the pre-election campaigns; but their conflicts do not extend to systematic tampering with the ballot box or falsifying of the count. Perhaps the causes which contribute to honest electoral practices can be summed up as these. There is, first, the homogeneity of the population which accepts the fundamental assumptions of a parliamentary democracy and no longer seeks any drastic changes in the structure of its governmental institutions. Second, the electoral legislation is well devised to deter or detect organized corruption of the vote. The officials responsible for administering

21. See below, pp. 235–37.

the laws are secure in their jobs, since they are not at the mercy of the spoils system. Lastly, there is a fairly even distribution of wealth as well as a relative absence of powerful and unscrupulous interests, two factors which reduce the potential sources from which bribery can flow. When measured by the yardstick of electoral integrity, modern New Zealand still merits much of that commendation for purity which Bryce bestowed after his visit in 1912.[22]

22. James Bryce, *Modern Democracies* (New York: Macmillan Co., 1921), II, 328.

CHAPTER IX

MODERN PARTIES

PARTY politics in New Zealand during the last fifty years have followed a well-defined trend. For two decades the Liberals triumphed over their rivals and enjoyed an unbroken tenure of office. From 1912 to 1928 the Reform party was strongest, although its supremacy was never so firmly established as that of the Liberals had been. In the depression of the thirties Reformers and Liberals coalesced to face the opposition of labor, whose power was steadily mounting. From 1936 to 1947 the Labor party predominated and has thrice been reindorsed at the polls. Three parties in succession have thus held the ascendancy. Only for brief periods has New Zealand experienced the awkwardness that arises when two or three parties are equipoised and deadlocked. Such periods did occur during the Liberal decline before 1914 and later during the twenties. But in most parliaments of the last half-century one party has held a secure majority. Each of the parties in turn has retained popular favor long enough to convert its program into laws and its laws into administrative reality.

The slowness with which the pendulum has swung from "ins" to "outs" is a striking characteristic of New Zealand politics. It can best be explained in terms of economic factors. Politics in this Dominion are concerned with economic problems to the exclusion of almost all others. Social and moral issues, it is true, have at times entered into the field of party warfare, but none of these has ever dominated political controversy, except possibly the prohibition question—and this latter has economic implications because the liquor trade is a powerful vested interest. On matters of defense and foreign policy parties have seldom been in conflict, since an overwhelming public sentiment clung to the imperial connection. Race relations, likewise, have been relegated to the background. Neither the troubles in the administration of the Samoan mandate nor the crises of the Maori renaissance ever provoked serious differences of opinion between parties. Only the economic issues have remained as the perennial battleground for politicians. It has, however, been New Zealand's good fortune to enjoy comparative prosperity during most of the last half-century. Party stability has merely reflected economic stability; and the long-term character of the economic changes made long-term ministries possible. Whatever party has been in power has usually retained office while economic conditions continued to be good, which means, in New Zealand, when the overseas prices for its four principal exports are high. But any shift in the relations of economic groups, or any catastrophic fall in prices, has brought an upset to the dominant party. Thus did Reformers replace Liberals in 1912; thus did Labor replace both in 1935.

The Liberals

The Liberal victory in the election of 1890 marked an event as decisive for New Zealand as was the passage of the first Reform Act for Britain. The consequences of each event permanently charted the future course of the country's history. It was unprecedented in New Zealand that one party should control the government for two uninterrupted decades, emerging from no less than seven consecutive elections with consistently high majorities. That was a record which even the "Continuous Ministry" could not match. Moreover, the use to which the Liberals put their majorities left on New Zealand a stamp it has always retained. In a sense, their achievement consisted merely in applying a principle adopted by previous ministries, namely, that the power of the state should embrace new services if required in the public interest. So many, however, and so far-reaching were the additional state activities which the Liberals introduced that the balance between public and private enterprise was decidedly tilted in favor of the former. Although the state had reached out into many fields before 1890, its activities all told were still of less consequence to the community than those of private individuals and nongovernmental organizations. Once the Liberals had carried their program to fulfilment, the state was established as the paramount influence in shaping New Zealand's destiny. Even after the decline and fall of the Liberals, party politics can still be accurately described in relation to what they accomplished. Reform left much of their work untouched and itself carried on the Liberal principles by application to further spheres. Some modifications and even some reversals of policy were attempted by Reform. But those were restored by the Labor party, which since 1936 has followed in the steps of the old Liberal tradition.

The underlying assumption of that tradition was basically democratic. The Liberals rode into power by attacking privilege. They stayed in power by driving their attack home. Their ideal community was one in which benefits and advantages would be equally shared and widely diffused. Since the state was the only institution which represented all citizens on a roughly equal footing, its powers were to be increased. The state was to determine what benefits would be shared and how they would be distributed. It resulted from these Liberal ideas that as many persons as possible would be brought into direct economic dependence upon the governmental machinery, which politically they could control. Privilege was to be assailed wherever found, and in the early nineties it was most easily discovered among the land monopolists and the industrial employers. A radical party cannot come into being until a strong vested interest exists which it can charge with abusing its position. In New Zealand radicalism flowered later than in the mother-country, since the Colony lacked a hereditary aristocracy and an established church. But the aggregation of land, the sweated industries, and the unemployment of the eighties at last supplied the progressives with something to fight against. In attacking a system, the Liberals also opposed the class which had profited from it. Into the political struggle they brought with them the representatives of the underprivileged. Hitherto the participants in politics had belonged exclusively to the middle class and mostly to its upper section. Now the lower middle class and workingmen were elected to Parliament. The Liberals thus wrought a social as well as a political and an economic change.

It must be kept in mind that the party which succeeded in the election of 1890 blended together diverse groups and aims. As long as their aims remained compatible, the groups stayed united to promote their common interest, and the Liberal party was supreme. But when their interests ultimately diverged, the groups fell asunder and the party collapsed. One section consisted of those whose chief concern lay in the utilization and ownership of land. These were either small owners, who envied or feared the big runholders, or farm laborers or town workers who wanted land and could not afford to buy. The object of the land reformers was simply to force monopolists to sell some of their holdings through a policy of steeply graduated taxation and compulsory state purchase. Land so acquired was to be split up and leased by the state, which would also provide loans at low interest rates to help the poorer colonist in getting his farm started. Large estates, in Reeves's phrase, were "social pests." The long-term effect of the land reform would create a widespread state tenantry cultivating small farms.

Combining with those who hungered for land were the workers in New Zealand's nascent industries. A trade-union movement had taken big strides forward in the eighties. It sought better labor conditions and higher wages and strongly supported a protectionist tariff. In Otago especially many craft unions had come into being and had loosely organized into a Trades and Labor Council. This body held a conference in 1885 attended by labor representatives from other parts of the Colony. Its future link with the Liberals was to be foreseen in the presence of Stout, then premier, who favored removing the legal disabilities under which unions suffered. By 1890 industrial unions had taken their place alongside those of a craft character. That momentous year witnessed the first labor attempt to gain its demands by a major strike. A maritime strike which had started in Australia spread to the New Zealand watersiders as a sympathetic effort. Atkinson and the employers strongly opposed the workers, whose funds were soon exhausted. But this defeat stimulated the growth of organized political activity among the working class. Beaten in the industrial sphere in the month of September, they sought redress by political action in the December election. Workingmen rushed to have their names registered on the electoral rolls. The trades and labor councils made an alliance with the Liberals, putting up some candidates of their own under the Liberal label and, for the rest, voting solidly for middle-class, Liberal candidates.

The propertied groups had lost their sense of political dominance and economic security in the culminating sequence of events from 1888 to 1890. Dillon Bell, a leading Conservative who then represented New Zealand in London, wrote thus in 1889 expressing his fears and hopes to his son, who was later famous in Dominion politics: "It seems early even to conjecture what policy Ballance and his side will bring out, yet they will really be governed by Stout . . . . and he will not let them run amok against property. In vain the Socialist leaders will cry out that they pledge themselves to do this and do that. Stout has been before, and will be again, a moderating influence against mere confiscation schemes."[1] But the Conservatives were to find that their reliance on Stout was valueless. Although the Liberals did refrain from "mere confiscation schemes," they were moving farther to the left than the type of liberalism which Stout represented. A man with ideas more advanced than Stout's formulated much of the new Liberal policy. This was William Pember Reeves. They differed in that Reeves trusted, whereas Stout mistrusted, the expansion of state activities. The new liberalism had emerged from the negative into the positive phase, shifting the emphasis in its theory from liberty to equality. The intellectual architect of the new Liberal order has recorded in many passages of his writings the sentiments of that time, and, when he came to write the history of the Dominion, he summed up his impression which fits in with the anxieties of Bell: "In the voting in December 1890 there was an uncomfortable approach to a clean cut between the richer and the poorer."[2]

The choice that lay before the voters in 1890 was expressed in

1. Letter of December 28, 1889 (quoted in W. D. Stewart, *Sir Francis H. D. Bell: His Life and Times* [Wellington: Butterworth & Co., 1937], p. 20).

2. W. P. Reeves, *The Long White Cloud* (3d ed.; London: Allen & Unwin, 1924), p. 278. Siegfried similarly writes: "An indefinable sense of revolution was abroad in the land" (André Siegfried, *Democracy in New Zealand*, trans. E. V. Burns [London: Bell & Sons, 1914], p. 82).

the official policies of the principal contending parties. If you voted Liberal, you were asking for all these: "The stoppage of 'dummyism' in land sales. No more borrowing. Self-reliance. Thorough retrenchment. The prevention of the acquisition of land in large holdings. The resumption by the State of land urgently required for settlement, and vigorous settlement of the land. The discouragement of absentee landlordism and of speculative land purchasers. Better treatment of workers in factories. The use of railways to develop the agricultural and pastoral industries rather than as a means of imposing taxation. The establishment of technical schools. Reform of the Legislative Council. Measures to improve the condition of the workers. The repeal of the property tax and the introduction of a land and income tax."[3] For a party to pledge itself to so much was ambitious. To carry out faithfully all its pledges, as it subsequently did, was unheard of. But that was the reason the Liberals held power for twenty years.

By contrast, here is what Atkinson had to offer as the swansong of the old conservatism. If you voted for Atkinson, you preferred to have: "Strict, but not parsimonious, economy, combined with cheerfulness and a firm belief in the unbounded resources of the colony. Further borrowing within the colony. The purchase of Maori lands. Retention of the property tax. Non-interference by the Government or Parliament with industrial disputes."[4] Politically it was a choice between governmental action or abdication. The majority were suffering economic wrongs which could be remedied by exercise of their political rights. They chose action. The outcome of the election in 1890 was a victory for the Liberals but not a walkover. The party received 56 per cent of all the votes cast, besides carrying one district without a contest.[5] Their opponents, whose percentage of votes was far smaller, won four seats without opposition. The new Parliament contained only thirty-eight avowed Liberals, as against twenty-five Conservatives, seven members of miscellaneous faiths, and four Maoris.

3. See J. Drummond, *The Life and Work of Richard John Seddon* (Wellington: Whitcombe & Tombs, 1907), p. 133.
4. *Ibid.* 5. See above, Table 12, p. 187.

The clue to interpreting any election results lies in the distribution of the votes cast for the opposing parties. Since parties are the political expression of economic and other interests, and since town and country earn their livelihood in different occupations, voters may easily be separated into urban and rural. Economic interests in turn are connected with such geographical factors as climate, soil fertility, and lines of communication. In New Zealand the bulk of the dairy industry is in the North Island on the wetter, western, side of the central mountain range. Sheep farming is mainly concentrated on the drier side of the North Island and in the South Island to the east of the Southern Alps. The principal cities are spread lengthways down the two islands at roughly equal distances apart. They are all on the coast and all possess harbor facilities.[6] They are the gateway for the transportation and distribution of the country's commerce. The North Island, with its bigger population, contains the two largest cities and most of the Dominion's industry. So, besides the urban-rural division, there is also a regional distribution of the parties' voting support from which much can be learned. To discover, as far as the statistics permit, the economic and regional bases of the New Zealand parties, I have analyzed the results of every election held since 1890. The same classification of districts into entirely and mainly urban and rural as was used above in Table 11 serves to group the constituencies in an intelligible economic pattern. For each of these groups of districts I have worked out the percentage of votes obtained at every election by the respective parties (see Table 13). Another set of calculations records the regional variations of party voting strength. The two islands have indulged in different political preferences for the climatic and economic reasons mentioned above. At various stages in their history parties can virtually be identified as belonging primarily to one island. Table 14 shows the percentages of votes obtained over the Dominion as a whole and in each island taken separately. From these two tables, read in conjunction with those in chapter viii, emerges a statistical narrative of fifty years of political history.

A glance at Table 13 reveals that the Liberals in 1890 were

6. With two exceptions (Hamilton and Palmerston North), every New Zealand city with over twenty thousand inhabitants is on the coast.

overwhelmingly strong in urban electorates. The cities and towns recorded a heavy protest vote against the economic depression and the government's inadequate recovery measures. In the rural constituencies votes were more equally divided, though the Liberals were ahead of their rivals. Liberal supporters were distributed equally between the two islands, but the Conservatives were weaker in the north than the south. In more than one constituency, where the contest was close, the Liberals benefited from the act which had abolished plural voting in 1889.[7] Some of their seats in the new Parliament were won by the barest of majorities. Ballance himself, the leader of the party, carried the Wanganui district by only twenty-seven votes. Had plural voting still been permitted, the well-to-do landowners could have ridden in from surrounding districts and cast extra votes against him. So, too, in the Masterton district situated beyond a range of hills fifty miles from the capital. At previous elections as many as forty wealthy voters were known to go there by train from Wellington on the election day and vote for the Conservative candidate. In 1890 they could not do this, and a Liberal topped the poll eighteen votes ahead of his opponent.

Subsequent general elections, while they ratified and confirmed the Liberals' tenure of office, exhibit a changing pattern in the distribution of their votes. When the time came for the election of 1893, the country was presented with stirring issues. For three dramatic parliamentary sessions the Liberals had tried to convert their pledges into legislation. Though they could induce the lower house to pass their land reforms and labor bills, they had been repeatedly obstructed by a Council packed for many years with Conservative nominees. Add to this the enfranchisement of women, the rising vigor of the prohibitionists, the death of Ballance, and Seddon's accession to the premiership —such was the context in which the Liberals sought popular indorsement of their efforts.

And indorsement they received. The Liberals emerged from the election of 1893 with 58 per cent of all the votes cast and with fifty-one of the seventy European seats. Yet their support was now differently distributed. In urban areas they were still dominant,

7. See above, p. 26.

TABLE 13*

PERCENTAGE OF VOTES OBTAINED BY POLITICAL PARTIES
IN URBAN AND RURAL DISTRICTS, 1890–1943

Date of Election	Party	Entirely Urban	Mainly Urban	Mainly Rural	Entirely Rural
1890.........	Liberal	62	78	48	42
	Conservative	20	11	40	42
	Miscellaneous	18	11	12	16
1893.........	Liberal	57	70	57	51
	Conservative	18	21	18	40
	Miscellaneous	25	9	25	9
1896.........	Liberal	41	49	52	49
	Conservative	34	37	34	46
	Miscellaneous	25	14	14	5
1899.........	Liberal	47	55	64	55
	Conservative	37	28	31	40
	Miscellaneous	16	17	5	5
1902.........	Liberal	48	60	59	50
	Opposition	14	0	36	28
	Labor and Socialist	6	0	0	0
	Miscellaneous	32	40	5	22
1905.........	Liberal	41	81	53	53
	Opposition	18	19	37	38
	Labor and Socialist	4	0	0	0
	Miscellaneous	37	0	10	9
1908†........	Liberal	59	70	54	51
	Opposition	10	22	38	42
	Labor and Socialist	11	6	1	0
	Miscellaneous	20	2	7	7
1911†........	Liberal	33	45	39	45
	Reform	27	28	36	48
	Labor and Socialist	21	16	0	1
	Miscellaneous	19	11	25	6
1914.........	Liberal	40	40	48	45
	Reform	39	46	52	53
	Labor and Social Democrat	21	14	0	2
	Miscellaneous	0	0	0	0
1919.........	Liberal	23	29	30	34
	Reform	21	29	44	50
	Labor	40	27	17	12
	Miscellaneous	16	15	9	4

* This table does not include the four Maori constituencies; nor are any figures for 1946 included, since the districts can no longer be precisely classified. Mixed districts are also omitted because, by definition, they do not indicate either a rural or an urban basis.

† First ballot.

TABLE 13—*Continued*

Date of Election	Party	Entirely Urban	Mainly Urban	Mainly Rural	Entirely Rural
1922..........	Liberal-Labor	12	24	33	43
	Reform	29	39	49	50
	Labor	44	34	9	3
	Miscellaneous	15	3	9	4
1925..........	National (Liberal)	7	19	30	27
	Reform	41	44	55	55
	Labor	44	33	12	15
	Miscellaneous	8	4	3	3
1928..........	United (Liberal)	30	31	31	26
	Reform	25	32	42	51
	Labor	39	34	15	11
	Miscellaneous	6	3	12	12
1931..........	Coalition (United-Reform)	32	48	49	56
	Labor	49	44	23	4
	Miscellaneous	19	8	28	40
1935..........	National (Coalition)	21	28	38	46
	Labor	57	52	39	33
	Democrat	9	5	9	8
	Miscellaneous	13	15	14	13
1938..........	National	32	41	49	48
	Labor	64	59	48	47
	Miscellaneous	4	0	3	5
1943..........	National	35	42	49	58
	Labor	53	50	46	38
	Democratic Soldier Labor	6	6	2	2
	Miscellaneous	6	2	3	2

TABLE 14*

Percentage of Votes Obtained by Political Parties in the Whole of New Zealand and in Each Separate Island, 1890–1946

Date of Election	Party	Percentage of Valid Votes Obtained in All New Zealand	Percentage of Valid Votes Obtained in North Island	Percentage of Valid Votes Obtained in South Island
1890.........	Liberal	56	57	56
	Conservative	29	26	31
	Miscellaneous	15	17	13
1893.........	Liberal	58	51	64
	Conservative	24	34	16
	Miscellaneous	18	15	20
1896.........	Liberal	46	47	45
	Conservative	37	37	38
	Miscellaneous	17	16	17
1899.........	Liberal	53	52	53
	Conservative	36	41	33
	Miscellaneous	11	7	14
1902.........	Liberal	52	50	54
	Opposition	21	30	11
	Labor and Socialist	2	3	2
	Miscellaneous	25	17	33
1905.........	Liberal	54	49	59
	Opposition	30	36	23
	Labor and Socialist	1	1	1
	Miscellaneous	15	14	17
1908†........	Liberal	58	52	66
	Opposition	27	31	21
	Labor and Socialist	5	4	7
	Miscellaneous	10	13	6
1911†........	Liberal	40	39	41
	Reform	35	40	29
	Labor and Socialist	10	10	10
	Miscellaneous	15	11	20
1914.........	Liberal	43	41	46
	Reform	47	50	43
	Labor and Social Democrat	10	9	11
	Miscellaneous	0	0	0
1919.........	Liberal	29	25	34
	Reform	36	44	24
	Labor	24	21	28
	Miscellaneous	11	10	14

* This table does not include the four Maori constituencies.　　　　　† First ballot.

206

TABLE 14—*Continued*

Date of Election	Party	Percentage of Valid Votes Obtained in All New Zealand	Percentage of Valid Votes Obtained in North Island	Percentage of Valid Votes Obtained in South Island
1922.........	Liberal-Labor	26	24	30
	Reform	40	42	37
	Labor	25	24	26
	Miscellaneous	9	10	7
1925.........	National (Liberal)	20	20	22
	Reform	47	50	41
	Labor	27	26	29
	Miscellaneous	6	4	8
1928.........	United (Liberal)	30	27	34
	Reform	35	36	34
	Labor	27	28	25
	Miscellaneous	8	9	7
1931.........	Coalition (United-Reform	44	44	44
	Labor	35	37	32
	Miscellaneous	21	19	24
1935.........	National (Coalition)	31	29	34
	Labor	47	48	47
	Miscellaneous	22	23	19
1938.........	National	40	39	42
	Labor	56	57	54
	Miscellaneous	4	4	4
1943.........	National	43	43	43
	Labor	48	48	49
	Democratic Soldier Labor	4	5	3
	Miscellaneous	5	4	5
1946.........	National	49	50	47
	Labor	51	50	53
	Miscellaneous	0	0	0

although they gained a slightly lower percentage of votes than before. But in the rural constituencies their votes rose by 9 per cent over the last election. Their decisive lead in the countryside was the electoral reward for the passage of Liberal land legislation. Parliament had at last enacted the law which imposed a graduated tax on large estates. Already the government had shown its intention to use its powers by the spectacular purchase and subdivision of the huge Cheviot estate in the Canterbury plains. Farm laborers and owners of small farms voted Liberal in gratitude. In the South Island, where most of the big runs were situated, the electoral repercussions marked the death sentence of the "squattocracy." As compared with the figures for 1890, the Liberal vote declined relatively in the north but increased in the south. Three years in office had made of the Liberals a South Island rather than a North Island party and had given them a rural following almost as strong as their urban support.

Fresh from victory at the polls, the party produced in 1894 such a bumper crop of new legislation that this has been called their *annus mirabilis*. A factories act, a trade-union act, industrial conciliation and arbitration, lands for settlement, and state advances to settlers—all these measures passed into law. But, after carrying out their pledges, the Liberals struck a succession of difficulties. They encountered a financial crisis (not of their own making) in which they had to come to the rescue of the Bank of New Zealand and reorganize it from a private into a semipublic institution. The Conservative opposition were consolidating their forces, aided by the prohibition movement to whom Seddon was anathema. In 1896 the premier lost two of his ablest cabinet colleagues: Reeves, who went to serve as agent-general of New Zealand in London, and Ward, who resigned because his private affairs had been too closely mixed up with the bank crisis. To add to these embarrassments, Stout, seated in Parliament as an independent Liberal, was vigorously charging the government with maladministration. In 1896 the Liberals skated near to the edge of defeat. As compared with the results in 1893, their proportion of the total votes cast dropped from 58 to 46 per cent, their number of parliamentary seats from 51 to 39. In the cities and towns their decline was sharpest and the Conservative gains the greatest. In rural electorates the Liberals maintained their position, for their policy of subdividing the big estates and of helping the small settlers with government loans was now well under way. Formerly powerful in the south, it was there that the old Conservative party regrouped and rallied their adherents to fight their last electoral battle. Consequently, in that island, of the total votes cast, those obtained by the Liberals amounted to 19 per cent less than in 1893.

Despite this setback Seddon pulled his party through the critical period and regained the lost ground. With great tactical skill and a shrewd electioneering eye, he introduced his Old Age Pensions Bill—a noncontributory scheme financed out of taxation—which the Conservatives obstructed with a last-ditch opposition. In a memorable parliamentary battle the Liberals outlasted the other side largely because of Seddon's unflinching tenacity and overruling will-power. Old age pensions accomplished what its author, the premier, intended. It insured the security of the aged and of his own ministry. At the ensuing election (1899) the Liberals recovered practically all their former majority. They resumed their ascendancy in the urban constituencies and collected a still higher margin of votes among the farmers. Between the two islands their supporters were evenly spread.

Thereafter, until Seddon died in 1906, all was easy. At the turn of the century the premier identified New Zealand with the imperialistic sentiments that found an emotional vent in the queen's jubilee and a martial setting in the Boer War. The elections of 1902 and 1905 were merely victory parades, in which the Liberal grip on the country was confirmed anew. In every class of electorate the Liberals were now by far the strongest party. Secure enough in the cities, they were no less potent in the countryside. The farmers whom Liberal legislation had placed on the land clung to their allegiance, especially in the south, where the Liberals in 1905 took 59 per cent of all the votes cast. For years afterward, even when the Liberals had degenerated into a spent force, the district where the Cheviot estate had once been situated consistently returned a Liberal member to Parliament. In 1930 George Forbes, the last premier to lead the rump of the Liberal party, was a farmer who had been one of the first to settle on Cheviot land.[8]

The return of prosperity assured a continuance of the Liberal supremacy in the opening years of the new century. The hard times which had beset the Colony ever since 1880 changed for the better in the late nineties. Refrigeration, a technological development, made possible in 1882 the first successful shipment of meat to England. Thenceforth New Zealand began to reap the benefits of an export trade in frozen meat. Sheep were now bred for food as well as for clothing. In the eighties disappointed settlers had left New Zealand to seek security elsewhere. But, when the tide turned, immigrants flocked in their thousands to the still empty spaces of the North Island. Finding there a climate admirably suited to the dairy industry, they were able to add butter, and later cheese, to the exports of lamb and wool. A rise in the world prices of such primary commodities encouraged an increase in production. To this extent, therefore, prosperity's arrival was hastened by external economic causes, and Professor Condliffe is justified in arguing that New Zealand's recovery was the result of "healing economic forces" independently operating. But he does less than justice to the work of the Liberal government by suggesting an antithesis between "the constructive organisation of economic life" and "the records of political interference."[9] On the contrary, the Liberals directly contributed to prosperity by wise political regulation. It was their land laws which freed much land of good quality for closer settlement. It was their provision of cheap credit through the state that encouraged the farming of this land by settlers who possessed a large capacity to work but little capital. Thus did the ministry assist the rise of the dairy industry which, unlike sheep-farming, could operate very profitably on a holding of far smaller average size. In the industrial sphere, too, the Liberals' machinery for conciliation and compulsory arbitration of labor disputes (Reeves's brain-child) promoted peace for the time being. Here, therefore, was a case where legislation and administration, intelligently

8. See his statement in *P.D.*, CCXXI (1929), 510.

9. J. B. Condliffe, *New Zealand in the Making* (London: Allen & Unwin, 1930), p. 139.

planned and boldly executed, deliberately harnessed economic tendencies to promote the greatest happiness of the greatest number. Had the great estates been suffered to remain, large profits might still have been garnered. But then the dividends would not have been so widely diffused.

The long Liberal hegemony splits, therefore, into phases, each with its own character. Between 1891 and 1898 there lasted what Reeves has called the "eight years' tussle." The party survived this period of clash and conflict because it strove persistently and energetically to fulfil its program. From 1899 to 1906 its legislative activity subsided, and the emphasis was now placed on the administrative application of the victorious policies. Less dramatic than the eight years' tussle, the second phase of quiescence has an importance of its own, since the Liberals gained time to establish their system as something familiar in the daily lives and accepted habits of New Zealanders. Liberal principles and laws were assured of sympathetic administration for long enough to guarantee that some of their effects would be permanent.

Opposition died down because it had no sense. Why turn out the government when times were good? Reeves mentions a comment made to him by a Conservative leader: "I would sooner have Seddon with prosperity than anyone else without."[10] Similar views were heard in trade-union circles from those who resisted attempts to set up a separate labor organization independent of the Liberals. The French observer, Métin, who visited the Colony in 1899, quotes the remark of an old and influential trade-union secretary: "These young fellows [who want a separate organization] may perhaps be right; but, if we listened to them, we would run the risk of overthrowing Seddon, and for whose profit? That's what we don't know. What we do know is that Seddon has done a lot for us and will do more still. Let's stick to him."[11] Seddon himself accurately summed up the prevailing mood in a letter written shortly before his death. This was his account of public opinion when he won his fifth consecutive electoral triumph in 1905: " 'With Seddon we know where we

10. *Op. cit.*, p. 298.

11. Albert Métin, *Le Socialisme sans doctrines* (2d ed.; Paris: Félix Alcan, 1910), pp. 143–44. (My translation.)

are, and he will not go to extremes. If anything happens to him
we might get a weak Government, and then what would happen
to us? It is better to be sure than sorry.' This is the keynote of the
situation that led to the great majority of December 6th last."[12]
On all sides, then, the majority were disposed to grasp prosperity
and trust the Liberals. Overseas prices steadily rose, and vistas
of ever expanding export markets stretched before an optimistic
colonial vision. Contented New Zealand basked in its good
fortune and left its politics to Seddon.

But this state of affairs could not last. Already before Seddon's
death, the symptoms of the future Liberal decline were appearing.
While he lived, his prestige was sufficient to prevent a rift in the
party's ranks. Yet it is doubtful whether even his shrewdness
could have held together much longer the alliance which was
disintegrating. The interests and aims of industrial workers and
small farmers, whose compatibility had underwritten the Liberal
supremacy, now forked into different paths. Each group pursued
what it envisaged as its own economic advantage. As their co-
operation gave place to competition, the weakening of the old
alliance led to a realignment of political parties.

On one side organized labor showed a desire to forge its separate destiny. Métin had been struck by the paradox of a country
which had "the most advanced labor legislation" combined with
"the least organized labor party." His illustrious compatriot,
Siegfried, who also studied New Zealand during the Seddonian
era, observed: "It is a curious fact that the New Zealand working
man is little interested with the choice of a representative: he
wants one, but it matters little to him whether it be a middle-class
man or not, so long as this representative will give him sufficient
guarantees."[13] True, the Liberals had included a number of workingmen in their parliamentary party, but, to all intents and purposes, these merged their identity with the rest and were satisfied
with the Liberal label. A new and younger group of labor leaders
was forming who questioned the wisdom of assimilation with the
Liberals. The remark of the old trade-union secretary, quoted
earlier, illustrates the clash of opinion. It was a strong argument

12. Quoted by Drummond, *op. cit.*, p. 358.
13. *Op. cit.*, p. 86.

that nothing should be done to weaken Seddon. Even those who hoped to dissolve the connection found it hard to counteract his influence in labor circles. Some of the early efforts to set up a distinct labor movement were told to the writer by a lifelong labor supporter who participated in them as a young man. He described a meeting which was held in Wellington in 1905 to support a Labor candidate for Parliament. In the middle of the meeting, Seddon suddenly appeared on the scene, although not by invitation. Naturally, as premier, he had to be asked to speak; and, after hearing a speech which listed dramatically all that the Liberals had done for labor, the meeting was swept over enthusiastically to his side!

Yet, despite his influence, a few labor and socialist candidates under various labels did stand for election in Seddon's lifetime. They polled 10,500 votes in 1902 and 3,600 in 1905 without winning any seats, and their candidates were almost entirely confined to the four big cities. Their participation in these elections did not affect the results. Yet it was a portent whose significance for the future could not be ignored. From 1906 onward this incipient labor breakaway from the Liberals gathered pace. Seddon had been succeeded as premier by Ward, his minister of finance. Both men had risen from poor circumstances by their individual energies. But Seddon remained ever a man of the people, while Ward nourished a flair for finance and associated himself with the business community. His was not the personality or the outlook to conciliate labor in its mood for political emancipation—a mood encouraged by the examples of the British and Australian Labor parties. Moreover, the trade-union movement at this very time was voicing its dissatisfaction with the industrial machinery which Reeves had designed. Industrial peace reigned serenely only as long as the Arbitration Court pronounced awards favorable to labor.

After 1905, however, labor's requests for higher rates of pay were not granted as readily as before, and in 1908 the Blackball miners signalized a new policy by striking in defiance of the court. Under the Conciliation and Arbitration Act it was left to the unions to choose whether they would register, and so fall legally under the court's jurisdiction, or not. The more powerful unions, representing seamen, watersiders, miners, and the like, thought that they could secure their aims more effectively by direct action. Influenced by syndicalist theories and by general Marxian doctrines of the class war, they assumed a militant temper, seeking not merely better conditions within the capitalist system but an onslaught on capitalism itself. The weaker craft unions composed of the skilled workers clung to the arbitration system, since their numbers were inadequate to insure success by direct action.

There was thus a dualism within the trade-union movement, analogous in certain respects to the division in the United States between the American Federation of Labor and the Congress for Industrial Organization. From the industrial sphere the schism extended to labor's political activities, separating the advocates of gradualism and of revolution. Stimulated by the miners, the militant industrial unions formed in 1909 a Federation of Labor. The next year, to match it, the older and less radical Trades and Labor Councils created a Labor party designed for parliamentary action. To contain this heady new wine was too much for the strength of the old Liberal bottle. In 1908 the various Labor and Socialist candidates received over 40,000 votes, bringing them four seats. The new party (or collection of labor groups, as it then was) concentrated its attention on the cities and already in 1911 could boast of one-fifth of the votes in the entirely urban electorates.

The Reform Party

While labor was pursuing its tactics of separatism, the farmers also were flocking behind a new leader into a new fold. Although they had acquiesced in Reeves's industrial code, their chief interest lay in the policies of land settlement and state loans. Once these were achieved, they were ready to call a halt to other Liberal measures. Reeves himself states that the party's right wing, comprising mainly farmers, thought even in 1896 that the Liberal experiments were going on "too fast and too far."[14] Their political advocate, the focus of their loyalty and the min-

14. *Op. cit.*, p. 297.

isterial representative of their views, was not Seddon or Reeves
but Jock McKenzie, minister of lands and of agriculture. When
this ardent farm-bloc leader died in 1900, the Liberal government lost some of its attractiveness to the farming community.
Having gained their original objective, the small farmers could
hope for little more from the Liberals.

The growth of the North Island dairy industry, moreover, and
the rise in the prices of primary products, were making the new
class of small farmers prosperous. Formerly radical when times
were bad, they now had something to conserve. Retrospectively
a member of Parliament has described the changing outlook of
that period: "I would just refer to one or two large areas of land
taken during the regime of the Liberal party compulsorily. . . . .
I have lived in that district for thirty-five years, and I knew the
men who took up that land. The bulk of them were working men,
taken from the ranks of labour, and eighty per cent of them were
Liberals at heart. . . . . Many of them went to the land with
no more than sufficient money to pay half a year's rent. Times
were good; they prospered; to-day most of those men although
taken from the ranks of labour, when they became possessed of
wealth kicked away the ladder by which they had climbed, and
now they are supporting Reform."[15] The spread of conservative
sentiment manifested itself in the desire for freehold ownership of
the land which was occupied on state lease.[16] Many leading
Liberals, strongly influenced by single-tax theories, proposed
nationalization of all land. But the more tempting alternative in
the eyes of the state tenantry was to receive a freehold tenure. A
campaign for freehold ownership of their land provided the nucleus of a new farmers' movement. This grew and flourished, especially in the North Island in the heart of the dairy region of the
Waikato. The Liberals, as has been pointed out, were tending to
become a South Island rather than a North Island party. But
after the turn of the century the northern population outstripped
the southern. Voting preponderance shifted from the areas where

15. *P.D.*, CXCIX (1923), 328.
16. See J. E. Le Rossignol and W. D. Stewart, *State Socialism in New Zealand*
(London: Harrap & Co., 1912), p. 51. J. C. Beaglehole comments: "The Liberal
land-policy was so successful that it ended by destroying the Liberal party" (*New
Zealand: A Short History* [London: Allen & Unwin, 1936], p. 65).

liberalism had its strongholds, and among men settled on new soil new loyalties grew.

Crushed by repeated Liberal victories, the old Conservative party representing the large landowners and well-to-do business-men broke up after the election of 1899. That appears clearly in our tables of the electoral results. When a political party disinte-grates, there are usually many politicians with local influence who float adrift from central direction. Candidates stand for election as independents and under labels of all sorts and descriptions. So in 1902 the officially styled opposition candidates—there was no longer a Conservative party—polled under 86,000 votes, while miscellaneous candidates of various types received around 105,000. Nineteen opposition members, as compared with ten independents, were elected to the lower house. The opposition, or what was left of it, was weakest in the cities, where large num-bers of votes went to the unaffiliated candidates. In the rural dis-tricts the opposition still managed to put up something of a showing; and it was relatively stronger in the North Island than the South. At the 1905 election the opposition ranks were more consolidated, this time under the new leadership of William Massey, a North Island farmer. They received 117,000 votes, while miscellaneous candidates polled 61,000. As before, the organized opposition fared better in the north than in the south. Most of their votes still came from the countryside, although they recuperated somewhat in the urban districts. In 1908 the Liber-als under Ward had the highest percentage of votes in all classes of electorates, but it was in the cities that their ascendancy was least disputed. The opposition vote increased slightly in farming areas and was again stronger in the north. As its party organiza-tion was being rebuilt, the votes of miscellaneous candidates dropped considerably.

For the election of 1911 the battle lines were manned in earnest. The opposition was now reconstituted as the Reform party. In this new guise it offered itself to the favor of the electors. The name "Reform" keynoted its criticisms of the Liberal ad-ministration. For years it had been charged that the Liberal ministry maintained its power by patronage and corruption. At public meetings Massey said that, if he could not promise roads

and bridges and railways, he could at least offer "clean hands."
One of the Reform planks was to institute nonpolitical control of
the civil service. Another was to alter the constitution of the
Legislative Council, effectively packed by that time with Liberal
nominees. But the most attractive carrot which Reform dangled
before the electoral nose was a freehold tenure for occupants of
state-leased farms. Descended from the old Conservatives who
had supported Atkinson, the party which now sought to dis-
possess the Liberals had first reformed itself. Like its parent, it remained first and foremost a farmer's party. But those now dominant in its councils were not the wool-producers of the large
estates but the small dairy farmers. Thus in the election of 1911
more of the Reform votes were polled in the North Island than
the South, and more in the countryside than the towns. All told,
the Liberals won a higher number of votes, but Reform captured
more seats. Labor split the vote sufficiently in urban constituencies to detract from Liberal majorities.

The election results could not be called a decisive popular
mandate for any party. The new Parliament contained thirty-six
Reformers, thirty Liberals, four Laborites, six independents, and
four Maoris. Ward, like Atkinson in 1891, did not concede defeat until Parliament assembled. Then he resigned, in the hope
that the Liberals might yet retain power under a new leader.
After a severe internal conflict the party choice fell upon a South
Islander, Thomas Mackenzie, who with a reconstituted ministry
struggled on for a few months more. But the disunited party
could not agree on a common policy; and Massey, aided by a
few Liberal turncoats, at last defeated the ministry by forty-one
votes to thirty-three. Taking office, but insecurely perched on his
precarious majority, Massey had the acuteness to realize that
he could establish his position only by boldly introducing his
legislative program. Bills were quickly proposed for removing
civil service administration from ministerial control, for permitting the holders of state-leased farms to acquire the freehold,
and for converting the Legislative Council from a nominative
into an elective chamber. The first two measures soon passed into
law, but the third was inevitably delayed and obstructed by the
Council itself. Reform at any rate had shown the voters that it

could provide the country with a government determined to fulfil its pledges and more capable of positive action than the disintegrating Liberals.

More determination and action, though of a less commendable character, were shown by Reform in its attitude to labor problems. At the very time when Massey succeeded to Mackenzie, a major strike was being conducted by the miners at Waihi. Belonging to the radical Federation of Labor, they were putting into practice the syndicalist theory of direct action. Since their union was not registered under the Conciliation and Arbitration Court, Massey resisted the strikers and eventually had the mines reopened by men who registered under the act as a "scab" union. One striker was killed by the police and others were injured in the restoration of law and order. The following year, however, labor militancy flared up anew on a still larger scale. The events of 1913 came nearer to a general strike, since more than one industrial union, and even some craft unions, participated. But the head and front was formed by the watersiders at the port of Wellington. In this case the menace to a farmers' government was even more direct than that provided by the Waihi coal stoppage. Farm produce lay idle on the docks and could not be shipped away for export. The Reform ministry handled the situation by taking forcible possession of the waterside. Using the police, and arming volunteer bands of farmers as special mounted constables, they loaded the ships in defiance of the strikers. As in the previous year, a new union was formed and duly registered under the Arbitration Act. Riots, violence by vigilantes, arrests of strike leaders, charges of sedition, and prison sentences were witnessed in the country which had boasted of finding a panacea for industrial strife. The government, the employers, and the farmers were victorious, and the unions were forced into submission. The crises of two years had proved the utter collapse of the foundations on which the Liberal supremacy had rested. In the early nineties the small farmers and industrial workers were economic and political allies. In 1913 their rivalries were arbitrated by force.

The display of strength reaped for Reform its electoral harvest. Held a few months after the outbreak of the first twentieth-century world war, the general election of 1914 was conducted amid an atmosphere of patriotic enthusiasm. The total Reform vote topped that of the Liberals, and Massey's parliamentary following increased. The political effect of granting the freehold was seen in the higher percentage of votes, as compared with 1911, cast for Reform in the country constituencies. In the cities, too, the Reform vote leaped upward, for employers applauded the forcible crushing of strikes. The votes of the Labor party, suffering from the recent industrial setbacks, remained almost stationary and were still confined to the cities. The ensuing four years of war were accompanied by a virtual truce in domestic politics. From 1915 Reformers and Liberals united in a national government which manifested the outward cohesion and the inward dissensions normal to most coalitions. Only the small Labor group was left to constitute an opposition. As in Britain and many other countries,[17] so in New Zealand, the war found socialism a house divided against itself. Some Labor leaders criticized the war *in toto*, either from pacifist convictions or viewing it as an imperialistic contest between rival members of the capitalist class. Others acquiesced in it as an unavoidable evil and confined their opposition to the government's treatment of the workers and to the policy of conscription. Under charges of sedition various Laborites were given prison sentences and even forfeited their civil rights, for war always intensifies the ever latent intolerance toward dissident minorities.

When international warfare temporarily ceased in 1918, it was time for party hostilities to be resumed. With alacrity Ward, whose personality jarred with that of Massey, seized his earliest opportunity to break up the coalition. Thereby the stage was set for the strange politics of the twenties. It was in this decade that New Zealand learned what it means to operate a parliamentary democracy under a three-party system. Elections were held triennially, in 1919, 1922, 1925, and 1928. Only at one of these did the popular vote record an overwhelming preference for any one party. Reform was the dominant party of the decade and amassed the largest number of votes at each of these four elections. But the

17. See Francis W. Coker, *Recent Political Theory* (New York: Appleton-Century Co., 1934), pp. 122 ff.

percentages of its votes to the total numbers cast fluctuated successively from 36 to 40, then up to 47, and down to 35. The number of its parliamentary seats changed from forty-three to thirty-five, from thirty-five to fifty-one, and thence to twenty-five. Although Reform premiers governed the Dominion continuously from 1912 to 1928, it remains a surprising fact that on no occasion did this party ever poll more than 47 per cent of all the votes recorded.

In the "khaki election" of 1919 Reform polled 50,000 votes less than in 1914, yet obtained four seats more. Reform gained somewhat at the expense of the Liberals, who were prejudiced by the clumsy eagerness with which Ward withdrew from the coalition. In the countryside, although their proportion of the votes sank slightly, Reform remained the leading party. In urban constituencies, particularly those of the South Island, the Reform vote slumped heavily, Labor being the gainer. The differences in the political complexion of the two islands were extraordinary. Of the North Island voters, 44 per cent supported Reform; of the South Island, only 24 per cent. The ministerial party was clearly based upon the good will of the North Island farmers. When the government again faced its masters in 1922, the result was one of those freaks which can be expected under the electoral system described in the previous chapter. Reform regained the 50,000 it had lost as well as winning unopposed in one district; but its seats dropped by eight. Although it had polled 40 per cent of all the votes and was still the largest parliamentary party, by itself it lacked a majority in the House of Representatives. This reverse, if it could be so described, was explicable by the public displeasure with the economic conditions of the two preceding years. When the effects of the postwar slump reached New Zealand, the government had pruned its budgets and cut its servants' salaries. By 1922, moreover, Massey was suffering from the general postwar reaction against wartime leaders which had already displaced Wilson's Democrats in the United States and Lloyd George's Liberals in Britain.

For these electoral vagaries Reform was duly compensated in 1925, when the system worked as much to its benefit as earlier to its disadvantage. The party now had a younger leader, Coates, also a North Island farmer, who acceded to power on Massey's death. The ministry was aided by that most potent of all electioneering arguments, a revival of prosperity. Furthermore, a newly hired secretary-organizer injected into the Reform campaign a volume of publicity, advertisements, and "ballyhoo" which was successful because it was novel in New Zealand. More popular votes and more parliamentary seats were accorded to Reform than it captured at any other election. In every class of electoral district the party advanced in voting strength. Fifty-five per cent of the country voters, and over 40 per cent of the city dwellers, made Reform their choice. But, as previously, the party was more popular in the North Island than in the South.

It appears from an analysis of the figures that Reform had at last succeeded in its bid for the support of urban business interests. This was not the first time that the party had angled for their votes. But hitherto many of the financiers, importers, manufacturers, and retail traders had preferred to follow Ward and his Liberals than to accept a party so obviously dominated by farmers. Yet the rising strength of Labor constituted in capitalist eyes a menace against which the weakening Liberals were an unsure bulwark. Induced, therefore, by the reassuring sound of an American-imported slogan—"More Business in Government and Less Government in Business"—the urban employers turned in large numbers to Reform. For the second time in the history of modern New Zealand the party conflict approximated to a horizontal division between economic classes. In the nineties the Liberal supremacy had depended on a combination of the urban and rural proletariates. In the mid-twenties Reform won its victory because it forged an alliance between urban and rural employers.

But the alliance was short lived and unsuccessful. The businessmen were irked by a partnership in which they felt subordinate. Disgruntled at some changes in the income-tax law, they reached the climax of their dissatisfaction in the liquor controversy. There had existed for some years in the city of Auckland a small but powerful ring which possessed the controlling interests in various

breweries, insurance companies, and industrial ventures.[18] This
group was one of those which swung to Reform in 1925. When
the long-delayed problem of revising the liquor laws was brought
before the new Parliament, the brewery interests sought legislative protection against the onslaughts of the prohibition movement. The ministry introduced a liquor control bill into the
House of Representatives, which soon split, not on party lines,
but into "wet" and "dry." The bill that finally passed a third
reading was so much amended as to affront the liquor trade. Controversial clauses were altered by the Council and again redrawn
by the House. In the end, the control of the ministry over
Parliament was greatly shaken by the confused divisions, and city
businessmen lost faith in the efficacy of the Reform party. The
coming depression was already casting its shadow forward; and
the slight economic deterioration during 1928 helped to discredit
the government. For Reform the election of 1928 was a debacle.
As compared with 1925, the percentage of their votes to the total
dropped from 47 to 35. Their parliamentary representation was
halved. Their urban supporters were 16 per cent less than before.[19] Even in rural districts, though they remained the strongest
party, their lead was reduced. Their votes were 7 per cent lower
in the South Island than in 1925 and 14 per cent lower in the
North Island.

The party which gained most at Reform's expense was not
Labor but Liberal; a surprising outcome, since in the recent
elections the Liberals had gone steadily downhill. They had received 43 per cent of all the votes cast in 1914, 29 per cent in
1919, 27 per cent in 1922, and only 20 per cent in 1925. But in
1928 they revived to the extent of receiving 30 per cent of the
total. How did this happen? In desperation at their successive
defeats the Liberals had sought an elixir of political life under
new slogans and labels, calling themselves first Liberal, then
Liberal-Labor, then National, and eventually rising as the United
party. Three times in those harassed twenties they changed leaders, switching from Ward to Wilford, from Wilford to Forbes,

18. Opponents have called this clique "the Kelly gang" after the name of Ned
Kelly, a notorious Australian gangster.

19. In the city constituencies of Auckland, where Reform received 40,000 votes
in 1925, they won only 17,000 in 1928.

and from him back again to Ward, for in postwar New Zealand
the Liberals were hopelessly wedged in a middle position, com-
promised between the more clear-cut alternatives of Reform to
the right and Labor to the left. To Labor were gravitating from
the Liberal ranks more and more of the industrial workers and
the progressively minded intelligentsia. Reform with its solid
Conservative core appealed to the "haves," to persons of "sound"
principles and material substance. After settling the freehold
issue, and forcibly compelling the submission of industrial disputes to the Arbitration Court, Massey had left most of the Liberal legislation alone. Why, then, could not the Liberals—or, at any
rate, their right wing—amalgamate with Reform?

The Liberal party, in short, was following the same fate as its
British counterpart. Both in the mother-country and in the
Dominion the Liberals had fulfilled their great mission before the
outbreak of war in 1914. In neither country did the party survive
the impact of war upon its philosophy and principles. When the
Conservatives in Britain and the Reformers in New Zealand
acquiesced in the Liberal accomplishments, those who desired
yet further measures of change pinned their faith to Labor
parties professing socialist theories. There was nothing more for
the Liberals to do, save write an epitaph to their own past glory.
The parallelism during the twenties between the party politics of
Britain and of New Zealand is amazingly close. Political ascendancy lay with the right-wing party; but the power of the left wing
was growing. Between them the Liberals were ground out of
existence.

When there was little to distinguish the program of the New
Zealand Liberals from that of Reform, coalition was naturally
suggested. And there were many arguments in its favor. Reform
was a party with one good campaign cry—the freehold. Its other
cry, the abolition of patronage, was suitable only for opposition
use, and soon dropped out of hearing when the party attained
power. After the war Massey could devise no new positive policy.
In default, he seized upon the negative tactic of being violently
antisocialist. Like the Seddon of the latter years, Massey appealed to such symbols as the flag, the empire, and the rights of
property. Labor, socialism, and communism he equated in the

same general denunciation. Indeed, if Reform's lengthy tenure of office be surveyed, the party's positive achievements were singularly unimpressive. The Liberals, likewise, could offer nothing in the twenties but the memory of their old tradition. On the questions of imperial solidarity and anti-bolshevism they concurred with Reform. For two parties united in their support of common principles and in their fear of Labor, coalition seemed the obvious solution. Thus Mr. Downie Stewart, the most scholarly of Reform ministers, advocated it consistently for many years. After the election of 1922 Massey himself stated: "It seems to me that the results of the election show the necessity for a reconstruction of parties. The three party system cannot possibly be satisfactory in any case, and it is simply folly for the Liberals and Reformers to go on fighting each other when so far as policy is concerned there is little or nothing between them."[20]

But coalition was delayed by numerous obstacles. One was the personal incompatibility of Massey and Ward. In the early twenties, when Ireland was aflame, repercussions of the Irish turmoil affected politics in New Zealand. For Massey was an Ulsterman and a Protestant, while Ward was a Catholic. Sectarian bitterness aggravated partisan disputes. An organization called the Protestant Political Alliance threw itself into the lists, giving most of its political support to Reform candidates. On their side, Liberals were unwilling to abandon their separate identity. Hard put to it to state their divergence from Reform, they posed as a stabilizing party of the center appealing to all moderates to reject the extremes of right and left.[21] Although their strength persistently declined, the Liberals managed to hold together a small nucleus of steadfast supporters. It was in the cities that their votes dwindled most rapidly at the successive elections of 1919, 1922, and 1925, for it was here that they suffered most from the combined effects of the rise of Reform and Labor. In the rural areas, too, the Liberals were weakened; although even in 1925, the year of their worst defeat, they retained the confidence of over a

20. Press statement (see *Evening Post* [Wellington], December 8, 1922).

21. Confronted by the same difficulty, British Liberals similarly presented themselves as a moderate center party. Ramsay Muir attempts to elevate this enforced necessity into a virtue (*How Britain Is Governed* [3d ed.; London: Constable, 1933], pp. 146–52).

quarter of the farmers. In the North Island, Reform's stronghold, the Liberal downfall was more precipitate than in the South Island. As a sign that a party was breaking up, there was repeated, as in 1902, the symptom of an increase in the number of votes cast for independents. The miscellaneous candidates received 1,000 votes in 1914; 62,000 in 1919; 56,000 in 1922; and 39,000 in 1925.[22]

In 1928, however, came the unexpected reversal, turning Liberal dirges into paeans. Under the title of the United party, the Liberals raised themselves from the depths. They took nearly as many votes as Reform, and they won the same number of parliamentary seats. The explanation lies principally in Auckland. It was here that the big business group, which abandoned the Reform party, founded a new organization. Ample financial backing was put up by the brewery and other interests angered at the government's handling of the licensing bill. The program was carefully planned to appeal to the business community. It was equally agreeable to the scattered remnants of the Liberal party which united with the Auckland group. The keystone for this none too solid arch was found in the aging and ailing former premier, Ward, who contributed the prestige of past glories and a policy of borrowing £70,000,000. The rest of the story is told in the electoral results. In Auckland City at the 1925 election the Liberals had polled only 8,800 votes and had taken no seats, for the two reasons that the "Kelly gang" was supporting Reform and the then Liberal leader, Forbes, was a South Island farmer unknown in the northern city.[23] But in the same city three years later 42,000 votes, and five seats, went to Liberal candidates. Of the votes cast in all the entirely urban constituencies, 30 per cent went to the Liberals in 1928, as contrasted with 7 per cent in 1925! In the rural electorates, on the other hand, the Liberal share of the votes stayed the same. They were still relatively stronger in the South Island, but in both islands the percentages of votes gained by the Liberals rose considerably.

The party, which was thus revitalized, soon had to shoulder

22. The figure dropped somwehat in 1925 because in that year various of the independent votes were absorbed by the preponderant Reform group.

23. A leading article in the *Evening Post* (Wellington) of November 6, 1925, quotes thus from the *Auckland Star:* "To Auckland . . . . Forbes is only a name."

the responsibility of the worst economic depression in forty years. Since the Liberal representatives in Parliament numbered less than a third of the whole membership, they took office with Labor support. As the depression deepened and budgetary deficits mounted, the bewildered ministry proposed to balance the unbalanceable by cuts in salaries and social services. Labor would have none of this; so the Liberals perforce turned to Reform. It took nearly a year of tortuous negotiations, of proposals and countersuggestions, of gestures and recriminations, before the heads of both parties could combine by a method which saved their faces. Finally, the example of Macdonald's so-called national government in Britain enabled New Zealand to act upon its fundamental instinct to "follow Britain's lead." In September, 1931, Liberals and Reformers at last coalesced. A few months later the coalition fought and won a panic election similar to that just engineered in Britain. Labor remained in opposition.

The Labor Party

The New Zealand Labor party was more fortunate than its British namesake. It did not attain office before the depression. Therefore Labor could not receive in New Zealand the political blame for that calamity. It was able instead to hold the conservative coalition responsible if natural laws of economics behaved unnaturally; and this redounded to Labor's advantage in the election of 1935. Viewing the last thirty years in perspective, therefore, the Labor party has much to thank for the fact that its political career started somewhat late and proceeded somewhat slowly. Their late start was due to the special circumstances of Seddon's lengthy reign. The slowness of their rise resulted from the industrial defeats in the big pre-war strikes. In 1913 the two wings of the Labor movement came together, creating a Federation of Labor for industrial action and a Social Democratic party for political campaigning. It was difficult, however, to gloss over the internal dissensions between craft and industrial unions, between the gradualists and the militant, between those who hoped to capture Parliament from within and those who preferred to attack it from without. But when Massey crushed the watersiders in 1913, he forced the party to concentrate on electoral victories in the same way that Labor had sought parliamentary remedies after the strikers' defeat in 1890. Henceforth, although the success of the Russian Revolution gave the militants an additional talking-point, the growth of Labor was characterized by the preponderance of Fabianism over Marxism and by the conversion of the industrial unions to a parliamentary strategy.

At the five elections from 1919 to 1931 there was a steady, although slow, increase in the electoral support for Labor. The percentage of Labor votes to the total moved from 24 in 1919 to 25 in 1922, to 27 in 1925 and in 1928, and then to 35 in 1931. The election of 1919 was a remarkable one, because, though Labor captured only eight seats, they received a quarter of all the votes. This was Labor's answer—the same in New Zealand as in the British election of 1919—to its wartime treatment; and, taken together with what was happening in Russia, it was a shock to conservative minds. In constituencies of an entirely urban character as many as 40 per cent of the voters supported Labor. At every election since then Labor has consistently gained the highest proportion of votes in the cities. In the electorates classified as mainly urban, the percentage of votes won by Labor rose gradually until it topped the other two parties in 1928. Rural districts showed after 1919 a slightly increased interest in Labor. But, apart from areas where miners or lumbermen were congregated, the countryside plumped solidly for Reform or Liberal.

The organization of the unions and of the political party changed in these early twenties in style though not in substance. The pre-war Federation of Labor was replaced by an Alliance of Labor composed principally of industrial unions organized on a national basis. The Social Democrats were remodeled as the Labor party with a definitely socialist program incorporating the ideas and phrases of Sidney Webb. Thus prepared, the party emerged from the election of 1922 with about the same proportion of the votes but double its former number of seats. For the first time Labor became a parliamentary force to be reckoned with. Its popular support, as before, was strongest in the cities and towns. The following election in 1925 produced paradoxical consequences for Labor. Their votes increased, both absolutely and relatively, yet they lost five of their seats. Such was the effect

of the Reform landslide on a minority party. Nevertheless,
Labor retained its lead in the city constituencies and even gained
a slightly higher percentage of votes than before in country areas.
Possessing more votes and more seats than the Liberals, Labor became the official opposition in the new Parliament. At the next
election the Reform collapse helped Labor, just as it helped the
Liberals, to recover its parliamentary representation. In the
urban districts Labor again led over its rivals. But the effect of the
Liberal resurgence can be seen in that the percentage of urban
votes cast for Labor was lower than in 1925. The countryside
apart from the miners and lumbermen was still slow to respond
to the party's policies. Farmers viewed with suspicion a party
dominated by city dwellers and big industrial unions and avow-
ing socialist aims.

The advent of the depression with all its serious economic implications produced politically at least one good result—it clarified the party alignment. During most of the twenties New Zealand had been afflicted with a three-party deadlock. Throughout
the thirties the comparative blessing of a two-party system was restored. Voters were presented with a far clearer choice, and parliamentary majorities were stable. Before the election took place
in 1931 many were anxious about its outcome. Thus Sir Francis
Bell, who for many years had been Massey's second in command
of the Reform ministry, wrote to Mr. Downie Stewart: "I fear
that whatever is done Labor will win the election next year, with
promises of alleviation of indigence from the pockets of those who
have means. The farmers are hopeless, and as I fear, will vote
for any Party offering such promises."[24] Nevertheless, the electoral results were a decisive victory for the coalition. They took
forty-two seats (four of them without opposition), and their votes
in the contested districts came to 44 per cent of the total that were
recorded. Most of the coalition's support came from country
areas and the smaller towns. In the bigger cities Labor strengthened its predominance.

However, two signposts pointing to the future disquieted
the victors. One was the general rise in the total Labor vote. The
other was the high proportion of votes accorded to the numerous

24. Letter quoted by Stewart, *op. cit.*, p. 278.

miscellaneous candidates, especially in the rural districts. This
indicated that many of the farmers, whose "hopeless" attitude
Bell deplored, were discontented with both wings of the coalition.
As they could not yet bring themselves to vote Labor, they cast
around for other loyalties, among which an organization called
the Country party attracted some support. It was a warning for
the coalition to conciliate these numerous strays from its fold or
suffer the consequences. So, too, in the cities, as well as the Labor
vote, there was a body of opinion skeptical about the coalition.
A fifth of the people in the entirely urban constituencies voted for
various brands of independents—a symptom that urban business
interest disliked a coalition in which the farmers formed the
majority.

These chinks in the coalition's armor developed into gaping
fissures during the next four years. Though the depression was already serious in 1931, nobody then knew how severe or long-
lasting it was going to prove. Not until 1932 and 1933 was its
full intensity felt in New Zealand. Compared with what came
afterward, the fraction of the depression which preceded the
election merely resembled the less dangerous portion of the ice-
berg that shows above water. Nor did the ministry retain the confidence of any major group by its attempts to handle a situation
which confessedly lay beyond the remedy of any one government
in any one country. The downward spiralling in the overseas
prices of New Zealand's exports was not adequately offset by
legislation relieving mortgagees of their obligations. Unemployment, which mounted alarmingly, was not cured by halfhearted
public works schemes. Organized labor was still further alienated
by amendments to the Liberal industrial code making arbitration of disputes voluntary, not compulsory. Even financial orthodoxy could not balance its budgets by cutting down the meager
allowance for old pensions and reducing the grants for education
and other social services. Civil servants had their salaries slashed,
and shopkeepers suffered from the drastic deflationary policy
which reduced purchasing power. Businessmen felt themselves
tied to the farmers' apron strings and resented the ministry's subordination to rural interests. Legislation which intrusted new
activities to state departments was denounced by the right wing

as too socialist, by the left as an inadequate palliative. Finally, when unemployed men in desperation called attention to their plight by rioting in the main streets of Auckland, the government, imaginatively mindful of tumbrils and guillotines, of soviets and Siberia, curtailed civil liberties.

Meanwhile the Labor party, active in its opposition, profited from the coalition's growing unpopularity. The Labor program was modified by the omission of socialism and the substitution of measures which revived the old Liberal tradition. So much did the ministry fear the electoral verdict that in 1934 over Labor's protests they extended the life of Parliament by another year. Eventually in 1935 came the reckoning. Labor swept into power with over 390,000 votes (47 per cent of the total) and fifty-three seats. The coalition, which now presented itself as the National party, received 260,000 votes (or 31 per cent), and their seats dwindled to seventeen. Labor's strength was unchallenged in the cities, where its triumph was a foregone conclusion. More remarkable, however, was the accession to its ranks in the country areas, where it received a third of the votes. Among the small farmers of the North Island the Social Credit movement had recently secured a footing, just as it attracted the farmers in Alberta when the depression hit Canada. By its proposal to establish a "national credit authority," as well as by its promise of a guaranteed price for primary products, Labor now captured many of the rural protest-votes which already were discernible in 1931.

The National party suffered heavy losses in all categories of electorates. The higher the degree of urbanization in the constituency, the lower the proportion of National votes. The resentment against the government of the depression years was partly seen in the large numbers of votes cast for miscellaneous candidates both in town and in country. It was also dramatized by the intervention of an unsuccessful third party which assumed the title of Democrat. Led by a lawyer, who was mayor of Wellington, this group represented the right-wing protest against the late ministry. Throughout the whole Dominion the Democrats polled only 65,000 votes and won not a seat. But their activity was quite an important factor in enabling the Labor party to

capture as many as fifty-three seats with only 47 per cent of all
the votes. Actually twenty-two of these fifty-three seats were won
on a minority vote; and in fifteen of those twenty-two cases a
Democratic candidate contributed to the splitting of the non-
Labor vote. It is reasonable to assume that, had there been no
Democrats in the running, most of the votes cast for that party
would have gone to National candidates. That would have reduced the Labor majority in Parliament, while leaving unaltered their percentage of the popular vote. In a poll of 828,000
votes, such can be the effect of a mere 65,000 ballots if they are
distributed in districts where contests are keen and close. It is a
lesson which every party organizer learns some time or other
under the single-member district system.

Thus for the first time in any British country a Labor party held
office with a parliamentary representation that empowered it to
do whatever it chose, and up to 1947 Labor had stayed continuously in power for twelve years. It emerged from another election
in 1938 with a great increase in its popular majority. For nearly
four years until the outbreak of war and in the subsequent period
of postwar reconstruction, Labor had the opportunity to carry
out its policy under peacetime conditions. That policy has been
a mixed one because the political sources of Labor's majority
were themselves mixed. Among the Labor voters in 1935 were
trade-unionists (both conservative and radical) shopkeepers,
civil servants, professional people, pensioners and unemployed,
office workers, small farmers, and farm laborers. Many of these
did not want socialism. What they did want after six years of
privation was immediate security and an early return of prosperity. Any extensions of governmental power were welcomed if they
tended toward this result. Accordingly, before the outbreak of
World War II, the Labor ministry of New Zealand initiated a
new catalogue of public enterprises, amplifying many earlier-
established state activities and inaugurating some untried experiments.

Among instances of state ownership and operation (i.e., socialism in the strict sense) may be mentioned the acquisition by the
government of the Reserve Bank; the placing of the broadcasting
service under direct ministerial control; the marketing of speci-

fied primary products at home and abroad; and an ambitious program of constructing and letting houses. In the sphere left to private enterprise governmental controls were extended by the introduction of compulsory unionism and by development of secondary industries under license. But it was in the domain of social services that the most spectacular advances were made. Education, which suffered in the depression years from the niggardliness of an economy-minded ministry, received some welcome increments in its grants from the exchequer. The school age was extended upward and downward; milk was given to the children daily; new buildings were erected; and better salary scales were offered to teachers. Equally ambitious was the enactment in 1938 of the Social Security Act from which Lord Beveridge later incorporated certain features into his noteworthy plan for Britain. This great act consolidated various piecemeal measures of public assistance introduced in the four preceding decades. Setting out to accomplish a full program of social security from birth to death, it added new classes of benefits not previously granted, liberalized the qualifying requirements for benefits still subject to a means test, and increased the amounts paid out to individual recipients.[25]

When this act was placed on the statute-book in 1938 as the climax of three strenuous years of legislative activity, Labor's reelection was made doubly sure. Recovery from the depression was the final clinching argument; and, though opponents could hold that it was not Labor who created the rise in overseas prices, the government could retort that its policies had stimulated internal welfare and had contributed to a more equitable spread of prosperity's benefits. At an election in which a record number of persons voted, Labor gained 56 per cent of all the votes cast—9 per cent more than in 1935. In the cities and towns the support for Labor was overwhelming.[26] The farmers registered their approval of the marketing schemes and the guaranteed price by recording 10 per cent more of their votes for the government than

25. For a detailed study see my articles: "How Social Security Works in New Zealand," (British) *Journal of Public Administration*, XXII, No. 2 (1944), 74–86, and "The New Zealand Means Test: An Appraisal," *ibid.*, No. 4, pp. 131–36.

26. In the four biggest cities the government carried every constituency save two.

in 1935. In short, Labor predominated in urban areas and almost
halved the vote in the countryside. The National party, which
could offer nothing except a continuation of the same services at
a cheaper rate, was heavily outvoted. Relatively, however, its percentages compare favorably with those of 1935, since it absorbed
many of the miscellaneous votes and the Democrats had faded
out.

It should be noticed that the distribution of Labor's support
in 1938 was practically identical with that of the Liberals in 1890.
Fifty years apart two progressive parties won elections in which
they predominated in urban areas and were evenly matched
against their opponents in rural districts. Since the same pattern
was repeated, this suggests that Labor succeeded in reuniting the
two important economic groups which were once allied during
the Liberal ascendancy. In the intervening period of roughly
three decades (1905–35), the industrial workers and the small
farmers were in separate camps, and all that time no party, save
Reform in 1925, was able to win a convincing popular majority.
That was why party platforms so frequently resembled each
other. The alliance of 1890 was born of a depression. Between
1935 and 1938 the alliance was reconstituted in answer to another depression. It so happened that during each depression a
Conservative government was in power. Thus, when the voters
registered their discontent, they swung inevitably to the left. But
economic adversity has always reacted in New Zealand unfavorably to those in office, no matter to which wing they belonged.[27]
The Liberal downfall in 1911 was hastened by a slump in 1909,
to which Ward responded by those measures of economy which
usually make depressions worse. Again in the early twenties
Massey's reverse in 1922 followed upon the postwar slump.

Here, then, is the conditioning basis of New Zealand politics
and the clue to understanding its party history. There exists a
solid central bloc of voters who want security first and foremost
all the time. They will swing leftward only if times remain continuously bad and will gravitate back to conservatism with

27. The writer disagrees with the odd contention of Leicester C. Webb in
Government in New Zealand (Wellington: Department of Internal Affairs, 1940),
p. 23: "Generally speaking prosperity brings a swing to the left and economic adversity a swing back to the right."

prosperity. Seddon, who thoroughly understood his country's psychology, had this to say: "There is no doubt that outside of the colonies capitalists are afraid of the workers. This is not justified. My experience is that when a worker has a cottage of his own and a few pounds in the bank he becomes very conservative. Let want and anxiety for the morrow be removed from the worker's life and there is nothing to fear."[28] So in 1941 a prominent Labor leader commented to the writer: "Some people still think that the workers are seething for a chance of revolution. They're not. What they want is security—a job, a place to live, and something to eat." This solid central core, which holds the balance of power through its sheer voting numbers, is not, strictly speaking, a proletariat. It is composed of all people with small incomes and slender reserves—of industrial workers, small shopkeepers, the lower paid of the civil servants and schoolteachers, the small farmers, and farm laborers. Never revolutionary, sometimes experimental and disposed to try out a novelty, always anxious and insecure, these form the essence of New Zealand. Most accurately defined, they are sociologically and economically a lesser bourgeoisie. To unite all their component groups, and to keep them long united, requires first a depression of some magnitude and then a period of recovery. When economic adversity does bring them together, their political strength is overwhelming. It is their needs and desires, their attitudes and aspirations, which are responsible for the peculiar blend of state enterprise and state-controlled capitalism that characterizes New Zealand.

The outbreak of the second World War, in which New Zealand was the first of the Dominions to side with Britain, constituted a temporary setback to Labor's social program. Although the government pressed on with the inauguration of the medical benefits under its Social Security Act, the war was too costly to permit of other major increases in social service expenditure. Nevertheless, the requirements of total mobilization, and the threat of invasion in 1942, speeded up the drive toward a planned economy. All vital commodities—of which manpower was the scarcest—came under stringent control; and the Labor

28. Quoted by Drummond, *op. cit.*, p. 362.

party, which in the former war had strenuously opposed conscription, now conscripted virtually everything and everybody.

When a general election was held in 1943, the government
suffered from a series of handicaps. The public were irked by
many of the restrictions that were necessitated by total war and
sought an opportunity for displaying their ill-will. Particularly
irked were the farmers, who, being now relatively more prosperous, swung back to their normal political allegiance. What is
more, the Labor party experienced internal difficulties. Mr. J. A.
Lee, who had been a leader of the party's left wing, but was expelled in 1940, formed a movement of his own called Democratic
Soldier Labor. He set to work to pay off old scores, to attract away
the Labor party's left wing, and to split votes. Also, some of the
largest and most powerful trade-unions, particularly the miners,
jeopardized the government's political position by unauthorized
strikes. Thus when the vote was recorded, the Labor ministry,
though returned to office, slipped from its pinnacle of 1938. The
number of votes cast for Labor dropped by 74,000; their percentage of the total fell from 56 to 48; their seats in the House
were fewer by nearly one-fifth. In the cities and mainly urban
constituencies they were still the favored party, though their
margin of superiority was smaller than before. In the rural areas,
where previously they had divided the vote with their opponents,
the decline was severe. Less than two-fifths of the electorate in the
purely farming constituencies were pro-Labor.

The National party, on the other hand, gained both in votes
and in seats, and their popular backing increased in practically
all types of constituencies. It was evident, however, that the
electoral verdict was more of an admonishment to Labor than a
preference for National. Some of the public discontent and war
weariness expressed itself in voting not for the official opposition
but for a vast and weird variety of miscellaneous candidates under
strange labels. This particular election, indeed, attracted in the
seventy-six European constituencies no less than 268 candidates,
and twenty-two seats were won on a minority vote. As many as
128 of the defeated candidates polled less than the 25 per cent of
the votes, required by law, and forfeited their deposit of £10.

Among the unlucky ones were the members of the Democratic Soldier Labor party, all of whom, including Lee himself, were badly beaten. But though the votes for this Labor "splinter-group" amounted to only 4 per cent of the total, they were so distributed as to affect the result in certain closely contested constituencies.[29] To be precise, the National party won four of their seats because of the split in the Labor ranks. Thus in 1943, as in 1935, the defection of an extreme wing from a major party had quite a significant bearing on the final outcome.

One further aspect of the 1943 election requires mentioning. At that time a large number of New Zealanders were serving overseas in the armed forces. The forces' votes were separately recorded, and it is therefore possible to compare their political preferences with those of the people in New Zealand. Witness Table 15, which I have based upon the official returns.

It is evident from these figures that the official Labor party as well as the Democratic Soldier Labor party (which was led by a disabled soldier of the first World War) made a stronger appeal to servicemen than to civilians. Actually, in nineteen of the seventy-four European electorates that were contested, the candidate who led on the civilian vote did not lead on the armed forces' vote. In six of those nineteen cases the forces' vote swung the election to the candidate who was second choice among the civilians. All these six instances represented a gain for official Labor. What is the explanation of these facts? The Labor view is that the soldiers, being drawn from the younger male section of the population, were more progressive in their outlook and so preferred the party of the left. The Nationalists replied that most of the soldiers had been overseas for so long that they were out of touch with home conditions, that they voted for the picture they retained of a few years back, and that in any case they were presented mainly with Labor party publicity. Probably there is some truth on both sides. As in the wartime elections of other countries, the younger men tended toward a left-wing program. But it does also appear to be substantiated that the troops knew much more of the Labor platform (through the armed forces' newspaper and visiting ministers) than of that of the opposition.

29. Hamilton, Masterton, New Plymouth, and Waitemata.

The results of the election were a shock and a disappointment to the ministry which was perturbed over the split in its own ranks and over the marked hostility of the farmers. When the new Parliament assembled in 1944, the opposition, strengthened both numerically and qualitatively, harassed the government of whose members only four possessed real debating ability. For the first time since they had taken office, Labor was on the defensive and uncomfortable. In 1945, however, the government made a bold attempt to recapture the initiative. The ending of the long war in Europe provided the opportunity to prepare for peacetime recon-

TABLE 15

VOTES OF CIVILIANS AND ARMED FORCES IN THE ELECTION OF 1943*

PARTY	TOTAL VOTES		CIVILIAN VOTES		ARMED FORCES' VOTES	
	No.	Per Cent	No.	Per Cent	No.	Per Cent
National..............	390,343	43	359,021	44	31,322	35
Labor................	439,207	48	390,091	47	49,116	54
Democratic Soldier Labor................	40,423	4	34,241	4	6,182	7
Miscellaneous.........	41,397	5	37,674	5	3,723	4

* In the seventy-four European electorates that were contested.

struction, and the collapse of Japan later in the year facilitated the introduction of some further radical measures. Taken all in all, the legislative session of 1945 ranks as one of the most productive and most contentious in the history of New Zealand. As was the year of 1894 to the Liberals, so was 1946 the *annus mirabilis* of the Labor party. The bills that went on to the statute-book inaugurated such novel instances of state ownership and operation as the nationalization of the civil airways, of the linen-flax processing industry,[30] and of the Dominion's largest trading-bank.[31] More regulation of private enterprise was manifested by

30. A wartime, state-subsidized, innovation.

31. In this bank—the Bank of New Zealand—previous ministries of other parties had already acquired one-third of the shares and two-thirds of the appointees to the board of directors. For a fuller account of postwar legislation see my articles on "Democracy and Socialism in New Zealand," *American Political Science Review*, XLI, No. 2 (April, 1947), 306–13, and "Reconversion in Australia and New Zealand," *Journal of Politics*, IX, No. 2 (May, 1947), 225–39.

a minimum wage law and a full employment act. Social services
were extended by an ambitious scheme for Maori welfare and by
removing the means test from the family allowances. How closely
the grand strategy of all this legislation was linked with the next
election could be clearly seen in the amendment[32] to the electoral
law that wiped out the country quota—the measure which along
with the nationalization of the bank provoked the most stubborn
resistance of the opposition. The ministry, however, used all its
powers for "taking urgency" and jammed through its bills in
the rush of the last few weeks of the session. Similar tactics were
repeated the following year, when the Labor majority, acutely
mindful of the coming trial of strength, offered some reductions
in taxation, but did little that was strictly socialist in character
except to convert into a state undertaking the marketing in New
Zealand of imported petroleum.[33]

In November, 1946, the Dominion plunged into one of the
most hotly contested campaigns in the course of its history. So
strongly were the public aroused that as many as 95 per cent of
the registered European voters went to the polls. Unlike the
battle of the ballots three years earlier, the 1946 election was a
straight fight between the two big parties. On the Labor side, the
ranks had closed and the Democratic Soldier Labor party did not
enter the field. On the other side, the Nationalists reabsorbed
many of the miscellaneous candidatures and "splinter movements" that had blossomed and luxuriated in 1943. Only in eight
of the seventy-six European districts did more than two candidates present themselves. As compared with the 1,008,846 votes
recorded for Labor and National in those districts, the 1,932 votes
cast for independents (including Communists) were utterly negligible. The final tally revealed that the parties had divided
equally the seventy-six European constituencies, each winning
twenty-five seats in the North Island and thirteen in the South.
Labor led National in the popular vote by the slender margin of
18,590. In the North Island, as a matter of fact, the Nationalists
actually polled a few more votes than Labor; but in the South

32. See above, pp. 181–84.
33. All the oil consumed in the Dominion is imported.

Island, Labor secured a majority of just over 20,000. Although the urban and rural strengths can no longer be calculated as exactly as before,[34] it is evident from the returns that the National party had the solid backing of the rural areas. Of eleven secondary urban centers, six returned a Laborite and five a Nationalist. Out of thirty-two urban seats in the four chief cities, Labor secured twenty-six.

While the European voters, therefore, were divided equally, it was the Maoris who decided the issue. In the four Maori electorates, a majority of the voters, remembering the consideration and the appropriations they had received from the government, elected four Laborites who between them polled 11,200 votes more than their rivals. Thus the Labor ministry stayed in office with a narrow majority of four votes in the House of Representatives. But it was the members who represented the Polynesian race that held the balance of power!

The election of 1946, as is clear, continued the trend that was observable in 1943. The government's decline can be attributed to a number of factors: to the swing of the pendulum that will normally occur when a party has held office for a decade, to the resentment and irritations that a wartime administration must expect when the fighting stops, to the failure of the Labor leaders to bring in enough new and younger personnel at the top, and to a growing liberalization of the National party which itself is a tribute to Labor's earlier successes. The legislation of 1945 and 1946 was sufficient to stave off defeat but not enough to gain a victory. Indeed, had the Labor party not changed the electoral system in its own favor, it would almost certainly have been beaten. The leader of the opposition was probably correct in his estimate that "alterations to electoral boundaries cost us at the very least three seats."[35]

Such, then, was the divided electorate, and such the divided Parliament, which faced three difficult years fraught with tangled issues of international reconstruction and domestic development.

34. See above, p. 184.

35. Press statement reported in the *Evening Post* (Wellington), December 9, 1946.

Party Organization

To maintain its continuous identity over a length of years, a party must represent politically the social needs, both articulate and inarticulate, of major groups whose material interests coincide to a large degree. A party will so generalize the economic aims and mental stereotypes of its supporters that they can be idealized as fundamental principles. To these principles it will attune its public statements, and, according to its standpoint, it will look to preserve or to regenerate the existing social order. Wise party leaders know from experience that their programs and policy declarations, their manifestoes and their platforms, have their political use, even if that be merely to provide an opiate to the skeptical and propaganda food for the faithful. But the wares which the party displays in the window are not necessarily identical with what it actually sells across the counter. An opportunistic party—and what political party has ever attained success in any country without some measure of opportunism?—will adjust its vision of long-term ideals to the demands of the transient hour. In a world in which the rapidity of change appears the only constant element in the structure of society, parties must needs respond to the impatience and anxieties of the people they serve. Better to grasp the morsel of prosperity here and now than plan the blueprints of a far-off promised land. Thus the strategy of distant goals is whittled down to the tactics and maneuvers of the moment. Regarding their own triumph as essential to the national well-being, parties take a practical view and make power their first objective. To win the coming election, and then to stay in office—these are the urgent, pressing needs.

The business of the opposition, as Disraeli said, is to oppose. A party out of power will therefore inveigh against the maladministration or the corruption of the government. It may insinuate that jobs and contracts are obtained through favoritism and may recommend reform of the civil service. It may assert that the allocation of public works among electoral districts is politically engineered and will propose, in the name of sound finance, a curtailment of borrowing and a reduction in public expenditure.

It will advocate the remodeling of any institutional arrangements which work for the time being to its own disadvantage. If its parliamentary seats are less than the number warranted by its popular votes, it will campaign for proportional representation. If an upper house has been filled with its rival's nominees, it will clamor for constitutional reform. Should the ministry dominate Parliament, the opposition will cry dictatorship; and, should the government be unsure of its majority, it will plead for leadership and stability. Finally when the opposition reaps its victory and positions are reversed, it may find itself doing much the same as what it previously condemned. Once it is established as the government, a party will condone any procedures and institutions which do not obstruct its plans and will merely insure that the benefits accruing from its tenure of office are distributed among its own supporters.

Such is an impressionistic study of the modern party system when stripped of the protective coloring that ceremonial formalism and constitutional platitudes afford. In most democratic countries most of the time most parties would fit the general pattern of the picture just sketched. Between the *Realpolitik* of Leviathan and the Utopia of government by the people and for the people lies a gulf which reformers, rejecting the defeatism of the cynics, ever seek to bridge. Modern politics, like total war, leaves nobody unaffected. Each individual is either a participant in or a recipient of the processes of government. Enveloping all within its ambit, majority rule embraces the commonplace and even the sordid, along with much that is noblest in the life of the community. Ours are the politics of large numbers, and for that very reason we are faced with difficulties from which earlier and simpler societies were freed. The sheer size of the modern state makes good organization essential for political success. Organization is the framework, giving structure and form to the collective aims and activities of clustering millions. It is this feature which distinguishes the modern party from its nineteenth-century ancestor. Party organization—a relatively recent growth—has exorcised some of the old devils from the body politic but has invoked others that are new and, as yet, untamed.

It was not until the extension of the franchise multiplied the number of voters whose wishes had to be consulted that parties found the need and the occasion for organizing themselves and their supporters. In Britain the national organization of the Conservative and Liberal parties originated as a direct result of the second Reform Act of 1867. The newly enfranchised voter was urged to register. Obliging party managers helped the uninitiated to enrol and then offered them guidance in exercising their newly acquired privilege. So, too, in New Zealand the widening of the suffrage encouraged parties to organize their followers if elections were to be won. That is the reason the democratization of the vote was described in chapter viii as the root cause of the modern changes in the political system. A huge electorate is merely an amorphous crowd unless parties exist to group together those who are like-minded and to tender rival bids for the attraction of waverers. When the electorate came to comprise the whole adult population, parties emerged as the instrument for performing this function.

While party organization was the outgrowth of these causes, it became itself the starting-point for further political change. Executive committees, secretariats, conferences, and constitutions are now the wonted paraphernalia of the party system. Those of the voters who profess a fixed political allegiance are linked by the party organization with their representatives whom they elect to the nation's Parliament. But therein lies the crux. What is the relation between the citizens who cast the ballots and those who represent their will in the legislature? Who really determines policy? Who controls whom? Is the decisive voice to be that of the parliamentary party or of the nation-wide organization of supporters? Those were the questions which in Britain were first raised to the forefront of practical politics by Lord Randolph Churchill when he sought unsuccessfully through the medium of the National Conservative Association to dominate the premier, Lord Salisbury. In the United Kingdom control of the party's representatives inside the legislature by its supporters outside has never yet been carried to the same lengths as in the United States. American democracy has too often witnessed, particularly in state and municipal politics, the usurpation and abuse of power by extra-legal bosses, rings, and machines. Under its cabinet form of government New Zealand has approximated to the British model and has avoided the worst excesses of boss rule and machine politics. It would, however, be an error of interpretation to underestimate in New Zealand, or for that matter in Britain, the importance of the role which party organization has played. Both Bryce, summarizing the impressions gleaned in 1912, and Morrell, writing in 1935 before Labor had attained office, minimize the significance of party organization in this democracy, while admitting an exception in the case of the Labor party.[36] Such views require adjustment, not only because Labor has now become the majority party, but also because organization was far more effective even in the twenties than has often been supposed. Many are the general elections of modern New Zealand whose results have been considerably modified by good or bad organization.

Like so much else in this country, the growth of parties has reflected the personality of one man, Richard John Seddon. His long supremacy was bolstered by clever mobilizing of his support in all constituencies. But the nexus between the parliamentary Liberals and the voters lay in the personal strength of the leader. Seddon never desired and never achieved a cohesive national association of Liberal groups. Local Liberal associations, however, did exist in the principal cities and in other electoral districts where they predated his accession to office. It was sufficient for him to bind each locality to himself by separate ties without connecting them to one another. Seddon's attitude toward local gatherings of partisans was expressed soon after he became premier when the Liberal Association in Auckland drafted a fourteen-article memorandum to which Liberal candidates in the election of 1893 were to subscribe. Considering their program too extreme, the premier told his supporters that "it was his function to lead the party of which he was the head, and he made them clearly understand that while he held that position he would decline to be led by any section of the people."[37] To the

36. See James Bryce, *Modern Democracies* (New York: Macmillan Co., 1921), II, 315–16, and W. P. Morrell, *New Zealand* (London: Ernest Benn, Ltd., 1935), pp. 224–28.
37. Drummond, *op. cit.*, pp. 176–77.

Liberal party Seddon was his own party manager, executive, and constitution; and all that one tireless man could efficiently do he did. With Seddon's supremacy, the Liberal organization lived and brought in victories. With his death, it died.

Frequently more than one candidate affecting the same party label offered himself for election in the same constituency. Nowadays it is the function of a central party organization to prevent such vote-splitting which inevitably aids the other side. Seddon, however, who had nothing to fear from the Conservative opposition, was content to make it known which of the Liberal candidates had his blessing, and usually that guaranteed their victory.[38] After 1906 as the opposition gathered strength under Massey, Ward sought to retain his vanishing votes by central direction of his supporters in the localities. In 1908 a member of Parliament protested to the prime minister for intervening in the choice of candidates at a by-election. Ward justified his action with the retort: "It is quite a proper thing for the leader of either party during an election contest to take upon his shoulders the responsibility attaching to the position of leadership, and if there are two or more candidates on one side to endeavour to get one or more to retire in favour of the other."[39]

It was during the twenties that organization and campaign methods assumed new forms. The immediate stimulus was provided both by the co-existence of three contending parties and by the increase in the number of potential voters. The means was found in the development of broadcasting and of advertising techniques. The election of 1925 proved convincingly that thorough organization, centrally directed and locally executed, could attract bigger majorities. A widespread publicity campaign boosted the qualities of the new Reform leader. "The Man Who Gets Things Done" and "Coats Off with Coates" were among the slogans employed. In 1928 the Liberal comeback was largely due to clever organization, carried out in an especially efficient manner in Auckland. The Liberal candidates received material

38. On one occasion a newly elected Liberal representative referred in Parliament to "my constituency." Audibly Seddon interrupted: "Your constituency! It's mine! I put you in" (told to the writer by a member of Parliament who was present).

39. *P.D.*, CXLIV (1908), 616.

for their speeches from a central office and were coached in their platform methods. This was even the subject of caustic references in the Parliament chosen at that election: "If I read the speeches of one [United party] candidate, and then those of others," said an opponent, "it was found that every one read exactly the same. They have a speech-making factory somewhere; and the speeches are very well written, I admit."[40]

Once the practice was started, and its value demonstrated by results, every party was forced into imitation. In 1931, 1935, 1938, and 1946, canvassing, advertising, and propaganda were extensively conducted. "Educational" work has thus become an important function of the local branches in between elections; and, when an election draws near, the central headquarters issue a regular flood of leaflets, pamphlets, and posters. Prominent members of each party speak in key electorates where the issue is doubtful and the contest keen. Radio time is allocated to the rivals. Newspapers carry full-page announcements of promises and photographs of the candidates. Hoardings and handbills exhort the voter. In 1938 the campaign was vigorously fought. The daily press was then anti-Labor, practically without exception. Broadcasting facilities, however, were available to both sides, since that is a state monopoly in New Zealand. Labor issued its leaflets, among them one with "constitutional democracy" for its keynote and "written especially for farmers, shopkeepers, merchants, professional men and all who render useful service to the community." "Economic security and social justice" was the party's watchword. The Nationalists printed pamphlets in which "these socialists" were excoriated, while "peace, prosperity, and security" were offered as a consequence of a Labor defeat. There can be no doubt that Labor's victories in 1935 and 1938 were as much helped by its good organization as were the Reform triumph of 1925 and the Liberal renaissance of 1928. Organization does not of itself produce electoral victories, but popular trends can be intensified, wavering voters can be captured, and a win can be made into a landslide by the party whose organization is superior to that of its rivals. This additional element can make

40. *P.D.*, CCXXI (1929), 298.

a doubtful contest certain and a certain one doubly so. On that point New Zealand experience is conclusive.

But all this apparatus and machinery need money. A modern election cannot be fought and won without its campaign fund. The essence of party organization, therefore, is its method of financing. To the truth of this let the Liberal party in the twenties bear witness. At the close of the last war the financial weakness of this party was a serious handicap at election time. Viewing the Liberals as a spent force, the moneyed members of the community did not wish to bestow their contributions where they were unlikely to yield a profit. The parliamentary leader of the party, Forbes, complained after the election of 1922: "We have not had the money at our command that our opponents possessed. For them money has been poured out like water to defeat the opposing candidates. . . . . There is no force able to do so much in an election as unlimited funds."[41] Three years afterward, when the Liberals' defeat was even more severe, their organizer stated: "From the beginning the want of funds prevented us from taking the platforms in reply to Ministers, who did a vast amount of travelling."[42] On the other hand, in 1928, when the Liberals had ample sources of finance, their organization was efficient and their electoral results brought the party back to power. More than finance is needed to win an election, but without finance success can rarely be achieved.

In all democratic countries, New Zealand included, the crux of the problem is this: Who supplies the funds to the political parties? Usually the answer to this question, though it be of vital significance to the operation of government, is shrouded in mystery. Democracy prides itself, and deservedly, on the measure of publicity and openness which surrounds the conduct of its affairs. Yet party finance is too often regarded as a private matter which none but a few may know. In Britain the Labor party has issued public statements of the subscriptions to its funds; the Conservatives have not. In the United States the funds collected for presidential campaigns are duly made public, and federal laws now impose a maximum of expenditure which no party may exceed.

41. *P.D.*, CXCIX (1923), 91.
42. *Evening Post* (Wellington), November 6, 1925.

But there are loopholes in the laws, and it is well known that various cash contributions are made which do not find their way into the published lists.[43] New Zealand has no rule, in either its law or custom, requiring a public scrutiny of party finances. It is difficult to say of this country with either precision or certainty who are the contributors and how much they pay. Rumors, however, abound after every election that this person or that firm has supplied a big donation to a particular party. Other stories allege that certain astute business companies ingratiate themselves all around by secretly contributing to both parties. Even the practice known in Britain as "the sale of honors" had its counterpart in New Zealand during the twenties. Frequently, too, it is insinuated that donations are the payment for governmental favors received or expected. Such are the episodes which will be recounted by anyone who claims to be "in the know." Party funds remain a twilight topic where all can whisper and none can prove.

On the Labor side this at least is public knowledge that there is the closest connection both in organization and in finance between the trade-unions and the political party. The advent to power of a Labor government enormously strengthened the union movement both by promoting greater internal unity and by widening its membership. In 1937 the Alliance of Labor, to which many of the big industrial unions were affiliated, was amalgamated with the older Trades Union and Labor Councils, composed of craft unions which had clung to their independent identity. Together they coalesced into a new Federation of Labor. The merger took long to negotiate, since the smaller craft unions of skilled workers feared to be smothered by the larger industrial groups of the unskilled.[44] Not only has the union movement ceased to be a house divided against itself but it has also enlarged its rooms to take in more boarders. For the Labor government made membership in a union compulsory, arguing that workers who received those benefits of higher wages and shorter hours for

43. See, e.g., V. O. Key, Jr., *Politics, Parties, and Pressure Groups* (2d ed.; New York: Thomas Y. Crowell Co., 1947), chap. xv.

44. As a concession to such anxieties, the craft unions were eventually granted higher voting strength at the annual trade-union conference than the numerical proportion of their membership.

which unions had fought should belong to the organizations responsible for that improvement.

Compulsory unionism, which has greatly extended the coverage of the trade-unions and has brought some huge new groups like the clerical workers into existence, has its bearing on the question of party finance. The Labor party is officially composed of unions, of local party branches, and of individual subscribers. Affiliated unions pay dues to the party amounting to one shilling per annum for each member—a fact that is mentioned in the party constitution and in the financial statements of the unions themselves.[45] Although union contributions are by no means the only source of Labor funds, they remain the largest, the most regular, and the most dependable item in the party revenues. Through their financial dominance, therefore, as well as through their numerical majority, the unions inevitably preponderate in all decisions on Labor strategy and policies. The conversion of the party from militancy to parliamentarism proceeded step by step with a similar switch in the unions from syndicalism to Fabianism. There is a strong tie-up between the personnel of the trade-union leadership and the parliamentarians. Leading positions within the party, including the chairmanship, are held by prominent trade-unionists. Many of the Labor ministers have been active in their past careers as union secretaries. The executives of the party and the unions hold joint meetings from time to time, and, since the Labor government has been in power, these meetings have been reinforced by the presence of the cabinet. The annual conference of the Federation of Labor is held a few weeks before that of the Labor party, and some of the delegates are the same on both occasions.

In practice there has been a much closer working relationship between the Labor cabinet and the executive of the Federation than between the cabinet and the party organization outside Parliament. Its early constitutions made the annual conference of delegates from all local party branches the supreme governing body of the Labor party. Of recent years, however, the conference has lost rather than gained in power. Because it convenes only

45. Thus between 1936 and 1941 the Wellington branch of the large clerical employees' union contributed over £1,200 to the party.

annually and lasts a mere week, and because its members are drawn from all parts of New Zealand and are often strangers to each other, the conference cannot be as potent a body as the cabinet or the parliamentary caucus. A convention meeting at long intervals—witness the Supreme Soviet in the U.S.S.R.—cannot govern. Thus the supremacy of the conference tends normally to be formal rather than real. On rare occasions, though, the conference may assert itself, as when in 1945 the majority of the delegates forced the cabinet and the reluctant minister of finance to agree to nationalize the Bank of New Zealand. But usually Labor's fortunes are determined by the cabinet, the caucus, and the executive of the Federation of Labor.

A feature of the Labor movement on which all observers have commented is the tightness of its discipline. The party is highly centralized, for it is the national executive which controls the campaign funds and approves the selection of parliamentary candidates recommended by the local branches.[46] The central executive does not always indorse the candidate nominated by the local Labor Representation Committee for the constituency. Nor does it permit open dissent, either in Parliament or outside, from the policies officially laid down for the time being. Expulsions of nonconformists from the party have occurred more than once, the most spectacular case being that of J. A. Lee, formerly parliamentary undersecretary to the finance minister, in 1940. In the Labor movement generally it is usually fairly simple to enforce the compliance of a recalcitrant backbencher because few Labor candidates can afford to pay their election expenses out of their own pocket. Complaints are voiced both within the party and without that the degree of central discipline is excessive. But it is worth recalling one point which mitigates this criticism. The New Zealand Labor party is not alone in this respect. Labor parties of other countries—including the British party which once expelled Sir Stafford Cripps—are cast in the same mold. The reason is partly historical, partly economic. The Labor movement is composed of people who are mostly poor or else have slender means. Their strength lies in their numbers, and

46. For the election of 1946 the central executive actually chose the local candidates, though after consultation with the branches.

their only cogent weapon is their solidarity. If Labor sacrifices its internal unity, it loses everything. That is the reason for Labor discipline. At times it may be coercive and not in New Zealand alone. But without it no Labor party or trade-union movement could ever have been built up or could continue to survive. "Scabs," "blacklegs," "traitors," and "independents" are unpopular on the Labor side because of the movement's long historical struggle for recognition and its precarious financial resources.

From the aspect of organization, the National party, descendant of Reform and Liberal, forms a contrast to Labor. It can be described as a rather loosely knit federation of local associations. Central control and discipline tend to be less rigid than with its political rival. Parliamentary candidates are chosen locally, and their expenses are often locally financed. The party leader may, however, arbitrate in a local dispute, as happened in 1941 in the selection of a candidate for an Auckland constituency. Access to the wealth that is scattered through the country among prosperous farmers and well-to-do businessmen gives the local National organizations a measure of independence denied to Labor. While the National party criticizes the link between Labor and the trade-unions, it does not lack its own contacts with powerful interests even though these contacts be less highly formalized. Thus if the Labor cabinet and party executive consult jointly with union leaders, so do National party leaders with representatives of the banks, the Farmers' Union, the Manufacturers' Federation, and the chambers of commerce. Each party has its own economic backing that reaches into the sphere of industry, agriculture, and finance. The Nationalists enjoy the strategic advantage of controlling virtually every newspaper[47] and a large portion of the nation's financial resources. Internal harmony, however, is not always easy to secure even among those united by a common interest to conserve what they possess. Just as Labor's followers are divided between right and left wings, between craft and industrial unions, so the National party contains its own inner conflicts. The urban business interests are still hard to reconcile with those of the farmers. The cities are themselves

47. Until 1946 there was no Labor daily.

split into manufacturers' and importers' groups, into big business and small. Among the farmers is a classic cleavage between sheep-owners and dairymen, the former sometimes regarding them-selves as a rural aristocracy and disdaining the "cow-cockies." To build a stable majority out of such diversity is the task con-fronting National party strategists. If the great problem for Labor is to prevent defection on the left and hold the powerful unions in line, so the principal headache of their opponents is to unite the farmers with the city businessmen and keep them united. As the past history of New Zealand shows, many a party and many a government has been more harmed by its friends, or near-friends, then by its enemies and has gone from power when splits developed within its own midst. For the New Zealand voter the choice lies between one political group whose aims are those of a social and economic democracy and whose organization is highly centralized and disciplined and another group whose organiza-tion is looser and freer but whose counsels are dominated by the vested interests of property, business, and finance.

Can a democratic system of politics be achieved through the interaction of two such bodies? Some modern critics of the democratic party system react so intensely against its abuses that they prefer to be rid of parties root and branch. But that would be no solution, since, with all their faults, parties do fill a real need. The size of the twentieth-century democracy requires its party groupings, and this is true even in a country of one and three-quarter million people. The peaceful alternation in office between opposed parties achieves in the long run a democratic dialectic which differs from the other dialectics of the Hegelian or Marxian variety. Certain current defects could be removed if more publicity were attached to party affairs, for the conception that the internal management of a party's business is purely its own concern is a juristic fiction devoid of political validity. Fur-thermore, the parties which seek to operate the democratic process must themselves be organized in concord with de-mocracy's principles. To democratize party organization is only one aspect of the question that is vital to the large-scale govern-ments of modern times. Dewey has well expressed in general terms truths that are equally applicable to the state, to its parties, to its legislatures, and to its civil services: "Individuals can find the security and protection that are prerequisites for freedom only in association with others—and then the organization these associations take on, as a means of securing their efficiency, limits the freedom of those who have entered them. . . . . We have now a kind of molluscan organisation, soft individuals within and a hard constrictive shell without."[48] How to harden the individuals and to soften the shell, both to the right degree, remains one of the outstanding political problems of our century.

48. John Dewey, *Freedom and Culture* (London: Allen & Unwin, 1940), p. 166.

CHAPTER X

THE CABINET

Duration in Office

OF ALL the contrasts in the operation of the New Zealand political system before 1890 and afterward, none is more immediately striking than the relative duration of ministries. Let the figures speak first. They reveal that in the fifty-six years from 1891 to 1947 fifteen different cabinets are officially listed in the records. Each, therefore, lasted in power, on an average, for three years and nine months. Expressed in tabular form, the analysis of cabinet longevity reads thus:

Duration in Office	No. of Ministries
Under two months....................	2
Two months to one year..............	1
One year to two years................	2
Two years to three years.............	1
Over three years.....................	9

Six ministries have remained in power for under three years, while nine survived for over three. Of those which were the longest lived, Seddon's cabinet held office for thirteen years, while Ward's first ministry (1906–12), Massey's third ministry (1919–25), and the Fraser ministry (1940——) each received a tenure of more than five unbroken years. Compare these data with those of the earlier period when twenty-five ministries had an average duration of under eighteen months and when only five kept in office for more than three years.[1] Admittedly, when the nineteenth-century figures were interpreted in the light of cabinet history, it was seen that ministerial instability, though excessive, was not quite so serious as the bare statistics indicated. A certain degree of continuity underlay many of the changes. Similarly a study of the modern changes will prove that cabinet longevity,

1. See below, p. 75.

which appears remarkable even on the showing of the figures, has been still greater in actual fact. It is only right to make allowance for the two ministries in the twentieth century whose duration is listed officially at under two months. Neither of these short-lived cabinets was due to any parliamentary upheaval or electoral defeat, nor in the realistic terms of party politics was either of them a distinctly new ministry. Both were stopgap ministries put in to fill a brief interregnum between the death of one premier and the appointment of his successor. When Seddon died in 1906, Ward, his principal lieutenant, happened to be away in Europe attending the Conference of the Universal Postal Union. Until he returned to New Zealand, the next most senior member of the Liberal cabinet, Hall-Jones, temporarily assumed the premiership. Likewise, in 1925, when Massey died, there was a slight uncertainty as to whether the Reform party would choose Coates or not.[2] For a fortnight, therefore, the senior minister, Bell, who was seventy-four years of age, acted as premier until the party caucus made up its mind.

Instead of counting the number of ministries, one can learn more from a survey of the occasions when their party composition was altered. On the fall of Atkinson's government in 1891, the Liberals came into office. For the next twenty-one years (1891–1912), it was a continuous ministry of Liberals that held power. In the official records, however, this continuous Liberal cabinet is labeled as five different governments under the successive leaderships of Ballance, Seddon, Hall-Jones, Ward, and Mackenzie. The year in which the first real change of ministry in the modern period occurred was 1912. Every single member of the Reform cabinet was new to office. There was a complete change of personnel and a partial change of policies. This Reform cabinet lasted until 1915, when, as a gesture of wartime unity, a coalition was formed. The coalition ended in 1919, after which cabinets composed purely of Reformers governed the country for a decade. The party composition of the ministry was once more altered in 1928, when the Liberals took office, first under Ward and later under Forbes. From 1931 to 1935 there was a new cabinet based

2. W. D. Stewart, *Sir Francis H. D. Bell: His Life and Times* (Wellington: Butterworth & Co., 1937), p. 237.

upon the depression coalition of Reformers and Liberals. In 1935 the Labor ministry was formed, and again the change of office-holders was complete. Since then a Labor cabinet has been in power, led by Savage until 1940 and after him by Fraser. Thus the ministerial "ins" and "outs" of the last fifty years fall into a very few phases. The successive ministries have been Liberal (1891–1912), Reform (1912–15), Coalition (1915–19), Reform (1919–28), Liberal (1928–31), Coalition (1931–35), and Labor (since 1935). Half-a-dozen shifts in over half a century! Surely a genuine symptom of political and economic stability!

The reasons for the contrast with the earlier period readily suggest themselves. The same cause which promoted the long and continuous ascendancy of successive parties—to wit, the slow swing of the economic pendulum—has contributed to the longer duration of ministries. Parties which are enjoying repeated electoral victories do not go about changing their leadership. The development of party organization has itself tended to bolster the authority of the cabinet, since, as was observed in the previous chapter, the legislative representatives of the party have customarily controlled the extra-parliamentary organization. Also the emergence in modern times of leaders who acquire national prestige has itself encouraged longer-lived cabinets. The premier is a party leader, and when the electorate is swayed by a popular personage—a Seddon, a Massey, or a Savage—his ministers and parliamentary followers are likely to share in reflected glory. Because of the party organization now established in every constituency of the country, the modern prime minister and his colleagues enjoy an expectance of far longer political life than could Vogel, Grey, or Atkinson.

Although the party complexion of the whole cabinet has changed but seldom, it is natural that continuous ministries of the same party will exhibit internal changes of personnel. When cabinets are of such long duration, deaths, illness, old age, and occasional disagreements over new policy issues will cause periodic reshuffles. In 1911 New Zealand still had a Liberal cabinet in office, but its membership was far different from what it had been in 1891. In the critical nineties the outstanding members of the Liberal ministry were Ballance, Seddon, Reeves, McKenzie,

and Ward. Of these, Ballance died in 1893; Reeves left in 1896 to
become New Zealand's agent-general in London; McKenzie retired in 1900 and died soon afterward; and Ward had to resign
from the cabinet in 1896 because of financial embarrassments,
but he returned to it in 1899. From 1900 to 1906 Seddon and
Ward were the only survivors in power of the five big men who
had steered the ministry through its early fights. When Ward
became premier after Seddon's death, he seized the opportunity
to infuse new blood into the cabinet. Men like McNab, Fowlds,
Findlay, and Hogg could contribute fresh ideas to a jaded administration. McNab and Hogg, however, held views so divergent from the premier's that their resignations were requested in
1908 and 1909, respectively. In 1912 the abortive ministry of
Thomas Mackenzie attempted a final reshuffle of the now effete
Liberals with an almost complete change of personnel.

The long Reform ascendancy also produced its inner ministerial permutations. In the years before 1914 the leading ministers were Massey and Bell, to whom Allen, Herries, Fraser, and
Herdman filled subordinate roles. After the war and the interlude of the coalition, the cabinet was reconstituted to satisfy the
demands of some malcontents and of some able younger men.
Herdman, the attorney-general, was placed on the bench of the
Supreme Court, and Allen, Herries, and Fraser, had all surrendered their portfolios by 1921. Their places were taken by a
group of new men, among whom Coates and Stewart were the
two most conspicuous for talent. Thus reformed, the Reform
cabinet lasted, still under the masterful guidance of Massey and
Bell, until the premier's death in 1925. When Coates became
prime minister, those on whose support he chiefly relied were
Bell and Stewart. The cabinet received further remodeling at the
hands of its younger leader. As Stewart describes it: "Coates set
about the difficult task of reconstructing his Ministry. The work
was carried out in piecemeal fashion spread over several months.
This slow process aroused strong criticism even on the part of papers that supported the Government. . . . . By May 4 [1926]
four new Ministers had been appointed and there had been a
general redistribution of portfolios."[3] In fourteen years the Re-

3. *Ibid.*, p. 246.

form cabinet had been almost completely changed from what it was in 1912.

Returning to power in 1928 with the too-optimistic title of "United," the Liberals supplied New Zealand with the most fantastic cabinet it had seen for over sixty years. Ward, re-emerging as premier after a long political eclipse, trailed with him clouds of glory from the Seddonian era. Only one other of his ministers, Wilford, had previously held a cabinet post. The native unsuitability of some of the remainder was heightened by their inexperience. Certain of the newly chosen ministers had never before sat in Parliament, let alone in the cabinet; and, when they first addressed the House as ministers responsible for administering important departments, they were at the same time making their maiden speeches.[4] Before long, Ward died, and Wilford took the dignified position of New Zealand's high commissioner[5] in Britain. That left a cabinet nominally led by Forbes but largely controlled by Masters, the party's leader in the upper house. When Liberals and Reform coalesced in 1931, leading lights among the ministers were Forbes, Masters, Coates, and Stewart. But early in 1933 Stewart, then minister of finance, resigned on the issue of devaluing the New Zealand pound to which he was opposed. Coates succeeded to his portfolios and remained the dominant member of the ministry, although Forbes was the titular premier.

The Labor government, which up to 1946 had already held power for eleven years, also underwent its inward reorganization. Prime Minister Savage died in 1940; Martin, the minister of agriculture, retired from politics in 1941; Armstrong, the minister of public works, died in 1942; Webb, the minister of mines and of labor retired in 1946. In each case as a consequence there was a newcomer to the cabinet. Other changes have been due to differences of opinion within the party. It was an open secret in 1939 that parliamentary Laborites included a left and a right wing. To the right wing belonged the prime minister and almost the entire cabinet, the older leaders of the party who had fought

4. See the reference of Taverner (minister of railways) to "our duty as new Ministers of the Crown, and, so far as I am personally concerned, a new Parliamentarian" (*P.D.*, CCXXI [1929], 353–54). Cf. the similar remark of Stallworthy, minister of health (*ibid.*, pp. 344–45).

5. Formerly called "agent-general."

its battles in the days of its weakness and had struggled for trade-union privileges in the teeth of hostile Conservative governments. These were men who for the most part had worked in industry and had served the labor movement as organizers. On the left wing were gathered some younger men who were outside the cabinet but who challenged the majority in the cabinet by proposing in the caucus more radical credit schemes and more thoroughgoing measures of socialization. Leading left-wingers were a minister of religion, Nordmeyer; a doctor, Macmillan; a journalist, Lee; and a lawyer, Barnard, who held the speakership. In the cabinet itself, the minister of lands, Langstone, was the one who approximated nearest to their views. These political divergences came to a head early in 1940, when Lee was dismissed from his post as parliamentary undersecretary to the minister of finance and was soon after expelled from the party at the annual conference.[6] Thereupon the speaker resigned from the party of his own accord and associated himself with Lee. The Labor cabinet, reconstructed by the new premier, Fraser, admitted to the rank of minister one of the other left-wingers, Macmillan, who had stayed within the party. When Macmillan subsequently resigned and went out of politics, Nordmeyer took his place in the cabinet and soon proved himself one of its ablest members. In 1943 Langstone's disagreements with his colleagues led him to resign from the ministry. Later in that year, although Labor won the general election, the minister of agriculture, Barclay, was defeated in a rural constituency and a substitute had to be found. By 1946 the three cleverest men—Fraser, Nash, and Nordmeyer—were bearing the main burden of government.

The Cabinet and the Electorate

The longevity of these modern ministries appears all the more remarkable in view of the greater frequency of modern elections. In the thirty-six years from 1855 to 1890 there were nine general elections, and each Parliament lasted on an average for four years. But from the election of 1890 up to that of 1946, there have been only eighteen general elections in fifty-seven years, which makes

6. In addition to disagreeing with the cabinet's policy, Lee had published a personal attack on the prime minister when he was dying.

an average duration of three years and two months for each Parliament. Voters in the twentieth century have had more frequent opportunities of ousting their government, yet they have seldom put their ballots to that use. At the great majority of elections since 1890 the people have indorsed the government of the day. At a few elections (e.g., in 1911 and 1928) the popular verdict has been indeterminate. Only rarely (e.g., in 1935) has the citizen body registered a sharp disapproval of those in power. Nor has Parliament shown any greater inclination than the electorate to unseat those whom the people have placed in office. Backbenchers' revolts would seem to be as extinct in New Zealand as the moa.

Before 1890, as a general rule, the ministry was subordinate to the House of Representatives. Nowadays it is normally the electorate that decides from which group of parliamentarians the cabinet shall be selected. Seldom in the last fifty years has the choice of a ministry resulted from the maneuvers of parliamentary parties and of independent representatives. The question of which party should constitute the government is left to the House only in the rare cases of an indecisive election. Thus, up to 1908 there was a clear public mandate for the Liberals. Even in 1896 they were the preferred party, although they led in that election by only a slight margin. The results in 1911 were unsatisfactorily vague. It was clear that the Liberals were losing favor. But they gained more votes than Reform even though they took less seats. So it happened that in 1912 the House had to settle the party composition of the ministry. First the Liberals tried and failed. Finally, Reform succeeded in establishing a majority sufficient to move onto the treasury benches. In 1914 it was evident that the ministry had won fresh public support, and it stayed in power. Next year it was again public opinion (together with the promptings of the governor-general), and not the action of Parliament, which spurred the creation of a wartime coalition.

During the twenties the three-party system complicated both the electoral results and the ensuing parliamentary relationships. In 1919 and 1922, although Reform appeared the most favored party, its votes were less than the combined totals cast for other parties. Especially in the awkward Parliament that lasted from

1923 to 1925 the ministry's position was shaky and precarious. Massey clung to office because two independents and one Liberal voted with him on every no-confidence motion in order to prevent Labor from controlling the balance of power.[7] Such were the effort and strain that they weakened the premier's health and hastened his death in 1925. On one occasion he remarked to Stewart, then his colleague in the cabinet: "Never try to carry on a Government of only two or three; it is hell all the time."[8] At the election of 1925 there could be no doubt that prevailing opinion wanted a Reform ministry. But in another three years' time votes and seats were so distributed that any pair of parties had a majority over the third. The electorate was as confused in its preferences as were the politicians. Inevitably, therefore, the establishment of a ministry was thrown upon the members of the lower house, who produced an alliance of Liberals and Labor up to 1930 and after that a coalition between Liberals and Reform. At the succeeding elections from 1931 to 1943 the voters did supply a clear decision, and no discretion in the choice of a ministry was left to Parliament. But in 1946 it needed the Maori votes to tip the scales for Labor's benefit.

Most ministries of modern times, in short, have won their mandate directly from the people and not from Parliament. What the people generally do at election time is to show their like or dislike of whosoever happens to be in power. The voting revolves principally around the merits and demerits of those in office. To a less extent the public simultaneously reveals its attitude toward the opposition. Electoral verdicts are usually recorded for or against the "ins" and indirectly for or against the "outs." The elections held during the thirties offer adequate examples. In 1931 the public voted, on the whole, for the coalition. In 1935 they voted, not so much for Labor, as against the coalition government. In 1938 the vote was a positive indorsement of Labor. In 1943 and 1946 it was a caution and a rebuke to Labor. The saying that possession is nine points of the law might well be applied to the results of New Zealand elections. The officeholders normally have the strategic advantage on polling day.

7. Stewart, *op. cit.*, pp. 229–30.
8. *Ibid.*, p. 231.

Collective Responsibility

When a minister proposes to Parliament the measures he thinks necessary for the departments under his charge, his colleagues are duty-bound to support him. When the government seeks another term of office from the electorate, although each minister stands as a candidate in a different district, together they speak for the same policies. This is the principle of collective responsibility, our modern version of the Roman principle of collegiality. In practice it operates to produce some good and some bad results. "All for One and One for All" is a slogan of unhappy consequences if the blunders of one incompetent individual prejudice the efforts of his abler colleagues. Yet, whenever a particular person—whether it be the premier or any other minister—achieves an outstanding success, the benefits of his prestige, power, and popularity may be extended to the cabinet as a whole. For instance, John McKenzie's personal following among the small farmers undeniably helped the Liberal cabinet at the elections of 1893 and 1896.

Cabinets tend to be strange mixtures for the simple reason that no premier has a completely free hand in selecting his team. Every ministry, as a general rule, contains a few really able members, the number varying from one to four. The remainder manage to win a portfolio either because they are the loyal representative of some powerful interest or because they are old stalwarts whose seniority and party service must be rewarded. Ballance's cabinet contained Seddon, McKenzie, Reeves, and Ward, and an entourage of lesser men. In Massey's ministry of the twenties, those who counted, besides the premier himself, were Bell, Coates, and Stewart. Similarly, in Savage's Labor cabinet, most of the decisions and the portfolios that mattered were taken by the prime minister, Fraser, Nash, and Semple. For the low-water mark of incompetence one would have to scan the personnel of the last Liberal ministry (1929–31). To all intents and purposes, the effectiveness of a cabinet depends upon the number of its abler members and upon their personal relationships. The inner solidarity of a group is made or marred by the compatibility, ambition, jealousy, friendship, strength of personality, and intellectual force of the few who supply the drive and the direction. Above all, success depends on the prime minister, who by sheer ascendancy as in Seddon's case, or by congeniality as in Ballance's, or by political experience as in Massey's, or popularity as in Savage's, or tactical skill as in Fraser's, can promote team work and avert ruptures.

Coalitions constitute a special case where it is usually difficult to achieve proper cabinet cohesiveness. New Zealand does not love coalitions any more than does Britain. Yet it has been driven to form them three times under stress of emergencies. In 1915 a National government was created with an equal number of Reformers and Liberals. Massey was premier, while Ward became minister of finance. Participants in this wartime experiment have described it as unsuccessful because the leading stars were antagonists, both temperamentally and politically. Massey's own opinion was revealed in 1920 when a bill was introduced into Parliament to have the cabinet elected by the House. As an argument against it he illustrated his own experience during the war: "I say you cannot carry on if there are strong men in the Cabinet holding diverse views. . . . . The honourable member opposite was one of my colleagues [in the wartime coalition] and he knows quite well that it was impossible for us to pull together or unite. It did not matter what opinions I may previously have held in regard to an elective Executive, my experience in connection with the National Cabinet . . . . would have cured me."[9] Bell was no less disillusioned than Massey. Although he once said that "some of the Liberal Ministers were more loyal to Massey than to their own chief, Ward,"[10] he was very chary of repeating the experiment when the depression of the early thirties hit New Zealand. Mindful of the war cabinet in which he had served, he then wrote to Stewart: "I do not believe that a coalition can effect any useful purpose in times of peace."[11]

Nevertheless, in 1931 there was formed a coalition which governed the country for four unhappy years. Though this body, too, suffered from internal differences, they were not quite so serious as during the war. This was perhaps due to the circum-

9. *P.D.*, CLXXXVIII (1920), 653.
10. Stewart, *op. cit.*, p. 121.   11. *Ibid.*, p. 280.

stance that the two leaders of the coalescing parties were not personal rivals. Coates so overshadowed Forbes that a clash in the leadership could hardly occur. Ironically enough the only sacrifice to the principle of collective responsibility was that of Stewart, who had himself for some years strongly advocated coalition. Appointed as minister of finance, he disagreed with various of his colleagues' policies and, like Sir Herbert Samuel in the contemporary British coalition under Ramsay Macdonald, openly criticized proposals to which he objected. Eventually he found a majority of the cabinet (including his own leader, Coates) against him on the question whether the New Zealand pound should be devalued. "Early in 1933," he writes, "Cabinet decided to depreciate the currency in spite of the fact that it had already introduced a Bill to set up a Reserve Bank whose duty it should be to control the exchange without regard to politics. On this issue I resigned from the Ministry."[12] A genuine example, rare in New Zealand history, of a man resigning his high office because of his disagreement on a matter of principle!

When war again broke out in 1939, democratic institutions were once more put to this test: Could national unity against external foes and internal opposition between parties be simultaneously maintained? Schemes for a coalition, mooted publicly in the early months of the war, were reinforced by the sense of danger in the critical months that followed Dunkirk and the fall of France. New Zealand Laborites pointed out that their ministry, unlike its predecessors in 1915 and 1931, had an ample parliamentary majority and needed no coalition to bolster its authority. Conservatives retorted, with the inevitable appeal to British precedent, that Winston Churchill might similarly have governed with his Conservative followers, but he had agreed to co-opt Labor into a national administration. Nothing was done until the year 1941, when some decision had to be reached simply because this would ordinarily have been the year for a general election. The choice over which the Labor party deliberated was whether to have a coalition without an election or an election without a coalition. The prime minister, Fraser, preferred the former alternative. But there were other Laborites who called for an election,

12. *Ibid.*, p. 285.

remembering that their own party had itself criticized the previous Conservative government for lengthening the term of Parliament in 1934. A compromise was then reached. No election was held in 1941; but there was set up, over and above the ordinary cabinet, a war cabinet composed of three Labor members (including the premier), and two from the National party (including the then leader of the opposition). This was presented to Parliament and the public as a demonstration of unity sufficient to justify postponing the election.

Such an attempt at yoking a bipartisan war ministry to the normal one-party cabinet (with the Labor members doing double duty in both) implied a distinction between wartime and ordinary administration which lacked validity under the all-pervading exigencies of total war. The experiment was a concession from the government to the opposition but proved inadequate to promote party harmony. Before long, the Nationalists chafed at a system which debarred their two cabinet representatives from voicing full public criticism while it denied them a proportionate share in governmental responsibility. Consequently, the opposition soon selected a new parliamentary leader, Holland, who did not enter the war cabinet and was therefore free to criticize it from outside.

Early in 1942 the southward advance of Japan led to a renewal of negotiations for a coalition. Again, the alternative to coalition was an election, since Parliament's term had been extended only for a single year. After discussions lasting several months, the parties agreed in view of the invasion danger to postpone the election once more and this time to establish a more ambitious war cabinet. The new body consisted of thirteen members—seven Laborites and six Nationalists—including both the premier and the new leader of the opposition. The ordinary cabinet continued to function as before. The administrative consequences of this set up were well-nigh chaotic. Ministers were allocated spheres of jurisdiction which inevitably overlapped. One agency—the National Service Department—had no less than six different ministers supervising various phases of its work! Nor did the political results of coalition produce a harmony that offset these disadvantages. Partisan divergences, persisting at first behind the closed doors of the cabinet room, flared eventually into the open. When the coal-miners in the Waikato region of the North Island went on strike in defiance of the government, of the law, and of their own union leaders, the Labor ministers gave in to their demands, while four of the six Nationalists, including their leader, resigned. The coalition having failed, the government was forced in 1943 to resort to the other alternative of a wartime election.

Apart from the special problems which coalitions create, a cabinet may find its collective responsibility strained when any one of its members publicly dissents from his colleagues without actually resigning. An instance of this occurred in the twenties during the protracted disorders that resulted from unintelligent administration of the Samoan mandate. When the Samoan troubles were being discussed in Parliament, the then cabinet contained a Maori member, Sir Maui Pomare, who was minister for the Cook Islands. He did not hesitate to speak as a Polynesian and criticize the policies of his colleague who was responsible for Samoa. In 1940 another curious episode occurred when Prime Minister Fraser interrupted and objected to the remarks of one of his own cabinet members, Macmillan, while the latter was addressing the House.[13] Surely, collective responsibility is a flexible conception.

On other occasions the principle has been invoked in the more normal manner. Ward had to resign from the cabinet and also from Parliament in 1896 because his own financial interests in a private bank and in certain companies were involved with the Bank of New Zealand crisis. Explaining his action, he stated that

13. "MACMILLAN: We have in New Zealand today a very real need for more girls and more young women in our factories. . . . . Some people imagine that by raising money for the Red Cross and similar organisations, by holding social afternoons or bridge parties, they are helping the war effort. It may be true that . . . .

"FRASER: They are doing really good work, and I hope no one will cast any reflections on them.

"MACMILLAN: I have no intention of casting reflections on them. But the point I make is that if a lot of these people would go into the factories . . . . we would be able to produce more goods. There is a wonderful field for activity in that direction, and I am sure . . . .

"FRASER: A lot of them are offering to do that, but it is difficult to fit them in.

"MACMILLAN: Yes, I agree" (P.D., CCLVII [1940], 362). Not long after this, Macmillan resigned from the cabinet.

he resigned "without the least pressure from any of my colleagues, or without pressure from the party of which I have been so long a member."[14] When Ward himself was premier in 1908, he compelled the resignation of his minister of lands, McNab, who advocated radical views concerning the use of paper money. In 1934 the native minister, Sir Apirana Ngata, a Maori, resigned from the cabinet after a royal commission had disclosed acts of maladministration in his department, for some of which he was held personally responsible.[15] Bell was the type of strong-minded statesman whose temperament led him periodically to threaten resignation unless he carried his point and whose law practice rendered him financially independent of his ministerial salary. Stewart has recorded in the biography many instances of Bell's defiance. When the New Zealand Expeditionary Force was leaving for overseas in 1915, a dispute arose between the government, which requested proper naval protection, and the British Admiralty, which replied that no ships were available. Bell, who insisted on the need for convoy, was in a minority of the cabinet and did actually resign. But almost immediately after the men had sailed, Massey received the news that enemy warships were supposed to be in New Zealand waters and recalled the force to home ports. Thereupon the entire cabinet told the governor-general that they would resign unless the Admiralty found a convoy.[16] Bell, whose stand had been fully vindicated, returned with honor to the ministry. Later on, in 1921 and again in 1928, he announced he would resign if his colleagues reversed the forestry policy which he had initiated. Stewart thus sums up his general disposition: "Often when he was thwarted by his colleagues in Cabinet and failed to get his way, he would threaten to resign. In this respect he resembled Lord Morley rather than Asquith, as the latter tells us he had a desk full of Morley's resignations which he wisely ignored, and Morley remained at work."[17]

14. *P.D.*, XCII (1896), 19. Ward's constituency subsequently re-elected him, and he resumed the portfolio of finance in Seddon's ministry.

15. See *Report of the Royal Commission on Native Affairs* (Parliamentary Paper, G-11 [Wellington, 1934]), p. 56.

16. The convoy was forthcoming and included, among others, a Japanese warship (Stewart, *op. cit.*, pp. 111–14).

17. *Ibid.*, p. 294.

On the whole, these illustrations suggest that cabinet solidarity has been maintained in New Zealand to much the same degree as in Britain. Coalitions are always a strain and modify the applicability of the principle. Other breaches and public admissions of internal disagreements may be tolerated at times when it is politically expedient to retain a dissentient colleague. For the rest, resignations, whether actual or threatened, whether compulsory or voluntary, will occur as individual idiosyncrasy or party opportunism may dictate. Cabinet government could not operate in New Zealand or anywhere else without a substantial basis of agreement among ministers on larger issues together with a willingness to compromise on details and on tactics. A strong premier, even though he may concede to an especially valuable colleague, must see to it that his ministers at least say the same thing when they face Parliament or the public. Having so few portfolios to bestow and so many office-hunters to placate, no premier will indefinitely tolerate the presence of a "colleague" who clogs the machinery. The practice of New Zealand prime ministers has certainly subscribed to this attitude of Dr. Johnson: "Were I minister, if any man wagged his finger against me, he should be turned out; for that which it is in the power of government to give at pleasure to one or to another, should be given to the supporters of government."[18]

The Size of the Cabinet

The customary size of the New Zealand cabinet facilitates a premier's efforts to preserve its unity. It is self-evident mathematical truth that, the larger the cabinet, the greater the difficulty in maintaining internal harmony. Because the premier of the Dominion leads a far smaller team than his analogue does in Britain, the complexity of his problems is proportionately lessened. In the mother-country the huge size of the ministry gives rise to a host of administrative problems. New Zealand has been wise and fortunate to retain at the apex of its governmental structure a committee which is still fairly small and therefore tolerably manageable. Nevertheless, in this Dominion, too, the

18. *Boswell's Life of Johnson* (London: Dent & Sons, 1933), II, 373.

cabinet has partially succumbed to its inherent tendency to grow larger. The Liberal ministry of Ballance, and of Seddon in his early years, numbered only seven—"the seven devils of social- ism" as their opponents delighted to call them. In his later period Seddon increased it to eight, a number to which Ward adhered, while Massey in 1912 raised it to nine. The wartime National government ran to as many as fourteen, since so many leading lights from each of the coalescing parties had to be gathered with- in the constellation. After the war Massey tried to reshrink the ministry. But, to satisfy the pressure of the younger Reform group, he was compelled to admit newcomers, and the cabinet stayed big. When Massey died, the ministry counted twelve per- sons. Around that figure it has remained, the Labor ministry comprising thirteen.

Fifty years have seen the cabinet double in size. It has not yet, however, become unwieldy, although a reduction to eleven or twelve, if politically possible, would bring administrative advan- tages. The present number of thirteen probably represents the uppermost limit for efficiency. To extend the ministry beyond this would decrease its usefulness in operating. More members, more talk. More portfolios, more jurisdictional rivalries. As far as it depends on the element of size, the solidarity of the cabinet is reasonably well assured. Given a premier who is a good com- mittee chairman, the cabinet is large enough to contain varied experiences and viewpoints, yet sufficiently small to remain united.

Cabinet unity is also facilitated by a physical arrangement, seemingly trivial but important in its practical consequences. In London the offices of the ministers of the Crown are situated in the separate departmental buildings scattered along and around Whitehall. In Wellington all ministers have their offices in the corridors of the building that houses Parliament. Not only is it easier and less time-wasting for a minister to see one of his col- leagues when they have a common problem to discuss but it is also far simpler to call an emergency cabinet meeting if it is suddenly required. The housing plan of the small New Zealand ministry encourages its acting as a compact unit and fosters more frequent contacts between its members. The effect of such arrangements on the working of a political system should not be ignored. Convenience of access between persons may help to develop the custom of consultation, while agencies located at a distance may be more likely to function in isolation. In the legislature of the third French Republic it will be remembered that conflicts and deadlock between the Sénat and the Chambre des Députés were all too frequent. May this not have been due in some degree to the circumstance that the two houses met in different districts of Paris? There was less chance for the growth of those informal relationships which sometimes help to smooth over points of disagreement.

Because of the size of the New Zealand ministry, there has been less occasion for the emergence of that "inner cabinet" which has necessarily evolved in Britain. It is understandable, however, that prime ministers will consult certain of their colleagues more frequently than others. Before raising an issue in the cabinet as a whole, a premier who needs advice will most likely talk it over with the wisest or the most powerful of his ministers. Stewart relates that Massey, after his setback in the election of 1922, discussed with him and with Bell what course the government should adopt.[19] That is an example of what occurs all the time. In any committee there are necessarily a few who count for leadership more than the others. But no clearly demarcated "inner cabinet" has yet hived off from the larger body.

Smallness of size, furthermore, imposes a conventional limit on the number of ministers in the Legislative Council. Every cabinet must contain one member at least from the upper house because the government needs somebody who can represent it in that body and pilot its legislation; and, once a councilor is added to the cabinet, it is natural—so great is the burden of administrative work—that he should be assigned some departments to supervise. The only question that can arouse dispute is which portfolios he should take. Not being subject to election, a councilor cannot claim directly to represent the people; nor can he be made answerable to the lower house. The members of the elected chamber, placed there as guardians of the public interest, strongly disapprove if any governmental activity of a controversial

19. *Op. cit.*, pp. 229–30.

character is placed in the hands of a minister beyond the reach of their criticism. Premiers are, therefore, careful in selecting which portfolios to give to the minister in the upper house, and the opposition will customarily argue that the portfolios so selected are the very ones whose administration it wishes to discuss. From one ministry to another the assignments have varied considerably. Under Seddon, a legislative councilor named Buckley was attorney-general, colonial secretary, and postmaster-general. After Buckley resigned, his successor, Walker, acted for seven years as minister of immigration and of education. Subsequently, however, the lower house decided that education was too important a subject to be relegated to the less important half of Parliament. Seddon yielded to protests and transferred this portfolio into his own hands.[20]

When Ward was premier, he conferred on Findlay, a councilor, the attorney-generalship and the ministries of justice and of internal affairs. Afterward, "in consequence of the strong feeling of the people's representatives,"[21] he gave the internal affairs portfolio to a minister in the lower house. Massey encountered the same form of criticism because of the status he assigned to Bell, the second most important figure in the cabinet and yet a member of the upper chamber. In 1912 he made Bell the minister of internal affairs and of immigration; and again it was objected that the holder of the former portfolio should not be in the Council. One representative insisted that the minister responsible for this department ought to be in the lower house because he "had control of the local government of the Dominion." "The leader of the Upper House," in his view, "should have charge of such non-contentious Departments as Hospitals, Public Health, and Mental Hospitals, together with the Attorney-Generalship."[22] Massey, however, ignored these complaints to such an extent that, at one time or other during his premiership, Bell filled the positions of attorney-general, commissioner of state forests, and minister of internal affairs, public health, immigration, education, marine, justice, and external affairs.

In the depression of the early thirties, when the Conservative

20. *P.D.*, CLX (1912), 23.
21. *P.D.*, CLVIII (1912), 399–40.   22. *P.D.*, CLX (1912), 22–23.

coalition determined to slash public expenditure on all forms of social services, the Education Department was once again assigned to the minister who enjoyed the more sheltered atmosphere of the Council. The Labor opposition fulminated in the lower house but was powerless to alter the arrangement. Finally, in its own term of office the Labor party itself, reversing its earlier attitudes, imitated the conduct which it had formerly criticized in others. Immigration—of all state activities one of the most vital to New Zealand—was intrusted before the outbreak of war to the minister in the Council, and he did little about it. During the war the ministries of broadcasting and civil defense were similarly allocated. When a special portfolio of industrial manpower[23] was created in 1942, it was conferred upon the president of the trade-union federation, who was thereupon appointed to the upper house and did not contest a seat for election to the lower house until 1946.

Governments of all parties have used the Council as a convenient storage dump for those portfolios which they consider either as unimportant, and therefore negligible, or else as important but better veiled from public view. The representatives can, it is true, voice their criticism of any department handled by a minister in the Council, and they can reduce its appropriations. But it is not so effective to criticize someone who is personally beyond reach and who, in the parliamentary decorum that governs relations between the houses, must be referred to with more respect since he belongs "to another place."

Representation in the Cabinet

Strictly speaking, the only "representative" portion of the state machinery is the lower house of Parliament. For political reasons, however, every cabinet, although confessedly its members are drawn from one party alone, maintains the pose that it "represents" all sections of the nation. A small-sized ministry can find room for only a limited number of the many claimants who seek a portfolio. Carefully the premier must pick and choose which interests or which regions he will satisfy by selecting their repre-

23. In 1945 the title was changed to "minister of employment."

sentative for his cabinet. If the city of Auckland has returned to Parliament a number of members adhering to the dominant party, it expects to see an Aucklander or two in the ministry. If the farmers have supported the government more strongly than the cities, they expect a due proportion of portfolios (including, of course, Agriculture and the Lands and Survey departments) to be assigned to men from rural constituencies. Ministries must be distributed in some rough relation to electoral support. The architect of the cabinet ignores his customers at his peril.

In a country whose small population is distributed from north to south in quartiles of diminishing size, it is to be expected that the voters will favor some degree of regional representation. Subtropical, expansive, erratic, Auckland stands poles apart, geographically and psychologically, from rugged, Scottish, tradition-bound, Dunedin. Not to this day have the separatism of the early settlements and the provincial loyalties disappeared completely from the political consciousness of New Zealand. Not yet is there any single region whose population or wealth suffices to dominate the Dominion. If it acts in isolation, even Auckland, whose rate of growth has outstripped other centers, is far from able to dictate what it wants.[24] The North Island could, if united, override the wishes of the South; and of recent years, it is true, southern interests, such as chambers of commerce, have claimed that more than a fair share of public works and governmental funds have gone to the north. From the south, now containing a minority of the population,[25] have been heard objections to the electoral system by which seats are allotted to each island on a proportional basis—objections which after the passage of sixty years repeat the identical arguments of the north in the days of southern predominance.[26] Yet, when all allowance is made, these teacup tempests do not constitute a serious interisland cleavage. Cook Strait is not wide enough to be a real threat to New Zealand's unity. In traveling time, Wellington is nearer to Christ-

24. It often tries, however. In many New Zealand organizations—both governmental and private—the Auckland branch tends to go its own way.

25. Under 33 per cent at the census of 1945.

26. See above, chap. ii, pp. 28–30. I recall a discussion in 1946 with an ardent and well-educated South Islander who strongly defended secession from the North Island!

church than it is to Auckland, and the plentiful contacts between the southernmost city of the North Island and the more northerly city of the South Island serve to link the islands.

It remains true, nevertheless, that a prime minister constructing his cabinet must, in the language of officialese, "have due regard" to the regional and interisland distribution of his portfolios. Otherwise of a certainty he will run into criticism for neglecting important areas. A complaint of this type—to quote one instance out of many—was heard in 1912 when Massey announced the personnel of his first Reform cabinet. Conforming to Disraeli's classic remark that it is the business of the opposition to oppose, Ward had to raise some objections to his rival's ministry, even before they had yet done anything. To point out that various districts are unrepresented in the cabinet is a simple device for a politician to ingratiate himself with their inhabitants. So Ward embroidered the theme that the ministry contained no member from the cities of Auckland, Christchurch, and Dunedin or the regions of Southland, Westland, Marlborough, Nelson, Taranaki, and the east coast. Invidiously he contrasted the "special attention" paid to Wellington City, which had three ministers to its credit.[27] From the standpoint of governmental efficiency, of course, it is an indefensible idea that a cabinet must be pieced together like a committee of regional delegates. Political expediency, however, and the forces of localism here, as often, may run counter to the dictates of efficiency. The problems involved were well stated by a representative in the debate which Ward's criticism provoked: "A man when called upon to form a Cabinet cannot choose the best man in the House for fear of offending Invercargill, or Auckland, or Christchurch. He cannot say 'There are seven men in this House that come from Auckland, and they are better men to carry on the business of the country than any other men in the House.' Unfortunately, he cannot take them all in; he can take in only one or two, and he must then go to the South and take a man who is not of the same intellectual calibre and who therefore cannot advance the national interests as the others might do."[28]

New Zealand is not the only democracy the formation of whose

27. *P.D.*, CLVIII (1912), 399.   28. *Ibid.*, p. 679.

government is influenced by such considerations. A British premier must decide which places he can bestow on Londoners and which on members "from the provinces," which on the south of England and which on the north, which on county members and which on those from the boroughs. And, when that is settled, there is the special case of Scotland. An undetermined quota of portfolios must go to Scotsmen, including necessarily the secretaryship of state for Britain north of the Tweed. For while Englishmen docilely submit to be governed by Scotsmen, it does not yet appear to be established that Scotland may have an Englishman for its secretary. In federal countries such as the United States, Australia, and Canada, it is inevitable that the cabinet should roughly reproduce the regional and cultural diversities of the population. Regionalism in the United States even affects the composition of that half-judicial, half-political, body—the Supreme Court. Microcosmic democracy in New Zealand illustrates in smaller compass many of the complexities of the macrocosm.

The principle of occupational, as distinct, from regional representation in the ministry also receives the homage of lip service but is usually honored in the breach. City versus country forms the obvious line of functional cleavage in New Zealand. The ministry must duly incorporate a blend of urban and rural representatives on pain of being subjected to editorial fulminations in the slighted areas. A country journalist will condemn a cabinet dominated by city interests no less vehemently than the city editor will attack a farmers' government. Analysis reveals, however, that alternate ministries have been predominantly of the one type or the other. In contrast to the Atkinson government, the Liberal ministers were mainly drawn from urban constituencies. As a reaction against them, Massey, who claimed to be a "small farmer" himself, formed his cabinet by preference out of men who were or had been farmers.[29] Ward's Liberals, resuscitated in 1928, were on the whole more representative of city than country. But their successor, the Coalition government, was overwhelmingly bucolic in personnel—especially after Stewart, the only important city representative, resigned in 1933. The Labor

29. *P.D.*, CLVIII (1912), 410.

ministers have been, with about three exceptions, urban representatives possessing a strongly urban outlook.

Changes have also occurred during the last five decades in the class composition of the ministry. The first such change came about in 1891 and has been commented upon by Siegfried.[30] The leaders of the seventies and eighties (Atkinson, Grey, Vogel, Stout, Rolleston, Hall, and Whitaker) all belonged socially to the middle or upper-middle class. But in the Liberal cabinets led by Ballance and Seddon, members of the lower-middle class formed the majority. (It is a significant fact that Reeves, the one whom Siegfried considered an exception to this generalization, left the ministry in 1896 and retreated to London.) The Reform cabinets were constituted from a mixture of small owner-farmers and middle-class professional men. Bell, however, second only to Massey in influence and prestige, was a direct descendant, socially and politically, of the old New Zealand aristocracy that ruled before 1890. The Labor ministries of Savage and Fraser marked the second big change. Although they contained one or two farmers and a few professional men,[31] they were recruited for the most part from the working class. Men whose boyhood, youth, and early manhood had passed in poverty and struggle; men who had worked with their hands in the factories, on the wharves, and down the mines; men who from manual laborers had become union secretaries and party organizers and thence had won election to Parliament—these were the source from which Labor's leadership flowed. Economic differences and social distinctions do exist in New Zealand to a certain degree, but they are not extreme enough to deny to any class its measure of opportunity to govern the country. That is a fact which the Dominion may recount with pride.

There is no reason to suppose that in New Zealand, any more than elsewhere, the men who attain cabinet rank in middle age or later can suddenly divest themselves of the sympathies, the prejudices, and the outlook acquired from their past occupational experience. Writing with the Reform government in mind, Cond-

30. André Siegfried, *Democracy in New Zealand*, trans. E. V. Burns (London: Bell & Sons, 1914), p. 78.

31. At different times a lawyer, a clergyman, and a doctor held office in the Labor cabinet.

liffe has mentioned that New Zealand politicians, while in office, retain their business directorates without offending public opinion: "In recent Governments, Ministers have continued to act as directors of coal-mining, insurance, and frozen-meat companies, while the Cabinet of which they were members has had to supervise State coal and insurance departments and the meat export control boards."[32] The modern practice has its roots well back in the past. Seddon himself did not shrink from utilizing some of the financial possibilities of his office. In 1896 he was taken to task in Parliament for accepting a paid position as member of an advisory board of an "Anglo-Continental Goldmining Syndicate" which intended to carry on business in New Zealand. Questioned by Russell, the leader of the opposition, whether the premier ought to hold such a post, Seddon retorted that he had the same right as Russell had to be director of the "Northern Investment Company." To this Russell replied: "The circumstances are entirely different. The Northern Investment Company is a private company, in no way dependent on Orders in Council. I was appointed a director when I was not a Minister. The Premier was appointed a director of the 'Anglo-German Gold Syndicate,' not because he is Richard Seddon, but simply because he is Premier of the Colony."[33] Stout likewise criticized the premier for appointing himself at a salary of £250 a year as a member of the directorate to deal with the Bank of New Zealand estates for realization. Seddon's attitude to these matters was stated thus: "He did not think that either the members of the House or the country demanded that a Minister should do nothing else but simply be a Minister of the Crown."[34] Another prominent politician, Ward, did not cease throughout his long tenure of public office to indulge in speculative private ventures. On one occasion, in 1896, such embarrassing publicity was given to his private affairs that resignation from the cabinet became unavoidable. Even during his last ministry in the late twenties he caused much comment because the government under his auspices bought many motor vehicles from an importing firm with which members of his family were closely connected.

32. J. B. Condliffe, *New Zealand in the Making* (London: Allen & Unwin, 1930), p. 312.
33. *P.D.*, XCV (1896), 83.   34. *P.D.*, XCII (1896), 74–75, 100.

All these instances can be cited in print because they have been the subject of parliamentary discussion. On hearsay evidence the writer has been informed of other examples of ministers in various parties using their official positions to enhance their own incomes or those of their associates. Although one may learn about such incidents from independent and reliable sources, in the nature of the case it is seldom possible to produce any documentary testimony. All that can be done is to state the general impression arising from a perusal of Hansard and newspapers and from many inquiries in business and political circles. This would be a fair summing-up. The great majority of cabinet members have probably departed from office no richer than to the extent warranted by their official salaries. Certain ministers, while holding portfolios, have drawn profit from their business connections, and this has not necessarily been illegal. But it is virtually certain that there have been some cases in which ministers did not abstain from using a public trust for private enrichment. Viewed comparatively, the governmental system in New Zealand does seem pure in relation to some other countries. But no one could certify that all its cabinets in the last fifty years have been 100 per cent devoid of graft and corruption. A royal commission of inquiry might bring to light some closeted skeletons.

Whatever deviations from the norm there may have been can be ascribed partly to the all-pervasiveness of state activities and partly to the insecurities of a political career. Reaching into every corner of the nation's economic life, the departments of state have many permits to grant or withhold, for which some individuals are willing to pay a price. If a less scrupulous businessman should light upon a minister of easy conscience, money could change hands, and yet the transfer could seldom be proved. Systems of state regulation (as distinct from full public ownership and operation) sometimes lend themselves to dishonest dealings if the regulators can be bought.

While the concentration of governmental power supplies opportunity for corruption, uncertainties about their tenure of office provides some ministers with an incentive. Few members of cabinets in the last five decades have been rich, even on New Zealand standards of wealth. Since the Liberal triumph in the

nineties the well-to-do have mostly abstained from direct participation in politics. To gain their ends they have preferred to
manipulate and maneuver, where they could, from behind the
scenes and jerk the strings that held their parliamentary puppets. The emoluments of a minister of the Crown are not at all
high, especially when one reviews the responsibilities involved.
As manager of a bank or private insurance company, as a successful lawyer or doctor, as an engineer or a fashionable architect, an
able and enterprising man can earn far more than by entering
politics and aspiring to a ministerial salary. Triennial elections
make a minister's position unstable and precarious. The grant of
a portfolio is normally his long-awaited reward for many years of
dutiful party service in the House on the meager salary[35] of a
representative. He holds office on a temporary lease and under
continual threat of eviction. Is it surprising that some may be
tempted to make up for past denial, to provide for future security, and to capitalize on the profits of power?

Of the New Zealanders who give thought to governmental
problems, many complain of the poor caliber of the cabinet personnel. It is a stock theme among citizens of all parties, and the
criticism applies not to any single government but to the general
run of ministries over half a century. Few propositions about the
Dominion's politics would receive wider acceptance than this
one: The cabinet has greater power for good or evil than any
other group of persons, yet it does not contain nearly enough of
the best talent in the country. Over the question whether talent is
really available, let there be no doubt. This small population does
produce its quota of individuals of pre-eminent ability (witness,
in three different fields, Lord Rutherford, Sir John Salmond, and
Mr. David Low) who have matched the best brains of larger nations. Let us omit, however, the greatest names whose reputation
is internationally established. Let us not attempt to compare
Seddon and Massey with Gladstone and Churchill. Let us measure only by the fair and proper standard, which is to rate the
members of New Zealand cabinets side by side with the leading
figures in other spheres of New Zealand life. Take the top-notch
men in business; in the civil service; in education; in law, medi-

35. See below, p. 329.

cine, and the other professions; in the farming community; and in the trade-unions. Set against these the last half-century's crop of ministers, and how many of them will stand up to the test of merit? The number of cabinet members who can be described as intellectually outstanding (e.g., Reeves, Bell, and Stewart) may be counted on the fingers of one hand. One of these alone, Bell, held the post of premier—and he only for a fortnight. Another smallish group of ministers would include men with minds far above the average in ability, though not of a scholarly turn. Nash and Nordmeyer are cases in point. There have been others who distinguish themselves from their contemporaries, not by intellect, but by force of personality and gifts of public leadership. For example, Seddon, John McKenzie, Massey, and Savage. For the rest, the cabinets have been stocked with a number of men who were able but not outstanding and with a residue who were merely ordinary. To certain ministries, where collective responsibility has shrouded some individual mediocrities, it would not be unjust to apply the lines of T. S. Eliot:

> We are the hollow men,
> We are the stuffed men
> Leaning together.

When democracy relies on state action to such an extent as New Zealand does, and then fails to attract its best human material in the service of the state, there is something seriously wrong.

Functions of the Cabinet

Under the cabinet form of government any inadequacy in the average standard of ministerial ability has particularly grave consequences. It is the characteristic of this system to concentrate in the hands of the cabinet all the really important powers and functions. The ministry is the dynamo and central switchboard for the whole machinery of government. In a mechanism so highly integrated the effects of any failure at the focal point reach out to all its subordinate parts. After all proper allowance has been made for the influence on political decisions of the caucus, the heads of the civil service, and economic pressure groups, it remains true that the ultimate responsibility for every

act and omission is squarely placed upon the cabinet. "Every act
and omission" is a big, but an accurate, statement. For the scope
of the cabinet's jurisdiction covers alike the formulation of legislative policy and the methods of administrative execution. It is
not confined either to the parliamentary or to the departmental
sphere alone. With equal authority the ministry controls both
phases of what is, when realistically viewed, a continuous governmental process. That is a necessary reminder, since some British thinking on the role of the cabinet is still influenced by Bagehot's classic description of the cabinet as "a committee of the
legislative body selected to be the executive body."[36] Some sixty
years later H. L. McBain corrected Bagehot with the retort that
it was "a committee of the legislative body selected primarily to
lead the legislative body."[37] The antithesis, however, was neither
more nor less accurate than the thesis. Each stated a half-truth,
exaggerating one important aspect and ignoring or understating
another. Only a synthesis of their views would properly describe
the cabinet as it has functioned in modern New Zealand or Britain. Surely the dominance of the cabinet is as marked in the legislative branch (provided it has an ample parliamentary majority)
as in the executive. Its place and role should be thus defined. The
cabinet is a committee of the party dominant in the legislature
designed to lead both the legislative and the executive bodies. In
that definition the significant word is "both." It is this dualism in
the function of the cabinet which makes its working so complex
and its results so profoundly important. Formally and effectively
the British version of democracy fuses and unites in the same body
the final authority over all the stages of preparing policy and
translating it into action. The British system has the great merit
of so consolidating governmental power that responsibility cannot be shelved or evaded. But it runs the danger of accumulating
too much authority in a body that might not use, or could abuse,
it.

Under the presidential type of democracy operating in the
United States, the federal and state constitutions were originally

36. Walter Bagehot, *The English Constitution* ("World's Classics," No. CCCXXX
[London: Oxford University Press, 1928]), p. 9.
37. *The Living Constitution* (New York: Macmillan Co., 1927), p. 121.

designed under the influence of Montesquieu's theory of the "separation of powers." What actually happened was that governmental personnel were separated in three distinct branches, and governmental functions were distributed among the three. But in practice the distribution modified the rigid logic of the theory in its extreme form. Most of the legislative function was given to members of the legislative branch, but portions of that function went to the President and to the Supreme Court. Similarly with the executive and judicial functions. In no case was a complete function given in its entirety to any one branch. That would have been utterly impossible to do, because all governmental processes are to some extent intertwined, and no perfect threefold division can be devised either in theory or in practice. Nowadays the dynamic of a modern democracy, responding to its citizens' many needs, has pushed the American system even farther from its framers' design. Despite outward differences of form and procedure, presidential government has at times operated in substantially the same manner as the British. More than one President of the Union, more than one governor of a state, has exercised for a while a combined authority over the legislature and the executive departments. But because neither presidents nor governors can be members of their legislatures, the methods by which they secure a joint control must often be more devious and indirect than those of a prime minister.[38] The American system is superior to the British in this respect that it can more easily impose curbs on an abuse of power. Yet it suffers from the inherent difficulty that deadlocks may occur between the legislature and the chief executive. Nor, when legal powers are so distributed, can political responsibility always be squarely fixed.

The legislative side of its work absorbs relatively more of the cabinet's time in Britain than in New Zealand. In the mother-country there is a far greater volume of business awaiting transaction at every parliamentary session. Parliament must remain assembled for more months of the year at Westminster than at

38. On this topic consult H. J. Laski, *The American Presidency* (London: Allen & Unwin, 1940); W. E. Binkley, *The President's Powers* (New York: Doubleday-Doran Co., 1937); also my *The American Governor* (Chicago: University of Chicago Press, 1939) and "The Dual Role of the American President," (*New Zealand*) *Journal of Public Administration*, Vol. II, No. 1 (1939).

Wellington. Nevertheless, both new legislation and amendments to existing laws do form a major item of cabinet activity in the Dominion. In preparing its program of government bills, the cabinet instructs the ministers in charge of particular measures to work out the provisions in detail with the aid of their civil servants and (usually) to consult any organized interests that may be affected. If the ministry is a Labor one, caucus will discuss the general principles of the program and may appoint subcommittees to be associated with ministers on their respective assignments. Some legislation may be preceded by research carried out either by civil servants or by independent investigators. But that is still rather infrequent in New Zealand, where the conception that effective action must be based upon systematic study has yet to receive proper recognition. Many of the faults in the laws and their administration are due to slipshod and overhasty preparation and to plain unawareness of the available experience of other countries. Once a bill has passed through the stages of exploration and drafting, it is scrutinized in cabinet and in caucus. After that, its guardian-minister must see it safely through the public ordeal of parliamentary debate.

The over-all supervision of his departments is another duty of a minister. And would that ministers confined themselves to this! Unfortunately, there has long existed in New Zealand a deplorable administrative tradition by which ministers preoccupy themselves with all manner of trivial minutiae. The time which they should devote to reflection on the largest issues is absorbed with attention to pinprick problems. Ministers personally handle many a question which should be disposed of by their clerks. What is still worse, the fault committed by ministers individually is committed by the cabinet collectively. Innumerable small items of an administrative nature find their way on the cabinet agenda paper, where they have no business to be. Ministries, as a rule, have lacked a proper conception of their executive duties. A cabinet should take the broadest and the longest view of national progress; it should adjust in a harmonious relation to each other the competing claims of sectional interests; it should initiate policies of economic and social development or stimulate population trends which may take a generation to show results.

Matters of administration should reach the plane of cabinet discussion only when major policy issues or relations between two or
more departments call for clarification. A wise cabinet would
leave the administrative details to individual ministers who
should with equal wisdom leave them to their permanent heads.

Such is a counsel of perfection. New Zealand is far from approaching it. Even when a broad line of policy has been laid
down, the cabinet as a body will often continue to deliberate
upon the application of policy to particular cases. To all cabinets
this general criticism applies in varying degrees. In Seddon's day,
as elderly civil servants have told the writer, each individual request of an official for a higher salary was often considered by the
full cabinet. Stewart has written of Massey's ministry that, when
the policy of settling returned soldiers on the land was inaugurated after 1918, the cabinet collectively administered the scheme.
"Not only was every purchase carefully examined by an expert
independent Land Purchase Board, but no single purchase was
made without a resolution of Cabinet. The valuations of the
property were read to all the Ministers with full estimates of what
the land would produce and its value."[39] In more recent years
the Labor ministry has continued this bad practice of its predecessors. There have been occasions when a departmental head,
wishing to create a new position at a salary of under £600, has
had to wait for cabinet approval before any appointment could
be made. It is even a standing regulation that a minister must
obtain the agreement of his colleagues before he can authorize expenditure on any item over £250. Time is the most wasteful com-
modity in New Zealand administration. Cabinets fritter away
their own time on minutiae, and all through the departments action is delayed pending the cabinet's approval. The two main
consequences of the system are congestion at the center and hold-
ups everywhere else.

Besides Parliament and the departments, another claimant has
demands on ministerial time. This is the general public, the sovereign Demos, the vote-possessing master of the politicians. In a
small country in which the state undertakes so much, a minister
dare not ignore a voter. He must receive perennial deputations.

39. *Op. cit.*, p. 139.

His office must be open to all classes in the community. He must be available for personal interview. He must reply to innumerable letters. He must promise "careful consideration" of every suggestion, and each crank proposal must "be kept steadily in view." In short, in a small democracy the government has to stay close to the people. A minister becomes, like Figaro, the factotum of the town. All this might euphemistically be called "public relations." From one election to another it never ends. Some of it, let us grant, is valuable; some is necessary. Ministers are elected by the people, are paid out of public funds, and do hold their positions as servants of the public. Citizens have the right to convey their wishes personally to ministers, and the latter should derive help from direct contact with public opinion. But the good is swamped by the bad, and the whole system is terribly abused. Cabinet members attend to the petty trifles of their constituents, for the latter expect it, and it may be politically risky to refuse. The tradition which requires ministers to keep their ears close to the ground invites the danger that earwigs may crawl in.

CHAPTER XI

THE PREMIERSHIP

ALTHOUGH the head of the cabinet cannot be severed from the body of which he is the principal member, there is every justification for devoting a special chapter to a study of his status. A modern prime minister holds an office that is uniquely potent both within the governmental framework and among the nation at large. In his hands are drawn together the three principal threads of power and influence. As the recognized head of the dominant political party, he has the support of the electoral majority among his fellow-citizens. The leading figure inside Parliament, he controls the supreme legislative authority of the land, directing it into the channels he desires. As first minister of the Crown and legatee of its executive functions, he is the prime mover of the administrative machine and master of state departments. No single individual can wield, for good or ill, as much power as he. The ambit of his direct authority and indirect influence is startling in its scope. If an outstanding person becomes premier, he enjoys unequaled opportunities of national leadership.

The Selection of a Premier

When a democracy intrusts so much power to one man, it must insure that he is appointed with public consent and is accountable to the popular will. Otherwise, behind the façade of democracy may lurk the realities of dictatorship. The method of selecting a premier that has now been evolved depends only to a small degree on the law of the constitution and is mainly a product of unwritten conventions. Legally viewed, the prime minister is merely a member of Parliament whom the governor-general requests to form a government. If, as is the customary rule nowadays, the premier belongs to the lower house, he gets there simply as the representative of one constituency out of eighty. He is not elected by the whole country but by a fraction of the voters. His legal authority as premier rests on twin supports: his membership in Parliament and his commission from the governor-general. The mandate to govern the country is an amalgam of popular vote and royal prerogative. In practice, however, the position is far different, and the rigid, unrealistic conceptions of constitutional law must be recast in the mold of political actualities. First, the role of the Crown, through its intermediary the governor-general, has ceased to be of any significance except under very abnormal circumstances. The formalism of the law requires that the Crown "send for" some member of Parliament to head the ministry. Nowadays such a procedure is merely a rite or routine picturesquely observed because of its antiquity and historical associations. Though the governor-general's participation in the choice of a premier is all-important for satisfying the due forms of law, politically it is nearly always irrelevant. In fact, the actions of the governor-general are dictated to him by the dominant party; he has no alternative but to send for the man already designated by the dominant parliamentary group. Never once in the last sixty years has any governor-general had any opportunity of using his own discretion. Thus the potentially undemocratic influence of an appointive official has not been brought to bear on the selection of the real political head of the nation.

This argument presupposes that one political party happens to dominate the others and that it has formed its own decision about who shall be its leader. Normally these presuppositions are valid. If, for instance, a ministry resigns after a defeat at an election or in a division of the House, automatically the governor-general must turn to the recognized leader of the opposition. In 1891 there could be no doubt that Ballance had to be invited to act as premier; in 1912, after Mackenzie's resignation, Massey was clearly indicated as the successor. So, too, in 1935 Savage was the governor-general's necessary choice. In each instance the party had previously chosen its leader, and the Crown could only ratify that selection. The governor-general can choose only if the party has failed to do so, and what party nowadays would abdicate from that function? Another and more serious possibility of gubernatorial choice can exist if no party possesses a decisive majority. Between three rival leaders of co-equal strength no one but the governor-general could act as arbiter. But in such cases the parties themselves normally come to a working arrangement and indicate who should be premier. In 1928, for example, the Coates government was clearly defeated at the elections, yet its parliamentary strength still equaled that of its nearest opponent. Labor held the balance of power. Since some form of two-party combination had to be found, Labor agreed on certain conditions to support the Liberals, without entering the cabinet. All that was then left for the governor-general was to send for Ward.

A similar position arises when the premier of an undefeated government dies or resigns. Usually either he or the cabinet or the caucus has designated who is to follow, and quarrels over the succession are rare. New Zealand ministries, in fact, have often accorded to the second most important member of the cabinet a post tantamount to that of deputy prime minister—a name which is sometimes used to describe him. Necessity has indeed compelled the selection of such a deputy. Every few years New Zealand premiers have to take trips abroad. They may be called to an imperial conference in London or elsewhere. They may be invited to a royal coronation, or they may have to negotiate a loan. In wartime they are consulted on the political aspects of higher strategy, and international conferences are now more plentiful than ever. If the premier is away from New Zealand for a couple of months or more, he must leave a colleague in charge of the cabinet to carry on the government in his name. The latter becomes, in the absence of his chief, "acting prime minister." When his chief returns, he is recognized, informally at any rate, as the premier's deputy. If the premier should die or retire, his deputy has a strong claim to succeed him. Thus Seddon had deputized for Ballance during the latter's illness, as had Bell for Massey, and Fraser for Savage.

While the governor-general has, to all intents and purposes, been eliminated as a factor in the selection of the premier, another agent has come into the picture. Nowadays the body whose wishes must be consulted is the caucus, the meeting of a party's parliamentary representatives. If the caucus favors a certain individual as premier, that person will in fact be chosen; if the caucus is opposed to anyone, there is no chance of his being sent for. In Seddon's case the cabinet confirmed him as acting-premier after Ballance's death, but this had later to be indorsed by the Liberal caucus. It was again the caucus which decided the succession in 1925. On Massey's death, the acting premier, Bell, was sent for by the governor-general. He accepted the premiership for the interim but publicly stated that his appointment was temporary because of his age. The parliamentary party soon held a caucus meeting to select the successor. Potential leaders were Coates and Stewart, the latter of whom happened at that time to be in the United States. The caucus duly met and chose Coates.[1] A similar procedure was followed by the Labor party when Savage died. Fraser, the deputy premier, temporarily accepted office. The choice of a leader was then referred to the parliamentary caucus, where two candidates were nominated, and Fraser received the majority of the votes. On one memorable occasion, after a premier resigned, the caucus could not agree who should succeed him. This was in 1912, when Ward surrendered the premiership after his electoral setback, and the caucus of a divided party hesitated long between two rival claimants. Although Mackenzie emerged victorious, his followers were so badly split that the Liberal ministry soon toppled.

The foregoing arguments point to the conclusion that the decisions of the majority caucus have nowadays supplanted any discretion that the governor-general might exercise. This is, in my view, an advance in a democratic direction, since the caucus is composed of popularly elected representatives, while the governor-general represents only the Crown, an agency not directly amenable to popular control. If the British method of choosing the head of the government is to become fully democratic, elimination of all influence of the Crown is a *sine qua non*. Some English political scientists have pointed to the facts that King George V was able in 1922 to choose between Curzon and Baldwin and that in 1931 he participated with advice in the negotiations by

---

1. See Bell's comments in a letter to Stewart. "Perhaps it is as well that you are absent, since I think that the South would have wanted you and there would be dissension. As it is Coates is a certainty" (quoted by W. D. Stewart, *Sir Francis H. D. Bell: His Life and Times* [Wellington: Butterworth & Co., 1937], p. 237).

which a Conservative-dominated "National" government was substituted for the Labor ministry.[2] Other authorities, however, arguing that this influence is desirable, develop the thesis that there still resides in the Crown a reserve power to act as "guardian of the constitution." For this purpose a considerable degree of discretion must be accorded to the sovereign or his representative. Constitutional lawyers of a more conservative tendency envisage the Crown playing at times an active part in the selection of a premier—a role which presumably they consider consonant with democratic principles. Carrying their point of view to its logical conclusion, they suggest that, if the Crown "guards" the constitution and may intervene in choosing a premier, it may also under some circumstances dismiss a holder of the office. That this is not merely a sample of casuistry was proved in Australia in 1932, when Sir Philip Game, governor of New South Wales, dismissed the Labor premier, Mr. Lang. On that occasion the governor contended that the premier was acting unconstitutionally and that he was justified in inviting the opposing leader to form a new ministry.

Such a doctrine involves very wide implications, for, once the principle is admitted that a discretionary power still remains in the Crown's hands, where is the line to be drawn? To express it in terms of practical politics, conservatives fear the possibility of socialist majorities in Parliament. Knowing that the upper chamber and the courts are inadequate checks on any cabinet with a majority, they seek to revive the monarchy or its agent as potential defenders of the status quo. Left-wingers, on the other hand, realize that the Crown and its representatives in the Dominions are more likely to be drawn by their affiliations—social, political, and economic—to the right-wing parties than to the left. They are aware that in many past instances in which the Crown or its representative has given advice or exercised discretion, it has often been to aid the more conservative side (witness New Zealand up to 1893, Great Britain in 1931, and Australia in 1932). Therefore, left-wingers favor the removal of all discretion from

2. See Harold J. Laski, *Parliamentary Government in England* (New York: Viking Press, 1938), pp. 339 ff.; W. I. Jennings, *Cabinet Government* (London: Cambridge University Press, 1938), pp. 38–40.

the Crown or the reduction of the Crown's choice to precisely stated rules.[3]

Both in logic and in practice the alternatives are clear cut. Either some unfettered discretion is to be vested in the sovereign, or there is no such discretion. If the former is the case, then it must be remembered that the political machinery allows for no possibility of popular control over the Crown's actions. To allow to the Crown an unfettered discretion is to admit within the governmental system an element that is not responsible to the people. The other alternative is to remove all discretion by making the Crown's actions purely automatic. A king or a governor-general could be required to act only on the advice of the premier for the time being. If that advice is bad or is unfair to the other party, the people ultimately have the means of reaching a premier through the elections; they cannot so reach the monarch. If there should be an interregnum in the premiership, the course of the monarch or his representative should be charted by precise and predetermined rules. This is not the case at present, since there still remains much doubt and uncertainty about certain aspects of the exercise of the royal prerogative. Fortunately for New Zealand, however, no case has been known for over sixty years where a governor-general influenced the choice or dismissal of a premier. Six decades of precedents support the thesis that the parliamentary parties are today the real premier-makers.

Besides virtually eliminating the intervention of its governor-general, New Zealand has further democratized the process of choosing a premier by restricting the available candidates to the lower house. More than one premier in the early days was seated in the Legislative Council. For the last sixty years, however, only one legislative councilor, Bell, has served as premier, and he merely for a fortnight. When Bell resigned the premiership after the two-week interregnum between Massey and Coates, he explained diplomatically to the Council that his reasons for resigning were purely private and personal and had nothing to do with the fact that he belonged to the upper, rather than the lower, chamber.

3. See the argument in H. V. Evatt, *The King and His Dominion Governors* (London: Oxford University Press, 1936), *passim*.

His party, as he stated, did not see "any constitutional difficulty in regard to any tenure of that great office in this Council."[4] Legally speaking, he was right, for there is no constitutional obstacle to the choice of a councilor as premier. Politically, however, it is no longer possible for the premier to be stationed in the upper house. Bell himself admitted that there were "practical difficulties, more in the matter of election and public address"; and it was even proposed that, if Bell continued in office, he might stand for election to the lower house in the constituency which Massey had represented. A democratic community would not tolerate in its highest political office a man who had not run the gauntlet of popular election. Public criticism and resentment in the lower house would prevent the appointment of a nominated, instead of an elective, premier. However they may actually use their power, prime ministers must at least convey the impression that they were originally the people's choice.

Previous Experience

In the mythology of ancient Greece, Athene, the goddess of wisdom in arts, sciences, and war, was born, already maturely grown and in full panoply, from the head of Zeus, king of the gods. The political genesis of a modern premier is lengthier, more devious, and further removed from the godhead. In haphazard, planless fashion democracy lets its leaders be picked in the rough sifting of everyday associations. What is it that raises an individual out of the rut, marks him as a "coming man," and designates him at sixty years of age to head the country's government? For its thoroughness and singleminded concentration on the end in view Plato's proposed education of his "philosopher-kings" is unparalleled in the history of human thought on governmental problems. The hope that power would be united with wisdom, that those would rule who have the knowledge, has ever been the philosopher's stone of the idealist's search. In this twentieth century we are not even within sight of the goal. The method—if it can be dignified by that description—through which our rulers emerge is often a challenge to the principle that the job should go to the fittest. Balance in the scales the concentration of power

4. Quoted in Stewart, *op. cit.*, pp. 238–39.

against the caliber of the top leadership, and the disparity in many countries will call for explanation and remedy. The gratification of private whim, ambition for power, lure of the limelight, failure in other occupations—such are some of the motive forces which are as likely to launch a politician on his career as any mission of public service.

If education be one prerequisite for high office, the New Zealand of this century compares unfavorably with its own past. Before 1890 thirteen men attained the premiership, of whom ten had received a university, and the other three a secondary, education. The modern period has witnessed eleven premiers. Of these, five attended primary school only, five were educated to the secondary level, and one (Bell) went to a university. What is to be said of a democracy in which in the last fifty years only one university graduate has held the premiership, and he for a mere fortnight?[5] The extension of free public education has been accompanied by a lowering of the average educational standards of the political leaders. The implications of this fact are discouraging. Democracy is right to insist that educational opportunities must be equalized, and to a very large extent this has been carried out in New Zealand.[6] Why, then, does democracy not proceed to utilize politically the recipients of higher learning? It would be quite wrong to assert that no man can be a good premier unless he has studied at a university. But it is surely surprising that no university graduate, with the exception of Bell, has attained to the premiership in modern New Zealand.

The occupations in which the premiers earned their livelihood have varied considerably. They constitute, in fact, a cross-section of the community's economic life—with the professions omitted. In the successive periods of Liberal, Reform, and Labor dominance the premiers have fairly represented in their own person the economic interests of their party following. Take the five Liberals who held the premiership between 1891 and 1912. Four had been in business: Seddon as a hotel- and storekeeper, Hall-

5. Bell, incidentally, was a law graduate of Cambridge, not of the New Zealand University.

6. New Zealand's educational system is on the whole more democratic than that of Britain, but it still preserves some relics of privilege (e.g., the survival of certain expensive private schools, known as "snob-shops").

Jones as a contractor, Ward as a merchant and financier, and Mackenzie as a storekeeper. Ballance, however, was a journalist. Throughout the next decades, the era of Reform, it was farming which led to the premiership. Massey and Coates were both farmers, as was Forbes, who coalesced with Reform in 1931. The one exception was Bell, a distinguished lawyer. Savage and Fraser, the two Labor premiers, began life under the severe economic handicap of poverty, worked as manual laborers and trade-union secretaries, and then became professional politicians.[7] Except for lawyers, teachers, engineers, and members of other professions, the different classes who serve the community's needs have all contributed their quota of premiers. As for their religious affiliations, the prime ministers accurately depict the relative strength of New Zealand's sectarian divisions. Nine of the eleven were Protestants; two (Ward and Savage) were Catholics. Vogel, who belongs to the older period, is the only Jew ever to have been premier.

Once they entered on a political career, all the modern premiers had to serve a long apprenticeship before winning the most coveted prize. Many have started in the sphere of local government, acting as councilors or mayors, or else doing duty on school committees, harbor boards, or road boards. Thus gaining experience and attracting attention in their own local bailiwick, they could secure a party's nomination and win an election to Parliament. It is in this capacity as a private member of the legislature that their real political training, such as they have, is obtained. Every premier, prior to his elevation, has served in the lower house for a minimum of twelve years—some, indeed, for as long as twenty. The sole exception, Bell, was in the lower house for only three years, but for thirteen years he sat in the Council. Prime ministers have been, therefore, experienced parliamentarians and old electoral campaigners. A man must survive many elections and legislative sessions before he can hope to be head of a government. By that time he is versed in every trick of the trade. Committees and caucuses, lobbies and log-rolling, pressure groups and platforms—these are his professional ABC's.

7. Cf. Savage's statement: "I believe that the school which sent me to this House is the mine, the workshop" (*P.D.*, CXCIX [1923], 116).

Many a premier, in addition, served as minister in someone else's cabinet before he himself took over the steering-wheel. Ballance had previously had four-and-a-half years of cabinet experience; Seddon, two years; Ward, twelve; Coates, nearly six; and Fraser, over four. But in the nature of the case, where a new party came to power for the first time, neither the premier nor his colleagues could be expected to have had an inside acquaintance with the running of a cabinet. This has happened twice: when Massey and his Reform ministry took office in 1912 and when Savage in 1935 formed his Labor government. But in neither of these cases did the lack of previous ministerial experience detract from their performance as premiers. As leader of the opposition during many sessions, Massey had established the basis of working relationships with the other parliamentarians of his party. Before becoming the ministry, they were already a group of like-minded politicians, accustomed to co-operate in legislative debate and in planning party strategy. So, too, with Labor. Savage and his colleagues had fought many elections together and over long years of uphill progress had played the role of "His Majesty's Opposition." A rough system of specialization had even been sketched out; and in the sessions of the depression period Nash was the chief critic of the Coalition's financial administration, Fraser of their educational policies, and Semple of their public works program. In caucus meetings, committee discussions, and conference debates, the ministry was already foreshadowed. A man who has led his party in opposition, and has promoted the loyalties that must exist between colleagues, can make a good premier without prior service in a cabinet. But nobody could possibly succeed as prime minister who was unversed in the ways of Parliament. Parliamentary government requires that a premier must be a trained parliamentarian.[8]

8. An instructive comparison can here be drawn with the American system which insists that its chief executives, both in federal and in state governments, must not be members of the legislature. It is noticeable that the presidents and governors who co-operate best with their legislatures are often men who have themselves previously served as legislators, e.g., Presidents Theodore Roosevelt and Franklin D. Roosevelt and Governors Smith, Lehman, Byrd, and Lowden. On the other hand, three modern presidents—Taft, Wilson, and Hoover—who notoriously failed to "hit it off" with Congress had never been in a legislature.

Duration in Office

Once he attains the premiership, a man is not easily dislodged, That, in a sentence, is the lesson of half a century. Successive prime ministers of all three parties have continued in power for long, unbroken terms. Continuity of tenure of its highest office is a significant feature of this democracy. Ward, Forbes, and Fraser remained at the head of the government for over five years without a break, while Seddon and Massey each enjoyed more than a twelve-year "reign." At the other extreme, Hall-Jones and Bell, who served for under two months, were only temporary stopgaps. The contrast between the average length of a premier's occupancy before and after 1890 is most striking. Two years and nine months was the average duration in the earlier period, and only Stafford stayed continuously in power for five years. But the average tenure for the modern period has been five years. In many cases it has been death that has terminated the premier's occupancy. Ballance, Seddon, Massey, Ward, and Savage—the list of prime ministers who have died in harness is long and contains conspicuous names. The two premiers of briefest duration resigned voluntarily as soon as the party had had its opportunity to elect the obvious successor (Hall-Jones giving up the reins when Ward returned from Europe in 1906, and Bell handing over to Coates in 1925). Ward in 1912, Coates in 1928, and Forbes in 1935 all resigned after an electoral defeat—only three such instances in five decades. Mackenzie, who tried in 1912 the impossible task of patching the broken Liberal party, resigned, not after an election, but after a switch of parliamentary votes had wiped out his precarious majority.

Premiers, in short, have enjoyed the same longevity in office as cabinets. Successful parties and stable ministries have no incentive to change their leaders. Only death or defeat brings a new general to the fore. Such, however, has been the tradition of New Zealand parties and the paucity of able men available that even after an electoral debacle the standard-bearer has often remained unaltered. Although Ward resigned after the election of 1911, he had no difficulty, once the Mackenzie interlude was finished, in regaining the leadership of the Liberals. Rejected by the voters of more than one constituency in the twenties, he nevertheless re-emerged as the Liberal head and prime minister in 1928. Coates, despite his reverse in 1928, continued to be chief of the Reformers and became in the depression the most powerful member of the Coalition. In office and out, New Zealand parties as a general rule have been loyal to their leaders.

The Premier's Leadership

Besides the qualities they share in common, premiers exercise a leadership which must in the last resort emanate from the in-dividuality of their own personalities. The authority of a prime minister is an attribute common to all and derives from the pow-ers of the office. But his personal prestige, the respect he inspires, and the confidence with which he is regarded, these are what the individual himself contributes.

Ballance, the first of modern premiers in chronological se-quence, illustrates how a man can lead a government without dominating it. Into his cabinet he collected the most able men his party could provide. Seddon, McKenzie, Reeves, and Ward were colleagues with minds of their own and with independent force of character. Himself disposed to mildness and conciliation, he earned their respect and won their co-operation. Condliffe aptly compares his premiership to that of Campbell-Bannerman, who, without being a brilliant person, led one of the most bril-liant cabinets that ever held office in Britain.[9] An appreciation of his chief was written later by Reeves, the minister of labor and education, who thus describes his own relations with Ballance: "Neither a Socialist nor with any marked interest in Industrial Democracy, Ballance left Labour matters to his colleague, the Minister of Education. . . . . So far from embarrassing his lieu-tenant in his difficult task, he strengthened his hands by making him Minister of Labour and providing him with competent de-partmental assistance. Then, after watching him closely for a while, he left him free to take his own course. . . . . His judgment and gift of conciliation attracted and united his party. . . . . Su-

9. J. B. Condliffe, *New Zealand in the Making* (London: Allen & Unwin, 1930), p. 174.

perior to personal vanity, he was the least jealous of chiefs and tried to gather strong men around him."[10] Ballance's natural mildness did not, however, prevent him from showing strength and determination when necessary. There was no hesitation in the way in which he introduced the controversial Liberal legislation and fought against the opposition party, the governor, and the Legislative Council. Even the men of iron in his cabinet admired their chief. Reeves mentions that Ballance was the only one who dared to differ from McKenzie, and the latter "had a real attachment" to his premier.[11] Intelligent and honest, conciliatory yet determined, Ballance was well fitted to govern a parliamentary democracy.

Ballance was succeeded in office by a still more redoubtable leader and man of very different stamp. Richard John Seddon, who became premier in 1893 and remained so until he died in 1906, is perhaps the most remarkable figure in New Zealand history. Judged by any standards—duration in office, power over his contemporaries, influence on the future—he was by far the most successful of all the Dominion's politicians. Only Grey and Vogel could be said to have affected the course of this country's development in a like degree. Under his leadership, or dominance, the Liberal party won five consecutive elections, the last three of which were a personal tribute to the prime minister. At his final victory in 1905 he received one of the largest majorities in his career.

For the power and the prestige which he eventually acquired, Seddon had to thank not only the favoring economic circumstances but also his own efforts. In 1893 his accession to the premiership was by no means assured, even though he had deputized for Ballance during the latter's illness. In the cabinet were two other potential premiers—McKenzie, as strong in personality as Seddon himself, and Reeves, whose intellectual qualities later brought him the directorship of the London School of Economics. Outside Parliament, moreover, was an influential claimant in Stout, the Liberal former premier, whom some members of

10. W. P. Reeves, *The Long White Cloud* (3d ed.; London: Allen & Unwin, 1924), p. 284.

11. *Ibid.*, pp. 264–65.

the party preferred to see as Ballance's successor. The details of
how Seddon came to be chosen are rather obscure and have to
be pieced together from different sources. Drummond in his biography states only that there was a rival candidate for the premiership and that Seddon was selected "after a long meeting" of the
cabinet.[12] The facts appear to be that the cabinet merely confirmed Seddon as acting premier, leaving it for the party caucus
to choose between him and Stout. Anxiously seeking support,
Seddon turned to the old Liberal leader, Sir George Grey, and
received his willing indorsement because Grey was personally
hostile to Stout.[13] Stout himself, however, made suggestions both
to Ward and to McKenzie that they should take office in a cabinet to be formed under his premiership. McKenzie at one stage
was inclined to favor Stout on condition that he received the
backing of the caucus. But eventually Ward and McKenzie both
adhered to Seddon, and the caucus confirmed him in his position
as party leader and premier.[14] These events are significant, since
they prove how insecurely Seddon vaulted into power. In the
Colony at large the choice of permier came rather as a surprise,
since he had still to prove his capacity. "The country," as Reeves
remarks, "gave a little gasp of mingled amazement and amusement, but on the whole was disposed to give the daring man a
chance."[15]

Thirteen years later when the daring man died at sea from a
heart attack induced by overwork, he had converted the government of New Zealand into something akin to a personal autocracy. For the last six years he enjoyed a position that was unassailable. He had broken the parliamentary opposition after five
years of hard fighting. His will was law in New Zealand. So great
was his power, so general his popularity, that he was known as
"King Dick." Admirers spoke of his premiership as a reign;
critics called it dictatorship. The qualities that made this pos-

12. J. Drummond, *The Life and Work of Richard John Seddon* (Wellington: Whitcombe & Tombs, 1907), p. 174.
13. See J. Collier, *Life of Sir George Grey* (Wellington: Whitcombe & Tombs,
1909), pp. 193–96.
14. For some retrospective sidelights on these negotiations consult *P.D.*, XCII
(1896), 31 and 50.
15. *Op. cit.*, p. 297.

sible deserve analysis, for they throw light not only on the general problem of democratic leadership but also on the special character of New Zealand. It must be beyond question that a country which acquiesced so long in such predominance by one man must have found in him a satisfying response to its political needs.

Seddon's outstanding trait was a complete singleness of aim. Ambitious beyond measure, he sought the highest political office he could reach. Once it was attained, he used every means to stay there. To his political career he devoted all his tireless energies. He was, in every sense of the term, a professional politician— the first of the modern kind to be seen in New Zealand and a thoroughgoing example of the type. He was as clearsighted in defining his objectives as in maneuvering toward them. What he achieved was due to his individual efforts, since advantages of birth, of money, and of education were not his. The semieducated son of two Lancashire schoolteachers, he emigrated as a youth, plunging into the hurly-burly of gold-mining in Australia and then in New Zealand. In the rough-and-tumble politics of the New Zealand west coast in its boom days he emerged as the vigorous and unpolished leader of a mining community. Elected to local offices, then to the Provincial Council, thence to the House of Representatives, he was an outspoken and long-speaking champion of his constituents. Concerning his determination to make himself master in the political field, Reeves, his colleague in the lower house and later in the cabinet, is a witness: "He concentrated absolutely on politics, seeming to live, move and think for them alone. Books, save blue-books, he ignored. . . . . I cannot recall hearing him talk of any non-political subject for ten minutes."[16] On similar lines his biographer records: "He learnt May's *Parliamentary Practice* almost by heart, and other standard works on the practical part of Parliamentary work were among the few books he cared to read or study."[17] Thus equipped, by his attention to detail, by his grasp of procedure, and by an intuitive flair for the psychology of politics, he could frequently override or outflank men with better brains and nicer scruples.

His courage cannot be called in question. He would take on any opponent with zest and, once starting to fight, would never

16. *Ibid.*, p. 305.   17. Drummond, *op. cit.*, p. 23.

surrender. His tenacity has become almost legendary. Some of his victories were gained by sheer feats of will-power, when he broke down an opposition by an endurance that was both physical and psychological. The most spectacular of such occasions came at the climax of the long-fought battle over his Old Age Pensions Bill when he sat in the committee of the House continuously for eighty-seven hours and won a war of exhaustion. To his colleagues, past and present, he was loyal. Unoriginal in his own ideas, he had the wit to appreciate the suggestions of others and the sagacity to estimate their political usefulness. He supported Reeves in his labor legislation and upheld it after Reeves went to England. He backed McKenzie's land laws and continued them after the old farmer resigned and died. The only measure that he personally initiated was the grant of old age pensions on a noncontributory basis—a measure typical of his aims and methods. Broadly humanitarian in his sympathy, he favored proposals that made life easier for ordinary men and women.[18] Ever mindful of the next election, he designed his schemes and arranged their timing to suit his electoral advantage. The introduction of the Old Age Pensions Bill was his means of extricating himself from a difficult political position.[19] From its passage the people benefited—and so did Richard John Seddon. His long ascendancy had the fortunate result of establishing and confirming the social service tendency in New Zealand legislation. Since his time there have been occasional episodes of whittling away the services provided by the state, but New Zealand has always swung back to the course which Seddon charted.

Seddon was determined that the state should serve its citizens; and, constituting himself the chief purveyor of services, he was at once the people's servant and their master. It was his unvarying practice to find out what the people wanted. If politically possible, he would give it to them, and he would make sure that it appeared as his gift. Unfailingly he toured the country from end to end, hobnobbing with local worthies, receiving deputations, hearing requests, and granting favors. His chief electoral asset was his own ubiquitousness. Seddon brought the activities of the

18. *Ibid.*, p. 327.
19. See Reeves, *op. cit.*, p. 298.

government—and himself—into the people's homes. "King Dick" was also "Our Dick."

But there is a reverse side to this picture of a man of the people serving the people. Seddon did not know the distinction between leading and dominating; or, if he did, he was disposed toward the latter. His power developed into a virtual autocracy, which, but for his death in 1906, might have been prejudicial to the future of New Zealand. To his cabinet and his own party he behaved in dictatorial fashion, being resentful of criticism and intolerant of rivals. His own attitude to newly elected Liberal representatives is revealed in a letter he wrote at the end of his life, where he discusses the results of the 1905 election: "I have my troubles before me, although with the whole of our party returned, and with only a few new members (or in other words 'young colts') to break in, the duties of the whips and the driving of the coachmen will not entail much anxiety."[20] As a private member he had himself been unruly and obstructionist. As premier, like all autocrats, he would not tolerate similar behavior toward himself. Even when one allows for the circumstances of political debate, there was much truth in the remarks made by Russell, the leader of the opposition: "It is necessary that the people of the colony should know also that by the autocratic will of the Premier his supporters in Parliament are not allowed an opinion . . . . ; they are not allowed to express the opinions of their constituents; they are made to sit silent; they are not allowed even to debate if the Premier wishes them not to do so. There is no limit to the autocratic power of the Premier, who resents criticism from either opponents or friends."[21]

The results of Seddon's dominance can be seen in various directions. The contrast between the personnel of his cabinet in 1893 and in 1906 speaks volumes. Reeves, McKenzie, and Ward were three valuable colleagues whom Ballance bequeathed as his political legacy to his successor. Reeves, the intellectual and the scholar, whose careful study and drafting produced the New Zealand labor code, left the ministry within three years. It has been said that when Seddon, the man of action, lost Reeves, the

20. Quoted in Drummond, *op. cit.*, pp. 358–59.
21. *P.D.*, XCIII (1896), 517–18.

man of ideas, it was the premier's greatest political blunder.[22]
Most probably the separation came about with mutual gladness.
McKenzie stuck to his post until ill-health forced his resignation,
but being cast in a Seddonian mold himself, and possessing a
loyal following among the small farmers, he was too powerful to
be dispensed with. His independence of the premier is illustrated
by an event told to the writer by a governmental official who
was personally acquainted with the circumstances. A file containing a proposal for a certain course of action was prepared in
the department of agriculture, approved by the permanent head
and by McKenzie, and sent forward for the premier's consent.
Seddon did not agree, wrote on the file "Not approved," and returned it to McKenzie. The latter merely added above Seddon's
comment the word "Proceed" and passed it on with this instruction to the head of his department. "King Dick," however, preferred to surround himself with "yes-men." When he died, his
ministry contained, apart from Ward, only a bundle of mediocrities obedient to his will. Ward, on becoming premier, had to
scrap a number of them.

In his party Seddon engineered the same deterioration in
quality as in the cabinet. For Liberals to oppose him in the caucus was dangerous; in the House, it was suicidal. New Liberal
representatives he considered, as his letter shows, to be young
colts who had to be broken in. Reeves significantly remarks that
"Seddon was not over-fond of intellectuals and had a propensity
for breaking with the clever young men of his party. He had an
exceptional power of attracting and managing ordinary men,
and usually preferred to trust to that."[23] It was not ordinary men
who built up the Liberal party to a strength with which it could
hold continuous office for twenty years. Nor could ordinary men
insure its future. Seddon's policies, as far as his party was concerned, were an endowment for his own security, designed to last
his own lifetime. He made no proper provision for the future.
An organization depending on the personal ascendancy of one
man could not outlive its autocratic master. Five years after

22. W. D. Stewart, Introduction to André Siegfried, *Democracy in New Zealand*,
trans. E. V. Burns (London: Bell & Sons, 1914), p. xiv.
23. *Op. cit.*, pp. 301-2.

Seddon's death his party had collapsed, and the utter ineffectiveness of Liberal leaders in the twenties was in large part the longterm result of his hostility to new talents. Seddon helped to create the Reform party by driving the able men away.

This dominance extended in like degree to the sphere of administration. At the time of his death Seddon held, in addition to the premiership, such major portfolios as labor, finance, defense, education, and immigration! Matters of detail, no less than questions of major policy, required his personal authorization. His tendency to amass all kinds of work into his own hands, and a temperamental inability to delegate, played havoc with the running of the administrative machine. Since the premier was perennially stumping the country, business piled up on his desk in Wellington awaiting a judgment on his return. Siegfried interviewed him just after he had come back to the capital from one of his political tours and was greeted with the statement: "See, I came back yesterday from a journey, and here I find this accumulation of papers; I shall run through them and then set out again to get an idea of what the Colony thinks, so as not to lose touch with public opinion."[24]

Particularly regrettable was the harm done to standards of political morality. Typical of the charges leveled against Seddon was the criticism made by an opponent in 1896: "He has, in his career as Premier and Treasurer, dragged down politics to a depth never before reached in any British colony I know of."[25] That statement is, of course, exaggerated, and New Zealand politics prior to Seddon were not all of the purest. The activities of persons like Whitaker and the general tone of Parliament during the eighties were not so edifying that Seddon could be held personally responsible for corrupting a lily-white community. There was much that was unsavory in the conduct of colonial politics before Seddon. What he did, however, was to systematize and organize a number of unwholesome practices. Certainly Seddon did not invent patronage in New Zealand, but it was he who for over thirteen years found and used unrivaled opportunities to fill the civil service with nominees of his political supporters. It was not Seddon who created the pork barrel, yet he

24. *Op. cit.*, p. 95.   25. *P.D.*, XCV (1896), 69.

assuredly mastered its full implications and applied them with
unsurpassed shrewdness and skill. In so doing, he was perfectly
frank, for he stated: "It is unreasonable and unnatural to expect
the Government to look with the same kindly eye on districts returning members opposed to the Government as on those which
returned Government supporters."[26] Perhaps he may claim more
originality for introducing the practice of part-time employment
on various public works projects. When an election was drawing
near, temporary employees would be taken on at £3 a week in
strategic areas. As one member pointed out in the House in 1896:
"We have the elections coming on, and to have a number of
voters employed washing gravel and making concrete will be
very handy in determining the next Rangitikei representative.
That is the object, no doubt; and that the viaduct has been delayed for that purpose, I verily believe."[27] Those familiar with
the politics of other democracies will find nothing surprising in
such a system. It has its counterparts in the political use of the
highways department by the Liberal party in the Province of
Quebec and in the manipulation of the W.P.A. in certain states
prior to the American presidential election of 1936. Seddon's art-
ful dispensing of the Public Works Fund was a by-word in his
day. Similarly the Railways Department with its huge staff was
taken away from the control of a three-membered commission
and placed immediately under a minister in 1894, a change which
facilitated a political administration.

Such is the portrait of New Zealand's leading prime minister.
Even today the appeal to Seddon still strikes a response in the
ordinary voter, as the Labor party has rediscovered. A journalist
who has been closely associated with New Zealand politics and
politicians for over forty years once expressed to me his view that
Seddon's has been the strongest personality in any Parliament
since 1900. It is unfortunate that, owing to this strength, the less
desirable effects have, along with all the good, become imbedded
in the political tradition of the Dominion.

The change from Seddon to Ward epitomized the declining

26. Quoted in J. E. Le Rossignol and W. D. Stewart, *State Socialism in New
Zealand* (London: Harrap & Co., 1912), p. 109.
27. *P.D.*, XCII (1896), 252.

fortunes of liberalism. The man with the broad popular appeal was succeeded by one whose sympathies were more circumscribed. Ward's personal limitations contributed to the restriction of Liberal influence. It enabled Massey to build up the Reform party out of the North Island farmers. A representative of the most southerly geographical region of New Zealand, Ward could not lead a country in which the north was then gaining so rapidly in numbers. His character and interests, moreover, made it certain that Labor would leave the Liberal camp. Although Ward, like Seddon, had made his own way in the world, he had quickly emerged into the class of the capitalist entrepreneur. Commerce in a big way, speculative finance, and private banking—this was his economic milieu. To the organized trade-unions, especially to their militant wing, such activities reeked of the bourgeois. To the ordinary man in the street, and on the farm, those whom Seddon had captivated by assiduous attentions, Ward seemed just another businessman. Under his premiership a two-party system quickly reappeared, bearing with it the future potentialities of a three-party deadlock. The subsequent episode of his reinvestiture with the highest office in 1928 was a merely pitiable return to the limelight of a man already ill and declining.

For thirteen years (1912–25) Massey was Ward's successful rival. His continuous tenure of the premiership almost equaled that of Seddon, and at the time of his death his national prestige was second only to that which "King Dick" had enjoyed. His political success was greater than Ward's and inferior to Seddon's because his popular appeal was wider than that of the former and narrower than that of the latter. His character lacked the flamboyant colors which make Seddon so arresting. Massey came to power at the head of a party pledged to reform the political institutions which liberalism was alleged to have corrupted. He was careful to cultivate a public reputation for honesty. A working farmer himself, he championed the freehold during long years in opposition; and, when he became premier, he took the portfolio of lands as his own charge. Despite the length of his premiership, neither his electoral nor his parliamentary position was ever as secure as Seddon's. His years in office coincided with a string of difficulties, first, in the sphere of labor relations, then in the conduct of the war, and later in the troubles attendant on the postwar slump. He clung to power, albeit precariously, and was actually the only British wartime premier to be holding the same office as late as 1925. Before the war the North Island dairy farmers made up the core of his political support. Antagonism to the militants among organized labor was a consistent thread running through his administration. He was quite prepared in 1912 and 1913 to use violence for breaking strikes. After the war he developed this tendency by skilfully exploiting the fears of bolshevism entertained by all who had property to lose. It was the aim of his propaganda to identify the Labor party as "red" and to brand its leaders as extremists. Thus he courted the urban business interests, hoping to ally them with the farmers in a common front against socialism.

Within his own party Massey acquired a thorough ascendancy. Liberal opponents tossed back the taunt of a one-man party which Reformers had flung at them in former days. How much truth underlay it was admitted by a Reform backbencher, who defended himself, as well as Massey, with the reply: "The reason why this party appears to be a one-man party is that every man in it is loyal to its leader, and that we focus on him the policy of the party."[28] Yet, partly because he had to face a stronger opposition, partly because he was less lustful for personal power, he showed more tolerance inside his party and his cabinet than Seddon. Throughout his years as premier he always relied heavily on Bell, so much so that to some the leadership appeared a dyarchy, while others believed that Bell really dominated Massey behind the scenes. The truth is, according to Stewart, that the talents of the two men aptly complemented each other; but Massey remained the chief. "He recognised," Stewart writes of Bell, "that on all question of political strategy and tactics Massey had a flair for knowing the trend of public opinion and what measures he could induce Parliament to adopt. This instinctive, practical, empirical knowledge of what the man in the street thought, Massey had gained by long years of arduous fighting and constant direct contact with all classes of electors, both in town and country. . . . . On the other hand, when it came to a

28. *P.D.*, CXCIX (1923), 98.

question of finding a solution to some difficult problem, or of drafting an intricate Bill, or of giving advice on legal and constitutional problems, Massey realised that Bell was a consummate master. Indeed, the qualities of the two men—the practical sagacity of the one and the profound learning and skill of the other—made an admirable political combination."[29] It is doubtful whether Seddon could ever have endured for so long this powerful figure close to his throne.

Apart from his dependence upon Bell, Massey was forced by circumstances to be tolerant toward the younger men of ability in his own party. After the war there was a group which showed signs of forming a "cave" within the Reform ranks. Massey wisely avoided trouble by taking some of the prominent members into his cabinet. In so doing, he strengthened his own position. During his last Parliament, when his majority was exiguous, Massey tried to impose discipline on Reform backbenchers. "Sometimes his exasperation," says Stewart, "led to outbursts that seem amusing in retrospect. When he was told that one member was absent from the House through sickness he exclaimed: 'I won't have members going to bed merely because they are ill. If they want to die, they must die in the House.' " The private members, on the other hand, found their own importance and bargaining power increased since the premier's hold over Parliament was so precarious. Massey resorted to at least some of the undesirable expedients which Seddon had elevated into a political system. He could not fill the lower grades of the civil service with political appointees, since his own government had instituted a nonpolitical Public Service Commission in 1912. Yet the Railways and the Post and Telegraph departments were under separate staff management and directly subject to ministerial control. Public works were allocated to districts on well-worn pork-barrel principles, and, if the parliamentary support of an odd Independent or two was necessary to bolster the ministry on confidence motions, Massey would enter into the needed bargains.

The Reform leadership passed, on Massey's death, to Coates, a farmer from the north of Auckland, who had served gallantly

29. *Op. cit.*, pp. 291–92.

in the war. After the war his political rise had been rapid if not meteoric. He entered Parliament in 1911 and was appointed as a minister in 1919, when Massey found it expedient to take a returned soldier into the cabinet. In 1925 he became premier at the age of forty-seven, far younger than the average for modern prime ministers in New Zealand. The hugeness of the electoral majority which he received in that year was perhaps unfortunate, since it inspired him at the time with excessive self-confidence. The slogans with which the campaign was publicized encouraged a belief that his administration would be characterized by energetic and bustling activity. Within three years the high hopes had fizzled out. Coates did not shine as a parliamentary leader. Committing various tactical blunders, he dissipated the party's confidence in his judgment. Unlike Massey, he did not rely to a very great extent on Bell, although he pressed Bell to remain in the cabinet. For his part, the elder statesman and one-time premier was careful not to obtrude his advice where it was not sought. He wrote at that time in a letter to a former colleague: "All the part I have taken for so many years past with Mr. Massey, I am carefully abstaining from entering upon."[30] Unfortunately for himself, Coates trusted to his own discretion, which at times led him astray.

Some of his better qualities, however, were seen during the depression years, when, as minister of finance in the coalition government, he ruled over Forbes, the nominal premier. Coates made a genuine attempt to grapple with the economic breakdown. Although some of his schemes were ill conceived and others rendered him personally unpopular, he was courageous enough to take difficult decisions and sufficiently wise to seek the best assistance offering. Like many other countries, including Britain, New Zealand tried to defeat the depression with "orthodox" budgetary conservatism. Nevertheless, in certain directions, the powers of the state were extended to alleviate distress. Some remedies of a mildly progressive nature were too radical for the right-wing conservatives, who decried Coates for being a socialist. To left-wingers, on the other hand, and in particular to the Labor opposition, the remedial measures seemed inadequate pal-

30. Quoted by Stewart (*ibid.*, pp. 242–43).

liatives. Inaugurating public works and relieving mortgagees of their burdens did not do enough to compensate for the drastic "economies" in social services.

In one respect Coates stands out almost alone in the line of New Zealand premiers. He brought to his office an appreciation of administrative problems which he had earlier displayed as minister of railways. During the depression he surrounded himself with an able group of young university-trained men, whom he utilized as a "brain trust." He preferred not to act until research had been conducted and plans investigated. He was aware to a greater degree than most prime ministers that a chief executive must delegate and that details must be handled by subordinates. Had his social sympathies only been broader and his human insight more profound, he might have been more concerned to mitigate privation and less interested in balancing budgets.

The Labor party, and its leader, were the beneficiaries of the odium heaped upon Coates. At the election of 1935 Savage was not widely known in the country, since only in the previous year, when Holland died, had he become head of the party. But during his first three years in office he succeeded in cultivating something of that broad popular appeal which was Seddon's speciality. The revival and expansion of social services brought him the good will of the majority—and their votes. The public's impression of the premier in the election year of 1938 pictured an elderly bachelor, simple, sincere, and benevolent toward his fellow-men. Extensively circulated photographs of a benignly smiling expression helped to build up the mass symbol. Sentiments of gratitude to the premier personally for the returning prosperity were frequently demonstrated and in many cases were genuinely felt. Head of the government which in 1938 put the Social Security Act through Parliament, Savage was viewed as a man brimming with the milk of human kindness and a giver of all good things. How intensely personal was his appeal can be illustrated from this incident told to me by a university student who saw it happen in a polling booth on election day. An old woman came in and told the official in charge that she wanted a voting paper to vote for Mr. Savage. She was given the voting paper, but it was ex-

plained, to her disappointment, that the premier was standing
for a constituency in Auckland and could not receive a vote cast
in Wellington. To vote for the Labor candidate in her particular
electorate seemed a poor substitute.

But the Pickwickian benevolence which appeared to signify a
mild and gentle man was combined with considerable strength.
When differences of opinion over financial policy revealed themselves in the Labor ranks, Savage remained fiercely loyal to his
minister of finance, Walter Nash. The premier would not be
moved by Labor left-wingers in the party caucus who assailed
Nash for being too orthodox and cautious. From one point of
view, this was a splendid example of a premier's loyalty to a colleague, and Savage deserved to be commended for standing by
his able subordinate. Viewed from another angle, however,
Savage could be considered obstinate in his deafness to the wishes
of younger Laborites. An old party fighter, Savage had rewarded
the stalwarts and veterans of past Labor campaigns with places in
the cabinet. Unlike Massey after 1919, he was unwilling to admit new talent to the higher councils. When a majority in the
caucus declared after the election of 1938 that they would choose
the cabinet for the prime minister, he retorted outright that he
would pick his own colleagues and threatened to resign unless he
had his way. The display of firmness reaped its temporary victory
—but at the cost of a secession from the party by some malcontents in and after 1940.

The examples of Seddon, Massey, and Savage indicate what
qualities are required of a New Zealand premier. The all-important essential is to cultivate the broad popular appeal. The prime
minister must build up a personal relationship with the citizens:
service to their needs in return for their electoral support. Bagehot considered the most successful type of British premier to be
"an uncommon man of common opinions." With a slight modification that judgment will apply to New Zealand. Here a premier must certainly have common opinions; he must, that is to
say, reflect the mass judgment. He must also be an uncommon
man where force of character and political shrewdness are concerned. But he should not possess uncommon intellectual ability.
If he does, he will find that his brains are, politically, a liability.

In an equalitarian democracy the prime minister must carefully avoid or conceal anything that sets him too far apart from his fellows. This applies to his social position no less than to his personal attributes. Seddon and Massey, who knew their people, lavished knighthoods on their colleagues but never added the prefix "Sir" to their own names. Ward, being less endowed with psychological insight, went so far as to accept a baronetcy, thereby offending colonial opinion, which does not approve of hereditary titles except when held by a British aristocrat. Although Coates did not make himself a knight, the rumor was spread around that he assumed social airs, and, whether true or not, this harmed him politically.

Successful premiers in this Dominion have been shrewd to sense popular feeling and anticipate public demands. They have shared the mentality of the average person and shown an understanding of his needs. Had they been intellectually brilliant, they would have been mistrusted, for the electorate is suspicious of minds that range to loftier spheres. Outstanding brain-power, in fact, may bring a man near to the top, but it will disqualify him from the topmost position. Seddon had to be premier, not Reeves; Massey, not Bell; Coates, not Stewart. Failures in the premiership have been persons like Ward or Coates, who neglected to popularize themselves with the ordinary voter, or someone like Forbes, whose abilities were just too mediocre in every respect. The successful premiers have not been endowed with learning or culture. Nor have they even been orators, if by that term is implied a noble and dignified style of speech. Oratory is virtually unknown nowadays in New Zealand politics. Instead a premier must be a forceful speaker. He needs not elegance but power; not eloquence but vigor. In debate he must be crushing to the point of rudeness. To bandy personalities is not against the rules. Some of the repartee with which Seddon, Massey, and others, retorted to criticism was the reverse of polite.

In the conduct of administration, a prime minister, while superior to other ministers, must share their tasks under pain of flouting the dogmas of equalitarianism. If they are loaded with portfolios and burdened with "administrivia," he must be the same. Most New Zealand premiers have not understood how to run the country's largest business, its government. They have not appreciated that the chief executive must be free to think, to plan, and to view all particular administrative problems in broad perspective. They have taken portfolios into their own hands and dealt with detailed routine and inconsequential minutiae. All this is over and above the supervisory tasks which necessarily fall to the head of the government: co-ordination of colleagues, receiving deputations, control of party strategy, and attendance at public ceremonies.

It is an accepted New Zealand practice, established by the Seddon tradition, that the premier's door is open to the individual citizen seeking redress of a grievance or the grant of a favor. To describe to what lengths the practice is carried would require the publication of any premier's weekly diary of engagements. But anyone who has any conversance with administration in the capital city has an inkling of the matters that come to the prime minister's desk and of the callers who consume his time. Hundreds of individuals and organizations seek interviews with the premier; many (far too many) receive a personal hearing. Read what John Gunther had to say about the president of Costa Rica, and you will have an analogy.[13] The effects of the system are a mixture in which, possibly, the bad outweighs the good. In principle, let it be admitted, the tradition of approachability, which successive premiers have fostered, is thoroughly democratic. Normally any citizen can, if he wants it, gain direct access to the most powerful man in the land. The individual's right of interview not only exists but is regularly exercised. Seddon encouraged it on a wide scale, for "King Dick" loved to hold court. The Epigoni have duly followed suit. Direct, day-to-day, man-to-man contact between government and the governed does exist in New Zealand. On that score the needs of democracy are satisfied. What is more, the premiers do not only sit and await their callers. Their visits around the country, their addresses to all manner of conferences, their attendance at a host of social functions—these are part of the stock-in-trade. The premiership requires an infinite capacity for shaking hands.

31. *Inside Latin America* (New York: Harper & Bros., 1941), p. 134.

But the abuses can be as serious as those already noticed in the discussion about the cabinet.[32] Even in a country with only a million and three-quarter inhabitants the calls on a premier's time are excessive. Once the practice of direct access to his office is established, where can the line be drawn? When all have the vote, who is to be shut out? It is true that the system's shortcomings are due in very large part to the unreasonableness of citizens who have no compunction in seeing a prime minister about matters which, though important to an individual, may be nationally insignificant. Some premiers, however, are themselves to blame for not discouraging the time-wasters.

As yet, New Zealand is a long way from a solution to the problem of securing effective, but democratic, leadership. The premiership has undeniably been democratized. It has become the instrument of popular rule which it was not before 1890. Today, instead of being aloof from the people, it is, if anything, almost too close to them. Both the average caliber of personnel in this office and the organization of its functions call for improvement. The apex of the governmental pyramid needs recarving to a new design.

32. See above, chap. x, pp. 282–84.

CHAPTER XII

PARLIAMENT

THE importance to democracy of a popularly elected legislature cannot be overemphasized. At one time or another in their history parliaments have been called upon to perform functions as vital as the petitioning for remedy of grievances, the authorization of taxation and expenditure, the enactment of laws, the control of executive departments, and the interpretation of public opinion. Every properly constituted governmental system which subscribes to democratic principles must insure that it contains due provision for all these functions. The institution charged with their performance occupies a central position in the machinery of state. Though this was furthest from their intentions, dictators have paid profound tribute to the significance of legislative assemblies. Their open hostility was shown by the carefulness with which they crippled the powers of parliaments and packed them with their uniformed gangs to *heil* and to applaud. The writings of Mussolini and Hitler's *Mein Kampf* go out of their way to dilate upon the weaknesses of elected legislatures, to belittle their activities, and to heap scorn on their personnel. An attack so elaborately devised reflects their awareness that the legislature did represent to the public mind a custodian of liberty and thus formed a menace to dictatorship. The burning of the Reichstag was more than a tactical trick; it was both a symbol and a challenge. The presence or absence of a freely functioning legislature is one of the essential criteria to distinguish democracy from its opposite. Hence the need for a careful appraisal of Parliament, of its members and their work.

But here enters a paradox. While the indispensability of the legislature to democracy would be readily accepted as a general proposition, it would be argued in many individual cases that this or that legislature has declined in effectiveness and repute. The French nation in the period between the two world wars did not highly esteem their national assembly. Britain's Parliament was much criticized in the same two decades, although it did retain greater public respect than its sister-body across the Channel. In the United States the federal Congress and the legislatures of various states have at times conducted themselves in a manner detrimental to their prestige. New Zealand offers one more example to add to the list. The Parliament of the Dominion does not stand high enough in the public regard. On a candid survey of the facts one must admit that there is a wide gulf between the importance which attaches to democratic legislatures in virtue of their functions and the repute which many of them actually enjoy among those they represent and serve. Such a discrepancy must provoke grave reflection among all who have at heart the preservation and improvement of democracy. It is in the legislature that democracy's task of adaptation to twentieth-century necessities has created its greatest strains and stresses. The institutions of democracy are in crisis because they are in transition,[1] and the legislature is passing through the transition less successfully than our cabinets, civil services, and other institutions. To realize that Parliament's various functions are no longer equally suited to its machinery, and that the relative need of legislative participation in these diverse functions has altered, is the key to an understanding of the problem. It is also the starting-point of an insight into the crisis within the institutional structure of democracy. The causes and the effects of this state of affairs, as they apply to New Zealand, are the subject of this chapter.

The Lawmaking Function

When the functions of the nineteenth-century parliaments were described, it was pointed out that in latter decades control over legislation tended to pass from the two houses combined to the lower chamber and from it to the cabinet.[2] That trend has been continued and confirmed throughout the fifty years since the Liberals took office. In modern times the only bills on a topic

1. See H. J. Laski, *Democracy in Crisis* (Chapel Hill: University of North Carolina Press, 1933), and W. E. Rappard, *The Crisis of Democracy* (Chicago: University of Chicago Press, 1938).
2. See above, chap. vi, pp. 127–31 and 139–42.

of importance that have any chance of enactment are those which the ministry chooses to introduce. Before they are brought into Parliament, government measures, as these are called, are prepared by the relevant departments, dissected in the cabinet, and, very often, scrutinized and debated at the party caucus. Parliament comes into the picture only at the later stages of the legislative process. It is not Parliament which selects the topics on which laws are to be passed or which drafts in detail the actual text of the bills. In all the preliminary arrangement and preparation of the legislative program the decisions that matter are taken for Parliament and not by Parliament. A British political scientist has stated in this realistic fashion how laws are actually drawn up in the mother-country: "The legislative initiative has gone from the private Member and now belongs to the Departments of State under the direction of the Cabinet, which together have become in practice the first chamber in our lawmaking mechanism."[3] In New Zealand, too, the first chamber is composed of the cabinet and the departments. But which is the second chamber? Is it Parliament or the caucus of the majority party?

The formal theories of constitutional law have their own explanation of what makes a law. The legal view holds that it is the observance of certain recognized procedures in Parliament (the three readings, committee stages, etc.) together with the royal assent that convert a bill, which is not legally binding, into a law, which is. The royal assent, of course, whether it be given by the king in person or by the governor-general on his behalf, is merely an antiquarian relic kept up for the sake of traditional form. It is possible—for there have been signs pointing this way—that the approval of Parliament may likewise be degenerating into a ceremonial gesture maintained only because it is traditional. When our legislative institutions have passed through their present transitional phase, it is not unlikely that their share in lawmaking may have dwindled to a purely formal ratification. Among the pointers are three well-known tendencies. One is the passing of the initiative in legislation from Parliament to the cabinet and

3. H. R. G. Greaves, *The British Constitution* (London: Allen & Unwin, 1938), p. 31.

the civil service. A second is the rise of disciplined party organizations which in New Zealand, at any rate on the Labor side, tend to substitute the caucus for Parliament as the effective lawmaking instrument. A third sign is the growing propensity to enact laws in very general terms and leave them to be filled in by executive regulations.

Though all these tendencies are unmistakably clear to view, they have not yet completed their full development. In any stage of transition an account of new trends must be modified and qualified by the partial survivals of older practices. It is true, for instance, that much of the subject matter and content of legislation is settled outside Parliament. Changes, however, are still made on the floor of the House and in committee. It may be that some constructive suggestions emanate from the opposition which a sensible government will want to incorporate in its bill. Or perhaps a measure was inadequately considered by the cabinet and too hastily drafted—as often occurs—and parliamentary debate lays bare the imperfections and inconsistencies. Or it can happen that an agitation will be stirred up in the press and at public meetings, so that the government will prudently offer concessions. When the Labor ministry in 1941 proposed an amendment to its Social Security Act which might ultimately have led to the socialization of the medical profession, it had an ample parliamentary majority to do what it wished. Yet it backed down before the vocal opposition of the doctors to a state medical service and accepted modification of the bill in committee. Or, again, a government may deliberately insert into the draft of a bill some stringent clauses which it does not really want and which it knows the opposition will pounce upon. By making the magnificent gesture of striking them out, it may partially satisfy the opposition and divert the criticism which would have fastened on other features. For all these reasons the act that emerges from Parliament may differ in various features from the bill that was introduced. The government initiates; Parliament amends. Yet amendments are normally confined to the less fundamental clauses. If Parliament succeeded in a major operation on a vital part, this would be tantamount to a defeat of the government. Amendments proposed by government backbenchers and members of the opposition may be adopted if they are confined to minor surgery—or, better still, to the plastic surgery of face-lifting and face-saving.

Apart from suggesting amendments to government measures, private members still retain and exercise their constitutional right to introduce their own bills. Practically none, however, of the private members' bills ever reaches the statute-book. As a representative complained in 1896: "In common with other members who have been some four or five years in this House, I have noticed a number of Bills brought forward by private members, numbering some seventy or eighty measures during a session. It is a well-known fact that many of these Bills which are introduced are never intended to pass the second reading. They are strangled at that stage, and are thrown into the waste-paper basket."[4] Since that date the legislative initiative of the backbencher has, if anything, further declined. In Britain it created almost a sensation in the late thirties when A. P. Herbert, as a private member, managed to secure some changes in the outmoded divorce laws. In New Zealand, of the very few private members' bills to become law in the last twenty years, perhaps the best known was the daylight-saving scheme of T. K. Sidey. But this persistent representative did not see his efforts rewarded until he had reintroduced the measure on the tenth occasion within fourteen years. Many a private member's bill has reappeared on the order paper at session after session without ever going beyond a second reading or the committee stage. Sometimes, of course, the opposition will announce its future program to the public by introducing measures in this manner. Thus the Public Service Act of 1912, which was fathered in the House by Herdman, the Reform attorney-general, had been proposed by him in various forms on more than one occasion during the reign of the Liberals. Seeking to embarrass the government of their day, many private members have brought in a bill providing for the election of the cabinet by Parliament. Others have drafted measures concerning Bible-reading in schools, further restrictions or prohibition of the liquor traffic, and a host of social and ethical problems. When, however, one surveys the actual legislative output of the private

4. *P.D.*, XCII (1896), 83.

members, one feels, with Horace, that they are in labor with mountains but bring forth mice.

Of recent decades the caucus has assumed a special importance in the lawmaking process. Later in this chapter the implications of the rise of the caucus will be discussed at fuller length. Here it is enough to say that, since Labor's victory in 1935, the caucus of the government party has virtually become an inner legislature. Its procedure is formalized with notices of motion, countermotions, amendments, committees, subcommittees, reports, and majority decisions.[5] It is here, in fact, that legislation is really "passed." After the caucus has decided, the disciplined party troops into the House to record the verdict already settled beforehand. If it is allowed to run its course, the trend, which has developed thus far, may make of the New Zealand system a government neither by cabinet nor parliament but by the caucus. Whether this result will emerge depends, in part, upon the future power of the Labor party, since within the National party the caucus is less rigidly established.

The third indication that legislation is ceasing to be primarily a parliamentary function is the growing predilection for orders-in-council issued under the authority of the cabinet or regulations authorized by a single minister. In this respect the two New Zealand parties, which differ somewhat in their use of the caucus, have conformed to the same pattern. When the National party, under its then guise of a coalition, was in power during the depression, it was repeatedly criticized by Labor for resorting to ministerial orders in lieu of statutory enactments. When positions were reversed, Labor behaved exactly in the fashion it had formerly condemned and was taken to task by outraged Nationalists. These facts can be explained in one or more ways. Either it is that politicians are incurably inconsistent, or that they are short both in memory and in foresight, or that modern conditions make this trend unavoidable for all governments no matter what views a party holds when in opposition. The last explanation is probably correct, since governments of all parties in New Zealand have followed the same practices in a snowball progression

5. See the pamphlets written by J. A. Lee after his expulsion from the Labor party in 1940: *I Fight for New Zealand*, etc.

for more than two decades. It is reinforced, moreover, by the fact that other democratic countries have exhibited just the same tendency. In Britain, for instance, so many tasks of a legislative and judicial nature have been conferred by act of Parliament upon administrative agencies that a former lord chief justice in an exaggerated protest discerned the rise of a "new despotism." Lord Hewart's generalizations, however, were effectively answered by the Donoughmore Commission on Ministers' Powers. Their report conceded that the trend was open to some abuses and disadvantages, for which they proposed remedies. But in favor of the use of ministerial regulations they advanced the strong reasons that it relieves the pressure on parliamentary time, allows for executive discretion to meet emergencies, and disposes satisfactorily of technical, scientific, or administrative detail. The United States has met with the same problem at both the federal and the state levels. Here, too, legislative and administrative convenience has fostered the use of executive orders, issued by presidents or governors. In America some constitutional purists in the legislatures and on the judicial bench have supported their resistance by invoking the concept of the "separation of powers." It is facile, though unrealistic, to twist Montesquieu's theory into the dogma that there exists an indivisible function of lawmaking intrusted in entirety by a written Constitution to a branch of the government called the legislature. Despite the many setbacks due to unsympathetic judicial attitudes, the resort to sublegislation and subjudication, as it is called, continues to pervade American governmental practice.

In New Zealand government by order-in-council is now a well-established procedure on which the arguments, both for and against, have been reiterated by each party. Certain obvious defects formerly observable have now been corrected. These orders are better drafted nowadays and are published in a uniform series which runs to bulkier length for every successive year.[6] The device much criticized in England and known as the "Henry the Eighth clause," which conferred on the minister a power to amend portions even of an act by regulation, has not yet been

6. The form of regulations and the procedure for issuing them were systematized in a Regulations Act of 1936.

employed in New Zealand. But while the arguments used in the Donoughmore report to justify ministerial regulations are applicable to this Dominion, there are, nevertheless, certain abuses of the practice in New Zealand, none of which, however, is irremediable or strikes at basic principles. A civil servant who has had much experience with these orders-in-council told me his belief that many of them would be declared *ultra vires* if someone cared to challenge them in the courts. Often an order, which may be invalid, stands for years merely because it is unchallenged. There was an important case in 1939 in which a business firm tested the legality of the government's policy of controlling foreign exchange and licensing imports. This step was taken by the Labor ministry early in 1939, immediately after their re-election, but before the new Parliament had convened. It was introduced by order-in-council under the supposed authority of earlier acts dealing with quite different financial and economic matters. The regulations were duly pronounced invalid by the court,[7] as indeed they were. But the new Parliament soon legalized the needed powers. Since Parliament is "sovereign," unconstitutionality presents few fears to any ministry with a secure legislative majority.

From the point of view of a cabinet which dislikes publicity, the advantages of incorporating contentious points in regulations rather than in the body of an act are obvious. Numerous New Zealand ministries have shown their preference for skeletal legislation conferring wide powers in broad terms. The vague, general clauses of the enactment then receive specific content from orders-in-council. The statute-book is cluttered with legislation of very general scope, for there has been a contagious habit of taking extensive powers to do all manner of things and of keeping these powers on the statute-book just in case it may be expedient at some time to use any of them. Many laws do little else than grant powers and establish an organization to achieve some vaguely stated objective. An example is the Full Employment Act of 1945, which is mainly a machinery measure and contains little about substantive policy. Both legislative and administrative convenience makes the order-in-council an indispensable

7. *Jackson* v. *The Collector of Customs*, G.L.R. 229 (1939).

tool of government. There are overwhelmingly cogent reasons to show why successive ministries have favored the use of regulations and why they should continue to be used in the future. But it would be wrong to deny that the practice can be abused or that it has been abused by both New Zealand parties. The abuses, however, can be remedied without impairing this valuable adjunct to modern administration.

The Control of the Public Purse

Simultaneously Parliament has also been losing much of the control it formerly possessed over finance. That conclusion follows inescapably from an analysis of the New Zealand system. Control over finance is a co-operative venture jointly managed by the Treasury, the spending departments, the cabinet, the House of Representatives, and the controller and auditor-general. Of all these authorities, the House, though formally supreme, is in actual practice a minor partner.[8] The machinery for the preparation of the budget is set in motion by the Treasury, which in May of each year sends round to all departments a request for their estimated revenue and expenditure. Since the new financial year begins on April 1, departments draw up their estimates during the first quarter of the year in which the money will be raised and spent. There is a standing legislative authorization in the Public Revenues Act permitting departments in the first quarter of the new financial year to spend up to one-quarter of their last year's appropriation. This is intended to tide over the interim period between the close of the old year and the passage of the new Appropriation Act. Often the minister of finance will tell the Treasury at this early budgetary stage whether the cabinet is ready to sanction a greater or smaller total of expenditure than in the previous year; and sometimes, when requesting each department to submit its estimates, the Treasury gives a rough indication of the amount that will probably be granted.

The next phase of the work is carried out within the depart-

8. The following account is based upon the writer's conversations with officials of the Treasury, of the spending departments, of the Audit Office, and of the House of Representatives, as well as with two former speakers and other members of Parliament.

ments, where the chief of the accounts branch collects estimates
from each branch, section, or bureau. Consulting the permanent
head of the department, the accountant tries to reduce certain
items if the total amount requested exceeds the sum mentioned
by the Treasury. Before their expenditure estimates are forwarded to the Treasury, departments will first show them to their respective ministers. (Revenue estimates, however, may not always
be submitted to ministers before being handed in to the Treasury.) Should a new departmental activity or some special increase of work make it impossible to keep within the Treasury's
allocation, the permanent head must negotiate with the Secretary of the Treasury and explain his need for more funds.[9] If
these two officials cannot reach agreement, then the issue is referred to the political heads, the minister of finance and the minister in charge of the department concerned. If these become deadlocked, the prime minister must give a decision either on his personal authority or after cabinet discussion. By this time all the
political, as well as the administrative, implications will have
been thrashed out, and proposals will be dealt with according to
their bearing on the state of the exchequer and on the government's future electoral prospects.

By the end of May the Treasury has received most of the departmental estimates, although certain laggard agencies may delay until June. The estimates of revenue, supplied by the tax-
collecting departments (e.g., the Customs and the Land and Income Tax departments), cause the Treasury less difficulty than
the estimates of expenditure. It is the experience of the Treasury
that revenue agencies normally understate their probable income, because they wish to be on the safe side and will be proud
if they can show a surplus at the end of the year. On the other
hand, spending departments usually overstate their requirements,
since they wish to have a margin for contingencies and since they
expect their requests to be cut down in any case. Thus, in balancing its budget, the Treasury will regularly add a percentage
to the estimates of revenue that are submitted and will lop off

9. Usually the Treasury prefers to tell a department that it must reduce its
grand total than to specify which particular items are to be cut. It is then more difficult for the department to throw squarely upon the Treasury the onus for reducing
individual salaries or curtailing certain activities.

something somewhere from the expenditure estimates. The total estimates, both of expenditure and of revenue, are laid before the cabinet by the finance minister. If the estimated revenue is inadequate to meet the proposed outlay, the government must weigh up the political effects of either decreasing the expenditure or increasing taxation or raising a loan. Once these decisions are taken, the completed budget is presented (usually in June) in highly itemized form to Parliament.[10] When it receives the estimates, the House of Representatives consigns them to the Public Accounts Committee, composed of ten private members drawn from both parties. Through this committee it would be possible for the House to exercise control over finance. In reality, however, as the system now operates in New Zealand, the work of the committee is absolutely inadequate. This criticism is conceded on all sides by the officials and the parliamentarians with whom the writer has discussed the matter. The committee, it is true, conducts hearings of the departmental estimates at which the permanent head of the department concerned and his senior officers are present. But these hearings are usually so brief that the estimates of a whole department, running possibly into several millions of pounds, may be disposed of in less than three-quarters of an hour. Some of the committee members are unversed in public finance, while others may want the whole business to be settled with the greatest possible speed. Department heads have told the writer that the chairman will turn over the pages of the estimates with rapidity, asking members of the committee if they have any questions about the items on each succeeding page. Such questions as are asked usually deal with small matters of purely local interest to the electorate of the individual member. The bigger issues are seldom raised. Even if a department head has come to the committee all prepared to answer some ticklish objection, the odds are that the point will not even be mentioned. Finally, to complete the sorry story, this committee, unlike its British namesake, presents its report not to the House but to the government. Its recommendations, if it troubles to make any, are merely advisory and can, of course, be ignored.

10. Supplementary estimates, containing new items, may also be submitted later in the session.

Summing it up, a high civil servant commented to the writer: "As a form of public control, the work of the Public Accounts Committee is virtually valueless."

In the House itself the procedure merely reproduces in larger compass what goes on in the Public Accounts Committee. Following traditional practice, the House considers the budget in its two committees of the whole: namely Supply (for expenditure) and Ways and Means (for revenue). Here again the work is perfunctory, and the discussion inadequate. Departmental votes totaling large sums and comprising many items may be authorized in a few minutes. Sometimes the Appropriation Act does not get passed until the end of July or even August, that is to say, in the fourth or fifth month of the financial year to which it applies. In that case, since the Public Revenues Act authorizes expenditure for only the first three months of the new financial year, a special measure called the Imprest Supply Bill must be enacted to bridge the gap between the end of the first quarter and the passage of the new Appropriation Act.[11] This system of deferring the estimates and the new appropriations until the new financial year is already well under way carries with it an advantage and a disadvantage. The later the estimates are prepared and considered by Parliament, the more accurate they are likely to be. But the effectiveness of public control is seriously hampered, for on some items the money will have been spent before Parliament even comes to discuss the departmental vote.

The Committee of Ways and Means normally performs its duties just as sketchily as the Committee of Supply. There is, however, a difference between their functions which may justify more haste on the part of the former body. It is perhaps excusable to speed up the debate on the imposition of new taxes because otherwise their object might be defeated. Alterations in the customs tariff, for instance, are ratified by resolution of the House in a single day (the first day on which they are made public) to prevent anyone from taking quick advantage of the proposed changes. Occasionally, nevertheless, such speed is contrary to the public interest, since new taxes, affecting many pockets, should

11. If Parliament is late in convening for its session, one of its first and urgent tasks is usually to pass an Imprest Supply Bill, or else no public funds may be spent after June 30.

be studied in all their economic and social consequences. Some years ago a government proposed to levy a sales tax and sought speedy parliamentary action. To have it passed by a certain Friday evening, they needed the unanimous consent of the House for suspending the standing orders. One member, contrary to the decision of the majority in his party caucus, refused his consent and so had the bill held over until the following Tuesday. During the week end protests, telegrams, and resolutions poured into Wellington, and the government was forced to amend its proposal. Such courage and independence, however, on the part of an individual representative are exceedingly rare. Usually the financial measures desired by the government are accepted without any substantial change.

In the authorization of expenditure the dominant questions that arise are those of party policy and social need. The budget is, or should be, a summary of desirable national objectives couched in terms of pounds, shillings, and pence. The preparation and the passage of the estimates involve choices between alternatives, preferences for one set of values over another. During this stage the positive contribution of Parliament is, as has been seen, very slight. There is yet another stage to mention, one that is subsequent to the legislative appropriation. It is the review of how the money actually was spent. Here, too, Parliament is directly concerned, according to the theory of the constitution; and, in this case, its interest is somewhat better safeguarded, since it has established a reviewing agency, the Audit Office headed by the controller and auditor-general. Like the British official with the same title, he is a servant of Parliament, not of the ministry. Appointed for an indefinite term by the governor-general in Council, he holds office subject to good behavior and can be removed only by a majority vote in both houses. His functions are generally to supervise expenditure and in particular to see that public funds are paid out only by a lawful procedure and for the objects which Parliament authorized. His control may take one of two forms. In certain cases, before payments are made, his consent must be obtained (preaudit).[12] For the rest, his task is to

12. Preaudit is required for the salaries of new appointees; claims for more than one month's salary at any time; interest, loan transactions, and return of deposits; transfers between government accounts; and payments out of the item (£750,000) known as "unauthorized."

check vouchers, receipts, and bills after payment and to certify that all financial transactions have been conducted in due legal order. Legality, in short, not policy, is the province of the controller and auditor-general. No one could gainsay its importance, nor would anyone assert that the holders of the office in New Zealand have inclined toward laxity. As a matter of fact, complaints are heard at times that the controller-general is over-zealous and prone to magnify minutiae into big issues. The truth seems to be that serious defalcations seldom occur simply because the payment of public money is strictly supervised, and the chance of not being found out is slender. Since large-scale misdemeanors are rare, the controller must, to justify his presence, find something to expose and criticize. Hence peccadilloes must be pounced upon and, in the absence of grosser faults, may be enlarged to bigger dimensions. The value of the office lies not so much in the detection of little faults but in the prevention of the bigger frauds which might occur if it did not exist. You do not measure the value of the police by referring solely to the statistics of crimes committed and criminals apprehended. You must also add to your estimate the number of crimes never committed just because the police are there to stop them. For that reason the controller and auditor-general is necessary to the Parliament he serves, but his usefulness, it must be conceded, is limited. His reports, though presented annually to Parliament, are not referred for the study of any special committee. The majority of members probably never even read them at all. Moreover, in any case, a parliamentary supervision which confines itself mainly to the aspect of legality as seen in a postaudit is not enough. It is a bigger political assignment to have the power to choose the objects for which public money may lawfully be spent than to be able to punish those responsible for illegal expenditure. Parliament has little say in determining financial policy in the preparatory stages. It has virtually lost control of the public purse.

The Authority of the Cabinet

In the last fifty years the tendency, noticeable even before 1890, for the ministry to assume greater powers over the House of Representatives has steadily continued. It is from the ranks of parliamentarians that the members of the cabinet are selected, but it is the smaller body which dominates the larger. Nowadays the problem of parliamentary organization is to find some means of protecting the majority. Private members are an inferior caste with a depressed status. Their relations, however, with the cabinet differ according to their party affiliation. One must consider separately the means by which the cabinet controls backbenchers of its own party and those by which it overrules the official opposition and any independents who may happen to hold a seat.

For handling representatives of its own political persuasion the cabinet finds its strongest weapon in the party machine. Normally the ministry, composed of the party's outstanding parliamentary representatives, dominates the party organization both within the legislature and without. Thereby it retains a hold over any member who seeks the party's reindorsement at the next election. Since elections are held every three years,[13] the position of a representative is precarious. Politicians and public servants who are "in the know" describe the profession of parliamentarian as the most insecure white-collar job in the Dominion. Probably less than half the members of the lower house could afford to pay from their own pockets the expenses of an election recurring triennially. Naturally, the cost of a successful candidature varies with the constituency; a newcomer with a less extensive reputation may have to spend more than the old campaigner. The strength of the opposition, the difficulties of canvassing, the concentration or spread of population—all these are elements in the cost of an election. I was told by a veteran member who represented a mainly urban constituency for two decades continuously that he used to spend on his campaign from £100 to £150. Another member, who had only recently won his seat in a mainly urban district where parties were evenly opposed, admitted to me that his election cost from £200 to £300. In exceptional cases the expenses may run much higher. A candidate who captured an important rural seat after a hard struggle is said to have spent £800.

When one considers all the financial outlay and psychological insecurities on the debit side of the ledger, the compensation on

13. See below, pp. 351–52.

the credit side appears quite inadequate if not stingy. Colonial democracies are exacting in their demands on politicians and niggardly in their rewards. In 1892 the Liberals raised the member's annual payment to the munificent sum of £240 (plus traveling expenses). It was increased in 1901 to £300 and in 1920 to £500. From this high point it was later reduced by 10 per cent and was further cut during the depression. Since then it was restored by Labor to the level of £450, and in 1944 it was raised to £750, of which £250 are intended to cover expenses and are nontaxable. To anyone who depends upon his stipend as the main source of income that is still an inadequate remuneration. A member of Parliament receives innumerable financial calls which he dare not turn down. "I have heard it said," one representative remarked, "that it sometimes cost a member £300 to get into the House, £300 in subscriptions, and £300 to get out of the House."[14] Another observed: "I know members who do not get anything out of their honorarium at all, and who spend a great deal more than they receive by way of honorarium."[15] When a candidate succeeds in entering Parliament, his previous occupational activities may have to be sacrificed. Lawyers, like Sir Robert Stout and Sir Francis Bell, have often found it impossible to reconcile a parliamentary career with an extensive legal practice. Businessmen cannot attend to their private affairs if they are assembled in Wellington for four or five months of the year. In fact, there are really only two groups who can become parliamentarians without serious detriment to their other interests. On the National party side, the farmers are able without undue hardship to sit in the House, which, to suit their convenience, always meets over the winter months. In the Labor party, trade-union secretaries can readily combine their work with the requirements of attending the legislative session. Otherwise, unless a man has independent means, he throws himself financially upon his party when he becomes a representative of the people. With few exceptions the professional politicians are tied hand and foot—and mouth—to the cabinet-controlled party organization. One way, then, by which the ministry can bring to heel a backbencher of their own party is to threaten that the party will select another

14. *P.D.*, CLXVIII (1914), 732.   15. *P.D.*, CLVIII (1912), 664.

candidate at the next election. As effective as this threat is, the
bribe offered not to the member himself but to his constituents is
in the form of local public works. The pork barrel is still a factor to
be noticed in the politics of New Zealand. Neither Liberal, Reform, nor Labor governments have neglected its potentialities.
Seddon, who had watched how the system was applied by other
ministries during the eighties, saw to it in the nineties that public
works were allocated to the districts of his political supporters.
Ruefully a member complained in 1896: "It is within my own
knowledge that in districts represented by honourable gentlemen
who do not support the Government there is often little or nothing spent. I am one of those unfortunate representatives in this
House who have not been of the 'right colour,' and who have not
succeeded in getting any money worth mentioning for my electorate."[16] Another divulged the following information: "I think
not long ago a member was importuning the Minister for £6,000
for roads and bridges in his district . . . . and after a lot of unsuccessful applications he was cheered by the Minister with this
statement: 'I can give you that £6,000 just now, because so-and-
so "slated" the Government so much in that speech of his that I
have taken £6,000 off the votes in his district, and I will give it to
you.' Now, that is an absolute fact."[17]

When Ward became premier, he showed that he disapproved
of the practice and put the blame for its continuance on the localities and their representatives who showered him with requests for more largesse. Nevertheless, in 1908, anticipating the
general election of that year, he behaved no differently from
Seddon.[18] Massey, in all the righteousness of a leader of the opposition, commented: "Parliament, instead of being a Legislative Assembly, is now nothing more than a huge and unwieldy
Road Board."[19] But in 1923 Massey, who had watered down some
of his earlier principles after eleven years as premier, was himself
assailed with this very criticism: "All his arts," said Sidey of the
Reform premier, "were employed at the last election [1922].

16. *P.D.*, XCIV (1896), 197.
17. *P.D.*, XCVIII (1897), 260.
18. J. E. Le Rossignol and W. D. Stewart, *State Socialism in New Zealand* (London:
Harrap & Co., 1912), pp. 109 and 114.
19. *P.D.*, CXLV (1908), 502.

Look at the roads and bridges vote: it was a record in the history
of the country to sweeten the constituencies . . . . why, in former days he characterized that system as one of bribing the
electors with their own money, and yet at the last election we had
the roads and bridges vote—during the election year—nearly
£900,000."[20] Likewise under Coates's leadership the practices of
the pork barrel were not lost from sight. The most notorious case
was in his own electorate, where a new railway line was constructed and routed to take an extraordinary detour in a loop
shaped like a balloon.[21] Nor has Labor been any less adept in
utilizing the same methods to secure votes both in the House and
in the electorates. Its extensive public works program, managed
by Semple the minister for that particular department, was designed with political as well as economic ends in view. In more
than one constituency, the opposition asserted, the influx of public works employees during 1938 helped to swell the Labor vote
in the November elections. Provided that men were placed in
their camps six months before the day of balloting, they could be
deployed as mobile squads to reinforce weak local positions. Such
has been the tradition continuously maintained since 1870 that
members of Parliament are still expected by their constituents to
produce public works in their districts. This expectation can be
utilized by the cabinet as a club to keep a backbencher obedient.
It is the regular practice of the Post and Telegraph Department,
before building a new post office, to inform the member for the
district and allow him to make the announcement. Just before a
general election many representatives will write in to this department, asking for a list of post-office buildings constructed in their
constituency during the last three years. Then in their campaign
speeches they can cite these buildings as their achievement, even
though they may have had nothing to do with the decision to
erect them. The Railways Department may be asked by members for information about new station buildings, alterations in
the timetable, or addition of new trains that may have helped
their constituents. There is actually one train from Wellington
which is popularly known as "Field's Express" from the name of

20. *P.D.*, CXCIX (1923), 84.
21. See *P.D.*, CCXXI (1929), 246, 527, 632.

the representative who received the credit for it. A member who cannot point out to the electors some such list of accomplishments is not likely to be regarded as one who has the interests of his district at heart. He may fail to be re-elected. By its method of doling out the titbits from the pork barrel the ministry can control the private member. Unless he keeps in their good graces, the favors will not flow to his district. Therefore, he votes as he is told.

As long as it has an ample parliamentary majority and can control its own party, the cabinet has no fears of the opposition. With its voting predominance in the House, it can be certain of a successful reception for its measures. The opposition can criticize, but it cannot enforce acceptance of its criticisms unless the government prudently thinks that by a concession it will be strengthened politically. At the most the opposition can merely conduct delaying actions. But its opportunities for stone-walling and obstruction are now far less generous than of old. The standing orders of the House of Representatives have been twice revised in the last fifty years. The first occasion was in 1895, when Seddon saw to it that no one would be able to employ against him the tricks that he had used against the Conservatives. The Liberals when they were in opposition had gloried in the tactics of obstruction. "I have kept the Honourable Captain Russell," said one Liberal, "sitting on those Government benches for nearly fourteen hours before I allowed an iniquity to be performed by the honourable gentleman, and he knows it; and on another occasion the honourable member for Mardsen, Sir George Grey, and myself kept them here till nine o'clock in the morning."[22] The changes introduced in 1895 certainly increased the power of the ministry to control debate. Russell referred to the new standing orders as a code "under which freedom of debate was stifled and criticism curtailed to the very last degree."[23] Later, in 1899, he wrote in a letter that "business now regulates itself according to the whim of the Premier and the supineness of the Speaker."[24] A second revision of the standing orders was carried through un-

22. *P.D.*, XCIV (1896), 156.
23. *P.D.*, XCIII (1896), 517.
24. Quoted in W. D. Stewart, *William Rolleston* (Wellington: Whitcombe & Tombs, 1941), p. 196.

der the chairmanship of the speaker in 1929. It, too, cut down the privileges of members by placing a limit upon the length of speeches from both the front and the back benches. Every member, however, still had the right to have his limited say, and there was no closure or guillotine. Evening debates were made to terminate at 10:30 P.M., a welcome change from the former midnightly ordeals that had dragged on into the small hours.

Under present conditions the ministry has the power to get its business through the House expeditiously. By a majority vote it can change the order paper or "take urgency" for a measure; and with unanimity it can suspend the standing orders and pass a bill through all its stages within one day. The business of Parliament is arranged by the prime minister in conjunction with the party whip. Also by courtesy the speaker and the clerk of the House may be consulted; and, to smooth things over, the leader of the opposition and the opposition whip will be informed of what is pending. As Professor Jennings has pointed out in his book on the British Parliament, the system implies that give-and-take on which democracy in the last analysis depends. Under normal conditions, it operates smoothly enough, though the opposition is periodically inclined to charge the government with attempting to rush matters. At a pinch, however, any prime minister with a solid majority has enough authority to break through a deadlock and get his measures carried without hindrance.

Such is the arsenal of weapons which the cabinet can utilize against its own backbenchers and the opposition that private members are made to feel their impotence. It is discouraging to introduce a bill with the virtually certain knowledge that the government will block it. As a representative said in 1912: "We, the ordinary members of this House, are elected by the people of New Zealand to do the business of Parliament. And what say have we got in the business of Parliament? Very little indeed. The measures that have anything like a chance of going through must first emanate from the Cabinet, which is in its turn controlled by the Prime Minister."[25] Another stated in 1920 that he had a number of bills on the order paper but that it was "at the sweet will of the Government whether they will go through or

25. *P.D.*, CLVIII (1912), 674.

not." One was an amendment to the Destitute Persons Act, which was being blocked by a minister because his department objected to it. A second was a proposal for a war pensions appeal board which the government incorporated into its budget a week after the private member had introduced his bill in the House.[26] Caught in the grip of the party machine, members must swallow their convictions and compromise their principles. "I have known throughout my fourteen years' experience here that members have not infrequently had to vote for a proposal they did not believe in; and members themselves have not infrequently supported proposals emanating from a Government they did not believe in."[27] The grievances of the private member were summed up into an indictment voiced by a former minister when temporarily deprived of the sweets of office: "Under such a form of Executive control," said Hanan, "we know in this House that private members have little power or opportunity to initiate, amend, or carry through legislation. The Cabinet and the Government party machine autocratically govern the proceedings and the business of the Houses of Parliament."[28]

The Private Member's Defenses

Nevertheless, this does not complete the story. Although cabinet control over Parliament is a very real force, counterbalancing factors do exist. Undeniably the cabinet is potent; yet it is not necessarily or inevitably or always omnipotent. There are methods—sometimes latent but occasionally rising to the surface—by which private members can assert themselves against the ministry. Without considering what these methods are, and how they are employed, no one can correctly gauge the balance of forces within Parliament.

The backbenchers of the majority party, for example, possess in the caucus a potential weapon for resisting the cabinet. The caucus, as was noticed in chapter vi, is by no means a modern invention in the politics of New Zealand. In recent years, however, it has been put to new uses which may foreshadow radical

26. *P.D.*, CLXXXVIII (1920), 657.
27. *P.D.*, CLXVIII (1914), 726.   28. *Ibid.*, pp. 719–20.

changes in the institutions of parliamentary democracy.[29] The
caucus was firmly established during the regimes of the Liberal
and Reform parties. Both government and opposition then held
meetings of the representatives of their party in the course of the
legislative sessions. It was an opportunity for the cabinet to discuss its program with its supporters and to arrange the strategy to
be followed in the House. This is Massey's account of the procedure he followed when he came to office in 1912: "We asked
for an adjournment for three weeks to formulate the policy of the
party, to get it into what may be called legislative shape. The
policy of the party at that time was approved by every member
of the party; the Bills that were introduced were consistent with
that policy, and there was no occasion to bring them before the
party as a whole, though, as a matter of fact, they were discussed
on quite a number of occasions."[30] By taking this precaution, any
differences of opinion between the cabinet and the backbenchers
or between rival wings of the party might be adjusted *in camera*.
The speeches and the voting in Parliament itself normally presented an appearance of party unity which could not be attained
without preliminary discussions. On the opposition side the party
leaders met their followers to decide their tactics and choose their
line of argument for countering the government's measures. The
caucus, in short, provided machinery for consultation and discussion. To some extent also it reached decisions that were binding
on members of the party concerned.

But it was a feature of the caucus, as operated up to the thirties
by these parties, that the ministry—and especially the prime
minister—retained control. With Seddon in the chair few dared
openly to disagree with the premier. Votes were not taken in the
caucus, since "King Dick" wished to leave himself a free hand.
In the Reform party Massey maintained his leadership but in
the face of more criticism than was ever offered to Seddon. Two
former Reform members have told the writer that the proceed-

29. The internal organization and activities of the caucus are as secret as
those of the cabinet. Most of the information that follows has been gleaned from
parliamentarians in oral interviews. Almost the only written material on the caucus
is contained in the pamphlets published by J. A. Lee after he was expelled from
the Labor party in 1940.

30. *P.D.*, CLXXXVIII (1920), 654.

ings in the caucus of that party were quite informal. There was no regular system of tabling motions, moving amendments, and coming to a vote. The wishes of the caucus were interpreted by the leader of the party. Occasionally he would ask for a show of hands to test the general feeling; but the vote was not considered binding. Massey silenced many of his younger Reform critics who became vocal after the war by making them ministers. It takes a big man to get up and oppose the premier in the caucus— or even in the cabinet. He is likely to be blacklisted if it occurs too often. The system followed in the Liberal and Reform caucuses has been carried over into the present National party. There, too, votes are the exception rather than the rule. It is left to the party leader to sum up the views of members and, if possible, to state the collective judgment.

The Labor party, however, has given a new twist to the caucus system. It is possible in the light of recent tendencies that the caucus may even emerge as an instrument through which the rank and file of the majority party can dominate the ministry. Hitherto this potentiality has been partly, not fully, developed. But already it can be seen to have significant implications, which a sketch of the Labor caucus will reveal. The organization of the parliamentary Labor party has been based upon two principles, internal democracy combined with strong discipline. The former meant that policy and tactics were settled by majority decision after full discussion. The latter involved the loyal obedience of the minority within the party to the majority. In such a setting the position of the party leader could not be quite the same as in the parties built upon the lines of historical tradition. He, too, would be bound by the majority verdict, even if he had happened to disagree with it. He would be official spokesman for the caucus and the chief executive officer for carrying out its wishes. But in practice the Labor party has not functioned in the spirit of this intention. Its history is made up of conflicts between the tendencies of control by the leader from above and control by the rank and file from below.

The election of 1919 was the first at which Labor attained a parliamentary representation of sufficient numbers to create a problem of internal organization. Sixteen years elapsed before it

won the electoral victory that brought a Labor ministry into
office. The caucus functioned, therefore, and established its procedures during the decade and a half while the party was in opposition. While the principle of majority rule was recognized, it so
happened that Harry Holland, the party leader up to 1934, was
a man of ability with strong personality. He himself supported
the conception that a party leader—whether the party be in
office or out—is responsible to members of the party. "The Australian system of selecting the Ministry is, in my opinion," he
once stated, "the best system. The members of the Cabinet are
selected by the party in caucus by ballot on the preferential-vot-
ing system. The Premier . . . . by mutual arrangement with the
men selected, allots the portfolios, and the system works fairly
smoothly. I do not know how, under party government, you
could have a better system."[31] Holland's personal prestige, nevertheless, accorded him a leadership which made him more than
just a spokesman or executive officer for the caucus. In his time,
however, the only questions arising in caucus discussion were
those of the policy and the tactics for an opposition group. All
Labor representatives were then private members. Differentia-
tions of power did not yet exist.

The election of 1935 created two new problems. Since Labor
was now in power, there were ministerial positions to be filled.
This implied within the caucus a distinction between the ministry and the backbenchers. Further, the parliamentary representation of the party had more than doubled from twenty-four to
fifty-three. The caucus, therefore, contained another potential
line of cleavage between the newly elected members and the
party veterans who had borne the brunt of battle up to 1919 and
had since then served almost continuously in Parliament. Savage,
who had been leader for the eighteen months since Holland's
death, had to prevent the split that was possible on either of these
two grounds. As premier, he personally selected his ministers and
allocated their portfolios. Naturally enough those chosen were his
old colleagues, many of whom had for so long sat with him in
Parliament. None of the younger Laborites was included in the
cabinet. But it was arranged that private members of the party

31. *Ibid.*, p. 669.

should be attached to different ministers, assisting them in some of their administrative duties. Likewise, ministerial salaries were pooled and partly shared with those of private members. Labor's equalitarianism required that the sweets of power must tickle many palates.

If the practice of majority rule were to be followed within the caucus, it meant that the ministry could on occasions be outvoted. It meant also that the old Labor parliamentarians could be swamped by the newcomers. For awhile these possibilities of conflict did not show themselves. The Labor backbenchers wholeheartedly supported the ministry in all its initial tasks of restoring the services cut down during the depression. On their side, the ministry, suspicious of the public service and its permanent heads, leaned on its parliamentary supporters. But the change came. The men who had been made ministers after long years in opposition, liked their new-found power, and certain of them had no wish to share their authority with private members. Less radical in outlook than certain of the younger representatives, they preferred to pursue a course of moderate social reform and defer the introduction of socialism. Inside the caucus, backbenchers pressed for the fulfilment of the socialist program. A gulf threatened to develop between the ministry and the rank and file, between the older men of the right wing and the younger of the left. Seeking to counteract this pressure, the ministry turned to their department heads, most of whom had by now won their confidence. In the early days of the ministry the caucus more than once adopted proposals in defiance of departmental objections. Latterly the ministry came to rely upon the public service for resisting the suggestions made in the caucus. They would come to the caucus—or indeed to the annual conference of the party—armed with memorandums and material which their departments had supplied. As a sop to the left wing, the cabinet created, on the British model, the new position of parliamentary undersecretary and appointed Lee to take charge of housing under the jurisdiction of Nash, the finance minister. But this turned out to be an unhappy clash of orthodoxy and radicalism embittered by temperamental differences. Nor did it satisfy Lee, who felt himself worthy of full cabinet rank.

Matters headed for a crisis in the year that followed the party's second electoral triumph. At the first meeting after the election, the caucus claimed the right to elect the ministry, and asserted this by a vote of the majority. Fearing the left wing and knowing that the caucus would elect some of its members to the ministry, Savage refused to agree. The discontented left, thwarted by the premier, tried to win caucus approval for measures promised in the Labor program which the ministry would not introduce. Within the caucus the struggle for power between the ministry and the backbenchers—complicated by the split between right and left—continued during 1939. It culminated in public criticisms of the government and the premier by Lee and in his expulsion from the party at the time of Savage's death in 1940.

The selection of the new premier and the succeeding events have marked a new phase in caucus history. Fraser, who had been acting prime minister, was sent for by the governor-general and provisionally accepted the premiership subject to the approval of the Labor caucus. When the caucus met, with Fraser in the chair, three nominations for the premiership were put forward, and on a show of hands Fraser was elected. He then called upon the caucus to choose the cabinet, asking for nominations in turn for each ministerial position. As a result of this procedure, Mac-Millan, who had been the left-wing nominee for premier, was taken into the cabinet. In 1941 when MacMillan and Martin, the minister of agriculture, resigned, it was again the caucus which voted upon filling the vacancies. Barclay, who was minister of agriculture from 1941 to 1943, actually inserted in his biographical statement for *Who's Who* the point that he was "recommended by caucus for appointment to Cabinet." Of recent years the caucus has asserted itself not only in choosing ministers but also in debating policy. In some important matters of principle concerning the conduct of the war, the prime minister and cabinet were not always able to take quick decisions because caucus had to be consulted. One could not yet state definitely that the caucus now controls the cabinet, but it cannot be denied that the caucus has recently become a most important part of the governmental machinery, participating in the major decisions. It is in effect an "inner legislature" of the majority party through which the backbenchers may succeed eventually in controlling the ministry.

A purpose of the caucus is to remove differences among its own members so that the party, by acting in unison, can wield greater strength in the House. But this aim is not always achieved. At times the caucus may not be able to reach a decision which binds its members how to vote in Parliament. It may regard particular measures as nonpolitical or nonpartisan and allow each representative to act according to his individual judgment. Or, even if the majority do settle upon a policy, there may yet be some bold and independent spirits in the minority ready to flout their own leaders. For these and other reasons a study of the division lists reveals evidence of exception to the general rule of party solidarity.

Table 16 summarizes the results of my analysis of parliamentary voting in seven out of the twenty-one years when the Liberals predominated. All the figures were taken from the records of the divisions published in Hansard. The party membership of representatives has been determined by the allegiance declared when they were candidates for election to Parliament and is the same as was used in Table 12. A split in the party vote means, for the purposes of Table 16, that one-quarter or over of the declared party members voted on the opposite side to the rest of their colleagues.

This table, interpreted together with the data that were collected for it, leads to certain inferences about parliamentary behavior. To dispose, first, of the two more obvious conclusions that emerge from the evidence, it is clear that in all sessions the party vote was split on both sides of the House, although in different years the proportion of splitting varied from side to side. It is equally plain that far more splits occurred during divisions at the committee stage than during those on second and third readings and on confidence motions. Reasonably enough, the discipline of a party is not, and cannot be, enforced so rigidly in committee, where men who agree on general principles may differ over the details of particular clauses.

In 1892 party solidarity was strong among both Liberals and Conservatives but was stronger among the former. With a slender majority the Liberals were then conducting a great parliamentary fight against the opposition in the House, against the Legislative Council, and against an unsympathetic governor. They needed to close their ranks. In 1894 their majority was more se-

TABLE 16*

PARTY SPLITS IN THE NEW ZEALAND HOUSE OF REPRESENTATIVES

Session		Liberals	Conservatives†		Liberals	Conservatives†
1892	No. of members............	40	25	Total no. of divisions =157		
	No. of splits in committee...	23	34	Percentage of splits in committee to total divisions............	14.6	21.7
	No. of splits in House divisions....................	13	17	Percentage of splits in House divisions.....................	8.3	10.8
1894	No. of members............	51	13	Total no. of divisions =286		
	No. of splits in committee...	105	86	Percentage of splits in committee to total divisions............	36.7	30.1
	No. of splits in House divisions....................	16	21	Percentage of splits in House divisions...................	5.6	7.3
1896	No. of members............	51	14	Total no. of divisions =313		
	No. of splits in committee...	107	51	Percentage of splits in committee to total divisions............	34.2	16.3
	No. of splits in House divisions....................	30	18	Percentage of splits in House divisions.....................	9.6	5.7
1899	No. of members............	39	26	Total no. of divisions =127		
	No. of splits in committee...	17	23	Percentage of splits in committee to total divisions............	13.4	18.1
	No. of splits in House divisions....................	10	11	Percentage of splits in House divisions.....................	7.9	8 7
1904	No. of members............	46	20	Total no. of divisions =246		
	No. of splits in committee...	61	40	Percentage of splits in committee to total divisions............	24.8	16.3
	No. of splits in House divisions....................	17	14	Percentage of splits in House divisions.....................	6.9	5.7
1907	No. of members............	54	16	Total no. of divisions =321		
	No. of splits in committee...	131	57	Percentage of splits in committee to total divisions............	40.8	14.6
	No. of splits in House divisions....................	15	11	Percentage of splits in House divisions.....................	4.7	3.4
1911	No. of members............	45	25	Total no. of divisions =86		
	No. of splits in committee...	23	21	Percentage of splits in committee to total divisions............	26.7	24.4
	No. of splits in House divisions....................	6	8	Percentage of splits in House divisions.....................	7.0	9.3

* Allowance has been made for members elected at by-elections later than the general election. The data on which this table is based were collected by Mr. K. G. Reid.

† The Conservatives were called the Opposition in 1904 and 1907 and the Reform party in 1911.

cure, thanks to the general election, and they had won the opening phase of the battle in Parliament. Although the number of splits increased in both parties (especially in committee divisions), the proportion of splits actually decreased, since in that year 286 divisions were taken as compared with 157 in 1892. Two years later, in 1896, when 313 divisions were held, the Liberals' solidarity dropped to its lowest point, while the Conservatives became more cohesive. Seddon's difficulties, due to the loss of Reeves and Ward, were accentuated by the vigorous parliamentary opposition of Sir Robert Stout, who drew over many Liberals to vote against the ministry. In 1899 the Liberal majority was far smaller. But the battle was at an end; the most controversial legislation had been enacted; and only 127 divisions were taken. The figures therefore show a high degree of solidarity. Five years later, in the "King Dick" era, the number of splits in the House increased absolutely but declined relatively, since there were 246 divisions. The Liberal majority was enhanced by the fragmentation of the opposition. In 1907, when the divisions rose to 321, splits among the Liberals occurred very frequently in committee but less infrequently in the party. The opposition was becoming more compact than before, since it had less splits in the House. By 1911 the party battle lines were grimly drawn; only 86 divisions were held, and the leaders tried to maintain all the discipline they could before the general election.

These two decades of parliamentary history offer a clue, therefore, to understanding party votes in the House. The larger the majority of the government, the more likely that its party may split. A whip can allow a private member to follow his own conscience when the security of the government is not at stake. A party in opposition may be frequently split when it is on the decline, but it will close its ranks as it climbs to power. Lastly, it must be noticed that bills of certain types of content produce splits more readily than others. Party leaders seldom trouble to require disciplined voting on private bills that concern a special locality or a particular individual or organization. Thus in 1892, of the thirteen occasions when the Liberals split in House divisions, eight dealt with bills of this character. So did seven of the seventeen Conservative splits. It is usual, moreover, for measures that relate to social issues to cause a split. Almost invariably both sides of the House will be divided on bills for regulating or prohibiting alcoholic liquor, for introducing the Bible into schools, for changing the marriage or divorce laws, and for control of betting and gambling. In 1896 there were six divisions in which the Liberals and Conservatives alike were split on such proposals. When the bills on private, local, or social problems are removed

from the list, the splits on bills of a partisan political nature—
though they do occur—are not so numerous after all. The year
1896, however, provided some spectacular examples of lack of
party solidarity on political issues. For in that year, the Liberals
were divided even on a motion of confidence in the government—
the type of division which provides the basic testing-point of
party cohesiveness.

Without going into the same degree of detail, one can observe
a similar pattern during the two decades between the two world
wars. Throughout the twenties the Liberal party was in decline,
save for its partial revival in 1928; the Reform party was strongest of the three; and Labor was slowly building its strength. It
was, therefore, among the Liberals that the votes were most frequently split. Even on motions of confidence, the party found it
difficult to remain united. The Reform party was next in order on
the scale of solidarity. Massey was hard put to it after the war to
curb internal revolts; and, with the precarious majority that he
received in 1922, the marginal value of each single vote was greatly increased. After 1925 the very size of Coates's majority con-
duced to diminish the cohesiveness of the party. When the ill-
fated Licensing Bill was introduced in 1927 and 1928, the divisions both in committee and on second and third readings
showed that the government and the opposition parties were
hopelessly split. In the judgment of an experienced parliamentarian the voting on that measure was more confused than on any
other in modern times. The Labor party, although it too has been
split on occasions, has on the whole remained more cohesive than
its rivals. This is due to the relative rigidity imposed by its caucus
system. Labor, however, like the other parties will split occasionally on private bills and over social issues. The measures which
produced most instances of party splits during the twenties, were
the Gaming Amendment, the Licensing Amendment, Summer
Time, Religious Exercises in Schools, Industrial Conciliation and
Arbitration, the Customs Amendment, and Want of Confidence
motions. The first four of these bills concerned social or religious
problems; the last three were strictly political.

Not only does the whip dislike seeing members of his party in
the enemy lobby but he also resents the behavior of any individ-

ual representative who makes a practice of straying into the
wrong fold. Almost every Parliament contains a few members
who have been elected as independents. The true independent is
he who is allowed to use his own judgment even on confidence
motions. Consider the claim made by Statham before he was
elected speaker in 1923; "I was elected to this House absolutely
independent of party, and free to do whatever I pleased. I
was again and again asked how I would vote in the event of a
vote of no confidence being moved, and I refused to say."[32] On
the other hand, another representative stated: "At the last election I announced myself as an Independent, at the same time
giving my allegiance to the present Government on a no-confidence motion. Why? Because I found that unless I did so the
people would say, 'No, we do not want you. You are not wanted
in the House unless you are prepared to say how you will vote on a
no-confidence motion.' "[33] A few members, who at one time in
their parliamentary careers were adherents of a party, have found
themselves forced into a position of independence when their
party has adopted a policy contrary to the interests of their particular districts. For example, in the depression of the thirties, the
coalition government under the farmers' domination launched a
series of cuts in pensions and in civil servants' salaries which affected people in the cities more than in the country. So two Reform members—one representing a mining, and the other an
urban, electorate—frequently voted against their party because
of the attitudes of their own constituents. One of these was later
re-elected to Parliament as an independent in the full sense of
the term. In 1939 the House of Representatives contained only
two independents, each of them a veteran with powerful local
backing in his district. Eight years later there were none.

Though it is normal, therefore, for the cabinet to predominate
in Parliament, the private member can offer some resistance. In
the caucus lies a device of great potential significance for overruling the ministry by weight of numbers; and even in the House
some representatives can be found on occasion to vote publicly
against the majority of their colleagues. With his long experience

32. *P.D.*, CXCIX (1923), 9; *P.D.*, CLXXXVIII (1920), 650.
33. *P.D.*, CXCIX (1923), 45.

as an ordinary private member, as leader of the opposition, and as prime minister, Massey was well qualified to offer this judgment: "The House is a strange animal. You must learn to know that sometimes when it appears most dangerous it is really only mischievous, and will give way if you stand firm. At other times a slight squall may be the forerunner of a raging storm, and in that case you must be ready to compromise."[34]

To weigh up the relative merits and defects of control by the cabinet or independence of backbenchers is a delicate question for political analysis. Some will insist that cabinet control is inevitable if Parliament is to work efficiently. The legislature must contain within its midst, so the argument runs, the springs of leadership and organization. No democracy can be governed by an amorphous medley of Ciceronian eloquence and Catonian independence. Only if premier and cabinet are strong, will the people have confidence in their Parliament. The ministry should therefore place a curb on the activities of private members. Without such a curb no decisions could ever be reached. It may even be urged, on this view, that cabinet leadership injects into Parliament just the requisite tincture of authoritarianism. The democratic body politic, if healthy, can safely be innoculated with a limited dosage of the dictatorial principle. It is not unlike the arsenic in a medical prescription which may be a beneficial stimulant in small quantities, though fatal if administered in larger amounts.

To the advantages of organized leadership the opponent of ministerial control cites the blessings of independence, criticism, and initiative. Leave the decisions to the cabinet, he will argue, and only those measures will be enacted whose political usefulness to the men in power is directly demonstrable. The ministry will not allow the limited time of Parliament to be consumed on bills, however valuable, that show little prospect of an early political return. Unenviable is the position of the private member shackled by party loyalties. Representatives vote against their conscience to safeguard their re-election. The New Zealand Parliament, as the critic of cabinet dominance will explain, has on

34. Quoted in W. D. Stewart, *Sir Francis H. D. Bell: His Life and Times* (Wellington: Butterworth & Co., 1937), pp. 291–92.

numerous occasions debated and divided on the proposal that it should elect the prime minister and each individual member of his cabinet. A parliamentary committee set up in 1890 actually reported in favor of adopting the Swiss system. Other backbenchers have repeatedly tried at regular intervals over the last four decades to make the cabinet subordinate to themselves. The Elective Executive Bill, a scarred loser of many debates, is always recurring and is never enacted.

By all but the prejudiced it will be conceded that each case contains a sound argument whose worth is destroyed when carried to excess. Proponents of cabinet control can overdo their zeal for leadership; just as critics, like Ramsay Muir,[35] can exaggerate their charges of cabinet dictatorship. Conversely, the merits of independence can be so overstated as to end in anarchy. What is clearly desired is a balanced blending of organized leadership with independent criticism. Each has its proper place in Parliament; each would be vitiated in the absence of the other. Although I do not concur with all of Muir's strictures, I do agree that the powers of the cabinet are sometimes strained to abuse. That is true of this Dominion as well as of the mother-country. Where the parliamentary system in New Zealand fails to achieve the proper blend is in its lack of independent criticism and backbench initiative. Cabinet control already exists in full measure— or even too full. The need in New Zealand is to strengthen the parliamentary powers, not of the cabinet, but of the private members. Yet, in restoring the balance, the corrective itself must not be pushed too far. In some of the state legislatures of the United States one can find warning examples of what happens when the enterprise of the individual member becomes too assertive. Certain American legislatures fall short of giving social satisfaction because their own internal leadership and the external influence of the governor are inadequate.

A revival within limits of the powers of private members would be a gain for the legislature's prestige and for democracy. The voters and the party organizations will most probably continue to choose the ministry. The cabinet, caucus, and civil service will share the control of legislation and finance. It is not in these func-

35. See *How Britain Is Governed* (3d ed.; London: Constable, 1933), pp. 87–91.

tions that the private member can most usefully intervene. But if the Parliament of the future is to provide a public forum for varied opinions and for honest criticism, then a certain degree of independence must be granted to backbenchers. When cabinet leadership is carried to excess, criticism cannot thrive. At present any dissatisfaction felt by members of the majority party is normally voiced, if at all, in the caucus. Criticism from the opposition is expressed in Parliament itself within the bounds set by the order paper which the premier chiefly controls. The opposition may steer away from exposing certain ministerial faults through fear that it will provoke publicity of its own peccadilloes. Party organization thus makes cowards of us all. At times the parliamentary debates may degenerate into shadow-boxing with a tacit understanding not to hit at the really vulnerable spots. But when the battle is engaged in earnest (particularly in the session that precedes an election), the representatives meet their critics with the technique of the *tu quoque*. Parliament then becomes the public laundry where each party's dirty linen is washed. Such a spectacle is not a beautiful one. But democracy is right in insisting that, if there be dirty linen, let the washing be publicly done.

A subtle interplay of forces operates inside Parliament. It is here that the premier and the ministry, the government caucus, and the opposition meet together under the speaker's chairmanship. Even the civil service is silently present, since a convenient fiction allows department heads to be seated near the Treasury bench in an area that is not technically on the floor of the House. Like the prompters in the wings, they can coach their ministers and hand them hastily scribbled replies to awkward questions. It is no wonder, therefore, that Parliament, which is the key to democracy in New Zealand and elsewhere, is also in certain respects its most disappointing feature. The pressures that converge upon this focal institution have yet to be adjusted and co-ordinated. The prime minister's influence is potent because of the authority and prestige which his office assures him in his party and in the nation. The ministry, if it is united and contains good debaters, has tremendous parliamentary power, since the resources of the state, access to secret information, and the distribution of favors are all at its disposal. The caucus in turn can force some consideration from ministers of its own party, since they depend upon their backbenchers' votes. The opposition utilizes Parliament as a platform for a national debate on the iniquities of the government. Its power lies in the publicity weapon and in the attractiveness of its promises. Finally, the heads of the civil service, whose voice is the one least heard by the public, exert a very real influence by advising their ministers and by administering the policies that are entrusted to them. Parliament embodies the exact antithesis of what is implied in a "separation of powers." On this point converge all the governmental agencies into whose hands the powers and functions of the state are distributed.

One reason why Parliament's prestige is lower than its importance merits will readily suggest itself. Parliament is the one branch of our governmental system (besides the judiciary) whose activities are in large part conducted publicly. The searchlight of publicity is thrown on the sayings and doings of the legislature in a manner which conforms to the requirements of democracy but does not always enhance its repute. Apart from secret sessions, certain committee hearings, and caucus meetings, the official business of Parliament is carried on entirely in the public eye. The press supplies reports on the debates and, although its selections are always made with a partisan bias, prints the speeches of front benchers fairly extensively. The complete verbatim text of each session is published in Hansard, in whose pages anyone who is interested can find exactly what was said in the House and by whom. Since 1936, moreover, legislative proceedings have been addressed not only to the eye of the public but also to its ear. When the Labor government took office, it initiated the experiment, new to the history of representative assemblies, of broadcasting the debates.[36] From many sides the innovation was welcomed as a healthy application of democratic principles. Thanks to the miracle of radio, the whole electorate could now become one audience listening to its representative conducting the people's business. Cynics who reflected on the deficiencies of Parliament even ventured the hope that its standards might improve if its discussions were broadcast. However good the the-

36. In 1946 the Parliament of the Australian Commonwealth commenced to broadcast its proceedings.

ory, and however optimistic the hopes, they cannot be said to have been fulfilled. Since it has gone on the air, the quality of the legislature has not improved. The public were at first shocked and disillusioned and have now grown accustomed. Those who used to think that only one side of the House (i.e., the party they opposed) was unedifying found that both sides can be equally so. Broadcasting has encouraged members to electioneer and talk directly to the voters outside, often ignoring the merits of the issue under discussion.[37] Stump and soap-box oratory have taken the place of "talking to the gallery." Frequent references are made to "those people who are listening in"; and at times the premier and other members have rebuked the House for giving to the listening public a poor impression of how Parliament does its work.[38] All this places the legislature at a disadvantage in comparison with other branches of the government. Inside the cabinet and in the civil service there may at times be controversies no less acrimonious than those that take place in Parliament. But around the internal doings of the ministry and the departments is drawn an official veil of secrecy. Little leaks out to the public of their domestic dissensions. When the cabinet or the civil service appear before the public, it is under the outward guise of concord and unanimity. The legislature, on the other hand, by virtue of its *raison d'être*, must make known its inner disunity. Differences of opinion, conflict, and opposition are essential to its procedure; but they do not always create the best of impressions among onlookers.

That publicity is the *sine qua non* of the legislative process can be best appreciated when we ask just what function a modern Parliament is equipped to perform. The enactment of laws, the control over finance, and the making of ministries are functions which have now virtually slipped from the parliamentary grasp. This transfer or redistribution of duties among different arms of the state is a phenomenon with which all students of governmental evolution are familiar. In different eras to meet changing needs the role of each and every institution alters. Twentieth-century parliaments are not adequately fitted for some of the tasks which, when society was less complex, they could once under-

---

37. See, e.g., *P.D.*, CCLVII (1940), 10, 23, 40. 38. *Ibid.*, p. 52.

take. The metamorphosis of the legislature need cause no lament provided that some really worth-while function is left to it. Parliament's function should be whatever its personnel are able to do better than other branches of the state machinery. What useful activity, then, is left to it under modern conditions? Surely this: it can and must serve as a public forum for the presentation of criticism and the ventilation of grievances.[39] It is one of the major differences between democratic and dictatorial systems that the former insists upon public criticism as a duly constituted activity within the framework of the law, while the latter equates criticism with treason and punishes offenders with the concentration camp or the firing squad. Question time in the House, the long debate on the address in reply to the speech from the throne, the discussions of departmental appropriations in the Committee on Ways and Means—these occasions provide regular opportunities for a public airing of injustices committed or social needs unsatisfied. No other institution of state can satisfy these requirements as suitably as Parliament. The very existence of this machinery for continuous publicity itself forestalls abuses which might otherwise be attempted. By virtue of this function the legislature is in a very real sense the watchdog of the citizen's liberties. Complaints about the declining usefulness of Parliament frequently overlook the greatest service it can perform. Whenever anything is done to strip it of its opportunities for ventilating grievances, then democracy will indeed have been wounded in a mortal spot. In carrying out what is nowadays its major activity, Parliament can, to state it in its lowest terms, be like Bagehot's constitutional monarch possessing the power to advise, to encourage, and to warn. Developed to its highest potentialities, the legislature can be the center and the focus for the critical inquiries and the constructive energies of an alert democratic opinion.

Strategy and Tactics of Parliament

There are other factors yet to be considered which condition the effectiveness of the legislative branch and influence both its

39. See Harold J. Laski, *Parliamentary Government in England* (New York: Viking Press, 1938), pp. 119 ff.

methods of procedure and its internal balance of power. Consider the fact that the length of term of the New Zealand House of Representatives is still governed by the Triennial Parliaments Act passed in 1879. For six decades the general elections have been regularly held at the prescribed three-year intervals. To this rule the only exceptions have been occasioned by wars or the depression. The Parliament elected in 1914 lasted until 1919. The coalition government elected in 1931 postponed the next election from 1934 to 1935—ostensibly on grounds of economy but actually because they feared defeat in 1934 and hoped that economic conditions would improve within a year. The Parliament that was chosen by the voters in 1938 extended its terms for two years. These instances apart, the ministry and every private member must always prepare to face their constituents three years after they have been elected. In favor of this system it is urged that triennial elections make Parliament continuously responsive to the wishes of the people. That claim is a reasonable one, and the results justify it. New Zealand ministries are very wary of public opinion, since the prospect of another election is never far from their thoughts. The government which prolonged its own life in 1934 only added to its unpopularity and made its defeat in 1935 the more certain. Triennial elections were instituted as part of an effort to democratize the political institutions of the country. From this point of view, the design has been fulfilled.

But there are other consequences of the system which were not properly foreseen in 1879. One of these has been the disuse of the premier's discretionary power to dissolve Parliament. Not once since 1890 has a general election been held earlier than toward the end of the prescribed third year. No premier has had occasion to go to the governor-general with a request for a dissolution before the due date. When elections are held triennially, a dissolution at other times is scarcely ever needed. In the first year of a new Parliament, a dissolution is improbable, since the voters have just recorded their verdict. In the third year it is equally improbable because in any case an election will be held at the end of the year. Only in the middle year would a sudden dissolution be likely, if a new issue of major importance were to arise or if a

shift in the parliamentary strengths of the parties made a stable
ministry impossible. Nevertheless, whatever the likelihood, no
irregular dissolutions, either in the second or in any other year,
have occurred for sixty years. Modern New Zealand, in short,
has seen the term of Parliament lengthened but never shortened.

Whether the premier's power to request a dissolution has been
out of use for so long that it is now obsolete is a nicety of constitutional metaphysics. The political scientist can say only that the
power is dormant, not dead. If a premier thought it politically desirable to make the request, the governor-general would have to
consent. Indeed, premiers have from time to time thrown out
hints that they were considering a dissolution. Massey did so in
1923 and 1924, when his parliamentary majority was terribly insecure. But the private members knew then, and still know, that
a New Zealand premier, even if he has the power to dissolve, will
always avoid holding a general election before the three years
are up. Apart from the fact that he and his ministers, no less than
the ordinary representatives, risk their seats, there is the other
cogent reason that elections are expensive. As it is, a New Zealand party must build up its election funds every three years, and
that imposes a recurrent strain on its finances. To interpose an
extra election at a shorter interval might be financially ruinous
for the party which wanted it.

Since triennial elections have meant disuse of the power of dissolution, that weakens the position of the premier in relation to
his caucus. In Britain a ministry which can threaten a recalcitrant group of backbenchers with a dissolution will often bring
them to heel. But in New Zealand the private members generally
know that this threat need not be taken seriously. When Massey
tried to use it in the Reform caucus, some of the members successfully called his bluff. On the other hand, if the premier were really
determined, he could still employ this weapon against his own
caucus as much as against the opposition. No example of this has
yet occurred in New Zealand; but it did happen in 1940 in the
Australian State of Victoria. There the premier found himself in
the minority in his own caucus. He requested of the governor,
and was granted, a dissolution in order to re-establish his majority. Formerly it was well understood that a premier defeated in

Parliament might appeal to the people. Now that the caucus is evolving into an inner legislature it is a simple transference for a premier, defeated in the caucus, to gain his way through a dissolution of the whole Parliament. However, in such a course of action the risk of splitting one's own party is tremendous.

Another consequence of triennial elections may be seen in its effects upon the strategy and tactics of the ministry in Parliament. The announcement of government policies and the timing of the legislative program must be adjusted to the dates of the elections. Since these recur at three-year intervals, the ministry must devise a captivating bait in every third year. A saying has grown up that the first year of a new Parliament is for talk, the second for work, and the third for vote-catching. It is interesting to trace in retrospect the various social service measures with a humanitarian appeal which have been introduced by different governments in the last year of an expiring Parliament. A famous instance is that of the Old Age Pensions Bill, which Seddon proposed first in 1896. When this bill eventually passed into law in 1898, it contained a clause limiting its validity to three years, after which it was to be reconsidered. Reeves himself mentions that "the Opposition thought they saw in this three years' limit to the Act a clever electioneering move on the part of their astute old foe the Premier, and they pointed out that by it he would keep the most popular of his measures alive as a hustings cry when the House had to face the country in December 1899."[40] Similarly it was in the election year, 1911, that the Ward ministry introduced and enacted pensions for widows. A more recent instance was the Social Security Act which the Labor government passed in 1938. Its enactment was deferred until the year of the election; and it is generally conceded in New Zealand that its comprehensive promises of old age, unemployment, medical, and maternity benefits were a major element in the Labor victory of 1938. That such services should be provided is highly desirable. But it is not so desirable that every three years the government should seek to concoct a vote-catching law and distribute the expenditure on public works with an eye to the doubtful constituencies.

40. W. P. Reeves, *State Experiments in Australia and New Zealand* (2 vols.; London: Allen & Unwin, 1902), II, 247-48.

Not only does the frequency of the elections encourage such legislative tactics but it also upsets the even tenor of administration by holding up decisions until the election is over. When they are held too frequently, elections seriously disrupt the continuity of administration. Such is the complexity of modern society that most legislation must be administered and amended over a longish term of years before its social results can be adequately judged. Even if a new government enacts portions of its program during its first year in office, it is too early to appraise it only a few years later. It would be difficult to establish an optimum number of years which should be allowed to lapse between elections, but the three-year period appears to me too short. The British Parliament operates under a quinquennial term. That, however, is somewhat too long, since by the fifth year a government is very likely to be out of tune with the electorate. In practice this seems to be recognized, for Parliament is usually dissolved in Britain before the end of its fifth year. Indeed, between 1900 and 1939 the average Parliament lasted four years. The four-year term which the United States accords to the President and to about half the governors is a wise provision. If adopted in New Zealand, an earlier dissolution—say in the third year—would still be possible if the circumstances required. A longer cycle between electoral upheavals would enable both Parliament and the administrative departments to work somewhat more smoothly.

One result of lengthening the life of Parliament to four years would be to make the representatives feel slightly more secure than they do at present. Many worth-while persons are not willing to enter New Zealand politics when they have to face the hurly-burly of elections every three years. Considering, however, the frequency of elections since 1890, it is remarkable how many members have held their seat continuously in successive parliaments. The turnover of parliamentary personnel in the modern period shows a great reduction on the early figures. Let Table 17 bear witness. For the whole period the average intake of new representatives works out at 31.5 per cent. Up to 1890 the average was 49 per cent. This striking drop has resulted from the growth of party organizations and from the lengthy predominance of the different parties. It means that in every Parliament on an average

about two-thirds of the members are experienced in its procedures and one-third can infuse new blood. Since the constituencies receive so frequently the chance to change the sitting member, this record betokens a fairly steady tendency for the voters to
remain loyal to the man who is in, provided that he retains his
party's indorsement.

Nevertheless, it is only by constant service to the needs of his
constituents as well as by obedience to his party, that a member

TABLE 17

TURNOVER OF ELECTED PARLIAMENTARIANS, 1890–1946

Year of Election	Total No. of Representatives	Representatives Not in Preceding Parliament	Percentage of New Representatives
1890	74	28	38
1893	74	31	42
1896	74	27	37
1899	74	24	32
1902	74	25	34
1905	80	16	20
1908	80	29	36
1911	80	26	32
1914	80	18	23
1919	80	26	32
1922	80	22	28
1925	80	22	29
1928	80	35	52
1931	80	11	18
1935	80	34	44
1938	80	16	21
1943	80	22	28
1946	80	17	21

can gain relative security in his parliamentary profession. The
tasks that a representative is requested to undertake are multifarious, nerve-racking, and time-consuming. The public adhere
to the tradition developed by Seddon and appeal for their representative's assistance in their private affairs. He must be prepared
at all hours to receive them at his home or to talk with them by
telephone. Then, if it is a question of a pension, a mortgage, an
eviction, or some similar trouble, he must go to the appropriate
agency and seek a sympathetic hearing. Many a department is
continually beset by members of Parliament acting the role of
social worker or errand boy for their constituents. The system has

the same good features, and yet is open to the same abuses, as were noticed in the contact between the ministry and the citizens. Sometimes the departments may gain an insight into the effects of their actions on the welfare of individuals which otherwise they might not appreciate. Civil servants have told me that some representatives have helped them by their knowledge about local conditions in their districts. It is a contact which forces the breath of public opinion through the administrative corridors. At the same time, however, it is often grossly abused both by individual citizens and by the members. The public can be very unreasonable in the requests they put to their representatives, and the latter may attempt to exert unwarranted influence upon the course of administration.

The Legislative Council

So far this discussion of Parliament has been confined to its more important half, the House of Representatives. But, in referring to the dependence of representatives upon their constituents' good will, one must not overlook the existence of a second chamber whose selection and tenure are not directly decided by the public. Although the Council nowadays is little better than an antiquarian relic, it remained a political power at least up to 1893. Its reduction to impotence is a part of the story of how New Zealand democratized its institutions. Twice in the fifty years from 1890 to 1940 were efforts made to change the structure of the Council. The first of these, conducted by the Liberals from 1891 to 1893, succeeded. The second, attempted by the Reform party from 1912 to 1920, failed.

When the Liberals acquired their majority in the lower house in 1891, they had to contend with an upper house packed with Conservatives. As a last gesture of defiance, Atkinson, before resigning had nominated to the Council six new members—including himself. Thus the Conservatives, outnumbered in the popular chamber, retreated to the Council for a last-ditch fight. Although Ballance and his Liberals sent a written protest to the governor—before the change of ministry had taken place—Lord Onslow acted on Atkinson's advice and appointed his nominees. At the time when these additional six were appointed, the Council al-

ready contained over thirty-five members, of whom only five or
six could be relied upon to vote Liberal.

Very soon the Council gave a taste of its temper. In 1891 and
the few following years, the upper chamber provided, in Reeves's
words, "one of the most remarkable exhibitions of wrecking ever
given by a Colonial Second Chamber. . . . . Several measures of
importance were thus put back twice and a Bill to permit local
bodies to levy rates on unimproved values three times."[41] Among
the measures which the Council either rejected or wrecked with
its amendments were the bills for Land for Settlements, Electoral
Reform, Shop Hours, and Industrial Conciliation and Arbitration. Consequently, the Liberals realized, as did their British
namesakes in 1910 and 1911, that institutional reform must pre-
cede the social changes they desired. The lower house passed a
bill in 1892 altering the terms of appointment of future councilors
from life-tenure to seven years. It was, of course, defeated in the
Council. Ballance then requested the newly arrived governor,
Lord Glasgow, to appoint twelve extra members to the Council—
a number which would still have left the Liberals decidedly in a
minority. Glasgow refused to agree. The ministry referred the
dispute over his head to the Colonial Office and received its approval. When the twelve "peers" were created, four were workingmen, the first of these to be appointed to the Council. Supported by the Colonial Office against the governor, and triumphantly re-elected by the voters in 1893, the Liberals were now able
to curb the Council. This time the upper chamber did not dare
to reject the bill which shortened the term of future councilors to
seven years. Seddon then proceeded to fill the Council with his
supporters, including Liberal candidates defeated at the general
elections. Not until 1899, however, did the Liberals finally gain
a majority of their own party in the upper house.

When Seddon placed a person in the Council, he expected to
receive his votes on all government bills sent up from the lower
house. He had no power to influence them directly, but in reserve he held the sanction of refusing a reappointment when a
councilor's seven years were expired. The honorarium for mem-

41. W. P. Reeves, *The Long White Cloud* (3d ed.; London: Allen & Unwin, 1924),
p. 285.

bership in the Council was fixed at £150 per annum in 1892 and was raised to £200 in 1901. In many cases this sum was a sufficient inducement to inspire obedience. One councilor remarked in 1912 that the seven-year term had been a mistake because "there is a tendency to place members too much under the influence of the Ministry of the day."[42] But if a Councilor did not support his measures, Seddon would not hesitate to appoint someone else. An example of this victimization was Edward Richardson, who had formerly been a representative and a minister of the Crown. As one councilor said in a reminiscence some years afterward: "On some Bill which the then Leader of the Liberal party [Seddon] wanted passed Mr. Richardson could not see his way to support it, and he voted against it. That was a short time before his seven years tenure of office was expiring. I dare say some honourable members will remember what the measure was, but I know well that not only was he interviewed and begged to alter his decision and do as he was wanted, which he would not, but it was known that when the time came for his re-appointment he would not be re-appointed, and he was not. . . . . That case is well-known and I could speak of others."[43]

It was easy, therefore, for a determined ministry continuously in power for two decades to bend the upper house to its will. By 1912 the Council had become completely subordinate to the cabinet and to the lower house. It was then as fully packed with Liberals as it had been formerly with Conservatives. Its share in legislative activity and in shaping governmental policy had so diminished that the majority of its members ceased to attend debates. A councilor stated in 1912: "I have carefully looked over the list of those who regularly attend the Council at present, and I cannot find more than nine or ten members who regularly take their places here."[44] Hence, when Reform found itself in power, they were confronted with a situation analogous to what existed in 1891—a Council filled with the nominees of the party they had just ousted from office. The Reform party had proposed changes in the constitution of the Council as one of the principal planks

42. *P.D.*, CLIX (1912), 410.
43. *Ibid.*, p. 501; cf. pp. 240 and 521 for further confirmation.
44. *Ibid.*, pp. 399–400.

of their electoral programme. Complaining that the Council had become quite dependent upon the will of the lower house, they reinforced this observation of Siegfried: "It is a wretched assembly, quite without influence, which the progress of democracy has almost succeeded in transforming into a mere council of registration."[45] As one councilor pointed out in self-defense in 1891, the upper house had been criticized because under the system of life-appointment it had rejected bills passed in the lower house. Now it was being condemned because under the seven-year term it did not reject them.[46]

The proposals for reform of the Council were taken in hand by Bell, at whose insistence Massey had incorporated this item into the party's policy. Bell's own motives were quite clear. The Liberals had urged reform of the Council in the early nineties in order to weaken it. He advocated reform in order to strengthen it. Conservative by temperament as well as by philosophy, he wished to establish some agency strong enough to act as a brake on the lower house. Industrial unrest and the militancy of labor had made him and other advocates of property rights fearful of the legislation that a radical majority might enact. "There may come a time," he warned the Council, "it may not be far off—such as came in France, there may be a time when for the moment the country runs riot and mad—when a programme of absolute confiscation may be put forward, when the party in power in the other branch of the Legislature may propose legislation having that effect. I am not speaking of merely social reform; I am speaking of the possibility of a party being in power which may propose that which is advocated in front of the Post Office every day in the week here. I am not venturing to denounce those who hold those views; but on the part of these who do not, I want to see here established a Senate with power to interpose at least delay when—as I believe it is quite possible—that occurs."[47]

The essence of Bell's proposal was to give the Council its own mandate direct from the people by turning it from a nominative into an elective body. He favored an upper chamber smaller in

45. André Siegfried, *Democracy in New Zealand*, trans. E. V. Burns (London: Bell & Sons, 1914), p. 69.

46. *Ibid.*, p. 323.   47. *P.D.*, CLVIII (1914), 791.

membership than the lower and chosen by proportional representation in a few large electoral districts. In 1912 and 1913 the
Council resisted any change in its own constitution, but in 1914
they gave way and agreed to these principles in a modified form.
But, although the bill for reform of the Council passed into law,
it was never subsequently put into operation. Since an election
was due to be held at the end of 1913, Parliament accepted the
act with the proviso that it was not to come into force until 1916.
Thus if the Liberals were to win the election, they would have
time to repeal the act during 1915. Although Reform was re-
elected to power, the outbreak of the war provided a new com-
plication. As a condition of joining a national ministry, the Liberals stipulated that the application of the act was to be deferred
for the duration of the war. After 1918 the Reform cabinet apart
from Bell had grown lukewarm on the subject of altering the
Council; and, as Massey had now placed many of his own supporters into that body, he felt less apprehensive of it. The enforcement of the act was, therefore, made dependent upon the gazet-
ting of an order-in-council—and this has been allowed to lapse.[48]
The act remains on the statute-book and could be brought into
force at any time, but nothing has ever been done about it. The
Labor party, which was hostile to the Council when in opposition, and even suggested its outright abolition, has left it undisturbed. Following the precedents set by the Liberals and the Reformers, it has since 1936 made the upper house innocuous and
subservient by appointing a number of Laborites. In 1941 a piece
of amending legislation made women eligible for membership,
and in 1945 some women were appointed.

Such is the record of the New Zealand Legislative Council over
the last forty years that, judged from any point of view, this must
be considered one of the most futile and ineffective second chambers in the world. Composed as it is at present of members nominated for a seven-year term with prospects of reappointment, it
can always be controlled by a resolute cabinet. For interposing
the delays which Bell wanted, it is quite ill suited, because nowadays its membership could always be swamped. On his assumption that a check upon the popular majority is necessary, Bell was

48. Stewart, *Sir Francis H. D. Bell: His Life and Times*, pp. 98–100.

correct in desiring to see a Council elected directly by the people. But the assumption itself is highly questionable. If the lower house be fully democratic in its mode of election, any upper house that is differently elected must by definition be less democratic. In a modern democracy, however, no such upper chamber would or should dare to resist the will of the lower. At present the debates in the Legislative Council provide a faint and feeble echo of the arguments already thrashed out in the popular house. The voice of the Council is little heard, little considered, and little esteemed. It has no share in making the decisions that really count.

It may well be asked why such an upper house should have been permitted to survive so long. The answer appears to be that successive governments have derived a few minor political advantages from its continuance. It is useful, for example, to be able to bestow membership of the Council as a form of patronage. The post carries with it at present the salary of £375 per annum, as well as the title of "Honorable," and for these reasons some people desire to be councilors. As Stewart has observed: "Any Prime Minister will acknowledge that he has a pigeon-hole always crammed with letters urging for the most varied reasons the claims of the writers or their friends to seats in the Council."[49] Appointments to the Council serve as a dignified way of rewarding elder statesmen and loyal party stalwarts.[50] Moreover, the Council may be and still is at times deliberately used by the ministry for amending or rejecting bills which they prefer to deal with there than in the lower house. It is often politically convenient to pass a bill in the House of Representatives with the understanding that it can be pigeonholed in the Council. Bicameralism is admirably fitted for shelving responsibilities. A Liberal former minister, Wilford, expressed the truth when he said: "I am one of these who, if I had my way, would alter the whole Constitution and do away with the upper House. I think in that case we would do our work better: we would put fewer Bills through, but we would do our work more carefully. It is a common saying in this House, 'Oh, get on with the business; it has to go to the upper

49. *Ibid.*, p. 94.
50. The Council contains a number of persons who were defeated in an election for the lower house.

House, and it will be put right there.' That is a wrong principle."[51]

Apart from these two purposes—each of which is an abuse more than a merit—the Council does perform one useful function: namely, through its Statutes Revision Committee. There it reviews legislation from the standpoint of consistency in drafting; and errors in the text of a bill, due perhaps to the adoption of incompatible amendments, may be discovered. While, however, this is valuable, it is not a task for whose performance an entire second chamber with all its attendant ceremonial needs to be maintained. The Statutes Revision Committee could perfectly well be a standing committee of the House of Representatives. In fact, New Zealand democracy might just as well admit the realities and institute a unicameral legislature. It would require some alteration of the standing orders and the committee system of the House of Representatives to adjust the institution of Parliament to a single chamber. Such a change was made in the twenties in the Australian state of Queensland and in the thirties in the American state of Nebraska. If the present Council were to be abolished, nothing of importance would be lost. Nor is there any strong public sentiment in favor of its survival. Shadows cannot command respect.

The Character of Parliament

It is from the House of Representatives that Parliament as a whole takes its character. Those who have studied New Zealand's lower chamber during the last fifty years have almost universally exposed its deficiencies. To Sidney Webb in 1898 it appeared that "the great reproach which can be made against the New Zealand Government is without doubt its complete vulgarity. It is a failing common to all New Zealanders, although it appears under different forms with different people. With few exceptions, and without distinction of parties, there is a vulgarity of ideas and an absence of refinement among politicians which is the result of the pioneer life they have led."[52] Visiting the Colony around the same time, Siegfried indorsed this judgment and summed up his

51. *P.D.*, CLXVIII (1914), 155. 52. Quoted by Siegfried, *op. cit.*, p. 75.

own impression: "The sessions of the New Zealand Parliament are not always edifying. It is not that they are particularly turbulent, but personal allusions are very frequent, and the debates rarely reach a high level. It is clear that the members know each other at too close quarters, and personal quarrels thus have a tendency to take a prominent place, which often gives the House of Representatives of Wellington the appearance of a municipal council, rather than of a Parliament."[53] The judicious and world-traveled Bryce offered a concurring opinion in some penetrating phrases: "The House of Representatives is in one sense too representative, for its members are little above the average of their electors in knowledge or ability. . . . . The Assembly is left to persons five-sixths of whom do not rise above the level of the town councilors of an English town. . . . . These things being so, the standard not only of attainments, but of debates and of manners also, leaves something to be desired. Thinking bears a low ratio to talking."[54] A similar and unflattering comparison between the House of Representatives and the London County Council was made by Reeves, who considered New Zealand's Parliament in modern times to have fallen below its earlier standards. "No Smuts, no Laurier, no Deakin, or Bruce has appeared," wrote the former Liberal minister, "and lacking men of outstanding intellect, able both to inspire and to lead, legislation has on the whole become more commonplace, and expenditure has at times been sought almost as an object in itself."[55] Among more recent judges, such New Zealand writers as Condliffe and Morrell have themselves added their quotas to this unfavorable consensus.

With these opinions my own judgment, based on a reading of Hansard and inquiries about the past as well as on contemporary observation, is in full agreement. In the late thirties and early forties the New Zealand Parliament did not offer an inspiring spectacle.[56] Too many of the speeches are of low standard and

53. *Ibid.*, p. 76.
54. James Bryce, *Modern Democracies* (New York: Macmillan Co., 1921), II, 318–20.
55. *The Long White Cloud*, pp. 255 and 345.
56. Much of the effectiveness of Parliament, though, depends on the quality of the opposition. In 1944, when the opposition were considerably strengthened, Parliament as a whole improved.

poor quality even when the topic under discussion rises above the trivial. The average caliber of legislative personnel is not good enough even though a few members on both sides are outstanding. The general public do not regard their Parliament highly and tend to look upon it as a kind of national bore effort. Nor could they possibly do otherwise. Some of the reasons for this state of affairs must be considered in the concluding chapter, when certain general features of this democracy will be passed under review. But a few contributing causes and resulting effects can be mentioned here. It is undeniable that the tightness of party discipline and the growth of the caucus have detracted from the prestige of members singly and of Parliament collectively. The ordinary representative is viewed as a cipher or puppet, voting in the House as he is told and then beseeching a renewal of his constituents' favor. Debates are a mere forensic exercise, since the outcome is nearly always prearranged. A member said in 1929 that "during the whole time he had been a member of the House he had known few honourable members' speeches—no matter how eloquent those members might have been—influence votes. Honourable members voted with their party or according to preconceived ideas, and it was immaterial what arguments were brought forward."

A former minister of the Crown, who also served as leader of the opposition, once listed to me these three reasons for the poor standard of the Dominion's legislature. They were the low salaries paid to representatives, the uncertainty and insecurity of their profession, and the abuse to which they were subject. Another qualified observer, the permanent head of an important state department, gave as the two qualifications for a New Zealand politician "the gift of the gab and the hide of a rhinoceros." There can be no question that neither the personnel nor the structure of this Parliament is fitted for the tasks it will have to shoulder in these postwar decades. A representative democracy which does not produce a better legislature than this one is running a serious risk.

CHAPTER XIII
DEPARTMENTAL FUNCTIONS AND ORGANIZATION

I T WAS the Liberal legislation of the nineties which drew the
eyes of the outside world to this young British democracy in
the South Pacific and earned for it an international reputation
for boldness in conducting social experiments. Thereupon it became the stock theme for social scientists to discuss and explain
the readiness of New Zealanders to expand the functions of the
state. Visiting scholars of such eminence as Siegfried and Bryce
noted that the government performed here various activities
which elsewhere were cared for, if at all, by private enterprise.
Since then, under the accumulating stringencies of two world
wars and a world depression, the Dominion has fully kept pace
with the trend, now become universal, of intrusting ever more
duties to its public officials. Already at the time when the more
recent world war broke out, the state was undertaking all the customary functions of government and many more besides. Much
has been written about those of New Zealand's government activities which are at all novel and unusual. Their social and economic consequences have been somewhat elaborately described.
But surprisingly little attention has been paid to the administrative system which brings a promised policy or an enacted law to
the fruition of achievement. What methods have been devised in
this much-governed country for organizing its state departments?
What have been the administrative consequences of continually
extending the range of state action? What machinery has been
set up to carry out the legislative will?

The Scale of Public Administration

Throughout the last half-century New Zealand has exhibited
a general tendency to multiply the functions of government, but

this expansionism has taken place in a series of waves. Acceding to power after the economic slump and the ministerial timidity of the eighties, the Liberals were energetically expansive at least up to 1897, equaling in their first seven years of office, if not surpassing, Vogel's dynamic creativeness in the early seventies. Their agricultural and industrial policies, as well as their inauguration of social insurance, led the state into new pastures. More acts of Parliament called for more agencies of administration. The machinery of government soon acquired a complexity it had lacked before. By contrast with the bustling nineties, the first decade of this century was a period of relative quietism. Neither Seddon in his "King Dick" era nor Ward, on whom the Liberal mantle descended, displayed after 1900 the initiative he had shown before. The earlier liberalism was positive, constructive, and radical; its later form was more conservatively disposed to guard its gains and hold what it had. Even the advent to power of the Reform party produced at first but few legislative innovations. The change from a leasehold to a freehold tenure of state-provided farms and the inauguration of a merit system in the civil service were the two most important changes on the statute-book. A new agency which thus came into existence was the office of the public service commissioner. Otherwise, no drastic remodeling or extension of the state departments was called for until war broke out in 1914. Thereupon ensued the inevitable hectic growths with a mushroom crop of new controls, new agencies, and new staffs. While most of these wartime sprouts were pruned away when "peace" was declared, others appeared in their place in answer to the social needs of the troubled twenties. As head of a farmers' government, Massey was nothing loath to see the activities of the Agriculture Department widely extended or to introduce various boards for regulating primary production. The development of road transport in competition with the rail services, the control of civil airways, and the commencement of broadcasting exemplified the impact of the new technology on the machinery of state. At the beginning of the turbulent thirties the economic depression led to the curtailment of many governmental functions, even though the severity of the capitalist breakdown itself brought into being a handful of new agencies such as the Reserve Bank.

But once again, in 1936, with Labor in office and overseas prices rising, the tendency to expand reasserted itself with a vigor analogous to that of the nineties. Continuously up to 1939, then during the war years and its immediate aftermath, the state extended its sphere of operations and assumed ever more responsibilities.

Modern New Zealand can fairly be described as one of the most elaborately governed democracies in the world. Among the activities already undertaken by its government in 1939 were some (e.g., control of foreign exchange and licensing of imports) which were not introduced into other countries until at the compulsion of war. Viewed in over-all perspective, the functions of state departments were as wide in their scope as they were varied in content. There could be found a public trust office, a state advances corporation, a government life insurance and a state fire insurance department, an industrial arbitration court, an internal marketing department, a country library service, and a social security department. These and other *rarae aves* of the political scientist's museum had their place alongside such familiar species as the Treasury and the departments of Education, Agriculture, Labor, Customs, etc.

Infinite indeed are the services which the government of the Dominion of New Zealand supplies to its citizens. While it educates the children in its primary and secondary schools, it takes care of their teeth in its own dental clinics and distributes free milk and apples. It will lend you money to build a house of your own or allow you to rent one which it has constructed and owns. It will give you insurance on your life or on your property and effects. It provides you with the services of the telephone, the telegraph, the mails, and a commercial bank. It will sell you the coal, which it has extracted from its own mines, or a palatable light wine that is produced in its vineyards. It will transport you on its railways, buses, or airplanes and will invite you to spend a vacation in its own tourist hotels and holiday resorts. It will entertain, and possibly instruct, you with its broadcasts; and, if you live in the country, it will provide you with books. Should you wish to erect a factory, import materials or manufactures from overseas, or send money abroad, you must obtain the state's permission. If you are a laborer, it fixes your minimum rate of wage,

determines the hours and conditions of your work, and compels
you to enrol in the appropriate trade-union. If you are a farmer,
it offers the assistance of its agricultural experts, buys certain of
your products at a price it guarantees, and markets them in the
Dominion or abroad. It plants forests, cuts its timber at its own
sawmill, and sells it. It organizes the growing of linen flax and
processes the fiber at its own plants. When there is an addition
to your family, or whenever you visit a doctor, it contributes a
portion of the medical fees; and, if you are unemployed, widowed,
orphaned, aged, or totally invalided, it pays you a benefit. It
will give you a career for life as a public servant working in its
employ. It can make your will, execute your estate, and administer any trust you desire to establish. If you commit a crime and
are found out by its police, it will incarcerate you in one of its
prisons. If you go insane, it will commit you to one of its mental
hospitals. Finally, when you die, it will take its share of what you
leave and will include your demise in the published statistics of
its invaluable *Year Book*. From birth to burial you may be a voter
at its elections, a subject of its laws, a contributor to its revenues, or a recipient of its services. Leviathan in New Zealand is a
well-nigh universal provider.

The Departmental System

To organize and correlate the numerous departments which
perform all these and other governmental activities is a genuine
problem of large-scale administration. That is a statement which
might conceivably sound exaggerated to inhabitants of countries
in which single cities have populations larger than that of New
Zealand. In the United States the number of federal civil servants
alone has come to exceed the total number of New Zealanders.
In 1938 there were in New Zealand 81,052 persons whose salaries
or wages were paid by the central government and 38,922 by the
various local bodies (see Table 18). Compared with the scale of
larger democracies, that does not seem such a tremendous problem to handle. Yet, consider that these 81,052 central and 38,922
local employees were organized to serve a population of 1,618,313
scattered over two islands almost the size of Britain. In that population at the census taken in 1936 half a million persons were

found to be gainfully occupied. Thus in 1938 approximately 16 per cent of all salary- and wage-earners in the Dominion were employed by the central government and approximately 8 per cent by local authorities. Centrally and locally the state provided a livelihood to almost a quarter of all working New Zealanders. Moreover, the services offered to the public in New Zealand are exceptionally numerous. Within this small and dispersed community the volume and the variety of governmental functions are phenomenal. Public administration in New Zealand can justly be

TABLE 18
NUMBER OF PUBLIC EMPLOYEES, 1913–38

Year	Total Central Government Employees*	Total Local Government Employees*	Total Population	% of Total Central Government Employees to Population	% of Total Local Government Employees to Population	Total Wage-earners in Census Years	% of Total Central Government Employees to Total Wage-earners	% of Total Local Government Employees to Total Wage-earners
1913......	37,501 (68.7)	17,067 (31.3)	1,134,506	3.3	1.5			
1916......	41,402 (73.8)	14,663 (26.2)	1,146,004	3.6	1.3	302,161	13.7	4.8
1918......	40,765 (73.5)	14,660 (26.5)	1,158,149	3.5	1.3			
1921......	45,613 (71.4)	18,291 (28.6)	1,126,428	3.6	1.4	370,692	12.3	4.9
1923†.....	46,955 (68.5)	21,563 (31.5)	1,343,021	3.5	1.6			
1926......	52,635 (65.7)	27,484 (34.3)	1,408,139	3.7	1.9	414,673	12.7	6.6
1928......	56,087 (65.1)	30,122 (34.9)	1,467,370	3.8	2.0			
1933†.....	49,692 (45.2)	60,256 (54.8)	1,547,124	3.2	3.9			
1936......	57,777 (55.6)	46,227 (44.4)	1,573,810	3.7	2.9	499,797	11.6	9.2
1938......	81,052 (67.6)	38,922 (32.4)	1,618,313	5.0	2.4			

* The figures in parentheses in these columns are the percentages of central and local employees, respectively, to the total number of public employees.

† Depression years.

called large-scale administration because—to convert the Churchillian phrase—so many are doing so much for so few. Here is a democracy of miniature compass with all the complex appurtenances of the modern social service state. The internal intricacy of its machinery involves all that tangle of structural and personnel relations which has defined and brought attention to the study of administration.

New Zealand, therefore, has this peculiarity. Where the population is small and where so much is done by the state, the field of private enterprise is *pro tanto* restricted. It is correct to say that in this Dominion virtually the only large-scale administration is of the public type. Large-scale private administration is almost nonexistent. One or two banks or insurance companies, a shipping firm, a construction company, and a few organizations that finance, sell to, or buy from farmers—these are about the only private undertakings in the country exhibiting problems of large-scale administration. In the United States or Great Britain, the student of administration can find domestic analogies and parallels between public and private organizations on an equally large scale.[1] In New Zealand those interested in large-scale management have only the government to study. Its administration is far and away the most vital and potent factor in the well-being of the community.

Here, however, arises the paradox which forms the present subject of inquiry. In the scope and variety of its functions New Zealand public administration has a large-scale character and content, but in its structure and style of organization it has not. The Dominion still adheres to principles of administration and to a departmental system which are unsuited to its modern needs. The machinery of government is arranged on fundamentally the same lines as several decades ago. It is bigger now than it was; but it has become so by mere addition, by accretion, by agglomeration. More parts have been tacked on, and that is all. No proper plan has been introduced for redesigning and recasting the pattern of the whole. There has been a little reshuffling; there has never been any reorganization. The government in New Zealand is carrying out mid-twentieth-century functions with nineteenth-century tools. Its functions have outgrown its structure.

This is merely the outcome of the administrative expansion that has persisted over fifty years without system or plan. Governments of all parties have contributed to the same tendencies. Liberals, Reform, and Labor in turn have inherited the legacy of an unwieldy machine and have each left it a bit more cumbrous. New functions have been assumed by the state. Sometimes a new department has been created to administer them; sometimes they have been placed in existing agencies. Gradually more than one department has become internally unmanageable because it has

---

1. See, e.g., Marshall E. Dimock and Howard K. Hyde, *Bureaucracy and Trusteeship in Large Corporations* ("Temporary National Economic Committee Monographs," No. 11 [Washington, D.C.: Government Printing Office, 1940]).

not been rebuilt to carry its heavier load. Likewise the whole administrative machine has become formless and unmanageable. It is an example of large-scale management conducted with small-scale instruments.

There have been times when a ministry or a royal commission has noticed the need for remodeling this "sorry scheme of things entire." Some recommendations have been put forward, and a few halfhearted efforts made to apply them. Yet the basic defects have remained. It has usually happened that suggestions for structural alterations have been advanced at times when governments were hard pressed for revenue. Administrative reform, consolidation of departments, and reorganization have been seriously considered only when expenditure must be curtailed. An attempt along these lines was made when the overseas prices of the Dominion's main exports fell in 1907 and 1908, and Ward decided to retrench. One of the devices then adopted was to group separate departments together in the hope of reaping administrative economies. How the accomplishment fell short of the aim was set forth authoritatively in 1912 by the Hunt Commission: "Three years ago there were in existence thirty seven different Departments under as many different heads. In the interests of economy and efficiency it was thought desirable to reduce the number of Departments and the number of heads, and with this object in view an amalgamation of many of them was brought about, reducing the total number to sixteen. . . . . This amalgamation was, in many cases, more nominal than real, and while certain Departments were grouped under one heading they really continued separate existences."[2] One year afterward in his first annual report the newly appointed public service commissioner stated: "The main Departments, with few exceptions, do not appear, so far as I have been able to ascertain, to exercise even a casual control over their so-called subordinate Departments. Theoretically, there are sixteen main Departments, but there are actually thirty three, which are practically independent in all respects."[3] Again in the slump of 1922 and the depression of the

2. "Report of the (Hunt) Commission on the Public Service, 1912" (appendix to the *Journal of the House of Representatives* [1912], H-34), p. 25.

3. "First Report of the Public Service Commissioner, 1913" (appendix to the *Journal of the House of Representatives*, H-14), p. 3.

thirties conservative governments under financial stress saw in administrative reconstruction a possible way of saving money; but the only structural changes actually accomplished were minor ones.

On such occasions the Dominion has been made aware that it could choose between alternative principles of departmental organization. It could establish either a large number of separate small departments or a small number of separate large ones. Now and then it has shown some inclination to choose the latter alternative. Apart from the attempt in 1909 to create a few broad groups, some individual departments have actually been built by the merging of scattered divisions or bureaus. An example is the Department of Scientific and Industrial Research, which was pieced together in 1926 out of the Dominion Laboratory, the Dominion Observatory, the Geological Survey, and the Meteorological Branch, and has since been greatly extended to cover other scientific research.[4] In general, however, the pull has normally been in the other direction. There is a much stronger propensity for branches to split off from the parent-body and become separate agencies than for distinct departments to consolidate. The reason for it can be found in the psychology of the civil service. The point was aptly put in the Hunt report: "There is a great tendency for each Department to magnify and glorify itself. The Secretary for each of the main Departments desires to make his Department an important one, because it means a more important position for himself. He is assisted in this way by all the officers of his Department, for raising the status of the Secretary means raising the status of all the principal officers under him. The head of every minor Department wishes to magnify his office and make it appear as important as possible, in order that he may break free from the leading-strings of the Secretary of the Department under which he is grouped, and become a Secretary on his own account."[5]

Political considerations, too, will sometimes determine the splitting of departments. The Electoral Department is a case in

4. See "Fifteenth Report of the Public Service Commissioner" (appendix to the *Journal of the House of Representatives*, H-14), p. 2.
5. *Op. cit.*, p. 13.

point. Up to 1918 this agency was a branch of the Internal Affairs Department. The minister of internal affairs in the wartime national government was a Liberal, and Massey, knowing that the coalition would soon be dissolved, wanted this strategic bureau under his own supervision as soon before the election as possible. Consequently, the Electoral Department was shifted to the office of the prime minister. The story of the creation of the Forestry Service will also illustrate the influence which a powerful cabinet member can bring to bear on the administrative structure. Until the early twenties the care of forests was dealt with, if at all, by the Lands and Survey Department, one of New Zealand's oldest agencies. Its policy, however, was to encourage settlement on the land and to open up new territory for agriculture or pasture. In its desire, quite laudable in itself, to increase the farm population, it had often sacrificed the Dominion's forests. Bell became concerned in the early twenties with the need to conserve the fast-dwindling forested areas and had legislation introduced. It was at his insistence that the Forestry Service was instituted as an agency under its own director quite independent of the Lands and Survey Department. Bell himself assumed the ministerial responsibility as commissioner of state forests. An agency which might have, but has not yet, been separated from the parent-body is the Child Welfare Branch of the Education Department. It is a branch whose potentialities have never been fully developed because the Education Department tended in the past to consider it a sideline. Proposals to constitute the Child Welfare Branch into an independent agency have emanated sometimes from the officials within the branch, sometimes from parliamentarians.[6] But they have always been successfully resisted by ministers of education.

This tendency to multiply the number of departments, to which all parties have contributed their quota, is not the only outstanding issue of New Zealand public administration. It is one question to choose between having many small agencies or a few large ones; it is another matter to determine whether the various departments of state should be closely integrated under cabinet control or not. This is one of the contentious problems of modern

6. See, e.g., *P.D.*, CCXVI (1927), 267.

administration arousing analogous controversies in many countries. Should departments be placed immediately and directly under ministerial (i.e., political) control? Or should they be to some extent insulated from political direction and be organized under boards or constituted into semiautonomous corporations? Over these questions the policies and practices of the major parties have differed markedly. Subject to some exceptions, one may state that the more radical parties (the Liberals in the nineties and Labor in the thirties and forties) have usually favored the principle of a closely integrated administrative system with ministerial control of departments. The Reform party, on the other hand, and the coalition of the depression years, preferred the opposite arrangement.

It will be recalled that the Conservative Atkinson ministry handed over the management of the railways to a board during the slump of the late eighties when administrative economies were in the vogue. Seddon, however, was irked to find the railways outside his control; and, once his power was established, he abolished the board and reinstated a minister in charge. Following the same line of theory and expediency, the Liberals throughout their twenty years of office objected to the establishment of a nonpolitical agency for personnel management in the civil service. The cabinet, as they insisted, must retain its supervisory authority unimpaired. It was, therefore, left to the Reform government in 1912 to create the office of the public service commissioner with a status semi-independent of the ministry. During the twenties, when the regulation of primary production and marketing came into vogue, the Massey and Coates ministries instituted several agricultural boards manned by representatives of the government and of the producers. In the depression the United-Reform coalition manifested the same preference in four cases. These were the Reserve Bank, which it created *de novo* and placed under a semiautonomous board; the National Mortgage Corporation,[7] under board control, which was substituted for the Advances to Settlers Department; the administration of broadcasting, which was taken over by the government and put

7. The capital of both the bank and the corporation was subscribed by private shareholders.

in the hands of a commission; and the railways, whose management once more reverted from a minister to a board.

When Labor took office, they made plain their policy that every activity of government must be politically and administratively subject to the ministry composed of the people's elected representatives. The boards that controlled broadcasting and railways were promptly abolished, and ministers assumed direct charge. For the National Mortgage Corporation was substituted the State Advances Corporation. Its capital is supplied by the state; the managing directors are appointed by the ministry; and the instructions of the minister of finance are binding. Also reconstituted was the Reserve Bank. It, too, operates now with state-provided capital. The board of directors and the governor are ministerial appointees who must execute the policy of the minister of finance. Of the new agencies established in 1945, the overhead organization followed much the same pattern as before. The Hydroelectric Branch of the Public Works Department was separated from the parent-body and was independently constituted under a minister. The wartime National Service Department blossomed forth into a peacetime National Employment Service, directed by a minister of employment. On the other hand, when the government took over the ownership of the Bank of New Zealand, the linen-flax industry, and the civil airways, it accorded to each of these the legal status of a public corporation. All three are owned entirely by the state and are operated by boards, but their general policy must conform to the wishes of the minister concerned.

At the outbreak of war in 1939 the machinery of government consisted of numerous departments that were separate from one another but somehow integrated under the authority of the cabinet. A description of the departmental system, as it then was, will show the administrative equipment with which New Zealand entered upon a streamlined, total war. The official list for 1939 numbers no less than forty-eight[8] distinct departments. But that is a figure which, like all statistics, requires interpretation

8. This figure is based upon the *Government Year-Book* (Wellington, 1939), pp. 864, 869–70, and upon the "Twenty-seventh Report of the Public Service Commissioner" (1939), p. 31. It includes the Social Security Department, which was organized in March, 1939.

and explanation before the true picture can be understood. There were six of these so-called "departments" whose staff comprised less than twenty-five persons, while three other agencies contained between twenty-five and fifty. The smallest of them all were the Prime Minister's Department, with only six members, and the Crown Law Office, the Public Service Superannuation Department, and the External Affairs and Cook Islands Administration—each with a personnel of eight. Such diminutive bureaus are to be contrasted with the agencies at the other end of the scale: the Police Department, composed of a force of fourteen hundred persons; the Mental Hospitals Department, staffed by fifteen hundred; the Post and Telegraph Department, with over eleven thousand; and the Railways, twenty-two thousand strong. The pygmies and the giants, Lilliput and Brobdingnag, unicellular organisms and mastodons, are incongruously combined in the departmental pattern. It is useless even to state what is the "average" size of a department, since the standard deviation is so high.

In yet another respect the number of forty-eight fails to correspond with the administrative realities. Many an agency is charged with functions so diverse that little or no connection may exist between its various branches. When it is administratively severed from the remainder of the organization to which it supposedly belongs, a branch virtually becomes a subdepartment and its head acquires a status of semi-independence. Such has been the Child Welfare Branch of the Education Department, a branch which has often in the past operated in self-contained isolation.[9] Such, too, is the Fisheries Branch of the Marine Department. "Marine" is a name for an ill-assorted miscellany of activities. This department regulates navigation in New Zealand's territorial waters, administers certain harbors, and operates a number of lighthouses. Being concerned with the general supervision of shipping, it conducts inspections of vessels and is staffed by engineers who examine the safety of boilers and other machinery. But this type of inspection is not confined to ships alone. The Marine Department also inspects machinery on land in fac-

9. In this case the isolation is geographical as well as administrative. Child Welfare is remotely housed at the end of the business center of Wellington opposite from the rest of the department.

tories and industrial plants and issues permits for the elevators in office buildings. Very loosely tacked on to these functions is the Fisheries Branch, which conserves and develops the Dominion's piscatorial resources in both fresh and sea water. Between the supervision of fish and ships there is no connecting link save their common predilection for water.

A third case in point is the Patents Office. Nominally this falls under the purview of the Justice Department on the ground that patent administration involves legal problems and Justice is the lawyer's agency. Actually the Patents Office has operated with little supervision by its parent-body. At one time it became so inefficient that the public service commissioner had to intervene and dry-clean an Augean stable of muddle, delay, and confusion. The Department of Scientific and Industrial Research exemplifies an internally heterogeneous agency created out of a collection of scattered bureaus and institutions whose activities were mainly technical or scientific. Even today some of the various branches enjoy such autonomy that the department could hardly be described as an integrated whole. More miscellaneous still are the weirdly combined interests of an Internal Affairs Department that "deals with practically any subject which happens to be outside the functions of other Departments."[10] Besides attending to the ceremonial and official aspects of government—the certification of public records, the commissioning of ministers, appointment of governor-generals, etc.—it is Internal Affairs which issues passports, conducts the censorship of films, grants licenses for game-hunting, supervises local government, administers a library and art collection, and controls lotteries and racing, to list only a portion of its wide-ranging activities. This department is the inevitable wastebasket which reappears under similar titles in every governmental jurisdiction to absorb the functions that can be fitted nowhere else.[11] Thus the term "department," as this survey shows, may be merely a compendious description for a loose federation of bureaus whose union, like the British Commonwealth of Nations, consists chiefly in their common allegiance to the Crown.

10. "First Report of the Public Service Commissioner, 1913," p. 26.

11. In Britain the "wastebasket" is the Home Office; in the federal government of the United States it is the Department of the Interior.

Cabinet Co-ordination

This congeries of departments and subdepartments was controlled in 1939 by a twelve-membered cabinet. Chart I shows the
departmental plan (or lack of it) and depicts the distribution of
portfolios among the ministers. There are several features in the
political and administrative arrangements of the executive
branch which call for comment. It will be noticed that, with two
exceptions, every agency was definitely assigned to the charge of
some member of the cabinet. The exceptions were the offices of
the controller and auditor-general and the public service commissioner, each of whom was appointed for a fixed term of years
by the governor-general in Council and was removable only by
parliamentary action. The controller was given independence of
ministers, since his audit might have to expose irregularities in
the financial administration of the department they controlled.
The commissioner also received a measure of autonomy in order
that public officials might be appointed on the basis of merit and
not of political influence. The supreme political authority was
the cabinet composed of the premier and ministers with portfolio. In addition to these, two persons were attached to the cabinet in 1939 with a quasi-ministerial status. One was the government's leader in the upper house, who was designated "member
of the Executive Council without portfolio"; the second was a
parliamentary undersecretary appointed to assist the minister of
finance. In practice each of these subministers was assigned some
function to administer in order that the duties of government
might be spread around.[12]

Despite these latter palliatives a valid criticism can be directed
against the general failure to distribute administrative burdens
with equality. One minister, a Labor stalwart in bygone strikes,
had under his care nothing but the departments of Internal Affairs and of Pensions—a very meager dole. At the other extreme
were two hard-worked and capable men on whom fell the bulk
of the burdens. Mr. Peter Fraser, who subsequently became

12. The cabinet member in the upper house took care of the State Advances
Corporation and of Immigration. The parliamentary undersecretary to the minister
of finance was responsible for housing.

CHART I

ALLOCATION OF MINISTERIAL PORTFOLIOS, 1939

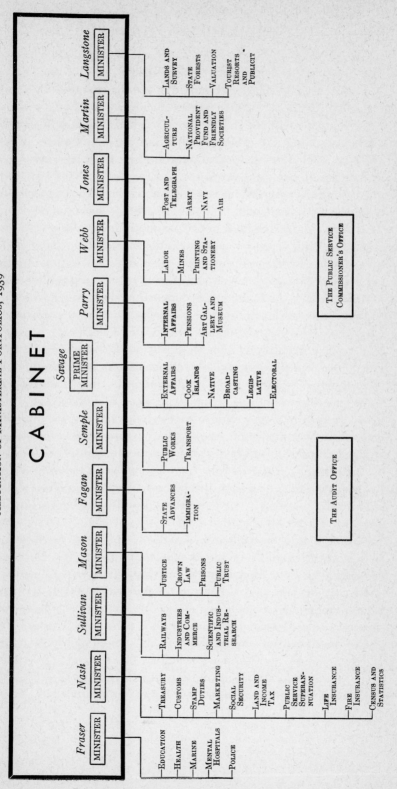

Fraser MINISTER

- EDUCATION
- HEALTH
- MARINE
- MENTAL HOSPITALS
- POLICE

Nash MINISTER

- TREASURY
- CUSTOMS
- STAMP DUTIES
- MARKETING
- SOCIAL SECURITY
- LAND AND INCOME TAX
- PUBLIC SERVICE SUPERANNUATION
- LIFE INSURANCE
- FIRE INSURANCE
- CENSUS AND STATISTICS

Sullivan MINISTER

- RAILWAYS
- INDUSTRIES AND COMMERCE
- SCIENTIFIC AND INDUSTRIAL RESEARCH

Mason MINISTER

- JUSTICE
- CROWN LAW
- PRISONS
- PUBLIC TRUST

Fagan MINISTER

- STATE ADVANCES
- IMMIGRATION

Semple MINISTER

- PUBLIC WORKS
- TRANSPORT

Savage PRIME MINISTER

- EXTERNAL AFFAIRS
- COOK ISLANDS
- NATIVE
- BROADCASTING
- LEGISLATIVE
- ELECTORAL

Parry MINISTER

- INTERNAL AFFAIRS
- PENSIONS
- ART GALLERY AND MUSEUM

Webb MINISTER

- LABOR
- MINES
- PRINTING AND STATIONERY

Jones MINISTER

- POST AND TELEGRAPH
- ARMY
- NAVY
- AIR

Martin MINISTER

- AGRICULTURE
- NATIONAL PROVIDENT FUND AND FRIENDLY SOCIETIES

Langstone MINISTER

- LANDS AND SURVEY
- STATE FORESTS
- VALUATION
- TOURIST RESORTS AND PUBLICITY

CABINET

THE AUDIT OFFICE

THE PUBLIC SERVICE COMMISSIONER'S OFFICE

premier, was responsible for Education, Health, Marine, Police, and Mental Hospitals—all of them, taken together, a cornucopia of thorns and troubles. Even that bundle of bureaus was surpassed by the collection of Mr. Walter Nash, in whose hands were concentrated no less than ten departments: Treasury, Customs, Stamp Duties, Marketing, Social Security, Land and Income Tax, Public Service Superannuation, Life Insurance, Fire Insurance, and Census and Statistics. Small wonder that his office was known as a notorious bottleneck where files piled high and decisions were perennially delayed, where memorandums were for so long "under consideration" and planning was drowned in the sea of detail. Nor was the prime minister himself devoid of a share in departmental administration. Under his wing came the departments of External Affairs, Cook Islands, Native, National Broadcasting, Commercial Broadcasting, Legislative, and Electoral—these in addition to his duties as general co-ordinator and supervisor of the entire machine!

Further scrutiny reveals that portfolios whose subject matter was essentially connected were distributed in different hands. Take as an example the administration of the various pensions and superannuation schemes. These were handled by five different ministers, of whom one dealt with the superannuation of teachers and policemen, another with social security benefits and life insurance and public servants' superannuation, a third with war pensions, a fourth with the national provident and friendly societies, and a fifth with the Pensions Department. Agriculture was administered by one minister; Lands and Survey and the Forest Service by another. The four agencies concerned with communications (Railways, Transport, Marine, and Post and Telegraph) were in the hands of as many different ministers.

If the lack of rationale in the distribution of portfolios prevented the comprehensive planning of policy, confusion was worse confounded by the practice of placing more than one minister over different branches of a single "department." For example, the Industries and Commerce Department included a branch called Tourist and Publicity. The permanent head of the department was responsible to one minister for Industries and Commerce and to a different one for Tourist and Publicity. The control of immigration is vested in the Labor Department; but the minister who supervised immigration was not the same as he who administered the labor laws. The official who was head of the Mines Department (under one minister) was also head of Housing Construction and so came under a second minister. In 1940 an example of inefficient wartime organization was seen in the case of one official who, as permanent head of the Justice Department, was also head of the Prisons Department and was further intrusted with the control of sugar supplies. In these three capacities he served three separate ministers. Such tangled administrative relationships are surely indefensible. How can one man properly work under more than one minister? And what happens to the civil servant's duty of loyalty to his ministerial superiors should they happen to disagree?

Existing Defects

Such, in brief, was the structure of New Zealand's executive branch in 1939. That year has been chosen for purposes of illustration because the departmental system was then at the height of its peacetime expansion. But the administrative defects outlined above are not peculiar to that year or ascribable to the Labor government only. One could just as easily analyze the same faults in preceding decades, when Liberal or Reform cabinets were governing the country. These very weaknesses are the recurring decimals of administration in this democracy. The question then must be posed: In what manner should the departmental structure be altered?

It might be argued, as certain civil servants do, that existing defects could be remedied by changes which would not involve a drastic reorganization of the entire system. It would be quite possible to keep the number of separate departments approximately as it is at present but to group them in such a fashion that all connected activities are placed under the same minister. Nor would it need any structural modifications to provide that each permanent head should be responsible for all branches of his department to one minister and only one. To some degree the machinery of administration could be improved merely by regrouping portfolios, by clarifying the lines of responsibility, and here and there by transferring an ill-placed branch or two. Proposals of this type are mooted from time to time by those who give any thought to the problems at issue. I agree that they would result in some improvement. But I am sure that they would not remove enough of the present defects. Such remedies, though they may be good as far as they go, do not reach deeply enough. They merely tinker with the superficial consequences of a system which from the foundations up is wrongly conceived.

There are two cardinal faults in the present structure of which only one would be in any material degree affected by such changes. The cardinal faults are these. First, many functions of government relating to a single social problem, which should be planned and administered as a unity, are spread over several agencies. All too often this results in the problems being treated as separate ones, in the lack of co-ordinated planning, and in acute clashes of policy and jurisdiction between the agencies concerned. I shall later give numerous examples of this failing, but for the present it is enough to cite one glaring case. A country whose wealth is primarily agricultural and whose welfare depends principally on the export of pastoral products is manifestly concerned with sound administration of its greatest natural resource —the land. A comprehensive, long-term, national policy of land conservation and development should underlie the programs of any and every ministry. But what is to be done when the administration of different aspects of land policy is separated into four major departments (Lands and Survey, Agriculture, Marketing, and State Forests) and is distributed in further driblets to at least three others (Internal Affairs, State Advances Corporation, and Scientific and Industrial Research)? Instead of a solo performance on a single instrument, there is a disharmonious septet —without even a clearly recognized first violin.

The second fault is to be discerned at the topmost tier in the governmental hierarchy at that crucial level where the execution of policy merges indistinguishably with its political formulation. Under an administrative system where fifty-odd agencies are directed by a cabinet of twelve politicians, it necessarily follows that each minister receives several departments to supervise. The departments are organized into distinct entities, each constituted under its own act of Parliament and vested with its own authority and power. Each is therefore co-ordinate with the other. Though their political importance may vary, their administrative independence is guaranteed. They are like sovereign states, as the fictions of international law conceive them, endowed with a conventional equality of status which masks the reality of their divergences. And as the heads of states are equal in international usage, so are the permanent heads of governmental departments in New Zealand's administrative law. Every minister deals with a group of heads all reporting to him autonomously. It is a union of sovereign departments which the cabinet co-ordinates or, rather, fails to co-ordinate. When social issues arise, as rise they must, which cut horizontally across the several departmental jurisdictions, upon the minister or upon the whole cabinet falls the duty of securing co-operation. Let it be granted that in any administrative system, however perfectly constructed, much interaction among agencies will at times be required. The modern community and its problems are continuous living tissue, and our departmentalization is at best a knifelike act of surgery. But let it be also admitted that the more agencies that are established, the more co-ordination that is required. Administrative relationships multiply by geometrical progression as the number of administrative units increases. The result of the New Zealand system is that far too much co-ordination, both of agencies and of functions, is thrown up to the ministerial level which could and should be settled farther down the pyramid of authority.

The combined effect of these twin faults may be summarized into a general indictment against New Zealand cabinets for failing to perform their proper role in the sphere of administration. Neither long-term planning nor co-ordination of the policies of separate departments is much in evidence in New Zealand. Ministries have been preoccupied with the issues of the moment; and ministers, like horses wearing blinkers, have had their vision narrowed into the compartments of the many agencies they supervise. The problem of modern public administration has become not unlike the great controversy of early Greek metaphysics. It is to reconcile the one and the many. Society is one; but its major need—to promote the general welfare—has many aspects. The cabinet, controlling body of the state machinery, is one; but many are the departments, the jurisdictions, the policies, and the interests under its management.

Nor is this all. Lack of integration is one harmful product of a poorly constructed organization. Another product, no less regrettable, is the constant tendency to overburden the ministry with attention to detail. That has been and is still the besetting sin of cabinet government in the Dominion. For the last fifty years the work thrown on the ministry as a body and on the majority of individual ministers has exceeded the human "span of control."[13] Quantitatively, this means that a greater volume of jobs is undertaken by the cabinet than it can efficiently handle; qualitatively, that matters determined by ministers are often of a type which should be relegated to subordinates. The Hunt Commission of 1912 enlarged upon this failing in words that are every whit applicable to cabinets of recent decades: "At the present time heads of Departments have to refer all sorts of minor details to the Ministers in charge of their particular Departments. This not only wastes the time and hampers the operations of the Department itself, but it takes up the time of Ministers attending to a mass of detail which, in many cases, they can know very little about, and which would be done very much better if they were relieved of them altogether, and the responsibility thrown on to some one else. We think we can safely say that very few managers of large businesses, even when they have had their lives' training in the business, would attempt to cope with the mass of detail with which a Minister in charge of a Department, who has not had any lengthy training with that particular Department, attempts to deal."[14] The very persistence of this fault, its stubborn survival through Liberal, Reform, and Labor regimes alike, is one of its most curious aspects. Evidently a practice to which all parties have conformed must indicate a national characteristic genuinely deriving from the New Zealand environment. To probe the causes, therefore, is to understand New Zealand.

13. For an illuminating discussion of this administrative and psychological principle see Marshall E. Dimock, "Executive Responsibilities," *Journal of the Society for Advancement of Management*, January, 1938.

14. *Op. cit.*, pp. 18–19.

Upon analysis a pair of explanations suggest themselves: (1) the outcome of political traits and (2) the administrative structure. The demands of a clamorous public on vote conscious parliamentarians have been discussed earlier. The citizen has the right of access to a minister's office to discuss his personal affairs which are affected by some activity of government. This habit, so democratic in conception but so abused in practice, brings many a minor file to ministerial desks. When confronted with an indignant citizen pleading his private case, the minister must show himself a sympathetic listener and be conversant with the details of his file. Is this democracy? Or vote-getting? Or the humanizing of government? Demands for rights, pleas for favors, threats of public opposition, offers of political support—these are the stuff of many an interview with ministers. Details come to the ear and eye of the political all-highest because the voters require it. As a corollary of this it may be mentioned that much legislation includes clauses which impose on ministers personally the onus of discharging certain duties. It is, of course, the ministers themselves who have such provisions put into the laws in the first place. They do so because it increases their own power to be in a position to grant or withhold favors and also because they know what the electorate wants. The voter prefers to deal with a minister, against whom he can exercise a kickback on election day, than with a public servant whose position is unassailable.

For the administrative explanation one must look into the inner structure and operation of the departments. It is the general rule in New Zealand public administration for matters to be thrown upward for decision by a higher authority than their intrinsic importance deserves. The mischief begins within the departments, some of which reproduce in miniature the same defective structural pattern that exists in the government as a whole. Expanding over the years as new activities were thrust upon them, a number of the older and larger departments have become federations of bureaus, divisions, and branches, mostly coordinate with one another. Inside such departments are a group of branch chiefs separately reporting to the head of the whole concern. Few are the agencies which have been replanned and rebuilt in modern times. Seldom has the allocation of functions to

branches been systematically devised or the relations among
branches suitably co-ordinated. A correct picture of the fundamental failing can be obtained by using an architectural analogy
and comparing the structure of a department to that of a pyramid. The all-important feature in the design of a pyramid is the
slope of the sides. The height of the apex from the base must be
adjusted to the length of the base, or the proportions and the
balance will be all wrong. Apply that same principle to administration. The usual fault in a departmental structure is to have
too long a base, composed of a series of malconnected branches
strung side by side along the same level of authority. The apex,
consisting of the department head and his immediate deputies,
normally lies too close to the base. There are insufficient grades or
posts of intermediate rank to canalize the flow of work from the
bottom to the top and relieve some of the pressure that is exerted
upward. The structure requires the department head to embrace
more activities and handle more work than can humanly fall
within his span of control.

A structure, of course, is made what it is by the persons who
organize and operate it. Its failings are merely the formal expression of the inadequacies of improperly trained administrators.
There have been heads of departments who themselves contributed to the overloading of work at the top by a stupid insistence
that all manner of trifles be brought to their desk. One head, appointed a few years ago to an agency faultily organized under his
predecessors, told me that in his first few weeks in the top position
he was aghast at the files, piled two feet high, brought in to him
by staggering messengers. It even happened that at the time for
the usual quarterly payment by each male wage-earner of five
shillings into the social security fund, members of his staff, senior
and junior alike, came to show him the stubs of their social security books as evidence that their quota had been paid. Department heads are held responsible for seeing that their subordinates
duly pay their contributions, and the previous director of this
particular agency had so literally interpreted his duty that he
personally inspected everyone's receipts! Not all the permanent
heads carry the mistake to this absurd extreme. Yet the undeniable fact remains that most heads deal with far too many trivial

or routine matters, partly through habit and in part through the faults of the departmental structure. And so it proceeds all the way up to the cabinet, the political apex of the whole governmental pyramid. A minister handles details that should be left to department heads, and the entire cabinet concerns itself with issues that the individual ministers ought to settle. Thus, at the top of the pyramid, business is congested, decisions are delayed, permanent heads and ministers are overworked. Were the system organized aright, at the peak of the structure the general layout of the whole machinery would be reviewed and the broader horizons of national interest scanned. But the peak in New Zealand is too frequently enveloped in cloud and mist, and the panoramic view is obscured.

The reason for all this can be put succinctly. The government of New Zealand is conducting a complex enterprise of large-scale proportions, but the structure and many of the methods are still adapted to small-scale activity. In a way it is only to be expected that some ministers will find it awkward to adjust to the implications of large-scale management. In other democracies where large-scale private enterprises exist side by side with governments, the men who become ministers are likely to have had experience of large-scale administration outside the sphere of public affairs. Few, however, of the New Zealand ministers come to their office from such a background. Most of them cannot previously have learned the secrets of large-scale direction and organization. There have been many cases of men attaining ministerial posts who never before had a secretary to work for them, and some have even insisted on personally opening the envelopes of all their numerous letters.

In administering a large-scale enterprise like the government of a Dominion, those in the highest positions must know the art of delegating responsibility. The economic use of time is indispensable to the successful administrator. Reserving his own attention for matters which really require his personal scrutiny, he must see that the time of his staff is duly apportioned according to the status of each official and the urgency of the business in hand. The minister or permanent head who thinks to unload his own desk by overloading those of his subordinates has learned only a small part of the game. For the work of government, which is sometimes dissected into the two phases of policy and administration, is in fact a continuous process. From top to bottom it consists in choosing between alternative courses of action, each choice being made in a sphere more restricted than the previous and each itself narrowing the scope within which the next choice will be made. Between the voters indicating at an election their general preference for one broad line of policy over another, and a postal clerk handing a one-penny stamp across the counter in return for a coin, lies a whole network of decisions within ever smaller concentric circles of choice. The processes of government resemble the puzzle boxes which can be opened at the middle to discover a smaller box inside, while that in turn contains one still smaller, and so on. When the people put a party into power, and a legislature selects what it will enact into law, and a cabinet fills in the gaps of the laws with regulations, and a minister applies the cabinet policy within lines laid down for him, and a permanent head chooses between alternative methods of administration, leaving to his section heads some discretion within the limits he prescribes—through all this at different levels of authority choices are made which set the bounds for the choices that are to follow. The task of large-scale management is to insure that choices are scaled to their appropriate levels. It is no less incongruous for a minister or department head to decide a policy in a narrow area of choice befitting a division chief than for the latter to settle what properly belongs to the "higher-ups." If work is to be properly scaled, administrators must possess the intellectual capacity to distinguish between the essential and the unessential as well as a temperamental willingness to relegate less important matters to less important officials.

Drastic change is needed if the Dominion's administrative system is to be re-equipped for managing functions of a large-scale character. Efficient public administration results from the fusion of three indispensables: the best organization, the best information, and the best personnel. In each of these elements much remodeling will have to be undertaken before the problems of peacetime reconstruction and future development can be satisfactorily handled. It is not enough to see that ministers and public servants are well informed, that they are imbued with a knowledge of the technique of large-scale management, and that merit receives its due and morale is kept at a high pitch. Good personnel often find their effectiveness frustrated by faulty structural systems. The organization of each single department and of the departmental machinery as a whole should resemble a channel through which the energies and the knowledge of administrators can pour freely, and not an imprisoning chain which cramps initiative and stifles enthusiasm. The structure must be geared to the qualities of those who are to operate it. For the rest of this chapter, therefore, administrative reform will be considered in its structural aspect. The next chapter will deal with the management of personnel. The mobilizing of information in the administrative process is a topic which straddles both chapters.

Principles of Reorganization

Any reorganization must keep in mind the different types of administrative functions for which a modern government should find a place. These functions are four in number. First, there is the activity of planning and research. Under this head are included the preparation of long-term programs for developing the human and material resources of the nation, the task of fact-finding, and the supply of information to the ministry. The numerous departments which come directly into contact with the public form a second class. These are the agencies which stand in such varied relations to the citizens as regulating, policing, trading, educating, and serving. To this class belong the bulk of state departments. A different type of function is performed by agencies which partly assist and partly control the second group. A treasury or a central personnel office deals rather with other government agencies than with the public, and its relation to them is a mixed combination of aid and supervision. Postauditing, fourthly, is a watchdog, inspectorial activity. It is a final check or safeguard to assure the legality of all public expenditure. Together these four groups embrace the main classes of administrative work.[15] The problem, then, is to devise a departmental pat-

15. It might be urged that the function of revenue-collecting constitutes a fifth and distinct type, but it seems better to include this in the second group. A land and income tax or a customs department deals with the public and serves other departments by raising funds for them to spend.

390 THE POLITICS OF EQUALITY

Assuming that the personnel system attracts to the government
service the men and women of the best capacity, can a form of
organization be suggested which will permit them to use their
abilities effectively? It need not be arbitrarily supposed that precisely the same structure will suit each of the four groups. It is a
basic principle of public administration that a structure must be
determined by the functions to be performed. Different functions
call for different structures.

An agency charged with the task of planning and research
stands, as is evident, in a special category. Its purpose is to provide the government with a continuous supply of up-to-date information as a guide in mapping out long-term policies and in
formulating administrative decisions. Government is a species of
social engineering. It is an inexact science, since it depends on
the indeterminate and unpredictable factors of human wants and
aspirations. The knowledge of all the social scientists combined
can yield only probabilities, never certainties. Yet the probabilities approximate ever nearer toward certainty as they become
based on wider knowledge and longer experience. The administrator cannot dispense with the fruits of study and scholarship if
his plans are to be something more than wild guesses or flukes
which might just hit the target. The agency intrusted with research and planning performs staff work.[16] It is advisory to the
ministry and other departments, lacking the administrative authority to execute policies. Its powers are limited to making recommendations based upon its research. It discovers the facts,
forecasts possible trends, and initiates suggestions. But the responsibility for deciding what is to be done lies elsewhere. Any
planning or research agency which steps across the boundary
line between tendering advice and wielding authority is doomed.

Nowadays it no longer needs arguing that modern administration must have this function adequately performed by a well-con-
stituted agency manned with a competent staff. In Britain the
Haldane report on the machinery of government and in America
the Brownlow report on administrative management have

16. Military organization provides the analogy of the "general staff" (originally
the "general's staff") which plans operations but does not execute them.

mapped the outlines of this field which is further surveyed by the authoritative exponents of public administration.[17] New Zealand has already made some preliminary moves, but it needs to do a great deal yet before research and planning have been placed on a proper footing. In the Department of Scientific and Industrial Research it has already established an agency for co-ordinating technical research in various of the physical sciences. Among its branches are included the Dominion Laboratory, the National Physical Testing Laboratory, the National Chemical Laboratory, the Soil Survey, the Geological Survey, and the Plant Research Bureau. In addition, there are associated with it certain other research institutes financed and controlled partly by the government and partly by the wheat, wool, and dairy industries. Each institute is located in a university center, under the composite direction of a professor and of a committee representing the department and the industry concerned. The whole department is headed by a secretary responsible to a minister. Attached to it at the top is an advisory council, containing members from other state departments and from outside the public service. The advisory council can initiate and discuss the research policy of the agency. But everything is so arranged that the minister can have the final say if he wishes.

The department's usefulness has been fully demonstrated in different fields, in which its scientific studies have been a necessary preliminary to policy decisions. Before the war, for example, when the government was planning to inaugurate an iron and steel industry, it relied upon the reports which this department presented. During the war its services were used in such tasks as the development of radio location and the introduction of the linen-flax industry. It is well-known, however, that this agency does not fully satisfy the requirements of a research body. Its history has been marked by a tendency to go beyond the limits of finding the facts and making recommendations. It has at times pressed for administrative authority in spheres in which it con-

17. See *Report of the Machinery of Government Committee* (Cd. 9230 [London: H.M. Stationery Office, 1918]), pp. 22–35; *Report of the President's Committee on Administrative Management* (Washington, D.C.: Government Printing Office, 1937), pp. 25–27; Leonard D. White, *Introduction to the Study of Public Administration* (2d ed.; New York: Macmillan Co., 1939), pp. 29–31, 63–73.

flicts with other departments. These efforts have caused friction, in particular with the Department of Agriculture, which also conducts a certain amount of agricultural research and regards some of the activities of Scientific and Industrial Research as encroachments on its own preserve.

On the side of social science New Zealand governments have been far more backward in providing for research. It is true that Coates, as minister of finance during the depression, organized a small "brain trust" of university-trained economists. It is also true that certain departments have their own modest research sections, which in some cases are whittled down to the duties of an "information officer." It must be mentioned, too, that under the Labor ministry, the Department of Education has called upon the assistance of an independent agency, the Council of Educational Research.[18] Moreover, the same ministry did establish a Social Science Research Bureau designed to fill a role similar to that of the Scientific and Industrial Research Department. This bureau was placed under a director responsible to the minister of finance, and to it was appended the customary advisory committee of public servants and persons from outside. Unfortunately, this agency, created with happy hopes, was blocked and frustrated after it prepared a survey of standards of living among New Zealand dairy farmers. The minister of finance objected to the publication of certain facts, which might, he thought, lend color to unfavorable political interpretation. For a long period the printing of the bureau's report was delayed; and, when finally a public version was released, offending passages and unwelcome facts had been duly censored. Since then, shorn of its appropriation and staff, the bureau has remained as incorporeal as the smile of the Cheshire cat.

Only once was a serious attempt made in New Zealand to establish a central planning body for long-term social research. This was the Organization for National Development, whose establishment in 1944 held out some real promise, since its scope embraced three kinds of work: economic, regional, and town

18. This body was originally established with the aid of money from the Carnegie Fund. In 1945 it became a statutory corporation and is now financed by annual parliamentary appropriation.

planning. Unfortunately, it did not last for longer than a year. After this brief and undistinguished term it disintegrated as rapidly as it had been put together. The reasons for the failure deserve analysis. In the first place, it was constituted as a branch of the Prime Minister's Department, in the hope, apparently, that its status as an over-all, co-ordinating, agency would thus be securely recognized. Such a location, carrying with it the prestige of the head of the government, would have been excellent if the range of its work had been primarily of short-term character. But, as its duties were to undertake long-term research, the Organization for National Development failed to obtain the needed co-operation of many groups in the community at large. In particular, those who were politically opposed to the party in power were suspicious of an agency reposing immediately under the wing of the premier. Although a network of advisory committees, including representatives from outside the civil service, was established, few of these overcame their initial mistrust and settled down to harmonious co-operation.

Equally faulty was the method of supplying overhead supervision of the Organization for National Development. Subject to the prime minister, policy was guided by an executive committee composed of five leading permanent heads and the organization's administrative director. In other words, officials like the secretary of the treasury and the director-general of agriculture, who were already overburdened with multifarious duties, received the added charge of formulating plans for long-term, national development. When there was added to this handicap the further difficulty of obtaining a suitably qualified research staff, it is small wonder that the organization failed to establish itself. The ministry wanted quick results, especially with an election in the offing. The organization was unable to convince the politicians that long-term programs could not be hastily improvised. On announcing its demise to Parliament, the premier criticized the impracticability of such planning and the delays involved in its preparation. The organization was accordingly dissolved, and its fragments scattered.

If New Zealand, then, is to profit from the lessons of its own experience, how is the function of planning and research to be organized? That question can be answered only by distinguishing the different purposes which this function is designed to serve. In the first place, it is clear that many of the evils with which modern governments cope are the product of long-term trends and are soluble only by long-term remedies. Any diagnosis of current social maladies must analyze their origins and symptoms over past decades. This is true in the field of the physical sciences, which may be exploring such a problem as soil erosion; and is equally true of social science investigation when it tackles, let us say, a question like slum clearance. Likewise a corrective policy for problems of this nature may take a couple of decades before it shows results. Any such planning, therefore, involves decisions on paramount national issues, and the application of remedies demands an intelligent and sympathetic continuity from successive governments. As examples of research into long-term developments I would cite the report of the Committee on Recent Social Trends, set up by President Hoover in the United States, or the excellent series of studies prepared by the National Resources Planning Board. If research and planning of that kind are to be successful, the investigation must be conducted by independent and politically disinterested analysts, and their findings must be made available for discussion by the general public. Then, when action is agreed upon, it should rest on a broad basis of popular consent, since the same long-term plan may have to be operated by ministries of different parties.

Another important use for a similar agency is to serve the government of the day as a "brain trust." Every government needs an expert corps of political scientists, statisticians, economists, sociologists, and others, on whom it can call at short notice for memoranda and information to guide it in formulating policy. In this case, however, the questions requiring decision are of short-term duration; and consequently the research work and any plans based upon it have a more limited scope. The brain trust cannot be dispensed with by modern democracy, despite all the silly criticisms which sections of the press and the public sometimes level against it. It should form a civilian general staff aiding the prime minister and cabinet in fulfilling their political program. It should utilize as its master-plan the proposals of the long-term research agency and should elaborate the short-term tactics and priorities for its execution. Since the advice of the brain trust must be confined to the chief executive and his colleagues, its work cannot be open to the public.

If this distinction between the long- and the short-term aspects of planning and research is accepted, agencies must be devised to suit each purpose. For short-term work the research agency must evidently be very closely associated with the prime minister and placed in his department so as to assist both him and any of his ministers.[19] It must be directed and manned by a staff answerable to the government. Long-term planning, on the other hand, should not be so closely attached to the dominant party or the government of the day. Its direction should, therefore, be in the hands of a board or council, representing not only governmental experience but also the best minds with the broadest vision wherever they are to be found in the community. This board or council should be financially independent of annual parliamentary appropriation; and it should possess full discretion to choose research topics, to obtain its staff from the Public Service Commission, and to publish its findings. The ultimate and separate responsibility both of the board and of the prime minister in their respective spheres of control should be well defined. Research into physical as well as social sciences would be combined in different branches of the same agency. To create the nucleus of such a planning and research department, there should be amalgamated, for a start, the present departments of Scientific and Industrial Research and of Census and Statistics. The establishment of this agency would not preclude individual departments from organizing their own research sections for more detailed and special work in their own particular fields. Every department, indeed, should be encouraged to have its own research section. The central planning agencies, both long and short term, should keep in close touch with the research branches

19. The beginning of a response to this need may be found at the present moment in the Information Branch of the Prime Minister's Department. This is a survival of the wartime Publicity and Censorship Office, and its work consists partly in giving information to the people (i.e., public relations) and partly in informing the government.

of other departments and should draw on their knowledge and personnel.

The Prime Minister's Department is the next to be considered, since it forms the link in the administrative structure between the function of planning and research and the group of agencies which provide services directly to the people. It is significant that the British literature on public administration, including even the Haldane report, pays much attention to the supervisory role of the cabinet but less to that of the premier as co-ordinator of the governmental machinery. In the United States, however, where the office of a president or a governor is designated by constitutional provisions, the importance of a chief executive per se has been amply recognized. The Brownlow report advocated for the federal government the proposals already laid down in numerous surveys of state governments that the chief executive should be accorded greater authority, *de facto* as well as *de jure*, over all departments of the executive branch.[20] As one method of arriving at this result, it recommended that the President's own staff be strengthened by the addition of six administrative assistants and that under him should be placed the three "managerial arms" of planning, budgetary, and personnel control. Such suggestions apply to the cabinet form of government in New Zealand to this extent—that the premier needs to be buttressed with a corps of executive aides and his department freed from all activities of routine administration.

It cannot be disputed that the premier would benefit from the help of a small number of efficient administrative assistants. Directed by the permanent head of the department, their task would be to act as liaison officers between the Prime Minister's Department and other agencies. They would handle and draft replies to much of the correspondence addressed to the head of the government. They would dispose tactfully of many of the callers seeking a personal interview with the premier. Together they would comprise his own secretariat. This suggestion is comparable in purpose and design to the executive assistants to the President proposed in the Brownlow report and authorized by Congress in the

20. See *Report of the President's Committee on Administrative Management* and my *The American Governor* (Chicago: University of Chicago Press, 1939), chap. v.

Reorganization Act of 1939. It is analogous, also, to the French administrative practice of instituting a cabinet to assist the minister in charge of a department.[21] Distinctly and emphatically, the secretariat is not intended to interpose its own authority between the premier and other ministers and the permanent heads. It is purely a staff agency. It is the eyes and ears of the administration, just as the planning and research department is the brains.

Besides this secretariat, the premier's department should contain three branches, each responsible for an activity which is properly located under his direct control. As was discussed above, the function of research and planning, where it deals with short-term issues, rightly belongs in the department of the prime minister. A second branch would take care of the duties which devolve on the premier as leader of the dominant party in Parliament. The administration of legislative business, the preparations for a forthcoming session, and the arrangement of the program during the session—in these matters the premier's wishes are necessarily decisive.[22] This legislative branch would absorb some of the work carried out by the clerks of the two houses. It would also include the Law Drafting Office. Possibly it might take in the administration of the Government Printing Office on the ground that so much of all the material officially published is devoted to legislative business, i.e., bills, regulations, statutes, departmental reports, Hansard, etc. It could be further argued that the Electoral Department fits properly in this place, since its concern is to administer the elections by which parliamentarians are chosen. A good case, however, can be made out for allotting to this agency a status, like that of the long-term planning agency, independent of ministerial control. If the government of the day, composed of the dominant party, controls the Electoral Department, there is a latent possibility of dishonest elections whenever the issue is in doubt. Instead of the ministry, where the opposition is unrepresented, a bipartisan committee of Parliament, rep-

21. On this point note the experience of the International Labor Office as described in E. J. Phelan's *Yes, and Albert Thomas* (London: Cresset Press, 1936), pp. 65–67.

22. The premier consults with the speaker and the leader of the opposition. In general, of course, what he says, goes.

resenting both government and opposition, should have sway
over the electoral procedure. Lastly, the third branch to come
under the premier should certify and record all constitutional
acts on the Crown's behalf, a function now assigned to the Department of Internal Affairs.

The virtue of these proposals is to relieve the prime minister of
all the day-to-day administrative detail with which at present he
is overburdened. The only functions placed in his charge under
this scheme are certain general activities affecting the government as a whole and properly adhering to the principal figure in
the ministry. Freed from any necessity to supervise departments
which deal directly with the public, he should be able to supervise and co-ordinate the entire administrative system. As far as
structural provisions can insure, these changes should enable the
premier to be truly the chief executive.

The prime minister is leader of the cabinet, and the cabinet
members, individually and collectively, exercise direct political
control over the more than forty departments which come directly into contact with the people. It is proper, therefore, to discuss
next the changes which should be introduced into the organization of this large group of agencies. What should be their relations to one another and to the cabinet? Co-ordination of administrative policies cannot proceed alone from the top downward.
The pyramid of responsibility and authority must also be soundly
constructed from the bottom upward, or the cabinet cannot efficiently manage its huge job. The defects of the existing system
that was outlined above may be summarized in the phrase of the
Haldane report as those of "Lilliputian administration." The
remedy is to change this faulty structure in accord with the principles which were suggested in that report and have been partially introduced in the federal and certain state governments of
the United States. This would mean having fewer but larger departments. It would involve the introduction of an intelligible
rationale into the structural pattern of administration. The cabinet
should be kept at its present size. It might possibly be reduced, but
it should certainly not be expanded. It will be found on examination perfectly feasible to group together many of the agencies that
are now distinct and consolidate them into bigger units. As a

general principle, all governmental activities which are concerned with intimately related subjects should be combined for purposes of administration. The total number of departments should not be fixed arbitrarily but must be determined by two criteria. First, the number must be such as will not exceed the cabinet's span of control or preclude effective ministerial direction. Second, the work of government must be subdivided into the classes in which its activities naturally fall. Each departmental grouping must then be classified around some major service to the community. Existing departments whose functions closely impinge on each other must be amalgamated. Individual branches or bureaus should be transferred, wherever necessary, to the department in which they best fit.

All functions at present undertaken by the state for the public of New Zealand can be broadly divided into the following types of services: finance, land utilization and primary production, industrial production, transport, post and telegraph, public welfare, education, native affairs, justice, external affairs, public works, and trading. (Perhaps to these should be added a thirteenth—the control of local government. This could figure more prominently than at present if ever the central government boldly decides to prune, weed, and landscape the matted undergrowth of local authorities in the Dominion.) If one department were constituted for each of the twelve (or thirteen) groups of activities just listed, the number would harmonize admirably with the size of the ministry. But how would the transfer be effected from the old to the new? How would the existing organization be recast into this vastly different mold? What structural changes would be required? These questions can be answered if each group is surveyed and discussed in turn.

The proposed finance department would embrace four agencies, now separate from one another, and half of a fifth. It would, of course take in the Treasury. One of the principal branches in the finance department would consist of a budget bureau to prepare the estimates, to supervise the expenditure of appropriations, and to prescribe the accounting system of the state departments.[23] The Treasury's direction of government investments and the

23. These tasks are all undertaken at present by the Treasury.

flotation of loans would logically fall in a different branch. Here it should be closely linked with the operations of the Reserve Bank. This latter institution is the government agency described above which receives deposits of public funds, administers the national currency and note issue, and regulates financial trans- actions with overseas countries. To associate the Reserve Bank with a branch of a unified finance department is to accord open recognition to realities. A third branch should be constituted to handle the collection of revenue. At present the principal reve- nue-collecting agencies are the departments of Land and Income Tax and of Customs. These should be amalgamated, with the proviso that the control which the Customs Department at pres- ent exercises over tariff administration must be transferred to an- other agency, as will be discussed below. Less important, yet concerned with the same function, are the Stamp Duties Depart- ment and those sections of the Internal Affairs Department which collect the taxes on beer and on the totalizator.[24] For administra- tive convenience these activities should be combined into a single branch of revenue collection. A fourth branch can administer the stabilization policy, if, as is probable, this remains in some form a permanent feature of modern economic life.[25] This, to- gether with the branches of the budget, of loans and currency ad- ministration, and of revenue collection, would make up a unified department of finance.

The second department to be considered must contain a group of functions which are of vital importance in the New Zealand economy: the use of the land and the disposal of primary prod- ucts. The core of this proposed agency can be formed out of the existing departments of Lands and Survey and of Agriculture. The former has always been principally concerned with survey- ing the country and clearing land for new settlement; the latter's interest lies in the productivity of the farmers. With these depart- ments will rightly be attached the Forestry Service, whose origins

24. In New Zealand betting with a bookmaker is illegal. Bets can be laid only at the race course and through the totalizator. The government takes 5 per cent of the totalizator's proceeds, a lucrative source of revenue.

25. The existing Stabilization Commission is in effect already a branch of the Treasury.

were described above. It is true that in the past there have been political and administrative conflicts between the Forestry and the Lands and Survey departments. But in the future their opposite biases must be balanced and adjusted to suit a national policy of land utilization. It is better to organize a single department for ironing out such differences and viewing in broad perspective what are really phases of a single problem. To the same agency should be intrusted the Primary Products Marketing Department, which purchases and sells specified farm produce both in New Zealand and overseas. Although its functions are those of a business or trading operation, the marketing of primary products is properly located here, since that activity involves continuous contacts and contracts with the farming community.[26]

Following the British analogy of associating fisheries with agriculture in the same ministry, one may assign to the new department of land use and primary products the Fisheries Branch of the present Marine Department. Fish, like land, can be considered a primary resource, since, like the products of the land, they provide food for human consumption. Moreover, the control over lakes, rivers, and streams that is exercised in conserving fresh-water fish bears on the fertility of the surrounding countryside. Linked up, too, with the preservation of crops, pastures, and forests is the regulation of game and wild life. This subject includes the eradication of pests (rabbits, deer, etc.) and the provision of suitable and sufficient live animal targets for sportsmen. Hence the administration of the game laws, which now lurks in a branch of the Internal Affairs Department, should be transferred to the suggested new agency. With two exceptions, all the functions of government which concern primary production and the use of the land would thus be amalgamated into a unified scheme. Those exceptions are a pair of agencies whose work is vitally important to rural finance: the Valuation Department and the State Advances Corporation. The former, as its name makes clear, conducts valuations of all land throughout the

26. The Linen-Flax Corporation might, for similar reasons, be included with this group. Or it could be merged with the trading group, as described later.

Dominion. A leading function of the latter is to provide loans to individuals for building houses or developing their property, whether in town or country.[27] Holding the first mortgages over innumerable farms, the State Advances Corporation is in a position to execute policies which closely affect the farmer's capacity to work his land at a profit. For that reason, both the Valuation Department and this corporation should constitute a rural finance branch of the proposed department.

A third broad class of governmental activity clusters around commerce and manufacturing. A single department of industrial production should, therefore, be contemplated, its task being to plan and administer a comprehensive policy for the future industrial development of New Zealand. At present, however, the various functions falling within this sphere are scattered among some five or six agencies. One of these is the Customs Department, which for many decades, besides collecting customs duties, has been the custodian of the Dominion's tariff policy. Its outlook is ingrained with protectionism. Nowadays the work of this agency, one of the oldest in New Zealand's administrative family, is to some extent duplicated by a much younger department. A by-product of the war of 1914–18 was a Bureau of Industry, designed to license and encourage local manufacturing under the authority of the Industrial Efficiency Act. For over a decade the bureau remained insignificant. Nor were its potentialities fully realized until the Labor government extended its scope and authority. Faced in the years 1937–39 with a shrinkage in New Zealand's overseas assets, the ministry decided after the election of 1938 to inaugurate a policy of exchange control and import selection. The Bureau of Industry, which had earlier blossomed into a Department of Industries and Commerce, was catapulted from relative unimportance to a position of power in the nation's economic life. This was the department charged with stimulating the growth of secondary industries. When war broke out again in 1939, its ambit was once more enlarged, since the functions of supply were added to its other activities. On grounds of avoiding overlap and duplication a strong case can be made out for amal-

27. The State Advances Corporation at present also administers and leases the houses and flats constructed by the state.

gamating the Industries and Commerce Department with the branches of the Customs Department that control tariff policy.[28]

Another agency concerned with industrial development is the Labor Department. Caring for the safety and welfare of the workers,[29] it inspects factories, registers unions, supervises labor conditions, and regulates relations between employers and employees. It is also intrusted with administering the immigration program. Prima facie it would appear that this department could well be combined with Customs and with Industries and Commerce, since its subject matter is so closely bound up with theirs. Why cannot the problems of industry be administered by a single agency which attempts in its different branches to harmonize the points of view of capital and labor? Viewed from the aspect of administrative organization, this suggestion has much to commend it. Standing in the way, however, are obstacles of a political nature. In most democratic countries employers and employees regard their respective interests as competitive rather than complementary. Each side has been strong enough to secure the creation of a separate agency devoted to its own service. Thus in Britain the Board of Trade has been dominated by the owners of capital, while the trade-union outlook has received more sympathy in the Ministry of Labor. The same dualism occurs in the federal government of the United States, where the agency which was originally a single Department of Commerce and Labor was split in 1913 into two separate departments. If it be politically possible in any country to overcome the modern world's great schism between employers and workers, then a single agency should and could be created for the administrative regulation of industry. If, however, the clash of interests approximates to the unhappy conditions of "class war," then separate departments will in all probability have to be established.

The Marine Department, as already explained, at present undertakes the inspection of machinery. It is anomalous, as well as inconvenient, that factories should be visited by different groups

28. As suggested above, the revenue-collecting function of the Customs Department should be transferred to the proposed finance department.

29. Farm workers, in so far as they are organized and protected by law, fall under the Labor Department's jurisdiction. But most of its activities are concerned with industrial labor.

of inspectors following on each other's heels; those from the Labor Department viewing machinery from the standpoint of the worker's safety, those from the Marine Department judging it for its technical and mechanical adequacy.[30] Plainly it would be preferable for the government and industry alike to have one corps of inspectors charged with both jobs at one visit. Inspection of machinery, therefore, must be moved from the Marine Department to the proposed agency for industrial production. Another branch of this suggested department could well take over the Mines Department, which at present operates such coal mines as the state owns. Here, too, could be placed the proposed iron and steel works, a state enterprise which the government is contemplating to exploit the ores at Onekaka, as well as the inspection of explosives which is now undertaken by Internal Affairs. Still another agency which should be assigned to this group is the Patent Office. At present this small office reposes under the aegis of the Justice Department, on the assumption that patent administration is primarily a lawyer's job. While such administration must entail legal considerations, one may doubt whether these are the most important aspects to stress. Most patents have to do with modern technological developments which in some way or other affect industry. Were the Patent Office to be shifted to the department of industrial production, the industrial value of inventions would doubtless receive the primary emphasis that is their due.

One last agency belongs with the others just listed. During the war the government set up a National Service Department to administer the program of military and civil conscription. Unlike the mother-country, which tacked on this function to the Ministry of Labor, New Zealand constituted it as an entity separate from the Labor Department. The reason was just simply that the Labor Department was so out of date and poorly organized that it could not do the job without a more thoroughgoing reorganization than the government was ready to tackle.[31] At the conclu-

30. This point has been cogently argued by a pair of independent English observers. See the report by J. M. Davidson, "Industrial Hygiene in New Zealand," *Annual Report of the Health Department, 1945*, Appendix II, and A. E. C. Hare, *Industrial Relations in New Zealand* (Wellington: Whitcombe & Tombs, 1946), chap. xiii.

31. On this point consult Hare, *op. cit.*

sion of the war, when the Labor party enacted a bill to promote full employment, they assigned the execution of the policy to a National Employment Service, which was in large measure the National Service Department in a new dress. The ostensible pretext for not giving this program to the Labor Department was that an agency which had to police the employers could not also secure their co-operation in maintaining employment.[32] The real reason, however, was the same as before, namely, that the Labor Department was too ineffective. Not until 1947 were the beginnings of reform belatedly initiated. In that year at long last the Labor and National Service departments were merged and Labor administration was gradually overhauled.

The communications system constitutes a fourth sphere of governmental enterprise. Its administration, however, is nowadays divided into four agencies. First, the Railways Department handles the rail traffic, all of which in New Zealand is publicly owned and operated. Road services[33] are licensed and regulated by the Transport Department. Shipping is the province of the Marine Department. The civil airways, a public monopoly since 1946, are managed by a National Airways Corporation, subject, as to general policy, to the minister of air. The defect of this haphazard arrangement is that it discourages any national planning of all transport facilities as a single, co-ordinated system. The different methods of transportation, which should be treated as parts of one problem, are handled separately from, and sometimes in competition with, each other. Travel by rail, road, sea, and air ought all to be amalgamated into a unified transport department. Such an arrangement will not infallibly guarantee, but it should at least facilitate and promote, a broad view of the entire system of communications. This same agency would be the appropriate home for services to tourists, which in 1945 were made into yet another independent department.[34] Apart from managing and publicizing various state-owned resorts at Rotorua

32. Nevertheless, the provision of a service is combined with policing in the Agriculture and the Industries and Commerce departments.

33. The railways also operate some suburban bus services and some "feeder" services elsewhere.

34. Up to then it was loosely, and incongruously, attached to the Department of Industries and Commerce.

and elsewhere, tourist administration is largely a question of transport arrangements and so belongs properly to a department of transport.

There is another department—and an all-important one—whose work is connected with the same group of agencies. The Post and Telegraph Department conducts enterprises which fall under the rubric of communications, and the postal timetable must be ever adjusted to fit in with the transport services available. It would be quite reasonable, therefore, for this department to be amalgamated with Railways and the others just mentioned. But in this special case there are countervailing factors which lead to the conclusion that Post and Telegraph is better placed in a distinct group by itself. This agency with its 12,000 employees, and Railways with its 22,000, are the two giants—from the points of view of personnel and geographical dispersion—in New Zealand administration. Each by itself is a big enough managerial problem. Joined together, they might prove unwieldy. Indeed the Post and Telegraph Department holds a peculiar position in the governmental machinery because it is a maid-of-all-work for other departments. The savings bank was assigned to it in 1867 for the simple reason that the Post Office had more local branches throughout the country than any other department of state. Since that beginning, Post and Telegraph has undertaken numerous services for other departments; and its "agency function," as it is called, has been ever more widely extended. To gain some conception of the manifold activities of the state in New Zealand one need only visit the local post office around quarter-day. There you may see John and Mary Citizen paying their income tax, their radio or automobile license, or their telephone bill; or else receiving from the state one of the many social security benefits provided in New Zealand legislation. During the war this same department was utilized for organizing national savings campaigns, for registering for national service, for selling "bomber bonds," for the distribution of food ration books, and so on. Its ubiquitousness and its size give it a place of its own. It must form the fifth in this series of proposed departments.

Sixth should be a department of public welfare. This would incorporate three existing agencies in entirety and take over two branches from other departments. The Health and the Mental Hospitals departments, which in 1947 were consolidated into a single agency, clearly come within its ambit. So does Social Security. It should, moreover, include the administration of Child Welfare, now organized as a semiautonomous branch of the Education Department. The experience of modern social service administration has shown that child welfare problems are better handled by professionally trained social workers than by schoolteachers. Permeated with the social work approach, this public welfare department would co-ordinate the care of physical and mental health with the treatment of socially maladjusted individuals, whether they be children or adults. Hitherto New Zealand has done very little to modernize its conceptions and its practice in this all-important field. It is lacking in professionally trained social workers; it possesses not a single child guidance clinic; and it still regards psychiatry with suspicion, indifference, or fear. In short, it has not adequately handled the resources of the community for treating the maladjustments of a generation emotionally strained by depression and war. When and if such a public welfare department is instituted, to its care should be confided the administration of prisons. At present assigned to a rather soulless Justice Department, the Prisons Department is still managed more with the intention to punish than to reform. The prisons and their inmates would be better transferred to an agency that could apply the principles of modern social work.

Education, both of children and of adults, is the guiding purpose of the next major sphere of state activities. The nucleus is already formed by the present Education Department, which, save for the removal of its Child Welfare Branch, would remain intact. Besides educating those of the nation's children who go to the public[35] schools, this department should undertake certain activities that are designed to enlighten the adults. Thus it should incorporate the National Library Service (an enlargement made in 1945 of the Country Library Service set up in 1938) and be responsible for bringing books to the adult population outside the cities and larger towns. There are two other agencies, however,

35. New Zealand has in addition to these a number of private schools (primary and secondary), both denominational and nondenominational.

to which are at present consigned functions that touch upon the educational field. Massey's Reform government, trembling in the early twenties at the specter of revolution, imposed restrictions on literature imported into New Zealand. Persuaded by the reasoning that the jurisdiction of the Customs Department properly covered all imported articles, the ministry strangely assumed that its customs officials were the fittest judges of the intellectual content, and possible social effects, of foreign publications. This arrangement has never since been disturbed, so that to this very day the books and pamphlets suspected of being politically or sexually subversive are scrutinized by customs officials. It would be far better that this work should be transferred to the Education Department. The same agency should also take the responsibility for the film censorship now vested, for no apparent reason, in the Department of Internal Affairs. Such changes are recommended in the belief that a broad-minded attitude is more likely to pervade the Education Department than others. Should that belief be unfounded, which is not entirely impossible, there is little hope for any country's cultural development.

A difficulty arises when one considers the proper location of broadcasting which in this Dominion is now entirely controlled and operated by the state. From 1925 to 1931 the broadcasting service was conducted by a private company licensed and regulated under act of Parliament. In 1932 the Coalition government bought out the company, and up to 1935 a seven-membered board was placed in charge. This board was abolished when Labor came to power, and the broadcasting service was then converted into an ordinary department under a minister. It was financed by the sale of licenses (costing twenty-five shillings each) to owners of radio sets. For its director the government selected a professor from the New Zealand University. In 1937, however, the same Labor ministry erected side by side with the existing service and subject to the same minister a second broadcasting department to be financed commercially by advertisements and business-sponsored programs. Such an indefensible duplication was partly motivated by the desire to reward a skilful political partisan who was appointed at the head of the new department in return for his electoral campaigning in 1935. For a number of years, therefore, New Zealand continued to possess two rival networks each operating four major stations as well as subsidiaries. One organization, the National Broadcasting Service, has combined a fair proportion of educational and cultural items with its amusement programs. The other agency, called the National Commercial Broadcasting Service, has been devoted almost wholly to low-brow amusement.

It is evident that amalgamation of the two services was the proper solution of a duplication which should never have been allowed to arise. Eventually in 1943 the political wheel turned full circle. The director of the Commercial Service, a prominent member of the Labor party's left wing, gradually fell foul of his minister and the cabinet. Embarrassed by their former supporter, the government omitted to lodge an appeal against his doing military service when men of his age group were called up. With its head out of the way, the Commercial Service was thereupon placed under the director of the National Broadcasting Service— a step on the road toward an ultimate fusion of the two organizations.

Leaving aside the past history of broadcasting, one must still consider whether for the future this function should continue as a separate department and whether it should remain under a minister or revert to a board. New Zealand has so far tried both types of experiment, board control and ministerial supervision. Neither system has worked well, since neither has permitted a completely free and vigorous public airing of major issues. What happened, as a result of the structural change, was that control by a minister succeeded control by a board. Even in peacetime too much censorship has been exercised over the opinions that could be voiced on the air. The discussion of controversial topics and clashes of view have not been welcomed. The experience of direct ministerial control over broadcasting leads me to oppose its continuation. On the other hand, it must be conceded that the particular board which held sway in the depression was no model of intellectual tolerance. My own preference is to place broadcasting under a more enlightened board which will be independent of the government of the day, in the same way as the board proposed for long-term planning and research. The broadcasting board should have five members (two nominated by the premier, two by the leader of the opposition, and one by the chancellor of the university), all to hold office for concurrent terms of five years. The board would appoint and control a director of broadcasting, and its finances would be assured by a single appropriation spread over the quinquennium. It is possible, though it cannot be considered certain, that by such a system the control of radio would be placed under a body representative of many shades of opinion. Democracy must utilize the radio as a medium for community education and as a vehicle for free and full public discussion. Broadcasting, therefore, should form an autonomous unit outside the sphere of cabinet jurisdiction.

There is one remaining activity whose claim to be included in the Education Department must be reviewed. That is the encouragement of physical recreation, an idea that was taken up by the Labor government in 1939. Its administration was intrusted to the Department of Internal Affairs, the accepted home for miscellaneous oddities. Yet at the very same time the ministry was creating a new branch of physical instruction within the Department of Education. Thus the physical recreation of adults, their games and sporting pursuits, have been separately handled from the physical development of the nation's children. If the machinery of government is to be reorganized, why should these two branches not be brought together? But, if so, where should they be located after their amalgamation. There are good arguments for assigning physical recreation to the Public Welfare Department because of the obvious connection between this activity and health. But there are cogent reasons why the Education Department could handle it just as well. In caring for the physical, as well as the mental, development of children, this agency will unite the *music* and *gymnastic* which the Greeks considered equally essential to human growth.[36] Similarly, in encouraging physical exercise among adults, the same department can contribute to a solution of that urgent modern problem—the use of leisure. Physical recreation is a genuine case of a function which straddles two classes of governmental activity and could reasonably be assigned to either of them.

36. Plato, *Republic*, chap. ii, secs. 376 ff.

The welfare of the Polynesian peoples within New Zealand's jurisdiction provides the basis for yet another departmental grouping. The work of the existing Native Department is confined to Maori problems. During most of its history this old agency has been mainly preoccupied with the legal issues surrounding the ownership of native lands and their sale to white purchasers. Since 1929, however, the department has adopted the newer policy of assisting the general development of the Maori people as a whole and of their agriculture in particular. Under the energetic stimulus of a minister of the Maori race, the work of regenerating a people proceeded apace—so quickly, in fact, that ordinary administrative procedures were sacrificed in the rush. Appointed in 1934, a royal commission unearthed various irregularities in the departmental administration which caused the resignation of the minister and a reorganization of the department. Much still remains to be done if Maori welfare is to be sympathetically and intelligently aided by the organized resources of the whole community.[37] In general, the Maoris have viewed the Native Department with some suspicion and reserve. They consider that it has not always been managed in a spirit conversant with their own attitudes and interests. Sensitive to the superiority of Europeans in matters of material technique, they are irritated by such a *faux pas* as the very title "Native Department," implying, in the English language, that the Maoris are a "native," and hence an inferior, race. A possible structural change would be to transfer to the Native Department the special Maori schools which are now run by the Department of Education. The development of the Maori, from childhood on, could then be studied and administered as a continuous problem and be handled by officials (both Maori and non-Maori) steeped in the lessons of anthropological investigation. If, however, the main purpose of native schools be primarily to help the Maori adapt himself to occidental culture, it could be well argued that they should be under the same authority as other state schools and draw upon the reservoir of teaching experience accumulated by the Department of Education.

37. The Maori Welfare and Development Act, 1945, represents a noteworthy advance.

An appropriate structural change would be to amalgamate the administration of the Cook Islands and of Samoa with that of the Maoris. New Zealand has administered the Cook Islands as a colonial dependency, while it has held Western Samoa first under mandate from the League of Nations and now under United Nations' trusteeship. Both the Cook Islands and Samoa are supervised by the Island Territories Department, a small offshoot of the Prime Minister's Department. In the middle of the twenties New Zealand experienced considerable trouble in managing the Samoans, who have been called "the Irishmen of the South Pacific." The Dominion's difficulties as a colonial administrator were due not so much to any lack of benevolence and good will as to a failure to acquire a psychological understanding of another type of human being. Public officials and ministers, mostly[38] ignorant of Polynesia, shouldered a problem which they did not trouble to study scientifically and bungled it through plain stupidity. In the thirties and forties the administration has been improved, but much remains to be done. It is reasonable to propose that one department be created to tackle the problem of the Maoris, the Samoans, and the Cook Islanders, all of them being branches of the one Polynesian race. Such a department, constituting a small colonial service, should be staffed by officials, both Polynesian and European, who have been trained in anthropology.

To maintain law and order, to administer justice, to detect and punish crime—these are traditional functions of government. New Zealand possesses an attorney-general who is also minister of justice and supervises the Justice Department (an arrangement analogous to that proposed for Britain in the Haldane report). Affixed to this Justice Department are the Patent Office, which should be transferred to the industrial group, and the Prisons Department, which should go with the public welfare agency. The remainder of the Justice Department can be left, as at present, to supervise the administrative aspects of the courts and the judicial process. With it should be grouped the Police Department, which is now constituted into an independent

38. On one occasion the New Zealand minister for the Cook Islands was a Maori (Sir Maui Pomare).

agency under a minister other than the attorney-general. Police and Justice together could comprise a department of law enforcement. This could also suitably absorb the Crown Law Office, a bureau of small size and composed entirely of lawyers which conducts cases on the Crown's behalf and supplies other departments with legal opinions.

A tenth department is needed for the conduct of external relations. New Zealand now possesses a Department of External Affairs. Originally this was a branch of the Prime Minister's Department, but in 1943 it was constituted into a separate agency of which the premier retained the portfolio. The functions of this department are to conduct relations with Britain, the Dominions, and other nations, as well as to control New Zealand's small but growing diplomatic service.[39] In 1946 New Zealand maintained a high commissioner and staff in London, Ottawa, and Canberra; a minister and legation at Washington and Moscow; and trade commissioners or agents in some other countries. At Wellington, Britain, Canada, and Australia maintain a high commissioner; the United States, the Soviet Union, and France have sent a minister; and many countries are represented by consular officials. To the same class of duties belongs another function of government: the military defense of the Dominion against invasion. New Zealand has one minister of defense, but three separate departments for the army, navy, and air force. The lessons of the recent war point unmistakably to the need for a single military service unifying the three forces into one organization, for was it not the separation and rivalry among the services which in part contributed to that fatal lack of co-ordination in Allied campaigns during the first three years of the war? Whatever armed establishment is maintained by New Zealand in the years to come —whether it be a national fighting force or part of an international service or both—must be consolidated into one agency. Moreover, for political and administrative purposes it could well be amalgamated with the Department of External Affairs. Upon the conduct of foreign relations depends the need, if any, for armed defense. Army, navy, and air force can form three

39. The issue of passports, however, was left with the Department of Internal Affairs.

branches of External Affairs, the military chiefs of staff being subordinate in authority to a civilian head of the amalgamated
agencies.

Quite another category of state enterprise—the eleventh in this
list—includes five trading concerns which compete with private
business in offering services to the public. The quintet is made up
of the Public Trust Office (Vogel's creation), the Government
Life Insurance Department, the State Fire Insurance Department, the Bank of New Zealand, and the Linen-Flax Corporation. It is self-evident that the two insurance agencies have much
in common and would fit conveniently under one head. The state
can surely incorporate them into a single department no less easily
than the private companies can combine fire, life, accident, and
other types of insurance. The Public Trust Office, the Bank of
New Zealand, and the Linen-Flax Corporation are not so obviously connected with the two insurance agencies or with one
another. Yet there is some justification for yoking them in the
same harness. These are all departments which trade with the
public in competition with private enterprise. Without seeking, as
yet, to monopolize the whole of the field in which they engage,
they form a yardstick for measuring the quality and the cost of
similar services offered by their privately owned competitors. The
State Fire Insurance, for example, was introduced by Seddon's
ministry in order to protect the public against the exorbitant pre-
miums charged by insurance firms. The administration of such
departments as these varies with the hostility or friendliness of the
ministry to private business. Liberal and Labor governments
have, on the whole, favored brisk and energetic competition by
these trading departments, while ministries more inclined to the
right have sought to restrain state activity for the benefit of private profit. According, therefore, to the social outlook prevailing
in the cabinet, these departments will receive their "stop" or
"go" signal. If they are placed under one minister, he can co-
ordinate their advances into, or retreats from, the spheres of the
private firms. He can similarly co-ordinate and direct their investment policies—a factor of great importance to these agencies
which have ample funds at their disposal.

A twelfth group of governmental functions surrounds the need to build and construct a young and developing country. The job is already handled by the Ministry of Works, whose widely ramifying activities have left their physical impress on the landscape of the Dominion. This is the agency which has built the railways, roads, and bridges and has erected state buildings and public schools; which assisted the armed forces in constructing fortifications, camps, and airdromes; and which, up to 1945,[40] engineered hydroelectric projects and sold the power thus produced. In 1945 the construction of state houses and flats was rightly transferred from the State Advances Corporation to the Ministry of Works. This agency, if the Hydroelectric Department is reincorporated in it, will be broad enough in scope.

One final possibility is to establish a distinct department which can assist and co-ordinate the various local authorities of the Dominion. In New Zealand at the present time "local government" is a euphemism to describe a planless maze of nearly seven hundred separate jurisdictions, with overlapping areas and widely diverse administrative standards. Many a ministry has dallied and delayed over the problem of local body reorganization. All have shrunk from inciting the opposition of vested parochialisms. But the day must come when the cities, towns, and counties, the harbor and the tramway boards, the hospital boards, rabbit boards, and drainage boards will be consolidated. Then a central department of local government co-ordination will be required.

The general effect of the reorganization proposed in the foregoing pages is to convert along functional lines an administrative system of some fifty-odd agencies into the more manageable number of nineteen (see Chart II). Of these nineteen departments suggested, thirteen would be placed under the immediate charge of ministers and one under the premier. The other five departments would be semiautonomous units not directly amenable to control by the cabinet. For it is to them, and to them alone, that "special considerations apply": to long-term planning and research because its range transcends the purview of any

40. In 1945 legislation established a separate State Hydroelectric Department, yet one more example of the bad tendency to multiply agencies instead of merging them.

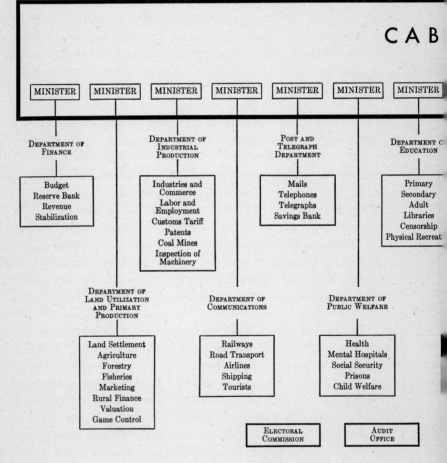

CAB

MINISTER MINISTER MINISTER MINISTER MINISTER MINISTER MINISTER

DEPARTMENT OF
FINANCE

Budget
Reserve Bank
Revenue
Stabilization

DEPARTMENT OF
INDUSTRIAL
PRODUCTION

Industries and
Commerce
Labor and
Employment
Customs Tariff
Patents
Coal Mines
Inspection of
Machinery

POST AND
TELEGRAPH
DEPARTMENT

Mails
Telephones
Telegraphs
Savings Bank

DEPARTMENT OF
EDUCATION

Primary
Secondary
Adult
Libraries
Censorship
Physical Recreat

DEPARTMENT OF
LAND UTILIZATION
AND PRIMARY
PRODUCTION

Land Settlement
Agriculture
Forestry
Fisheries
Marketing
Rural Finance
Valuation
Game Control

DEPARTMENT OF
COMMUNICATIONS

Railways
Road Transport
Airlines
Shipping
Tourists

DEPARTMENT OF
PUBLIC WELFARE

Health
Mental Hospitals
Social Security
Prisons
Child Welfare

ELECTORAL
COMMISSION

AUDIT
OFFICE

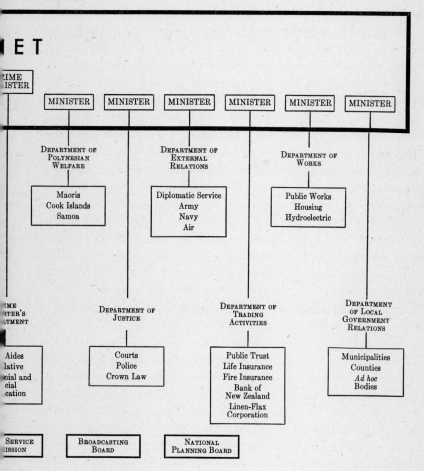

ET

RIME
ISTER

MINISTER   MINISTER   MINISTER   MINISTER   MINISTER   MINISTER

DEPARTMENT OF
POLYNESIAN
WELFARE

DEPARTMENT OF
EXTERNAL
RELATIONS

DEPARTMENT OF
WORKS

Maoris
Cook Islands
Samoa

Diplomatic Service
Army
Navy
Air

Public Works
Housing
Hydroelectric

ME
STER'S
TMENT

DEPARTMENT OF
JUSTICE

DEPARTMENT OF
TRADING
ACTIVITIES

DEPARTMENT
OF LOCAL
GOVERNMENT
RELATIONS

Aides
lative
nial and
cial
cation

Courts
Police
Crown Law

Public Trust
Life Insurance
Fire Insurance
Bank of
New Zealand
Linen-Flax
Corporation

Municipalities
Counties
Ad hoc
Bodies

SERVICE
ISSION

BROADCASTING
BOARD

NATIONAL
PLANNING BOARD

single ministry; to broadcasting because a democracy must zealously safeguard all opportunities for free and full discussion of opinions; to the electoral process, which must be nonpartisan; to the audit department, which must necessarily be independent in its investigations; and to the personnel agency,[41] which must resist the pressure to grant patronage. It can be socially harmful if the cabinet controls any of these five agencies. It is equally harmful if it does not control any of the other fourteen. Under the proposed reorganization many of the existing departments which now operate in independence of one another would be merged into single units and lose their separate identity. In some cases the regrouping of functions would be such that certain departments, as they are now constituted, would be split into their component parts and the parts redistributed. The work of the Customs Department, for instance, would be scattered over the departments of finance, industrial production, and education. The Marine Department would be parceled out among the departments of primary production, industrial production, and transport. Internal Affairs would find its bureaus reallocated between the agencies of primary production, industrial production, education, external affairs, and local government. There is no reason to criticize the proposed reorganization on the ground that it involves so great a redistribution of functions. It is rather a strong point of criticism against the present administrative arrangements that so many departments are now charged with varied and ill-assorted activities.

It might be thought that these suggested changes would prove unworkable because certain of the newly established departments would include conflicting interests. In the primary production department, for example, could the competition of forestry with land development be reconciled? Would the department of industrial production harmonize the points of view of employers and of labor? Could the transport department really co-ordinate rail, road, air, and sea travel? The answer to these questions is that the proper task of government is to attempt to create a general will or public interest by synthesizing special and limited claims. Although it is often said that every bureau has its clien-

41. Its functions and organization are discussed in the next chapter.

tele, it is hard to see how any conflicts that arise between private pressure groups in the community are mitigated if parallel, and often rival, state departments are established to represent those conflicts. Antagonism between rival sections of the community is surely not lessened by organizing separate administrative agencies, each an advocate for a different set of interests. On the contrary, if social conflicts are to be ironed out at all by the machinery of state, one and the same department should embrace all functions falling within the same broad field of activity. Opposed interests must be somewhere adjusted if social progress is to be achieved with the minimum of friction. Under the present system, where departments are often organized separately to care for opposed pressure groups, any adjustment between them has to be promoted by individual ministers or by the ministry as a body. The distribution of connected activities among distinct departments necessarily throws up all the more issues for settlement at the ministerial level. To amalgamate connected functions within one and the same department does not guarantee that there will no longer be rival interests in the community or that such interests will not require adjustment at the hands of the state. But it does mean that a better chance exists to reconcile divergent claims on a lower step of the governmental pyramid and not at the apex. It does mean, too, that a single department covering a wide field of social enterprise is more likely to take a comprehensive view of each interest and its appropriate place in the life of the whole community. If an Agriculture Department, as now constituted, is thought adequate to deal with the varied claims of wool-growers, dairy farmers, and meat producers, as well as producers of fruit and honey, can it not also widen its horizon to include fisheries and forestry?

That leads to another objection which might be raised. It could be argued that this chart for a proposed reorganization is logically devised and makes a precise and symmetrical blueprint but that it is impracticable. Are these suggested departments too large and unwieldy to be administratively efficient? This criticism has already been voiced by some New Zealand public servants with whom I have discussed my suggestions. But the answer is that New Zealand must adapt its organization to the large-scale character of the functions which its government undertakes. If the British Colonial Office can group together under its jurisdiction all the peoples of diverse culture who inhabit the British Colonial Empire, it is no insuperable problem for New Zealand to amalgamate its administration of Maori, Samoan, and Cook Islander. The size and the intricacy of even the largest of these proposed departments do not exceed what can be found in the administration of other democracies. Given the administrative capacity of its public servants, together with a proper personnel system for selection and training, there is no reason why New Zealand could not operate the machinery outlined above and derive corresponding benefit.

But a reorganization that applies to the formal structure alone is not enough. Should the machinery of New Zealand administration be redesigned on a large-scale pattern, it will require men and women of large-scale minds and personalities to operate it. Hence the personnel system—as it is and as it might be—forms the next subject for discussion.

CHAPTER XIV
THE CIVIL SERVICE

THE argument of the previous chapter can be summed up in a series of contrasts, which at first glance seem rather odd. Many of the functions undertaken by the state in New Zealand are advanced and progressive, yet the machinery of government contains much that is outmoded if not antiquated. The young nation which has boldly pioneered in many fields of social reform has initiated relatively little in the sphere of administration. On matters of policy the Dominion prides herself on being a leader; in administrative techniques she has been content to be a follower. An examination of the civil service will reveal that the same truth applies to personnel management. Here, too, New Zealand has in general lagged behind the most modern trends and has belatedly copied what was originated elsewhere. To cite but one example, a central personnel agency and a civil service based on merit were inaugurated in Britain in 1870; in the federal government of the United States and in New York State in 1883; in New South Wales in 1895; and in the Australian Commonwealth in 1902. New Zealand did not follow suit until 1912.

These paradoxes, however, can be explained. As was mentioned earlier, outside of the government there is little in New Zealand that qualifies for the description of large-scale management. Few ministers in their early careers have had any experience, or acquired any proper conception, of administrative problems; and few after taking office have contributed personally to improvements in the organization of the departments. The other source from which such improvements could emanate would be the top-ranking officials of the civil service. But, because of the methods of recruitment and education, too few of these have had a broad enough outlook or were disposed to reorganize the system to which they had grown accustomed. A survey of New Zealand's public personnel will corroborate these generalizations.

The Era of Patronage

If the delay in the introduction of a central personnel system can be attributed to one person more than others, much of the responsibility must lie with Richard John Seddon. The masterful Liberal premier succeeded in holding up reform of the public service both by his dominance over the party during his lifetime and by the impress of his ideas upon it after he died. For at least a decade prior to 1890 the civil service, subject to the mercies of ministries and Parliament, had been reduced and retrenched. Notorious among the habitual backbench critics of officialdom was Seddon. He it was who, when he became a minister in 1891, carried out his threats by ejecting some forty employees of the Public Works Department. From fear and dislike the public servants called him their "chief executioner."[1]

However, as Seddon became more acclimatized to the Treasury bench and more determined never to leave it, his attitude to the civil service changed. In it he saw an instrument of great utility for bolstering his own political ascendancy. Without a willingly co-operative corps of officials, the Liberal legislation could be administratively hamstrung. Without their loyal votes on election day, some closely contested seat might be forfeited by the Liberals to the opposition. Moreover, the expansion of state activities and the emergence of new departments meant jobs to be bestowed, and the premiership was worth some patronage. Seddon's consistent policy was to give to the largest possible number of individuals an interest in preserving his government in power. So thoroughgoing a political strategist was not like to exclude the civil service from his calculations.

When Seddon took office, the most recent laws governing the conditions of public employment were those enacted by the Stout ministry in 1886 and 1887. Seddon was in no haste to alter them, since they were pliable enough for his purpose. Permanent appointments to the public service were open to all who could pass an examination of easy standard. Other appointments could be offered on a temporary basis to those who had not

1. J. Drummond, *The Life and Work of Richard John Seddon* (Wellington: Whitcombe & Tombs, 1907), pp. 146–47.

qualified through the examination. In addition, experts could be placed in positions that required special skill or training. The premier had no need to interfere with the status of the permanent employees. All he had to do was to infiltrate through the gaps of the "temporary" and "expert" clauses in Stout's law. Nor did he take long in showing his hand. Seddon's own attitude and outlook are well crystallized in an incident which still circulates as a good story among New Zealand government departments. An old crony from his political bailiwick, the west coast of the South Island, came to ask him for a job. Seddon sent him to the head of the census and statistics department with an instruction that the man must be given employment. The department head took him on as a messenger for delivering letters and files— only to find that he could not read. Accordingly, Seddon's man was dismissed, and the department head sent the premier an explanatory memorandum: "I cannot employ this man. He is unable to read." Back came Seddon's reply: "Learn him!"[2]

As early as 1896 there were frequent criticisms in Parliament of this spoils system. One member complained: "Sir, I say that with regard to appointments to the civil service, appointments have been made in defiance of the law. Why do we send our boys to the public schools and enter them for the Junior Civil Service Examination? There are only about twenty or thirty who can go on the permanent list each year; and why are they to struggle to pass the examination if they are to be passed by, and the children of parents of the 'right colour' are to be shoved in?" The next year another parliamentarian reiterated: "The Service has been filled up with supporters of the government, independently of competence, and if this is not what is called 'spoils to the victors' I do not know what it is. . . . . It is well known, I have no doubt, to all members in this House that in all the clerical departments of the civil service it is necessary that youths should pass the Junior Civil Service Examination, and in accordance with the law they must be taken on in rotation in accordance with the pass they get. Young lads who have passed their examination and stand

2. This incident has been frequently related to me as an anecdote. But a veteran journalist and parliamentary reporter vouched for its authenticity, assuring me that he was told it by Seddon's own secretary, who knew the circumstances and saw the premier's minute on the memorandum.

well up in the list have been passed over and other lads who failed to pass appointed in their stead. . . . . It is a cruel thing to punish a boy because of his father's political opinions. . . . . In this matter the Government evade the law by making temporary appointments."[3]

The huge staff of one important agency was at first out of Seddon's grip. That was the Railways Department, over which Atkinson had erected the protecting umbrella of a three-membered commission. Replacing the trio by a minister in 1896, Seddon assured to himself, among other things, the direct control over many thousands of men and their jobs. Soon the practice was introduced of appointing the railways staff on the nomination of members of the House. More than one representative recounted in Parliament how he had been circularized by the Railways Department for a list of his nominees who would be placed on a rota for appointment as vacancies occurred.[4] So regular did the system become that in 1906 a list of test questions in English, supplied officially to the inspectors of primary schools, contained the following candid evidence: "Write a letter to the member of Parliament for your district, applying for a position on the railways."[5] In later years Sir Francis Bell, confessing from the lofty pedestal of an elder statesman the errors of his political youth, admitted that he, too, had conformed to the prevailing usages. "I myself" he repented, "have been guilty when a member of the House of asking the Minister of Railways to take some boys into the railway workshops, and I got them there; and it was not fair to the boys who had not behind them the political influence I had at the time."[6]

The Liberals offered various reasons and explanations for their encouragement of this practice. Openly and frankly some of them argued that government jobs should go to their friends and not to their political enemies.[7] Some insisted that the departments had been packed for many years by Conservative appointees and that

3. *P.D.*, XCVIII (1897), 219–20.

4. Cf. the retrospective remarks of the minister of customs in the Reform Cabinet (*P.D.*, CLX [1912], 63).

5. Quoted by J. B. Condliffe, *New Zealand in the Making* (London: Allen & Unwin, 1930), p. 200.

6. *P.D.*, CCXVI (1927), 517.   7. E.g., *P.D.*, XCVIII (1897), 64.

the time had now come to "liberalize" its personnel. As one member put it: "While we have got upon these benches a Liberal Government, and Liberal legislation as the outcome, we have got Conservative administration in the public service. It cannot be disputed that 70 or 80 per cent of the public service of the colony are undoubtedly conservative."[8] Even if that were, however, the genuine motive at the start of the Liberal regime, it could hardly continue to serve as a justification ten or fifteen years later. Long after his dominance was established beyond challenge in the electorate, in Parliament, and in the public service, Seddon persistently vetoed all attempts to curb ministerial control over appointments.

Because of the political accident that the same party enjoyed continuous power for twenty-one years, the effects of the spoils system were not quite so harmful as they have been in certain states of the United States. Although political influence was brought to bear in making appointments, rotation in office was scarcely known, since the Liberals were intrenched for two decades. Appointees who originally secured their jobs through party favoritism could not be ousted under the same party's regime. The Reform minister of customs, Fisher, thus reminisced in 1912: "When I went into the public service—now sixteen years ago—I remember a man in the employ of the Government at that time who addressed envelopes all day and received a salary of £275 a year. He came to the office when he liked, and his work was actually being done by a cadet at about £50 a year. Nothing in the world could have got that man out of the service: the political power behind him was too great."[9]

Nevertheless, the effects were bad enough. Some gladly, others reluctantly, the members of Parliament used their influence to secure jobs for their political supporters. The general public, fully aware of this method of entry into the service, besought the representative of their district to prefer their request to a minister. Depending upon the favors of the ministry if he was to satisfy his constituents, the representative was under pressure to toe the line in divisions and debates. The patronage system was a shrewd device enabling the cabinet to keep the voters grateful

8. *P.D.*, XCII (1896), 85.   9. *P.D.*, CLX (1912), 65.

and their representatives obedient. For their part, many members resented the embarrassing solicitation to which they were subjected. "Members of Parliament," said one of them, "are to a large extent labour agents."[10] Another eloquently vented his feelings of indignation thus: "It harrows my very spirit to be urged to importune Ministers for privileges and concessions that ought not to belong to any one shade of politics. . . . . I hate patronage in the gift or the receipt. I want to be rid of it, and I will hail with delight anything that will enable me to say, 'there is only one legitimate avenue to Government employment. Fitness is the pass; go one, go all.' "[11]

The spoils system was equally degrading to public servants themselves and destructive of their morale. It was discouraging to see persons appointed to junior jobs because of political backing and still more discouraging to see so-called "temporaries" or "experts" advanced to the more senior jobs. Permanent officials who qualified for entrance by passing the examination did have the advantage of being eligible for superannuation rights. On the other hand, they suffered from disadvantages. In 1900 the ministry put through a Civil Service Examination Act, further defining the methods of qualifying for permanent employment. But the same act laid it down that any public servant with permanent status had to pass a Senior Civil Service Examination or some equivalent before he could receive a salary higher than £200 a year. Temporaries, however, as the Hunt Commission was later to point out, "received their periodical increments of pay in the same way as those officers who joined as cadets, with this difference—that the temporary hands could be paid any salary that their work was considered to be worth, although they had passed no examination whatever."[12]

The injustice to the permanents can be seen by comparing the figures of the totals in the two groups. Seddon himself stated in 1906 that, between 1893 and 1904, 548 permanent cadets had

10. Quoted by J. E. Le Rossignol and W. D. Stewart, *State Socialism in New Zealand* (London: Harrap & Co., 1912), p. 202.

11. *P.D.*, XCVIII (1897), 90.

12. "Report of the (Hunt) Commission on the Public Service, 1912" (appendix to the *Journal of the House of Representatives*, H-34).

been taken into the service as against 439 experts.[13] As for the
temporaries, they were such only in name. Ward mentioned in
1912 that certain of them even predated the Liberal era and had
been in the service for as long as thirty years.[14] It is no wonder that
they came to be called "permanent temporary clerks." The situation in the public service at the time of Seddon's death was so
anomalous that his successor was forced to pass remedial legislation. An act of 1907 took the rather obvious course of converting 334 temporaries, who had over five years' service, into permanents. It also gave to an extra 293 temporaries the right to become permanent when they had completed their five years.
Thus 627 officials altogether were transferred to permanent status, a number which formed nearly a third of the 2,000 clerical
officers then in the service of the state.

In the following year the ministry responded to the slump by
retrenchment in the public service. Ward held out to business
interests the hopes of economies in the service amounting annually to £250,000. Actually, 940 officials were dismissed, but
only £98,970 were saved. At the same time the new law provided
for a classification system which hitherto had been attempted
only in the Railways and Post and Telegraph departments. The
task of classification, however, was intrusted, not to a central personnel agency, which New Zealand still lacked, but to a committee of department heads. Their efforts at rationalizing the relationships of existing employees resulted in the lodging of 1,760
appeals against their decisions; and either in fright or in disgust
they gave up the effort.[15] The Ward ministry, as the Hunt Commission noted, did not abuse the still surviving "temporary" and
"expert" loopholes to the same extent as Seddon had done.[16] Yet
a return prepared for the House in 1912 showed that in the preceding years 167 persons had been appointed to government

13. See Le Rossignol and Stewart, op. cit., p. 199. In 1912 the Hunt report
stated that the service then contained "539 officers who entered under the 'expert'
clauses of the various Acts, and of these 51 came in as short-hand writers and
typists" (op. cit., p. 23).
14. P.D., CLX (1912), 56.
15. "Report of the (Hunt) Commission," p. 17.
16. Ibid., p. 15.

positions on the nomination of Liberal parliamentarians, as against 23 on the nomination of the opposition.[17]

Hence at the close of two decades of Liberal supremacy, New Zealand had failed to infuse into personnel organization the modern principles underlying its extension of social services. When the newly appointed public service commissioner presented his first annual report in 1913, he revealed that "the Public Service had been working on the regulations of 1873, to which few amendments had been made, except as regards travelling-allowances."[18] The worst sins of omission were the absence of a central personnel agency and of a classification system spread horizontally across the vertical departmental divisions. The most grievous sin committed lay in the political manipulation of appointments and promotion. From all these factors resulted an unsatisfactory public service. In general, the morale of public employees was at a low ebb. Through the absence of a horizontal classification plan, conditions of work and salaries varied disproportionately from one agency to another. It was discouraging for a man to be carrying out duties in one department at less pay than a corresponding official elsewhere. The welfare of public servants and their chances of promotion depended principally on their own department head, on his good will toward the individual concerned, and on his popularity with the ministry of the day. An aggressively ambitious head would build up his staff, since his own prestige was thus enhanced. One who was politically influential could obtain from the cabinet a more favorable hearing for his own personnel. Transfers, for those who sought them, were hard to obtain, since each head tended to erect a Chinese wall of isolation around his agency. The transfer of an incompetent or of a mediocrity would always be encouraged; but the more able official often found an avenue of promotion in another department blocked by his own superior, who would not consent to his release.[19] Castigating such conditions in the service, the Hunt report enunciated this sound principle: "The Public

17. *P.D.*, CLX (1912), 50.

18. "First Report of the Public Service Commissioner, 1913" (appendix to the *Journal of the House of Representatives*, H-14), p. 5.

19. See "Report of the (Hunt) Commission," pp. 13–14.

Service should be treated as a whole and not as a number of separate watertight compartments, and officers of the Service should feel that they are officers of the Public Service as a whole, and not officers of special Departments only."[20]

When, in addition to all this, a public servant suddenly found a "temporary" or an "expert" brought in over his head, the sense of grievance and resentment can well be imagined. Such "back-door" entry into the civil service became the center of a controversy. Public servants openly argued that it was in their own interest to slam and bolt it; the ministry covertly maintained that it was their political interest to keep it open. The anomalies of status as between permanents and temporaries were too glaring to be perpetuated. Seddon merely brushed aside—for his lifetime at least—the recoil of the evil which he had aggravated. Ward toyed and tinkered with the problem but failed to solve it. The attempt at classification in 1908 proved abortive merely because the ministry was unwilling to surrender its control of personnel to a properly constituted agency. Harassed, vexed, and aggrieved by such cavalier treatment, some of the bolder spirits among the public servants had already formed a Public Service Association to press for the long-delayed reforms. Only in the Railways and the Post and Telegraph departments had a measure of classification been introduced. The great size of their staffs, and their readier facilities for combined action, made it politically necessary that they be placated. It is true that the methods of initial appointment to those departments still remained subject to political influence, but, once appointed, the employees of these two agencies were, thanks to their classification system, somewhat more assured than the members of other departments that no temporaries or experts would be brought in to bar their progress up the promotion ladder. Reacting to all these political influences, the employees themselves tended to seek a safeguard in the seniority principle, regarding this as their best alternative for determining promotion policy. Another possible alternative was to recruit individuals in the first place, and subsequently to promote them, on the sole basis of merit. But until a central personnel agency had been established, who could evaluate merit?

20. *Ibid.*, p. 23.

The political influences that surrounded many appointments, the uncertainty of gaining promotion on the basis of merit, the lack of any central personnel agency to institute uniform standards—these were all factors detrimental to the education and training of public servants. The civil service examination, which candidates for permanent status were required to sit, could be passed by any mediocre intelligence. Nor was the senior examination, which barred their promotion to a salary higher than £200 a year, at all exacting. The educational minima demanded of permanent employees could scarcely have been set much lower. New Zealand prided herself on being a democratic country. Although free primary schooling was now available to all, free secondary schooling was not. Hence the principle of equal opportunity was so interpreted as to mean that the standard of entrance must be reduced to the educational level where all stood an equal chance.

A presage of future trends, however, was contained in requirements that candidates for specified posts must possess advanced professional qualifications. Particularly was this the case in agencies which employed engineers. New Zealand's internal geography made much of its early history center around the problem of communications and thereby placed a premium on the technical ability of its engineers. Thus the Railways, the Public Works, and the Post and Telegraph departments were three which could not risk muddling along just on native common sense tinctured with literacy. Striking evidence of this is provided in the figures of civil servants in 1913 who were holders of degrees or diplomas. These were distributed as shown in Table 19. The engineers, it will be noted, comprised half of the total— a convincing illustration of the impact of a technological age upon a young colonial democracy. Other courses of university study found less favor in official eyes. Nor, under the conditions then governing promotion, had public servants, once they were appointed, any strong incentive to seek higher education. "Merit does not count as it should," complained the Hunt Commission. "The passing of the Senior Civil Service Examination is necessary for those who have come in as cadets if they wish to get more than £200 a year, but, except for this, the passing of examina-

tions, either departmental or outside examinations, such as Solic-
itors' and Accountancy Examinations, do not carry weight and
bring the promotion that might reasonably be expected."[21]

In-service training, likewise, had made only an embryonic
start, though the need for it was somewhat acknowledged in the
departments which relied on technicians. Both the Railways and
the Post and Telegraph departments had initiated their own
training program, of which the following is an example: "Correspondence classes for the instruction of officers of the Post and
Telegraph Department in technical telegraphy and telephony,
and in subjects of the Public Service Senior and Junior Examina-

TABLE 19

NUMBER OF PUBLIC EMPLOYEES HOLDING
DEGREES OR DIPLOMAS, 1913

B.A., M.A.	17
Law professional, LL.B., LL.M.	47
Accountants professional, B.Com., M.Com.	22
Engineering degrees and diplomas	136
B.Sc., M.Sc.	19
Miscellaneous	33
Total	274

tions and Sixth Standard were inaugurated in 1910. . . . . The
classes have been largely taken advantage of, the number of students for the years 1910 to 1914 being 2,001—861 technical and
1,140 general."[22] For the most part, however, public servants
were left to train themselves as best they might. The normal lot
of the new recruit was to be immersed in a monotonous routine
of dull minutiae, a process euphemistically known as "training
on the job." Commentary on the then prevailing system is contained in these authoritative words: "In some Departments no
foresight appears to have been exercised by training cadets. The
line of least resistance has often been to obtain temporary assistance, which in some ways has gradually become permanent. This
process of absorption is the most costly method that can be devised to recruit the staff of an expanding Department, and it is

21. *Op. cit.*, p. 16.
22. "Third Report of the Public Service Commissioner, 1915," p. 23.

not possible to calculate the additional expense which has been thrown on Departments by unsatisfactory methods of the kind. There are three or four large Departments which have strenuously resisted this, with the result that their staffs consist almost entirely of men who have been trained from youth in the Departments themselves."[23]

By 1912, in short, New Zealand had scarcely advanced beyond insuring that its engineers were adequately educated and trained. It lacked the prerequisites for a personnel system animated with good morale and functioning with high efficiency. How urgent it was to institute some form of systematic organization can be

TABLE 20

ESTIMATED NUMBER OF EMPLOYEES IN VARIOUS
BRANCHES OF THE GOVERNMENT, 1909

Railways	13,000
Co-operative laborers	10,000
Post and Telegraph	8,000
Schoolteachers	4,000
Police	850
Coal-miners	700
Lighthousemen	250
Other state departments	3,500
Total	40,300

understood by a mere glance at the size that the civil service had already attained. Table 20 gives an estimate (only approximate) of the number of employees of the central government in 1909.[24] For a population of about a million this figure was a large one. It was all the more imperative, therefore, for the ministry to attend to their welfare by offering fair opportunities and a life-career to the men and women who made service to the public their profession.

The Beginnings of Reform

The foundations of New Zealand's public personnel administration, as it is today, were laid in the year 1912. They are to be found in the recommendations of a royal commission and the

23. "First Report of the Public Service Commissioner, 1913," p. 8.
24. Quoted in Le Rossignol and Stewart, op. cit., p. 197.

provisions of a parliamentary enactment, two documents whose principles have now governed the organization of the civil service for three and a half decades. The commission, under a chairman named Hunt, was composed of intelligent businessmen, and in their own words "tried to look at the whole matter from a business point of view, bearing in mind certain differences which must always exist between private businesses and the business of a country."[25] Like so many royal commissions in New Zealand, it was rushed for time and had to skimp some of its investigation. Despite this drawback, it was able to present a good report[26] which combined a thoroughgoing exposure of existing defects with an intelligent understanding of personnel problems. Its principal recommendations can be reduced to four heads: Block all "back doors" of entrance to the public service. Promote from within the service. Appoint and promote on the basis of merit. Provide for free transfers of officers between departments.[27] With an enlightened and modern point of view, it defined the objects of personnel administration to include "entry by competitive examination, probation before final admission, security of tenure during good behaviour after admission, promotion by merit, and pensions on retirement."[28] To that excellent summary of essentials little need be added except provision for a classification plan and for in-service training.

With equally good sense the commission realized that it was useless to enunciate fine-sounding principles without instituting machinery for their enforcement. They pointed out that there was little to unify the service and offset the vertical divisions between departments. The Treasury was virtually the only agency with any authority to control its fellows, but its power was inadequate. Such co-ordination as was accomplished fell upon the cabinet, which was consequently overburdened by its attention to detail and routine. Drawing upon their business experience, the Hunt Commission suggested that a Board of Management responsible to the cabinet be created for the execution of its pol-

25. *Op. cit.*, p. 10.

26. Unfortunately the commission heard evidence *in camera* and subsequently had it all burned in order to prevent political embarrassments. A valuable historical source was thus irretrievably lost.

27. *Op. cit.*, p. 22.   28. *Ibid.*, p. 25.

icies. Composed of three members, two being men of business experience drawn from outside the service and the third a public servant, this board was to have charge of problems of organization and personnel.

The Hunt Commission was appointed by the Mackenzie ministry in May, 1912, at the very close of the Liberal lease of power. Its report was submitted in August of the same year. But in July the ministry had fallen, and Massey was already installed in office. For many years while it was in opposition, the Reform party had brought against the Liberals the accusation of political interference with civil service appointments; and future Reform ministers had, as private members, introduced bills to provide a satisfactory personnel administration. Indeed, reform of the civil service and of the Legislative Council, coupled with the grant of the freehold to the state tenantry, were about the only policies presented by this party to the electorate. Massey's cabinet was in such a hurry to get its program into legislative shape that a Public Service Bill was actually drafted and introduced to the House of Representatives even before the Hunt report had yet been submitted. By the time of the second reading of the bill, however, that report was printed and circulated; and its findings, which in general agreed with the bill, were extensively quoted during the debate. As Herdman, the minister of justice who took charge of the bill, stated: "Curiously enough, although on different matters the views I hold differ from those held by the Commissioners, yet on many other matters the Bill anticipated what the Commissioners have discovered."[29]

The parliamentary debate was a poor one and failed to do justice to the all-important topic of public service reform. Herdman informed the House that his bill was "modelled on the Australian legislation."[30] In an unsatisfactory opening speech he referred to civil service developments in Britain, Australia, and Canada, but he omitted any mention of the United States, being apparently quite unaware of the parallels between his own proposed scheme and the existing personnel agencies in the American federal and state governments. In one crucial respect the bill diverged from the recommendations of the Hunt Commission. Instead of a

29. *P.D.*, CLX (1912), p. 49.   30. *Ibid.*, p. 116.

three-membered Board of Management responsible to the cabinet, the bill provided for a single public service commissioner, whose status was semi-independent of the cabinet, and for two assistant commissioners subordinate to him. It was this feature which became the target for most of the Liberal attack. "I say it is awful," bemoaned the former premier, Ward, "to contemplate the autocracy which the Government is proposing to centre in one man, and it is entirely against democratic principles."[31] Riding the same hobbyhorse, another former Liberal minister, Hanan, declaimed: "Parliament should not surrender its rights to irresponsible Commissioners to control the public services of New Zealand. . . . . Therefore it is not democratic government to place, for instance, the appointments, promotions, etc., in the Civil Service entirely in the hands of, or allow it to be absolutely run by, Commissioners who are not elected by and representative of the people."[32] Apart from this argument, there was little for the Liberals to say against a ministry which so nobly avowed that it was divesting itself of political patronage. The bill accordingly passed through both houses, becoming the Public Service Act. Such, then, was the genesis of New Zealand's present system. There remains to appraise its merits and defects now that it has been in operation for three and a half decades.

The Public Service Commissioner

It should first be pointed out that at no time since the inception of the Public Service Act to the present have all the employees of the central government fallen under the jurisdiction of the personnel agency which it created. The judiciary and the legislative officials, members of the defense forces and of the police force, as well as the staff of the railways, were all specifically excluded from the operation of the act. The Post and Telegraph Department was at first subject to the commissioner, although his powers over it were restricted by certain exemptions which did not apply to other agencies.[33] Later, however, this department wriggled itself free from the supervision of the central personnel office and became a separate staff enclave. Reviewing the present-day

31. *Ibid.*, p. 59.
32. *Ibid.*, p. 74.   33. Public Service Act (1912), sec. 4.

system and leaving aside the military establishments of the defense forces, one finds that the civil employees of the state divide for purposes of personnel administration into six groups. The staffs of the Railways, Police, and Post and Telegraph departments are managed, respectively, by the heads of those agencies. Teachers in the state primary and secondary schools constitute a national career service administered by the director of education. The personnel of about forty-five departments, forming in New Zealand parlance the "Public Service,"[34] have been controlled first by the public service commissioner (1912–46) and since 1946 by a three-membered commission. In addition, however, there is a sixth group of public employees of a miscellaneous character who do not belong to any of the five services just mentioned. For example, the staffs of the Reserve Bank, the Bank of New Zealand, the Linen-Flax Corporation, and the National Airways are appointed and controlled by their various boards of directors. Ministers of legation, high commissioners, and all their staffs are appointed by the minister of external affairs without any advertisement at all.[35] This list of exceptions, if set out in full, would be a lengthy one, but no accurate record is available of who are included in the sixth group. Table 21, however, sets out the relative sizes of the five main groups and shows the development of a quarter of a century. Of these groups, it is the Public Service that most deserves attention. Since it embraces so many and such varied departments, the managerial problems of its personnel agency are the more complex and interesting.

The organization of the central staff office provides a convenient starting-point for a discussion of the Public Service. The act of 1912 went as far as legislation can go in guaranteeing the security and independence of the commissioner. Appointed by the governor-general in Council (i.e., the ministry) for a term of seven years, he could be reappointed for further terms. For misbehavior or incompetence he could be removed by the ministry; but only after a written statement of the reasons had been laid

34. The plural term "public services" covers all the employees of the central government.
35. External Affairs Act, 1943. However, the personnel of the External Affairs Department in Wellington were made subject to the public service commissioner.

before the House of Representatives and approved by it.[36] No commissioner was ever so removed, though one who became incapable of performing his duties was allowed to resign. The act further stated that the ministry "shall" also appoint two assistant commissioners. These were definitely to be subordinate in status to the commissioner and could not dispute his authority. In practice, however, despite the use of the mandatory word "shall," the act was consistently flouted by successive governments. At times there has been only one assistant commissioner, and on occasion not even one. Only in 1945 were the two assistants appointed.

TABLE 21

DEVELOPMENT OF CIVIL EMPLOYEE STAFFS OF THE
FIVE MAIN GROUPS, 1913 AND 1938

Staff Controlled By:	1913	1938
Public service commissioner...................	10,300*	16,000
Director-general of Post and Telegraph Department..	....	11,600
General manager of railways.................	14,200	21,900
Commissioner of police.....................	800	1,200
Director of education.......................	5,300	8,000

* Of this figure, the Post and Telegraph Department alone comprised 5,400. In the remaining agencies, still under the commissioner's control in 1938, there were 4,900 in 1913.

For one brief period there was a departure from the principle of single-headed control. From August, 1936, to December, 1938, two commissioners held office jointly with co-ordinate authority, an arrangement that worked only because one personality dominated the other. In 1939 the system of a single commissioner was restored, and this lasted for eight more years. But in 1946 a major alteration occurred. The government obtained from Parliament an amendment to the act, substituting a three-membered commission for the one commissioner. All are appointed by the ministry, but one of the three is nominated by the Public Service Association, which is the civil servant's trade-union. The first chairman is accorded a term of seven years; his colleagues, and all subsequent chairmen, a term of five. All are eligible for reappointment. Removals are subject to the same safeguards as previously. Just as the creation of the Public Service Commis-

36. Public Service Act, 1912, secs. 7, 10–11.

sioner's Office in 1912 inaugurated a new period in the public administration of the Dominion, so is another phase marked by the substitution of a commission for a commissioner. It is possible now, and necessary, to review the history of staff control by one man and to explain why a type of organization which persisted for three and a half decades (barring a two-year interlude) was eventually scrapped.

No one can fail to be impressed with the extent of the powers and the dignity of the status conferred on the public service commissioner. It was a position that constituted one of the plums of officialdom. Although less highly remunerated than such comparable posts as those of general manager of the railways, director of broadcasting, or managing director of the State Advances Corporation, it was the focus of many an ambition. Within the departments that comprise the Public Service, the commissioner was considered the head civil servant, ranking above even the secretary to the Treasury and the permanent head of the Prime Minister's Department. Indeed these last-named officials, as well as the heads of most other departments, were themselves appointed to their posts by the commissioner.[37] His powers included all aspects of personnel administration: the recruitment, examination, and appointment of new officials; the classification of all positions and the grant of salaries to individuals on a scale set by the ministry; supervision of recruits during probation and administration of in-service training programs; and promotion of the meritorious and punishment or dismissal of the unsuitable. To all these operations was added a broad power to investigate any department and inquire into its efficiency. Thus, at least in legislation, New Zealand amply provided for a central staff agency to supervise and assist the other departments.

When one asks how these powers have been applied and how the commissioner system worked in practice, the question moves from the aspect of legislative authority to that of administrative reality. My own conclusion, derived from many years of close study of New Zealand administration at the seat of government,

37. The ministry appointed, besides the commissioner himself, the director of broadcasting, the managing directors of the State Advances Corporation, the controller and auditor-general, and certain other high officials.

is the following. Although the public service commissioner necessarily played a major role in the administrative process, neither was the prestige of his office as great as its importance warranted nor were its powers ever developed to their full potentiality. This is perhaps paradoxical in view of the sweeping authority contained in the bald provisions of the Public Service Act. How did this contrast arise? How can one explain the gap between the act and the actuality?

An incident that occurred some years ago may serve as the beginning of an answer. I was in the office of a former public service commissioner on an afternoon when the House of Representatives were discussing a petition presented to it by a public servant whom the commissioner had dismissed for disobeying instructions. Since the debate in the House was being broadcast, the commissioner was able to listen in through his own radio set and supply his private commentary on the discussion. At one point a member declared: "The Public Service Commissioner has wide powers." At which the commissioner smiled and remarked to me: "Too wide!" That comment reveals and explains a great deal. The commissioner's effectiveness was never circumscribed by any lack of power. Instead the successive commissioners showed caution—sometimes even reluctance—in using the powers they did legally possess. They seemed fearful of displaying the full implications of their own authority. This should not be interpreted to mean that the commissioners in their thirty-four years of existence accomplished little or nothing. On the contrary, one must pay the deserved tribute to what was done. They put an end to the grosser forms of political patronage; they introduced a classification system; they increased the efficiency of many departments; and they encouraged the conception that the various agencies under their jurisdiction form a single service. All that is no mean record. Yet it is all too plain that the progress, however genuine, was insufficient. The reforms that were instituted were not pushed far enough. Some vital aspects of personnel work were almost entirely neglected until recent years, and others are still neglected. Perhaps the criticism may be best summed up in the terms that some scholars have applied to the development of personnel administration in the United States during the half-century from 1883 to 1933. Commissioner control was negative in outlook rather than positive. It tended to concentrate more on preventing certain abuses than on encouraging advanced ideals.

Those who are familiar with the historical evolution of central personnel agencies elsewhere will be well aware that in this respect New Zealand is by no means peculiar. Central personnel agencies have been called into being both there and elsewhere principally in order to remedy two common abuses: political patronage in appointments and promotions and the absence of uniform conditions among different branches of the service. Invariably, therefore, the initial tasks of such offices have been to eliminate patronage and to classify positions and salary scales horizontally throughout the departments. Once those jobs were achieved, for many years no further momentum stimulated the personnel administrators. Not until the economic depression and its aftermath placed a challenge upon governmental constructiveness was due care given to new aspects of personnel problems. Positive recruitment policies, higher standards in the education and training of staff, the nourishment of those intangibles that make for good morale—these are some of the more important forward strides of the last decade and a half. If the Public Service Commissioner's Office in New Zealand has been laggard in attending to these needs, at least there are similar agencies elsewhere which cannot claim to have wrought much better.

The reason New Zealand's various commissioners were circumspect in using their powers can be further understood by viewing their office in its political context. The high strategy that the commissioners mapped out for themselves was dictated by the balancing of different forces. They moved within an area defined by certain relationships. Those relationships brought them into contact with the cabinet, the permanent heads, the Treasury, and the rank and file of public servants organized into their Public Service Association.

In his dealings with the cabinet the commissioner was tugged in opposite directions by conflicting tendencies. Since his office was instituted partly to guard against political interference with the jobs of public servants, he had to maintain a certain degree of isolation from the cabinet. On the other hand, since the cabinet was supported by Parliament and represented the majority of the people, personnel policies had to be adjusted to ministerial requirements. Inevitably the intimacy of the contact between ministry and commissioner varied with different factors. It depended on the personal strength and standing of the commissioner, on the self-restraint or otherwise of the government, and so on. From a formal, legal standpoint, the commissioner appeared to be independent of political control. In executing his duties, he was not responsible to any one minister. His business with the government he conducted immediately with its head, the prime minister. Yet it would be wrong to suppose that the commissioner was as independent in administrative practice as the letter of the law might indicate. The truth was that the cabinet needed the co-operation of the Commissioner, while he wanted certain favors of them. Thus the ministry required his assistance in finding and organizing the staff to execute their policies. He, in turn, depended on their good will for obtaining amendatory legislation or new regulations or increases in the appropriation for his office. Proposals concerning personnel matters, which the commissioner could and should have settled on his own authority, were often sent up for the prime minister's approval. It is true that there was one commissioner who courageously defied a minister over the issue of inspecting a subdepartment and compelling the resignation of its head.[38] But such instances were rare. More often than not the commissioners were complaisant to the government of the day, and many of the promotions to high positions were determined by the personal or political preferences of a minister. Particularly during the war years the subordination of the Public Service Commissioner's office to the cabinet became ever more apparent.

No less ambivalent were the motives which governed the commissioner's relations with the heads of departments in the Public Service. His power to control them was sufficiently extensive, since he decided upon all staff questions within their departments. Without the commissioner's approval they could not promote a subordinate or alter his salary, create a new position, or make an appointment. In practice, of course, the commissioner neither re-

38. During this controversy the commissioner died of heart failure induced by the strain.

quired nor desired to administer his powers with a big stick. There was a great deal of informal discussion and unofficial consultation between the commissioner's inspectors and the personnel executives of the departments which paved the way for mutual agreement. The commissioner would usually try to meet the wishes of a department head in applying his powers over personnel. After all, it was the permanent head who was primarily responsible for the efficiency of his own department; and if his staff were not treated by the commissioner in the way he wanted, he could throw the blame on the commissioner whenever his department failed to run smoothly. A permanent head who failed to gain a sympathetic hearing from the commissioner might enlist the support of his minister. If that occurred too often, the commissioner could find that a majority in the cabinet were antipathetic to him. So powerful were such considerations that many department heads affected to take but slight notice of the Public Service Commissioner's Office. Some prided themselves on their freedom from his control; others referred to him as a "glorified staff clerk." But there were others again who welcomed his presence. They regarded him as a useful "buffer" to relieve them of the onus of discriminating between their subordinates when promotions were to be made. For their part the successive commissioners made it their policy to co-operate with the permanent heads. Only occasionally would they show their teeth; as, for instance, in 1933 when the commissioner, together with the controller and auditor-general, exposed to the prime minister the mismanagement in the Native Department, or in 1940–41, when the commissioner of his own initiative investigated the Patent Office.

Of particular interest has been the relation between the Public Service Commissioner's Office and the Treasury. Bearing in mind the machinery of administration in Britain, where the Treasury has such overweening power, one finds it unusual to contemplate a system where the Treasury has occupied a less exalted place. The Reform government in 1912 was wise when it consciously followed the Australian model (and unconsciously the American) of separating the central direction of personnel from the agency that manages finance. In Britain where control over personnel is vested in the department which also controls finance, two results follow. The Treasury tends to be overpowerful in relation to other departments, and within the Treasury itself the establishments branch tends to be subordinated to the financial side. New Zealand has balanced its Treasury against its Public Service Commissioner's Office; and, of the two, the latter was originally in the stronger position.

In various of the public service commissioners' reports—especially in the earlier ones—appear rebukes of the Treasury for its failure to perform its proper duties. Here is a quotation from the first report of the commissioner: "One of the most glaring examples is, or has been, the lack of co-operation between Departments and the Treasury. Although the latter Department is in sole charge of the accounts of the Dominion, it has not for a long time exercised its full powers. There has, for example, been no inspection by the Treasury and no examination of the method of account-keeping of Departments, with the result that a mass of work is unnecessarily duplicated at considerable expense and to the detriment of efficiency."[39] Comparing the powers over other departments exercised, respectively, by the commissioner and the Treasury, the Royal Commission on Native Affairs stated in 1934: "The Native Department is not, any more than is any other Department, an independent unit. It is subject to control in certain respects by the Treasury and the Public Service Commissioner, and also to a checking process by the Controller and Auditor General. . . . . The Public Service Commissioner has a more extensive duty than the Treasury."[40]

In recent years, however, the powers and influence of the Treasury have been considerably strengthened by a vigorous secretary. Originally an agency which did little else than prescribe departmental accounting systems, it has acquired a stricter control over departmental appropriations since the depression. In fact, the Treasury and the commissioner became, to a greater extent than before, mutually interdependent. The commissioner looked to the good will of the Treasury if he desired an increase in his appropriation. The Treasury required his sympathetic ear

39. "First Report of the Public Service Commissioner, 1913," pp. 2–3.
40. "Report of Royal Commission on Native Affairs, 1934" (appendix to the *Journal of the House of Representatives*, G-11), p. 47.

if ever it wanted more or better staff. It suited them both to co-operate, and this normally happened. For the spending depart-ments, however, it was something of an advantage to deal with two distinct control agencies, instead of with one as in Britain. It was also a definite advantage to allocate the function of personnel administration to an agency which was not predisposed to view all problems from the angle of cost.

But the body toward which the public service commissioner stood in the most crucial relationship of all was the Public Service Association. It must be recalled that the commissionership was established in 1912 in response to the wishes of the public serv-ants themselves. In the main it was designed to protect their chances of a career. Prior to 1912 the Public Service Association had already sprung up as a kind of trade-union for the civil serv-ice; and while it was the need and pressure of the civil service that brought the Public Service Commissioner's Office into be-ing, the establishment of that office gave a further fillip to the as-sociation, since the commissioner found it convenient to deal with one body that represented the rank and file. Since then the associ-ation has developed into a compact and powerful bloc, contain-ing over 90 per cent of the public servants and equally influential on the commissioner and the government.

In general, the considerations which have governed the rela-tion between the commissioner and the Public Service Associa-tion can be thus described. From the public servants themselves has come the political support for commissioner control of the service. For political reasons, therefore, any commissioner was bound to heed the wishes of the association, since it provided the main prop of his office. The association, for its part, depended on the preservation of the commissioner's powers through which political influence over recruitment and promotion was supposed-ly excluded. Each had, therefore, to work along with the other. Yet it was not always in the interests of either party that their concord should appear entirely harmonious. In order to satisfy their own members that they were being active, the executive and the general secretary of the association had from time to time to prefer requests to the commissioner and receive conces-sions from him. On his side, the commissioner, while often acceding to their requests, must not grant every point, or he might seem to be dominated by the association. Only rarely would an occasion arise for a real conflict between the two. An example of this did occur from 1939 to 1941, when the then commissioner sought to institute "efficiency tests," to certain features of which the association objected. Here was a controversy that came to deadlock and was more than once referred to the prime minister for settlement. But one further point should be noted. Even during such a conflict it was never the aim of either the commissioner or the association to push their differences to extremes. The commissioner, if he seriously antagonized the association, would weaken the basis of his power. And the association, if it thoroughly discredited the commissioner, would endanger its own greatest safeguard. Thus the relations between the two formed an amicable marriage, conducted according to tacitly understood rules and interspersed with occasional sparring bouts that were quite pretty to watch. The commissioner and the association might dicker, but they would never be divorced.

In a partnership, however, as in wedlock, it is always possible that one member may gradually take the lead at the expense of the other. Something of this nature did occur during the decade 1936–46. Reasons may be found in the relative strength of the personalities in the commissionership and the association and in the predilection of the Labor government for the claims of trade-unions. Thus in 1936, when the post of commissioner had to be filled, it was the association which objected to the appointment of a certain person as single commissioner and persuaded the government to put two joint commissioners in office, one of whom had the association's backing. In 1938, when the whole of the Public Service was regraded and its personnel were being interviewed, one of the joint commissioners toured all the cities and towns outside the capital in the company of the association's general-secretary. In 1944 it was on the urging of the association that the government appointed a joint consultative committee, with representatives of the commissioner and the association, to review the salary scale and the classification plan of the service. Finally, in 1946, an election year, it was the association which again persuaded the government to substitute a three-membered

commission for one lone commissioner. Their proposal was motivated partly by the desire to sidetrack the promotion of a certain official to the supreme rank and partly by the wish to have a
nominee of their own included in the tripartite commission.

Without unduly prejudging the new system, one may fairly
suggest that the change initiated in 1946 was a retrograde step.
In Britain the personnel management of the civil service comes
under the jurisdiction of one person, and the same is true of the
Commonwealth government in Australia. In the United States,
although the commission form still abounds, modern thinking
among authorities on personnel reveals a trend in favor of a single
staff executive[41] on the ground that a positive policy is more likely to be prosecuted. On the basis of New Zealand experience one
must concede that having a single commissioner will not necessarily
produce a positive administration and that the change to a commission marked the climax of a steady decrease in the authority
of the office. This deterioration was due largely to the personal attributes of successive commissioners, to their inadequate insight
into the needs of their job, or to weakness of character in pressing
their ideas. But it has yet to be proved that a commission will do
better.

A glance at the internal structure of the Public Service Commissioner's Office will offer ready proof of the aloof and negative
attitude which the central personnel agency tended to adopt toward the departments in its jurisdiction. Take the figures for the
financial year 1938–39, which marked the close of the period of
pre-war growth. Bear in mind that the commissioner then bore
the responsibility for promoting the welfare and efficiency of
some sixteen thousand officials distributed among over forty departments. Yet the staff of the commissioner's office numbered
only forty-five persons, and upon analysis even that exiguous
figure shrinks to incredible smallness. Let us take into account
only the controlling officials with administrative responsibility
who shared in the formulation of policy. They were the following:
the public service commissioner himself, the secretary of the
office, three inspectors, a superintendent of staff training, a chief

41. See my article, "Overhead Organisation of Central Personnel Agencies in
America," (*New Zealand*) *Journal of Public Administration*, IV, No. 1 (1941), 19–35.

clerk, and a women's inspector.[42] Eight persons to interpret and apply the Public Service Act to sixteen thousand civil servants! Surely it is self-evident that eight would be a ludicrously inadequate number to launch a personnel policy which aimed at being creative and constructive. The plain truth is that successive commissioners kept their staff below the bare minimum because a more positive policy was not to their wish. Equally striking is to translate this truth into terms of hard cash. In 1939 the total appropriation for the office amounted to £13,000—and that after the office had been operating for twenty-seven years. Was not that a niggardly allowance for the central staff management of sixteen thousand persons?

Even during the war, when added burdens were thrown upon the office, its administration, though it did grow, was still not fully commensurate with the need. In 1946 the Public Service had expanded to a total of 26,500 persons. The commissioner's office had a staff of eighty-five, only eleven of whom shared the responsibility for policy. The appropriation had risen to £30,000. Only in the field of training did the activities of the office show any genuine progress.

Nor should it be forgotten that, although the employees of the state are scattered throughout New Zealand, the commissioner's office and staff has been completely centralized in Wellington. In no other city, not even in Auckland, with over two thousand public servants, did the commissioner have a branch. All staff changes in districts outside the capital had to be referred to the capital for authority and approval. For information about the service in other cities the commissioner relied on the reports of his few and overworked inspectors who periodically made hurried trips from place to place. He was also partially assisted by some senior officials of other departments who, in addition to their ordinary work, represented his office in cities like Auckland and Christchurch and carried out specific tasks (e.g., interviewing prospective applicants for jobs). Apart from these slight exceptions, the fact remains that the personnel administration of the Public Service was concentrated in one city and managed by

42. The other thirty-seven consisted of clerks, typists, cadets, etc., none of whom participated in determining policy.

a handful of people for a parsimonious outlay.[43] Lastly, let it be added that the commissioners neglected to provide their office with a library and a research section on personnel matters. No concerted effort was made to keep abreast of staff developments overseas, nor was any member of the staff assigned to the duty of searching the current literature and latest reports for new ideas and new techniques.

The Functions of Personnel Administration

If such has been the organization of the central personnel agency, what are its functions and how were these carried out? Analyzing the various processes of personnel administration under the headings of classification, recruitment, education and training, and promotion, let us see how these have been managed in New Zealand.

It is necessary to take the system of classification first, since that constitutes the master-plan regulating the structure of the service. The arrangement into divisions and classes formalizes the relationship between positions and maps out the careers and lines of promotion to which public servants may aspire. The Public Service Act and its amendments provide for five divisions, called the administrative, clerical, professional, educational, and general. The administrative division, the highest in the hierarchy, comprised in 1946 the permanent head of every department, his deputy in six departments and, in one case, his second assistant. The salaries of members of this division are appropriated individually by Parliament. The clerical division ranges from high executive officials down to minor clerks and newly recruited cadets. Its salary scale extended in 1946 from £125 up to £1,000. In the professional division the commissioner was empowered by the Public Service Act to place anyone "whose duties involve special skill or technical knowledge usually acquired only in some profession or occupation different from the ordinary routine of the Public Service."[44] That is a clause which leaves room for a fairly

43. Since the commissioner was replaced by a commission, the top personnel of the office has been expanded. In 1947 three assistant commissioners were appointed, of whom one—at last!—is stationed in Auckland.

44. Public Service Act, sec. 20 (1).

wide discretion, but has in practice been applied to cover doctors, engineers, chemists, physicists, agricultural scientists, and some kindred groups. The educational division is somewhat anomalous, since it is composed of the teachers in the correspondence and native schools and a few other special schools which the state maintains.[45] The general division, lastly, takes in the residue. These are mostly technical and specialized persons who are not included in the professional division as well as a large class of manual workers, messengers, typists, and other subordinate ranks. In the professional division, salaries in 1946 ranged, as in the clerical division, between £125 and £1,000. Those of the educational and general divisions varied slightly. If the figures of the Public Service for the year 1939 be taken, these five divisions contained the following numbers: administrative, 39; clerical, 5,200; professional, 700; educational, 80; general, 3,900.

The total of the numbers just stated is under 10,000. The discrepancy is due to the fact that the figure 10,000 comprises only those with a permanent status. The remainder were temporaries. Despite the dangerous precedent which had been set under the Liberal regime, the Public Service Act of the Reform party did allow some provision for the engagement of temporary employees. It permitted these to be appointed for three months. There was, however, a loophole in the law[46] through which such temporaries could be reappointed and continuously retained in the service of the state. During the last quarter of a century ample use has been made of that opportunity, and in 1939 the service contained roughly 6,000 temporaries as against 10,000 permanents. Many of these temporaries were recruited since Labor came to power in 1936 to cope with the expansion of governmental activities. But many hundreds had seen over fifteen years of continuous service, being reappointed every three months. A large proportion of these temporaries consisted of women (or "female officers" as the Public Service is pleased to designate them). As will be emphasized later, in order to prevent women

45. Teachers in other state schools form a separate career service organized under the director of education. Officials of the Education Department are placed in the professional, clerical, or general division but not in the educational!

46. Sec. 45 (5).

from being promoted to the highest positions, it was found a convenient device to accord them only a temporary status. This glaring anomaly of "permanent temporaries" has in recent years proved as bad under the commissioner system as it was prior to 1912. The war intensified a problem that was already serious, so that by 1945 almost three-fifths of the public servants had temporary status.

Besides being grouped into five divisions and segregated into permanents and temporaries, the Public Service is further subdivided into classes within the divisions. Thus in 1946 the clerical and professional divisions both fell into seven classes, each stratum being assigned its upper and lower salary limits. The top one was named "Special." The rest, proceeding downward, were numbered consecutively from 1 to 6. Class 6, the lowest on the scale, had a top salary limit of £400. In 1939 there were 2,500 public servants in the bottom class of the clerical division, and 70 in the corresponding professional grade. Almost all the new recruits to the Public Service enter into this class. Thence they begin the long stiff pull up the hilly road to a permanent headship.

Such a classification system, as is evident, has nothing in common with the organization of the administrative class in the British Civil Service. The New Zealand civil service, in fact, has been based upon principles more analogous to those of Australia or of the United States. The Dominion insists, as a fundamental of her public service policy, upon the absence of any equivalent to the administrative class for entry into which an advanced educational qualification is required. It is this feature of its classification plan which has determined the methods of recruitment as well as the provisions for education (pre-entry and post-entry) and in-service training. The Public Service Act permits recruitment to the clerical division between the ages of fifteen and forty.[47] In practice the general custom prescribed by the commissioner's regulations has been to recruit new appointees with the status of cadets. Until 1931 the average age of these cadets was usually around seventeen. After 1935 more cadets were appointed at higher ages up to twenty-one. For appointment to the clerical division the normal peacetime rule of recent years has been re-

47. Sec. 41 (1).

cruitment under twenty-one; recruitment over twenty-one was the rare exception.

In the professional division the same rule, in general, applies; but, because of the need for technical and professional knowledge, the proportion of exceptions is inevitably higher. Recruitment policy in any particular year or decade will depend upon a variety of considerations. The decision of the ministry to expand or to contract the activities of government; the competing demands of business, industry, and the professions; the necessity to conciliate those who already belong to the Public Service—these and other factors determine the number of recruits to be brought in and the positions to which they are to be allocated. Table 22 shows the

TABLE 22

APPOINTMENT OF PUBLIC SERVICE CADETS, 1920–39

For Year Ended March 31	No. of Cadets Appointed	For Year Ended December 31	No. of Cadets Appointed
1920...........	318	1932...........	3
1922...........	170	1933...........	146
1924...........	336	1934...........	207
1926...........	338	1936...........	580
1928...........	167	1938...........	583
1930...........	256	1939...........	711
1931...........	92		

number of cadets appointed in different years between the two world wars. This table tells a clear story—the fairly high rate of recruitment immediately after the first war, the slackening-off during the slump of 1922–23, the return to the former rate during the prosperous years of the mid-twenties, the tapering-away as the depression loomed near, the virtual cessation of recruitment during the depression, and then, after 1935, the unprecedented expansion up to the record figure for the year 1939.

The educational standard that can be required of these recruits at the time of entrance has naturally been correlated to their age and to the prevailing demand for new staff. During the history of the commissioner's office, the minimum qualification for employment has been a passing mark in the Public Service Entrance Examination, which corresponds to three years' work at a secondary school. In the depression this examination was dropped; for, when so few cadets were recruited, the educational standard could be set higher. But, to cope with the increased demand after 1935, it was reintroduced. Preference in appointment, however, was given to applicants whose educational qualifications exceeded the minimum. Thus various examinations were rated above the Public Service Entrance Examination in order of difficulty: the School-leaving Certificate, obtainable after four years of secondary school; the University Entrance Examination; the University Entrance Examination or School Certificate and a Higher Leaving Certificate; the University Entrance Scholarship Examination with credit; a portion of a degree or a pass in two or more subjects of a professional examination—all representing less than the full completion of a university or professional course. During the years 1937 and 1938, cadets recruited into the clerical and professional divisions possessed the qualifications listed in Table 23.

In addition to these young recruits, whose education in nearly all cases had not advanced beyond secondary-school standard, some university graduates and holders of professional diplomas are also admitted to the Public Service. For the decade 1928–39 these totaled as many as 451, of whom 280 were appointed after April, 1936.[48] Upon analysis of these graduate recruits, the important conclusion emerges that exactly two-thirds of the number were scientists holding degrees in physics, chemistry, agriculture, medicine, and kindred subjects. The increasing demand for highly qualified specialists could be met only by appointing men who had taken their degrees or studied for their profession before entering the Public Service. Less than 100 out of the 451 held degrees in the liberal arts or in the social sciences.

The civil service, however, requires far more officials with a higher education than are represented in the number of those recruited after graduation. The hundreds of young cadets who enter the service at the scholastic level of the University Entrance Examination are therefore encouraged to continue their studies after they are appointed. It is the well-accepted practice for public servants to seek a university degree or a professional diploma

48. "Twenty-sixth Report of the Public Service Commissioner, 1938," p. 13.

as part-time students, working in their department during the
day and attending lectures and libraries in the evening. This
habit has received enthusiastic support from successive commissioners, who injected a pecuniary stimulus by conferring on those
who pass their examinations a special salary raise known as a
"double increment."[49] Yet another incentive for the pursuit of a
degree is the desire for promotion from the lowest class. Before
an official can move into the next class, he must satisfy a test of
efficiency by passing some examination of higher standard than

TABLE 23

QUALIFICATIONS OF PUBLIC SERVICE CADETS RECRUITED
IN CLERICAL AND PROFESSIONAL DIVISIONS
IN 1937 AND 1938

EDUCATIONAL STANDARD	YEAR RECRUITED	
	1937	1938
Public Service Entrance........................	....	144
School-leaving Certificate.....................	40	63
University Entrance Examination.............	493	318
Higher Leaving Certificate...................	52	43
University Scholarship Examination with credit.	2	2
Portion of degree or professional course........	51	13
Total.....................................	638	583

the minimum for entrance. A degree or a professional diploma enables its holder to hurdle this promotion bar. Such a very material bait has landed an abnormal catch of degrees. Table 24 represents, over twenty-five years, the grand total of all permanent
officials with degrees or diplomas, whether obtained before or
after entry.

Covering a quarter of a century, these figures illustrate both
the strength and the weakness of the civil service. They depict the
overwhelming predominance of men whose education is specialized and professional. Almost every year the several groups of
scientists, lawyers, and engineers have outnumbered the arts
graduates. Since the depression particularly, public servants have

49. It should be mentioned that "pot-hunters" are wisely discouraged by a
regulation which prohibits the grant of a double increment to any person more
than once.

rushed to take a commerce degree or an accountancy certificate. In 1938 the holders of these degrees and certificates formed one-third of the total, while scientists and engineers together formed another third. This emphasis on professional studies is largely the result of deliberate official policy. Successive commissioners complained of the shortage of specialists and have sought to increase the supply. Inefficiency in handling accounts, for example, met with severe stricture from the Hunt Commission, and the lack of qualified accountants was a serious weakness of the service during the early years of the commissioner's regime. An early

TABLE 24

PERMANENT PUBLIC SERVICE OFFICIALS HOLDING
DEGREES OR DIPLOMAS, 1913–38

Qualification	1913	1918	1923	1928	1933	1938
B.A., M.A....................	17	57	75	88	108	174
B.Sc., M.Sc., etc...............	19	49	63	101	133	256
Law professional, LL.B., LL.M....	47	77	135	166	222	282
Accountants, B.Com., M.Com....	22	57	150	187	348	665
Engineering and surveying diplo-						
mas, etc.....................	136	156	219	229	271	392
Miscellaneous.................	33	35	52	79	94	148
Total....................	274	431	694	850	1,176	1,917

report stated: "In many cases, it has been found that officers in charge of accounts have not received a proper training in accountancy. . . . . The Commissioners consider that this important matter should be taken up by the Treasury, and that a start should be made this year by the appointment of a number of cadets of special educational attainments, who are prepared to qualify in and follow accountancy."[50] Other professions, such as those of civil engineer, telegraph engineer, chemist, bacteriologist, and actuary, were likewise in demand among particular government departments, and study in these subjects was encouraged.

It thus became an accepted policy to offer special concessions to those seeking a professional education. In 1914 a course of physics lectures for telegraph engineers was specially inaugurated

50. "Fourth Report of the Public Service Commissioner, 1916," p. 3.

at Victoria University College[51] in Wellington. A more ambitious program to train civil engineers for the Public Works Department was later introduced. Combining a university education with thorough practical experience, this program extended over six years of work in the office, in the field, and at the engineering school of Canterbury University College.[52] Other specialized fields were catered for in the twenties and early thirties so as to provide the Agriculture Department with graduates in agricultural and veterinary science. More recently still a training plan was inaugurated for valuers (appraisers)—a profession previously neglected but indispensable to at least three agencies, the State Advances Corporation, the Lands and Survey Department, and the Valuation Department itself. Thus, there was instituted a postgraduate course in rural valuation and farm management at Lincoln Agricultural College, and a companion course in urban valuation at Auckland University College in conjunction with the school of architecture. It was a common feature of nearly all these schemes that young public servants were selected and sent to study their respective subjects as holders of scholarships which the government provided.

So actively, however, did public service commissioners for twenty years stimulate professional education that they eventually found it an embarrassment to place or utilize the graduates in liberal arts. This was avowed in plain terms as recently as 1938: "While the Commissioners encourage officers in many ways to undertake university studies, there are comparatively few opportunities of admitting to the Public Service students who have secured what may be termed a 'cultural' degree. There are wide and varied careers open to the specialist-degree holder, as medicine, engineering, law, commerce, and science; in fact in some few of these we are short of recruits."[53] Such testimony confirms the disadvantages from which holders of nonprofessional degrees have suffered. So urgently were specialists needed that scholarships were established for public servants to devote full-time

51. One of the six constituent colleges which together make up the federal university of New Zealand.
52. "Ninth Report of the Public Service Commissioner, 1921," pp. 9–10.
53. "Twenty-sixth Report of the Public Service Commissioner, 1938," p. 13.

study to various fields, while professional graduates who had not previously belonged to the service were eagerly welcomed. But no opportunities then existed for even the best clerical officers to take a "cultural" degree full time. Nor was it feasible, apparently, to fit an arts graduate into the administrative scheme of things. This ill-balanced policy was neither equitable nor wise. It concentrated on obtaining good technicians and paid little heed to the nonspecialized. It gave advantages to the best in certain groups which it denied to the best in others. Yet the tasks of general administration require a broader outlook than a professional degree alone can impart. If full-time study at the university was necessary for specialists, surely it was equally desirable for those who co-ordinated the technical skills of the experts. Prevailing tradition, however, considered a part-time education adequate for arts subjects and glossed over the cramming and the physical and mental strain which that entails.

This tradition was an unfortunate consequence of the New Zealand conception of democracy. It has its roots in the colonial antagonism toward the principle of an administrative class on the British model. New Zealanders have generally condemned the mode of recruitment to this class as undemocratic, and this attitude is mirrored in the commissioner's reports: "Although there is provision under the Public Service Act for the Commissioner to make special appointments to the Public Service in particular cases of persons holding University degrees or other special qualification, a cardinal feature of the New Zealand Public Service is promotion wherever practicable from within the Service and equal opportunity for all, merit, and merit alone, being the determining factor. The avenues of promotion are open to all officers who are qualified, and in this respect the New Zealand Public Service is more democratic than the English Civil Service, where all the higher positions are restricted to University trained men."[54] The same theme is further elaborated: "New Zealand is essentially a democratic country, and no practice which might be

54. "Eighteenth Report of the Public Service Commissioner, 1930," p. 4. It is not true that in Britain "all the higher positions are restricted to University trained men." From 1923 to 1935 nearly one-third of the new appointees to the administrative class were promoted from the executive or clerical class (see Herman Finer *The British Civil Service* [London: Allen & Unwin, 1937], p. 76).

inferred to give an undue advantage to those who can afford to
continue full-time studies at a University is likely to meet with
general approval. Due consideration must be given to the claims
of those already in the Service, who in their spare time attend a
University College and graduate therefrom."[55]

In her passion to be democratic, New Zealand sometimes carries to excess her own basic principle to equalitarianism. Is it
fair, ask the graduates of the university, to discourage men from
the service merely because they were not already members while
they were taking their degrees? Should not the Public Service
draw on all available sources of talent? Should it not also extend
to its nonprofessional members the opportunity of full-time study?
In fact, in her reaction against the mother-country, New Zealand
has overlooked the undeniable merits of the administrative class.
The charge that it is undemocratic to recruit that class principally
from graduates is really a criticism of the underlying educational
system, not of the method of recruitment per se. The remedy lies
in equalizing opportunities of entrance to the universities, not in
lowering the standard of entrance to the administrative class.
This defect apart, the British administrative class embodies excellent principles; first, that there is a function of general administration; second, that a good university preparation for that
function consists in subjects which "open, invigorate, and enrich
the mind";[56] third, that future administrative leaders must be
given early in-service training on responsible work. Any suggestion that New Zealand imitate some aspect of the administrative
class at once runs afoul of strong antipathy to the British method
of recruitment. Hostility against the one feature has colored the
attitude toward the others. Let it be proposed in New Zealand
that the function of general administration requires persons of
advanced education who should constitute a separate division
within the service and be trained early for their future responsibilities; assuredly the Public Service Association will assail this in-
sidious advocacy of a privileged class. Or intimate that a greater
number of the university's best graduates in arts could be absorbed with benefit to the service; back may come the retort that

55. "Twenty-first Report of the Public Service Commissioner, 1933," p. 4.
56. This is Macaulay's phrase.

they are hard to place or that the interests of those who joined earlier must be safeguarded. In general, those who have joined the service at the age of eighteen or under have felt that they had a prior claim on opportunities for promotion and have sought to exclude the holders of nonprofessional degrees.

Let us view some of the consequences of this system. Almost without exception, the members of the professional division hold a university degree or some professional diploma or certificate. In the clerical division the majority lack a qualification that represents the same standard of scholastic attainment.[57] Since the highest administrative positions may legally be filled by the members of either division, there is often a conflict between the professional and clerical sides in the struggle for promotion. In certain departments it is well settled, by practice rather than by law, that the head posts are reserved to the professionally qualified. Only engineers, for instance, rise to the top in the Public Works Department, and only a scientist has headed the department of Scientific and Industrial Research. Other agencies, however, offer a happy hunting ground to clerical officials and keep the professional men in a subordinate status. The most striking example of this latter tendency occurs in an agency which lies outside the jurisdiction of the public service commissioner—that composite and variegated body, the Post and Telegraph Department. There the clerical officials who fill the mails and accounts branches rigidly exclude from the supreme directive posts the highly qualified engineers who administer the telegraph and telephone systems. Where the clerical side predominates, it justifies its ascendancy with the argument that a department's policies should not be determined by mere specialists. Where the professional side rules the roost, it claims that the nonspecialized cannot properly supervise and direct the work of experts. Is this anything else than an effort by each of two distinct groups to make promotion its own vested interest?

Another consequence of the New Zealand practice can be traced in its effect on the university. From the irrefutable premise

57. In the clerical division in 1939 some five hundred had an accountancy certificate. Others had degrees which they obtained by part-time study at the university. A small minority were recruited to the service after completing their university course.

that a democratic university must be open to intellect not to wealth, the Dominion deduced that anyone unable to afford full-time study must be permitted to take a degree part time. The wiser conclusion would have been to provide all who deserve it with means for full-time study. Inevitably the preponderance of part-time students has lowered the academic standard. Hence there is a continual tug between the university faculty, who desire to raise their standard, and groups in the community seeking to lower it and thereby make the examinations safe for part-timers. Among the most important of such pressure groups is the Public Service itself, whose influence with the government cannot be ignored by a state-supported university. The university has often argued that part-time study cannot produce the best educational results and that the Public Service has not sought to attract enough of its best graduates. Scarcely one of New Zealand's former Rhodes scholars, for instance, has been appointed to a government department.[58] The public service commissioner did not offer them a salary high enough to induce them to enter, since this might be resented by the hundreds already in the service who were being paid less.

In such matters as the educational and promotion policies of the Public Service there is no impasse but thinking makes it so. The age-old controversy over the virtues of laymen or experts, broached long ago by Plato in the *Protagoras*, is now formalized into a contest between professional and clerical officials for permanent headships. If the clerical officer denies that a man of narrow specialization can grasp the implications of general management, the true solution is not on that account to deny a chance of promotion to any professional officials but to broaden their education and training. Conversely, when the latter seek to keep on top of the clerical men because most of these possess lower educational attainments, the remedy is surely to educate both groups

58. "The standard of salaries in the New Zealand Public Service," stated the commissioner in 1933, "in comparison with that obtaining in commercial undertakings, the teaching service, and in positions in other countries is very low. . . . . This is evidenced by the fact that not one New Zealand Rhodes Scholar has been attracted to the New Zealand Public Service although inquiries have been made from several as to whether they would be prepared to accept appointment" ("Twenty-first Report of the Public Service Commissioner, 1933," p. 5). One did accept subsequently.

to an equivalent intellectual level. In a word, the primary qualification for the holder of a high departmental post is his administrative capacity. Under that phrase I would include not only the ability to organize a system and manage the human beings who operate it but also the possession of a wide range of knowledge and deep social insight. It is both unwise and inequitable to exclude from an equal chance of promotion any group which may yield a supply of administrative capacity. It is wrong for either the professionally qualified or the clerical officers to grasp a monopoly of the high posts in the hierarchy. Nor is it any less indefensible for those who enter the service at eighteen or under to impose curbs on the recruitment of others who prefer to graduate first before joining a department.

The beginning—but only the beginning—of a solution along the right lines was found in 1940, when a special course for a diploma in public administration was inaugurated under my direction at the Victoria University College of the New Zealand University. Of postgraduate standard, this course includes subjects from the fields of political science, economics, and law, together with a close attention to the problems of public administration. The syllabus is intended as a liberal education in the issues of modern government rather than a specialized instruction in administrative technique. It comprises, as well as a thoroughgoing analysis of New Zealand problems, a comparative study of other countries, thus seeking to supplement the narrow confines of the Dominion's own limited experience. For the first time in the history of the New Zealand government, students were selected from the civil service[59] and granted scholarships for two years of full-time university study in social science. The scholars were chosen by a representative committee after applications had been invited from all departments. The requirements for selection included both academic ability and the qualities of character which would indicate the potentialities of future administrative leadership. During two and a half years from 1940 to 1942, twenty students in all, drawn from a wide variety of departments,

59. Although the scholarship scheme was fostered by the Public Service Commissioner's Office, trainees were selected from the Railways and the Post and Telegraph departments as well.

attended this course. The number was such that the proper educational methods of individual tutorials and seminar discussions could be applied. When the manpower crisis following on Japan's entry into the war compelled the temporary cessation of the scheme, the scholars who returned to their departmental posts fully justified their own selection and the principles on which the course was designed. With the return of peace the course was recontinued in 1947.

But this course in public administration was not the only means adopted for discovering and equipping the higher administrators of the future. It is evident that, by itself, no university syllabus can produce an administrator. The university can widen a circumscribed outlook. It can impart a much-needed insight into the social purposes served by the machinery of state. It can supply the stock of knowledge and information which the civil servant requires both as an administrator and as a citizen. Traits of character must be developed and a fund of practical experience be acquired which the university alone cannot provide. Complementary to education, whether professional or nonspecialized, is the system of in-service training obtained on the job under the instruction of senior officials. Any personnel organization which omits either the education or the training of its staff is omitting an indispensable form of social insurance. Up to 1939, however, the several commissioners paid scant attention to in-service training. The text of the Public Service Act, while it devoted some sections to recruitment and examinations, ignored the allied topic of training. Nor was this defect properly rectified by the first set of regulations which the commissioner issued in 1913. Department heads were vaguely told that "the progress of every cadet must be carefully watched." Yet little was done to translate a benign intention into positive fact for the simple reason that no one in the Public Service Commissioner's Office was specifically charged with the responsibility for training. Training was an area within the personnel domain claimed by formal proclamation to be under the commissioner's sovereignty. But a quarter of a century saw no sign of effective occupation.

In-service training, therefore, was relegated to the departments and varied according to the interest or apathy of each undersecretary. A few agencies, such as the Public Works Department, have instituted programs of their own for giving thorough practical experience to new recruits. The best organized of all such schemes was the one found in the Public Trust Office in the late twenties.[60] A proper staff training school was established to which young officials of the department were brought from all over New Zealand. They were placed under the care of qualified instructors, and their time was divided between lectures and study and practical administrative work. But, when the depression came, the training school was considered an expensive luxury which had to be discontinued in the interests of economy. Such efforts of the Public Trust Office and the handful of other agencies which cared to train their recruits should not be regarded as typical. Most departments made no systematic attempts to train the tyros. The early years of a young public servant's career were normally devoted to monotonous routine, a graveyard for his enthusiasm and initiative. Much of the blame lies with department heads, whose general apathy toward the need for training has been notorious. Some of the more conservative, remembering that they had received no formal training, were content to prolong into the future a system which had produced such men as themselves. Others rationalized the value of initiation by routine with the "democratic" argument that a future undersecretary must climb every rung of the ladder, not omitting to start at the very lowest. Such attitudes accorded well with the accompanying belief that for nonprofessional studies a part-time education sufficed. A day devoted to office minutiae could be suitable terminated with an evening of cram. Harmonious wedlock of training by routine and education by rote!

Not until 1939 did a freshly appointed commissioner undertake to care for in-service training and to raise the laggard departments to the level of the progressive. To give teeth to the principle that the training of every recruit would henceforth be planned by the central personnel agency, the commissioner created the new post of superintendent of staff training, a sign that the former policy of laissez faire was to be abandoned. Under energetic di-

60. See *Report of the Public Trustee* (Parliamentary Paper, B-9 [Wellington, 1926]), p. 23, and *ibid.* (1927), p. 21.

rection a comprehensive staff training plan, to be supervised from the commissioner's office and administered by the departments, was prepared. In each department a personnel officer was appointed to act in liaison with the superintendent of staff training. The departments under the commissioner's jurisdiction were divided into eleven groups, each group comprising agencies whose functions were akin and each being large enough to provide a varied administrative experience and offer an attractive career. Intensive training programs were then devised to suit the needs of the different groups. The objective was to insure to each trainee a broad knowledge of the several branches of his own department and of other agencies whose functions were closely connected. Thereby each recruit was to be under continuous observation from the time of appointment, and any special talent which displayed itself could be stimulated and developed. The ablest would be earmarked for promotion, the incompetents would be weeded out, and the misfits would be transferred. Such in general terms was the program inaugurated to compensate for a quarter of a century's neglect. This scheme was actually commenced in 1939 and 1940 with beneficial results and has been greatly expanded since 1945. The urgencies of rehabilitation have, of course, injected a new stimulus into the problems of training and retraining.

Without a sound educational policy and a thorough training scheme no personnel agency can properly apply the principle of merit in deciding promotions. Among the departments that comprise the Public Service it is the commissioner's office which has promoted men to higher positions. The commissioner's information has been derived from two sources. One is the periodic inspection of all departments conducted by members of his own staff. Each inspector is assigned a group of agencies which he must supervise; and every few years he is placed in charge of a different group so that eventually he acquires a knowledge of the whole service. The system would have worked well enough if only the commissioner had had more inspectors and if his office had been decentralized outside Wellington. As it was, the few inspectors available were so pressed for time that their visits both to the head offices in the capital and to branches elsewhere were perforce hurried and inadequate. The remedy is the simple one of appointing more inspectors, of whom one should be stationed in Auckland and one in Christchurch.

The second source of information is contained in the reports on each official which are furnished annually by the permanent head of every department to the public service commissioner. A reliable system of reports is essential to a career service which claims devotion to the principle of merit. How effectively the system operates will depend on the content of the report form itself and on the objectivity with which it is administered. Good reporting is a desideratum far from being achieved in the governmental administration of New Zealand. For over two decades a most unsatisfactory form of report was in use. Its content was poor, since it required a numerical appraisal of such vague generalities as "temperament," "conduct," "general culture." Its usefulness was further marred by lack of judgment on the part of those who filled in the reports. Certain permanent heads, being either too lenient in their standards or predisposed to view their geese as swans, grossly overrated the average quality of their staff and threw on the inspectors of the public service commissioner the difficult task of correlating the divergent averages of separate agencies. Other heads frankly assessed quality in terms of seniority, arguing that the experience born of long service (even if it were in a rut) was an index of efficiency. Again, as the commissioner had to state officially, "the tendency in many Departments has been to mark officers in direct ratio to their status— that is to say, Class I and higher officers were marked at 80 or over (out of 100), Class III and Class II officers at 70 or over, and so on in a descending scale."[61]

In 1943 a new type of report form was adopted which represented some improvement over the previous one but still left much to be desired. On the new form public servants are now rated out of a maximum of five points for each of fifteen "personal characteristics" (e.g., initiative, judgment, power to control staff, etc.). They are also assessed at a maximum of fifty points for quantity of work and another fifty for quality. The revised form suffers from some of the same vagueness as appeared in

61. Official circular from the Public Service Commissioner, No. 1943/20.

the old, and many of the items on which a numerical rating is required seem to overlap.[62] But the instructions which accompanied the form when it was distributed to permanent heads decidedly marked a step forward. The Commissioner's official circular concluded with these sentences: "It cannot be too strongly emphasised that annual reports have become a vital factor in the selection of officers for promotion. This fact should be kept continuously in mind by Permanent Heads and Controlling Officers. On the impartiality and the courage they display in marking officers will depend to a great extent the future efficiency of the Public Service." Courage has been sadly lacking in the past, for the simple reason that the person reported on is entitled to see the assessment of his superior. In fact, the back of the Public Service report, in the new as well as in the old version, reads as a series of retorts, rejoinders, accusations, and explanations. The form provides a space for the officer on whom the report is furnished to comment on the rating assigned to him; then a space for his controller to reply to that; next a further reply by the reportee; and finally, a summing-up by the permanent head. Quite a miniature diplomatic correspondence!

The procedure governing promotions is outlined in the Public Service Act and in an amending act passed in 1927. Everything is designed to accord to every employee a fair chance of having his qualifications considered whenever a vacancy occurs for which he would be eligible. All vacancies and appointments are publicly listed in an official circular which is printed monthly and is passed around every department. If there is a vacancy to a new or old position, the commissioner could fill it by the transfer or promotion of any member of the Public Service. When notifying of the existence of a vacancy, the commissioner could invite applications and state the qualifications needed. Of the applicants, "the most efficient and suitable" must be selected.[63] Against the decision of the commissioner an opportunity of appeal was allowed. The right of appeal is accorded to any unsuccessful applicant for a position to which applications were invited; or, if an appointment

62. E.g., "manner and temperament" and "personality"; "co-operativeness" and "adaptability"; "ability to delegate" and "organising capacity."
63. Public Service Amendment Act, 1927, sec. 8 (4).

was made without the inviting of applications, to anyone whose transfer to the vacancy would result in his promotion. An Appeal Board has been constituted under act of Parliament to hear appeals against any appointment, the onus being placed on the appellant to show positively that he was more suitable for the position in question that the commissioner's choice. It is the same board which has served as the tribunal to hear the cases of all officials who claim, but do not receive, a promotion on the classification list at the five-year intervals when the entire service is re-graded. The board is manned by three persons, one chosen by a vote among the public servants themselves and the other two appointed by the ministry on the commissioner's recommendation.

The chief characteristic of this whole procedure was its effort to protect the rights of public servants. The commissioner possessed a considerable degree of discretion, yet his powers are exercised with a constant eye to the Appeal Board. Each and every promotion must be justifiable before this tribunal. In practice, of all the appeals actually lodged, the majority were disallowed. But the value of the machinery was not to be measured merely by the small number of cases in which the commissioner's decision was reversed.[64] The true safeguard was to be found in the caution imposed on the commissioner and his inspectors.

A possibility of conflict could, and sometimes did, arise between the commissioner and the board if he and they should be wedded to different principles. Should promotion be determined by merit or by some other method? The law says by merit, but can this be always guaranteed and enforced? What are the threats which militate against the merit principle? More than one circumstance may in practice tend to violate the golden rule. Mere luck has brought many a mediocrity to the pinnacles of administrative power. Ministerial likes, based on grounds of personality or politics, may quicken the rise of others. At times, again, seniority will gild the careers of the undeserving. Of all these obstacles, seniority is the worst—for reasons that will be apparent to anyone who comprehends the ethos of an equalitarian democracy. The civil

64. The Appeal Board does not state the reasons for its decisions. When they overrode the commissioner, he was left in the dark as to the principles by which they were guided.

service contains tens of thousands of men and women who seek in it their life's career. But only few positions carry big salaries and confer great power. Democracy insists, and rightly, that all must be accorded an equal opportunity to reach the top and that the merits of the individual should pick the winners. Such is the ideal. But its application is influenced by two facts: the psychological one that the great majority of these tens of thousands are not fitted to occupy the highest responsibilities, and the political one that this majority, possessing voting power, can exert irresistible pressure through concerted action. Since the majority cannot rise by individual merit, they seek another principle which will increase their chances and find a ready alternative in the automatic operation of seniority. The government service necessarily contains innumerable positions requiring tedious and humdrum work which has to be done even though it cannot stimulate the performer. Many men and women seek in public employment not wealth (for they can sometimes get better pay elsewhere), or prestige (for the public servant in New Zealand is not singled out for especial social esteem), but the security of a sure job. Their prospects of advancement are those which T. S. Eliot has expressed in these deadly lines:

> Arthur Edward Cyril Parker is appointed telephone operator
> At a salary of one pound ten a week rising by annual increments
>   of five shillings
> To two pounds ten a week; with a bonus of thirty shillings at
>   Christmas
> And one week's leave a year.[65]

A personnel agency which shudders at elevating the commonplace will find that those who are unimportant singly are collectively powerful. The rank and file of the public servants gather strength by combination. Therein lies the political, and the administrative, significance of such a body as the Public Service Association. Undeniably many of the activities of this association are laudable and valuable. It has on many a matter protected the interests of the public servants, and it has enabled the commissioner to learn where the shoe pinched. But, in general, the collective policy of the association, as of the employee organizations in the

65. "Difficulties of a Statesman," *Collected Poems, 1909–35* (London: Faber & Faber, 1936), p. 137.

other personnel services, has tended to set a premium on seniority rather than on merit, on security rather than on efficiency.
The rank and file of their members are happiest if all go forward
at a regulated rate of promotion, just as the traffic moves in a city
where the street intersections have automatic lights. For anybody
to start off faster than the rest or slip through the lights is undemocratic. As for the plums, they must be distributed to as many as
possible. Permanent headships should be shared around for
senior officials to hold for one or two years prior to retirement.

To the five main personnel systems of the central government,
these points apply in varying degrees. For New Zealand, the
Post and Telegraph Department and the Railways are huge undertakings. Their branches and personnel are spread more extensively throughout the Dominion than those of any state enterprise except the public primary schools. They employ huge staffs,
of whom the great majority either perform manual labor or else
punctually observe the well-defined routine that is inevitable in a
continuous, night-and-day, service to the public. Their classification plans simply group their employees into two divisions, of
which the first corresponds to the clerical and professional divisions in the Public Service and the second to the general division.[66] Because their staffs are so large and because of the nature
of their work, these two departments recruit at an earlier age, and
consequently at a lower educational standard, than the Public
Service. The many departments of the Public Service carry out
more varied functions and contain relatively a higher proportion
of administrative posts than do the Railways and Post Office.
Hence the pick of the entrants to employment with the central
government usually gravitate to the Public Service.

Nevertheless, Post and Telegraph and Railways both depend
upon expert technicians for certain of their activities. These agencies have, for instance, sought the services of good engineers, of
whom some are recruited after graduation, while others, who are
recruited younger, are sent on governmental scholarships to study
at the university. Except for such professional qualifications,
these two departments have done little to encourage higher edu-

66. In 1939 the "first division" of the Railways contained 4,300 officials; that of
the Post Office, 3,300.

cation. Their staffs include, of course, a large number of accountants but very few holders of degrees in subjects other than science
and engineering.[67] Similarly in their in-service training programs, each department has taken trouble to train its technicians
and has even instituted special schools for this purpose. But training in general administration is little appreciated and still less attempted. In consequence the Railways and the Post Office are
usually headed by men who have grown up and served their
whole careers in a systematized clockwork routine. The staff
methods of both departments produce thoroughly reliable and
very efficient operators for a fairly mechanical undertaking.
Many of their employees—the postal clerks and ticket clerks, the
guards and the postmen—are schooled in direct contacts with the
public. They are well equipped to handle a multiplicity of forms,
to adjust the interlocking details, and to repeat the routine of a
complex administrative apparatus. Whether either agency encourages the use of imagination, stimulates inventiveness, or fosters a broad outlook is more dubious.

As its name reveals and its history indicates, the Post and Telegraph Department is a composite agency and provides one of the
few instances of amalgamation in New Zealand public administration. The telegraphic side (including telephones and radio) is
controlled by qualified engineers. These are responsible to a chief
engineer, who, originally the second man in the department,
now stands third or fourth in the hierarchy. The highest positions
are exclusively reserved, not by law but by custom, to the officials
who rise in the postal and savings-bank branches. Considerable
friction exists between the specialized, but well-educated, engi-

67. At the beginning of 1939 the following numbers of railway and postal employees held degrees or professional qualifications:

	Railways	Post and Telegraph
M.Sc. and B.Sc.	6	54
B.E.	7	1
M.Com. and B.Com.	6	4
M.A. and B.A.	1	1
LL.B. and law professional	5	....
Engineering diploma	86	27
Accountancy certificate	31	41
Surveying diploma	5	....
Total	147	128

neers, and the nontechnical, less-educated, clerical officials. Few in numbers, the engineers are qualitatively indispensable to the department. They are, however, overwhelmingly outvoted by the Post and Telegraph Employees' Association and Officers' Guild, which is the trade-union of this branch of the central government service. For the same reason, the engineers carry less weight with the minister to whom for matters of staff administration the director-general is responsible. It is votes that matter most in so large an organization directly subject to a political head; and, although its personnel system is formally dedicated to the principle of merit, actually an undue weight is attached to the factor of seniority desired by the bulk of the employees themselves.

The personnel practices of the Railways Department are superior to those of the Post and Telegraph in one important feature and are definitely inferior in another. The engineers of the Railways Department do enjoy relatively a higher status than their telegraphic confrères. They are not excluded from promotion to the topmost jobs. Of recent years, in fact, an engineer rose to be general manager. In other respects, however, the staff system of the Railways is woeful to behold, since it is wedded unashamedly to the principle of seniority. For this defect the principal blame must rest with the departmental trade-union, called the Railway Officers Institute,[68] which frankly disavows merit. Hampered by the policies of this politically potent body, and by the rigidity of the employee classification system, the general manager of the Railways is hard put to it to promote the meritorious. Since the Institute is represented on the board which hears appeals on questions of promotion, and since he is directly subject to a minister, the general manager can seldom, if ever, give rapid promotion "out of his turn" to a young man who shows promise.

To turn to the personnel policy of the police force is to reiterate the same complaints. In relation to the other branches of the central government's employees, the police have been poorly paid. That is the fundamental reason why the force cannot attract a superior type of recruit. It has to content itself with men of steady character, of good physique, but of mediocre intellectual abilities,

---

68. This is the trade-union of the clerical officials. There are other and bigger unions for the thousands of manual workers employed on the railways.

to whom security, the uniform, and the wielding of certain legal powers provide an attraction. The administrative system of this department could not be described as progressive. Successive commissioners have normally been appointed at an age when all they sought in the supreme office was a quiet niche before retirement. Seniority has been rampant in governing promotions and has appealed, since it is safe and automatic, to the majority among the rank and file. There are, however, some encouraging signs that a new spirit is stirring the Police Association and may eventually develop into a reformist drive.

Last to be mentioned of the five personnel services are the teachers in the state primary and secondary schools. The history of educational organization in New Zealand is told in the growth of centralizing uniformity at the expense of local diversities. Ever since the first Education Act was passed in 1877, the tendency has been to strengthen the central controls and whittle down the powers of the local education boards and school boards which still survive as relics of the former provincial autonomy. Nowadays in the forties, with the transfer of power to the central department not yet fully completed, the system still hovers in an intermediate limbo between centralism and localism. The department now possesses enough predominance, legal and financial, to be the major factor in New Zealand education. Yet the boards retain sufficient power to obstruct and thwart its will. As far as concerns staff matters, the fates and fortunes of those who enter the teaching profession now depend almost entirely on the department. For primary schools it is the department which undertakes the training of teachers at its four training colleges, which institutes a uniform salary scale throughout the Dominion, which periodically inspects and grades all teachers in descending rank on one national list, and which requires all promotions to vacancies to be determined by teachers' positions thereon. In the secondary schools it is again the department which institutes a uniform salary scale and inspects and grades teachers. But its grading of secondary teachers is arranged into broad groups rather than by individual rankings, and, in consequence, the various boards of the secondary schools have somewhat more latitude in making appointments and promotions. As is evident, such a system must depend for its efficiency on the judgments of the inspectorate. In the past much complaint has been directed against the inspectors by educationists. Inspectors have been selected from the ranks of the teachers and have not always been distinguished for enlightened and progressive attitudes on educational policy. Teachers who sought a higher grading are influenced, when their turn for inspection comes round, by the inevitable desire to satisfy whatever bias their inspector may possess. Safeness, conventionality, and orthodoxy have too frequently been the passwords leading to promotion. The remedy, of course, is to raise the caliber of its administrators and improve the quality of the inspectors. In short, against all these staff services—the postal, railways, police, and teaching—the same general charge can be leveled. Their prevailing personnel policies have impeded rather than assisted the rapid rise of new talent and the adequate promotion of well-qualified merit.

Any survey of personnel management in the central government must necessarily raise the question whether it is desirable to continue the division of public employees into so many distinct and separate services. Historical explanations, imbedded in the nature of New Zealand politics, will account for their coexistence. The Railways Department, as was discussed earlier, has always been involved in politics, and most governments have sought to retain control of its activities. Even the ministries, which for a while supposedly took the railways out of politics by placing them under a board, never contemplated such an aggrandisement of the public service commissioner as to place these thousands of employees under his power. The latter, too, have desired to constitute themselves into a distinct staff jurisdiction. Numerous enough to form a compact bloc, they have resented any transfers to the Railways from other parts of the civil service. Their voting power, a political potential of some magnitude, has enabled them to bargain directly with ministers and in that way gain what they wanted. For example, it was due solely to the pressure of the railways employees that the government established in 1944 a three-membered tribunal (including one employees' representative) to determine salary scales, to investigate working conditions, and to make decisions that are mandatory upon the ministry and the department.

Somewhat similar motives explain the separation of the Post and Telegraph Department from commissioner control. In 1912 when the Public Service Bill was before Parliament, the Reform government was hampered in its attempts to bring the postal employees under the commissioner. Their protests and pressure compelled the government so to amend its own proposals as to guarantee to the existing postal staff their opportunity of promotion in their own department. No public servant could be transferred from any other agency over the heads of those already in the Post Office. Thus, even while the commissioner did exercise jurisdiction over this department, he was forced to administer it as a separate personnel system. Later on, his powers were completely abrogated as a result of postwar political maneuvers by the Liberal leader, Ward. Having once been a telegraph boy and always regarding the Post Office as his special province, Ward was able to reinstate himself as the final arbiter over these many thousands of jobs. The postal employees, like those of the railways, acquiesced in the alteration, conjecturing that through their numbers they could wring more favors from a political head than from one who was nonpartisan.

The personnel organization of the state schoolteachers is again the product of history. The tradition of local control over education, derived from the mother-country, has persisted in New Zealand even since the provinces were abolished. National regulation by a central department has been subsequently developed in order to even out the disparate standards in the training of teachers and their remuneration. A completely centralized system, under which the education boards and the school boards would be reduced to merely advisory functions, is periodically mooted but encounters the opposition of intrenched interests. Different considerations from these have served to isolate the staff management of the police force. Because of their special function in maintaining law and order, they have always been treated as a disciplined body subject to stricter rules than apply to most other servants of the state. Unified control of the police has been considered necessary in order to insure their obedience to command if an emergency arose. The police are of extra importance to a country which in peacetime has had no standing army. Ministries have, therefore, retained full control over the organization as well as the personnel of this small but vital group.

The Need for Further Reform

Historical explanations of the genesis of the present-day system are not justifications for continuing the status quo. Personnel administration in New Zealand is hampered, not helped, by the present separation of powers under all these distinct staff authorities. The central government is really a single employer; but in practice it recruits, appoints, promotes, and pays its staff as if it were many employers. Disparities in standards have been offset only to a minor degree by a uniformity committee composed of the public service commissioner, the general manager of the Railway Department, the director-general of the Post and Telegraph Department, the director of education, and the secretary of the Treasury. While so many separate systems exist, the uniformity committee can do little about fundamental issues. It cannot, for example, successfully obviate competitive recruitment between the Public Service and the Railways and the Post and Telegraph departments. Nor can it do much to adjust some of the outstanding differences in salary scales. The salary scale for teachers is on the whole higher than the others; and the Public Service scale, while it allots to each class the same maximum and minimum as on the Railways and Post and Telegraph scale, operates in practice more generously than the two latter. A further disadvantage of the existing setup is that the various personnel jurisdictions become distinct career services so rigidly demarcated as almost to preclude any transfers. Finally, there is the disadvantage arising from the extra burden of work imposed on the heads of the Education, Police, Post and Telegraph, and Railways departments. To manage their own personnel systems these four agencies have organized their own staff divisions which cover the same type of work as the Public Service Commissioner's Office. Thus a great many issues affecting personnel in these departments go for final decision to the respective permanent heads, some of whom are known to devote several hours a day to staff matters. If these four independent staff jurisdictions were amalgamated into the central personnel agency of the Public Service, where they rightly belong, comprehensive personnel planning by the government would be encouraged; transfers between major branches of the civil service would be facilitated; salary scales could be harmonized; and the permanent heads of some of the Dominion's biggest departments would be relieved of a portion of their onerous burdens.

This proposal is administratively practicable as well as desirable. If in personnel matters the British Post Office is administered by the Treasury, the United States Post Office by the federal Civil Service Commission, and the Australian Postal Department by the Commonwealth Public Service Board, why cannot the postal and telegraphic employees in New Zealand be placed under the public service commission? If that be admitted, then on what principle can there be any valid objection to treating the railway staff in the same manner? To assimilate the existing classification plans would present no insuperable obstacles. For the most part, the first-division officers under the railways' and postal systems would become members of the clerical or professional division in the Public Service classification; while the second-division officers in the two former departments would be embraced in the latter's so-called "general division." The schoolteachers, likewise, could be satisfactorily amalgamated with the remainder,[69] and at the same time the residue of powers over staff now vested in the multifarious education boards and school boards could well be taken from them. It is anomalous that the public service commissioner has controlled the teachers in a few special schools like the native and correspondence schools, while the rest are within the province of the director of education. Since some of the Australian states have found it feasible to lodge the personnel management of their teachers in the agency that controls the bulk of their other public servants, New Zealand could very well make a trial of the same method. Similarly the central personnel agency which already administers the clerical staff of

69. This was actually proposed in the National Expenditure Commission's report of 1932.

the Police Commissioner's Office can suitably take over the recruitment, training, and promotion of the police force. The problems of discipline, so necessary in view of the special powers and functions of the police, would not present any serious difficulty, for the prison warders, who already form part of the Public Service, are under a discipline as strict as the police. There is no reason why the authority of the police commissioner or of the government in an emergency should be lessened by the fact that the police belong to a centralized personnel jurisdiction. If amalgamation of these independent systems was achieved, there would result a single personnel administration comprising one hundred thousand individuals. That figure is, admittedly, a far larger managerial problem than any now existing in New Zealand. But, as a matter of organization, what is it when compared with the half-million controlled by the British Treasury or the multitude under the aegis of the United States Civil Service Commission?

Along with amalgamation of the five staff systems a companion reform must be proposed. The civil service has yet to improve its methods of training the top-ranking administrators of the future. If the merit principle is to be thoroughly applied, let it be agreed that general administration requires education and training no less thorough than that of scientists, experts, and technicians. A civil service approaching the hundred thousand mark should form a pool ample enough to supply potential administrative talent. But the discovery, training, and promotion of the talented must then be organized in a systematic manner, not in the present haphazard fashion. The proper solution is to amend the classification plan of the Public Service by a downward extension of the present administrative division. In the lower grades of the classification system are many positions which involve administrative responsibility and call for a high order of knowledge and judgment. The position of a division chief, for instance, entails general administration, for its occupant must plan the work of his division, supervise his subordinates, and use his discretion in settling issues of policy. It would be quite feasible and practicable to pick out in each department the positions which call for administration in the same sense just described and then collectively designate all these posts throughout the Public Service as an administrative division. In addition, if proper emphasis is to be paid to the training of future administrators, understudies or executive aides must be assigned to the occupants of all these policy-forming positions. The understudy or aide would be placed under the direction of an administrative officer both to assist him and to learn from him. All positions filled by such understudies would themselves be comprised within the administrative division. That division would therefore extend horizontally across all departments and vertically from the top class downward, including both those who already fill administrative positions and the trainees who will possess them later. It must be open equally to men and women and equally to professional or to clerical officers.

Public servants should be appointed to this division at an age not older than thirty-five. They should be selected according to three criteria: personality, intellectual attainments, and previous departmental performance. Appointment to the administrative division should be open both to public servants who are recruited at eighteen years of age or under and to those who join the service after graduating at the university. But no one should be promoted to the division until he or she has been a member of the service for at least three years. In this proposal some may detect an attempt to foist upon democratic New Zealand the allegedly undemocratic administrative class of the mother-country. The unprejudiced, however, will see in it a method of engrafting on the Public Service only the valuable features of the British system and will recognize an analogy between this scheme and the one recently advocated in the United States by the President's Committee on Civil Service Improvement.[70] The pair of changes recommended above—amalgamation of the services and the establishment of an administrative division—are the principal structural changes required if the central government of the Dominion is prepared to recruit, train, and promote its available administrative talent. The size of the civil service and the importance of its functions make it imperative that the state should attract to its employ the best ability in the community and should

70. *Report of the President's Committee on Civil Service Improvement* (Washington, D.C.: Government Printing Office, 1941), pp. 56–62.

utilize it to full advantage, for, whatever else is doubtful about the postwar world, this at least is sure—the great mass of human beings in all countries, occidental and oriental, crave security. Security against military attack will dominate the motives of a generation which has emerged from the ordeal of two global wars, has lived uneasily through the shocks and crises of a twenty-year armistice, and is apprehensive of the atomic bomb. Security against economic hardship will be no less urgent for those who retain memories of the world depression and fear its recurrence. The demand for security is imposing yet more functions on the state and will call for more staff in their execution.

At present some of New Zealand's best talent, but not nearly enough, can be found within the civil service. Private employment and the professions compete with the state in recruiting many of the ablest, sometimes because of superior monetary rewards, and sometimes because of higher social prestige. It is certain that the public personnel agencies cannot maintain toward university graduates the attitude which guided them in the past, or they will continue to forfeit a splendid reservoir of potential administrators. Moreover, the inexcusable raw deal to which women servants of the state are at present subjected discourages the best members of half the population from seeking a civil servant's career. Even though they worked a lifetime for the state, the great majority of the women employed in the Public Service received in the past only temporary status. They have thus been shut off from any hope of appointment to the positions of real responsibility which are reserved to holders of permanent status in the classification list. Only about a score of women occupy positions of any importance in the departments of the Public Service, or in the Railways or Post and Telegraph departments. Except for school-teaching, which does offer more possibilities for a career, the central government holds out less attractive prospects to women of ability than private employment. The first country in the English-speaking world to enfranchise its women, New Zealand has been slow to grant them an equal opportunity of promotion in its civil service. There are women members of the British administrative class and women in big executive posts in the federal service of the United States. Why should New Zealand democracy treat its women differently?

If the Dominion were to adopt the proposals suggested in this and the previous chapters, it could possibly exhibit to the world a model administrative system. It possesses already one invaluable foundation on which such changes can be built: the generally high standard of personal integrity prevailing among its civil servants. A few defalcations or irregularities, some cases of misconduct or inefficiency, are uncovered and dealt with from time to time. But on the whole there is in New Zealand a commendable absence of graft and a strict code of honesty. For this fact, the knowledge that jobs are secure, as well as the installation of somewhat rigid accounting and auditing methods, are in part responsible. But there exists also that "inner check" which springs from the civil servant's professional devotion to the ideal of the public interest. The maintenance of such standards is essential to the social welfare in a country in which so big a proportion of salary- and wage-earners work for the government.

Finally, the relation of the civil service to party politics requires some comment. With the political parties the modern civil service has struck a mutually beneficial bargain. By guaranteeing to public servants a life's career and a pension, parties have forsworn the use of patronage and have guaranteed to the state's employees their tenure of their jobs. In return the parties expect, and the public servants owe, equal loyalty to any government which the people have placed in office. The New Zealand civil service forms a large cross-section of the community. Its members, who are citizens as well as state employees, naturally include representatives of all opinions and attitudes. There have been suggestions at various times that through its voting power the public servants can control the government. Thus, when Massey cut their salaries in the slump of the early twenties, it was definitely asserted in Parliament that many civil servants voted against Reform candidates at the election of 1922. Nor is there any doubt that this did happen. Again in 1935, after the coalition government of the depression years had repeatedly lowered salaries, large numbers of public employees undoubtedly gave their support to Labor. Since the great majority of public servants earn under £500 per annum, a government which has its eye on the next election must be careful how it treats these salaries.

Of equal importance to the government is the co-operativeness of the higher administrative officials, whose hostility could sabotage a legislative program. New Zealand has now passed through the acid test, since its civil service has worked under three parties in succession. Various Laborites, it is true, were suspicious at first of permanent heads who had served under non-Labor cabinets. In some cases there was friction between a Labor minister and the permanent head, but, in general, a close and harmonious working relationship soon developed. The Labor cabinet found that the civil service was fully prepared to carry out its instructions, and before long ministers grew to trust their administrative assistants and utilized their experience. There is no ground for charging the New Zealand civil service with undue political partisanship. Its political neutrality between elections has been abundantly vindicated by the manner of its performance. Neutrality at elections, or abstention from voting, is neither expected in the code of the profession nor required in the law of the land.[71] The civil servant is a citizen administering public affairs for his fellow-citizens, and in a country containing so many state employees the boundary line between the people and the servants of the people is necessarily imprecise. The civil service does not form a caste apart or a bureaucratic officialdom aloof from the community it is supposed to serve. Since in themselves they constitute a large segment of the public, the civil servants play many parts. They are citizens and voters, as well as servants of the state and administrators. If government by the people posits a high degree of participation, the sheer size of the New Zealand civil service helps to fulfil at least one democratic prerequisite.

71. The Labor ministry conferred on civil servants by legislation the right to obtain leave of absence from their posts and be candidates for Parliament.

CHAPTER XV

EQUALITARIAN DEMOCRACY: THE RECORD AND THE PROSPECT

THIS survey of New Zealand democracy both in evolution and in operation must be rounded off with an evaluation of the general results. The record of a century's development must be interpreted and the prospects for the future scanned if the Dominion's achievement is to be properly appraised. New Zealand has not yet, any more than has any country, produced a utopian society, and it cannot therefore receive uncritical praise. But it must also be remembered that any criticism will itself call for qualification. Burke's caution not to draw up an indictment against a whole people applies also to so small a group as one and three-quarter millions.

The central fact that conditions everything in the governmental system of modern New Zealand is the high degree of participation by its citizen body. In a country where all adults have been enfranchised since 1893, where elections recur triennially, where some 90 per cent of the electorate customarily vote, where over one-fifth of the working population are public employees, where the central government undertakes so much, and where seven hundred local bodies litter the map, democracy in the literal sense of government by the people has come as near to fruition as in the Athens of antiquity. Not only is the government exceptionally close to the people it serves but the proportion of the people who take a part in giving service to the whole is very high. On this score if faults exist, they are at least on the right side, being faults of excess rather than of inadequacy. It is arguable that elections recur too often, that there are too many public employees, or that there should be fewer local bodies. But no one could reasonably say that New Zealand places a gulf between the state

481

and the public, that it is run by an exclusive governing class, or
that its government is a remote and inaccessible *Ding an sich*.

It is this characteristic of plentiful participation by its citizens
which is both an effect of the extensiveness of state enterprise and
a reciprocating cause. The people, or at any rate most of them,
look upon the state quite healthily as being themselves under another form. When it acts, they feel that they are acting. What it
owns, they own. They do not endow it with metaphysical properties or ascribe to it any transcendental personality. To them it
is simply a utilitarian instrument for effecting their will. If something requires doing which cannot be suitably undertaken otherwise than by organized public endeavor, then let the state do the
job. From Vogel to Ballance, from Seddon to Savage, the same
refrain has been repeated. Once it was seriously pressed, the demand of all classes for equal political rights could not be refused
in a new country where population was scanty, land plentiful,
and a labor reserve nonexistent. The attainment of the adult
franchise led irresistibly to cumulative measures of state intervention in what had erstwhile been the sphere of private business.
Thus has New Zealand attempted during successive decades to
hyphenate the politics of democracy with the economics of socialism.

At the present time when the war and its aftermath have stimulated a swing to the left in so many countries, it becomes a matter
of international significance to inquire whether democracy and
socialism can and should co-exist. Two rival schools of thought, as
is well known, proclaim their opposition of views on this question.[1] One holds not only that socialism is compatible with democracy but that the former is a condition essential to the genu-
ineness of the latter, since private economic oligarchies impede
the possibilities of majority rule. Socialism, it is urged, consists
simply in transferring the principles of democracy from politics
to economics. Each, therefore, is complementary to the other.
The opposite argument contends that socialism and democracy
are mutually so incompatible that the latter cannot survive the

1. Contrast, e.g., H. J. Laski's *Reflections on the Revolution of Our Time* (New York:
Viking Press, 1943) with F. A. Hayek's *The Road to Serfdom* (Chicago: University of
Chicago Press, 1944).

attainment of the former. To operate a socialized economy, so it is held, involves a diminution of the liberty of the individual and aggrandizement of the state. From the accumulation of power, it is contended, would emerge a dictatorship.

If one swallow does not make a spring, the doings of one small nation cannot definitively settle a controversy of such amplitude. Nevertheless, the experience of New Zealand does deserve consideration just because the trend toward socialism has been so old and consistent a feature of its development. Let us then ask this question: If the establishment of democracy in New Zealand encouraged the movement toward socialism, in what way has socialism reacted upon democracy itself?

One evident result has been a growing centralization of governmental functions and, at the center, an integration of power under the cabinet. The reasons for this are not far to seek. Socialism entails the corollary of a managed or planned economy. In addition to the activities which it directly undertakes, the state is increasingly prone to regulate the sphere of action left to private interests. For, if the whole field of social conduct be divided into a portion that is planned and one that is not, the unplanned segment is likely to impinge unpredictably upon the former and throw the plans out of gear. Hence the tendency for what are called "controls" to multiply. Hence also the proneness to substitute uniform central standards for local diversities. And hence the desire to see authority tightly knit together and to avoid the clash of jurisdictions that militates against harmonious planning.

As a consequence the political[2] institutions of New Zealand have developed into a mechanism powerfully built and streamlined in design to execute the people's will. Constitutional checks that might impede the immediate translation of popular wishes into official policy have been largely removed or weakened. The cabinet and the caucus of the majority party possess ample means both for putting on the statute-book the legislation they desire and for following it up with administrative application. The upper house is completely subordinate to the lower. The governor-general is politically powerless to interpose a veto. The judiciary

2. The word "political" is used here in a limited sense. The administrative institutions, described above in chap. xiii, are not so powerfully built or streamlined.

are bound, and can be overridden, by act of Parliament. No federal system with a distribution of powers between legally independent authorities exists to thwart the central government. In
short, a New Zealand ministry which fails to fulfil its electoral
promises can never put up the excuse that it lacks the power.
Power is there in abundance for the using, and every voter
knows it.

That being so, it is right and proper to ask whether the people
have retained adequate means of control. The state in New Zealand may be likened to a high-powered automobile with a chauffeur in the driving seat and the owners sitting behind. Once the
car has gathered pace, the owners' safety depends upon their
chauffeur's skill. Periodically the gasoline tank must be refilled,
and then the owners can choose between alternative brands of
fuel or, perhaps, change their chauffeur. Democracy's problem is
to insure that the car will stop at the right intervals and that,
while it is moving, the chauffeur will follow orders from the back
seat.

On this point none need doubt that the advent of a large measure of socialism to New Zealand has not been accompanied by
the demise of democracy. The two-party system continues.
"Splinter parties" hive off, live their little hour, and are reabsorbed. Elections are held regularly enough. The press is vocal
and vehement but obviously not omnipotent, since the Labor
party has won four consecutive elections in the teeth of almost
every newspaper in the country. Question time in the House is as
searching as ever, and all proceedings nowadays are broadcast.
Governments in New Zealand, irrespective of party, have done
more than merely acknowledge a formal theory of responsibility
to the people. They have been responsive as well as responsible.
Where ministries have erred has been rather in their subservience
to the public than in their disregard of it. Many a cabinet, among
which the Labor one was not the first and will not be the last, has
been upbraided for its undue dependence on well-organized
pressure groups and for its yielding to sectional interests. The
structure of New Zealand politics, and particularly the frequency
of elections, make it difficult for any government to say "No"
firmly and to keep on saying it. Transient policies tend to over-

ride those of longer term, and partial goods encroach upon the common good.

But the problem of reconciling democracy with socialism and New Zealand's experience with this problem require further analysis at other levels. Because of the legislative policies on which it embarks, and the powers it confers upon the state, a socialistic democracy produces resounding administrative consequences. In the last resort it is in its administrative capacity that the state gives satisfaction or irritation to its citizens. In countless day-to-day transactions the state is personally embodied in the public eye, not as a parliamentarian, but as a civil servant. By its managerial methods do the people judge it—and to an extent, moreover, that makes integrity in administration a prime requisite for the success of a democratically planned economy.

It is the task of the civil servant to particularize the general provisions of a statute and apply the law without fear or favor. On the fairness and impartiality with which the law is administered depends in the large measure the citizens' respect for their government. Nothing is ever so destructive of public order as the awareness that the same rule is differently applied to persons in the same legal category. Yet the ideal cannot be attained by any automatic principle of enforcement, for, as all publicists know, the civil servant must possess discretion.[3] Flexibility is laudable in the laws that govern a complex and mobile society. But can the citizen be certain that discretion will be fairly and equitably applied, that the written letter will not be interpreted narrowly in his case and broadly in his neighbor's? In an administrative system headed by a political body, the cabinet, will partisan influences be brought to bear?

One may reasonably doubt whether any human association can ever entirely rid itself of influence. Governments are human, not mechanical. If a government is to act, someone's influence must carry weight in the making of decisions. He whose judgment is most highly regarded (either on its own merits or because of the person's status, wealth, or power) will in practice say what is to

3. See Marshall E. Dimock's essay on "The Role of Discretion in Modern Administration," in *The Frontiers of Public Administration*, by J. M. Gaus, L. D. White, and M. E. Dimock (Chicago: University of Chicago Press, 1936).

be done. To these considerations—and they need not be viewed askance—New Zealand is no exception. But influence may take on a less justifiable aspect. It may merge into an indulgence for ministers and their political coterie. It may enable citizens in a position of social prestige, citizens who wield economic power, citizens who sway the votes of others, to gain favored treatment. Probably no democracy yet established has completely overcome such influences. Assuredly New Zealand has not.

The occasions for administrative favoritism spring from two sources, of which one may be found among ministers and the other among civil servants. It is a customary feature of New Zealand politics to enact laws in broad terms. The laws are then supplemented with a string of regulations, and on many matters a final discretion is usually left with the minister. Now, it must be remembered that scarcely any group or institution is not subsidized or assisted or operated by grants from the public exchequer. Many an individual, moreover, conducts his business or supplies a service under some permit or license or recognition accorded by the government. Thus the ministry holds the strings that are tied in at countless points to the welfare of the citizens. The favor of a department subject to a minister must be repeatedly sought and its good will retained. In the hands of the members of the cabinet is concentrated a far-reaching power to promote this and to grant exemptions from that; to make one man's career or fortune and to curb that of another. Few ministers at any time either dare or desire to ignore the importunities of their friends, for they are ever mindful of the next election. All too often, the leading difference between governments of opposite party color seems to be this—that there are different sets of friends who prosper.

A second cause of the same mischief can be found in the failings of the civil service that are due to its system of recruitment and education. In the British civil service, with its predominantly university-trained administrative class, the higher officials possess an intellectual discipline that enables them to elucidate a general principle and apply it consistently through a labyrinth of individual cases differing in details. Among the higher personnel of New Zealand departments the same intellectual faculty has not, on the whole, been developed to a similar degree. Thus principles are less clearly formulated and less consistently applied. A tacit admission of this truth can be discerned in an explanatory formula that is much invoked by the Dominion's administrators. Their aim, they avow, is "to judge each case on its merits"—a euphemism that frequently glosses over the absence of governing principles.

Up to this point the appraisal of New Zealand's blend of socialism with democracy has been couched largely in terms of institutional factors. Since a politicoeconomic order, however, is indissolubly linked with other social fundamentals, and since institutions themselves embody and are animated by the prevailing spirit or ethos of a community, it is necessary to consider certain allied topics that impinge upon the central issue.

More than once in the course of this book I have had occasion to refer to that homogeneity of the population which so conditions the minds and mores of New Zealanders. The overwhelming numerical predominance of Europeans over Maoris and Orientals, of persons of British descent over those from Continental countries, of those with English and Scottish origins over the Irish, of Protestants over Catholics—these statistically verifiable facts have formed the mold in which is cast the character of New Zealand. The prevalence of a single national, racial, and cultural tradition—that of Britain—must enter into the final recapitulation. If, as Professor Laski has insisted, people think differently who live differently, the converse holds good no less emphatically. People who live alike tend to think alike. Resemblances that have their objective manifestations in language, in physical appearance, and so on, possess a subjective counterpart in the loyalties, attitudes, emotions, and sympathies that any culture imparts to its members. Thus if there can be said to exist a New Zealand way of life, the homogeneity of the population constitutes the root cause for its understanding and interpretation.

It was this homogeneity that first made possible, and then confirmed, the equalitarianism which typifies New Zealand democracy. In New Zealand, as in Australia, the proneness to apotheosize equality has been bound up with two facts, one psychological and the other economic. A Dominion which was colonized in large part by representatives of the laboring and lower-middle classes could be expected to react instinctively against any whiff of the mother-country's social stratification. When to this was added the economic opportunity of an almost empty land, the bargaining power of labor, and therefore its independence and its dignity, were amply secured. Privilege and deprivation, snobbery and subservience, could not be transplanted to a far-off terrain where the material basis for their being was no longer present.

Nourished in such favoring conditions, the seeds of equalitarianism struck deep their roots and grew lustily. Nowadays it is an ingrained equalitarian temper which dominates and regulates everything that happens in the community. Its all-pervading influence is both negative and positive, compelling certain lines of action and forbidding others. Insistence upon equality is, of course, basic to a democratic doctrine. Invoking this symbol, democracy has levied successful polemics upon caste, class, and capital. Equality of opportunity, the opening of careers to talent, the establishment of universal minimum standards—these are the beneficial results of equalitarianism. By aiming at all these and in large measure attaining them, New Zealand has done well and deserves a high tribute. But to equality, as to all social ideals, the truth holds good that *corruptio optimi pessima*. There is no foolproof formula to prescribe the amount of the dose. A wrongful use can set in train a sequence of harmful tendencies. Let us, then, try to assess the results.

Viewed from its most attractive angle, equalitarianism means a certain measure of fair play for everyone who belongs to the group. It means the fixing of minimum standards of treatment, to which all are entitled as of right, and then the adoption of deliberate measures to enforce them. It means the overthrow of the privileged and the raising of the underprivileged. It means the removal of class distinctions. It means both leveling-down and leveling-up. All of which may perhaps be best explained by saying that New Zealand has a genuine passion for social justice which is greatly to its credit. Poverty is well-nigh eradicated from the Dominion and in its worst forms does not exist at all. There is no underdog, nor is anybody exploited—unless it be the housewife and mother. New Zealanders insist that the essential minima for civilized living be guaranteed to all and shared around, that everyone be given an equal chance, and that the aged and the weak be cared for. Who shall say that in so doing they are not pursuing a genuinely democratic ideal?

It is, however, an ideal that differs in emphasis from that which finds favor elsewhere. If it be conceded, for instance, that democracy must seek to harmonize liberty and equality, it would be admitted that certain nations, of which the United States is the outstanding example, have traditionally placed a higher rating on liberty and have tended to subordinate equality to its requirements. New Zealand has reversed that emphasis. To the people of this Dominion equality comes first, and it is within its content that liberty has been redefined. Does this mean, then, as is asserted by some people in New Zealand, that liberty is thereby sacrificed and that in this sense the approximation toward socialism has involved a diminution of democracy?

The majority of New Zealanders would, I think, argue otherwise. Or rather, to be more accurate, since they have rarely gone to the pains of formulating a coherent philosophy of their own to explain what they do, they would probably accept the following argument as expressing the rationale of their social endeavors. "Liberty," in their eyes, is a broad generalization which acquires specific content from particular "liberties," that is, opportunities for individual persons to do certain things and resist certain compulsions. Now, there are some such liberties, for example, the right to vote, which in no way impede the exercise of a like right by others. But there are also liberties, especially in the economic field, whose use by some may restrict others in the development of their own potentialities. Thus it has arisen in many communities that liberty, or liberties, where pushed to excess, may eventuate in gross inequalities. Thus can a system dedicated to freedom finally be re-ensnared in the coils of privilege. Certainly in the modern world, where social power is so largely a function of wealth, the ownership of riches has usually conferred a number of liberties not available to the indigent.

Against such regimes New Zealand has reacted by attempting, in a word, to equalize liberties. It has sought to convert freedom from the privilege of a few persons at one end of the economic scale into an exact ration distributed to all alike. For bringing about the redistribution, the state has been employed as the mechanism. Hence the multifarious governmental controls which do restrict the liberties of some to act in certain ways are represented as enlarging correspondingly the liberties of other people to act in similar ways. Hence socialism becomes harmonized with democracy by a system of rationing liberties and by imposing on the state the duty of adjusting the ration.

Unfortunately, though, the beneficent tendency of such a social ideal has been marred, if not actually warped, in practice by some undesirable excesses. Devoutly believing that all men are created equal, most New Zealanders assert that in every possible way all must be equally treated. No one person or group may be preferentially favored. Rewards must be evenly spread. To set up distinctions is to be guilty of acting in an "undemocratic" manner, since these are the thin end of a wedge that drives class barriers into society. Not only must privilege be expelled but differences between individual abilities must be minimized. Rightly convinced that a basic minimum of fair treatment should be accorded to all, the Dominion tends toward the distortion that it is wrong to give different rewards to merit. Whereas democracy wisely avers that the government is everybody's business, New Zealand voters, in selecting members of Parliament, would seem to conclude that public affairs are the business of anybody to conduct. The theory which correctly insists that each has a right to his own opinion can become so twisted as to imply that everyone's opinion is equally right. Because of equalitarianism the civil service has not yet succeeded in training the needed type of administrator, since to promote the ablest "out of turn" is "undemocratic." Because every office boy has the right to become a permanent head, many believe that permanent heads must be culled only from those who started as office boys. The equalitarianism that may succeed in raising averages is also guilty of reducing standards. Whatever services be supplied to the public the same amount must be offered to all. Inevitably, therefore, the quality suffers. Socialists have rightly contended that none should eat cake until all have bread. But when everybody does have bread, as is certainly the case in New Zealand, what is to be done about cake? Either cake must be abolished altogether on the ground that it is undemocratic, or else some cake must be given to everyone, and then nobody can be allowed to receive more than a crumb. Under either alternative only one thing is certain: cake will not be enjoyed.

In at least two important respects the defects of a perverted equalitarianism are seriously detrimental to the Dominion. It is acknowledged by all judicious observers that New Zealand is notoriously ungenerous to talent. In its anxiety to raise minima, the country has deemed it necessary to lower maxima. Salaries and wages are so scaled that the gap between highest and lowest shall be as small as possible. The skilled worker receives under the basic wage precious little more than the unskilled, while some professional men earn less than some manual laborers. In the search for security, laudable though this be, incentives are being lost. There is not enough encouragement for each to do his best and for the ablest to display their full capacity. Everything tends toward a norm, and deviation from the average becomes a cardinal sin. All workers are protected, whether in their employment or out of it. But in place of the old fear of dismissal —often so harsh in its operation—no superior positive impetus has yet been substituted to elicit more work and better. Security itself can be pushed beyond the right degree; and, when this happens, such organizations as trade-unions and professional associations are concerned more with safeguarding jobs than with improving standards. An exceptional worker is a menace to his mediocre comrade. Group pressure, therefore, forces him to "go slow."[4] How to reconcile full security with good service and adequate incentives is a question urgently posed and not as yet resolved by the experience of New Zealand.

No less serious is the effect of equality and security upon intellectual life. The like-mindedness, which in any case would accompany cultural homogeneity, has been reinforced and accentuated

4. The historically minded may care to reflect on the lessons contained in the later evolution of the medieval guilds. Professor R. H. Tawney has alluded to "the defensive machinery of the guilds with their corporate discipline, their organized torpor restricting individual enterprise, and their rough equalitarianism" (*Religion and the Rise of Capitalism* [rev. ed.; 1937], chap. iii).

by the equalitarian attitude and the quest for security. In their
thinking, as in their methods of living, New Zealanders tend to
conform to type. The same convictions, prejudices, and stock
symbols predominate throughout the country. There is not
enough internal diversity to produce a clash of opinion. Nor, except to those few who have lived outside New Zealand and in a
country other than a British one, are there adequate means of
forming a standard of comparison and arriving at fair evaluations.
The mental world of New Zealand has been, on the whole, as
self-contained as its insular geography. Hence the spirit of critical
inquiry could not flourish without overcoming almost insuperable impediments.

As a consequence, many New Zealanders, when confronted
with differences, tend to be shocked and resentful. The equalitarianism that provides for all within the group can be hostile
toward those who reject the group standards or who are outside
the membership. Free-thinkers on religious matters, a handful of
oriental residents, refugees from European fascism, advocates of
heterodox social theories—all who do not conform are subject to
a suspicion and in critical times to a persecution that appear the
less justified because these minorities are so utterly impotent.[5]
To many a New Zealander it matters little that the representatives of such different cultures or beliefs are too few to be dangerous. Their very presence, involving a rejection of his ways, is itself a challenge to his security, since it is a reminder that other
patterns of living are possible besides his own. Thus the intellectual climate of New Zealand does not in general exhibit the
virtue of tolerance. Too large a proportion of the public resents
any criticism. When criticism is voiced, too many people, instead
of examining its validity, are accustomed to react defensively and
vent their displeasure in ways that can be harsh and even cruel.
Tolerance, after all, is a duty imposed upon the strong. In a
community in which dissidents from the established order are so
weak, the onus of being tolerant reposes on the shoulders of the
majority. By necessity the pygmy can do no other than be tolerant of the giant. The giant should tolerate the pygmy by grace.

5. New Zealand's record in the sphere of civil liberties during the two world
wars and the depression was none too creditable.

Here, then, in a small and culturally homogeneous milieu is the spectacle of majority rule producing some of the consequences so clearly foreseen eight decades ago by John Stuart Mill. The dulling effect of the mass mind, the dominance of conventional opinion, the despotism of custom, the intolerance of unorthodoxy, the sacrifice of talent to the worship of averages, a world made safe for mediocrity—all these tendencies are periodically manifested in New Zealand. The results are all the more unfortunate, since in its drive for conformism and in its lack of recognition for talent, New Zealand is acting of its own free will and harms no one but itself. On this score let there be neither mistake nor misunderstanding. New Zealanders belong to a fine stock and inhabit a magnificent country. A small nation that has achieved so much in the field of social services, and has given birth to men of the caliber of Salmond, Low, and Rutherford, cannot be dismissed as unimportant. Yet persistently New Zealand refuses opportunities to its most talented sons and daughters, denies them the chance of creative expression, and often drives them from its own shores in that annual "export of brains" which is its greatest tragedy.

There is an apparent exception to what I have just been saying which on a closer view serves rather to fortify than to weaken this argument. Perhaps the only spheres in which New Zealand really affords scope and assigns respect to ability are the professions of medicine and engineering. Their members at least are normally remunerated in a manner that indicates some appreciation by the community of their services. Now it is surely significant that doctors and engineers have this in common. They deal with a physical subject matter and produce results that are assessable in physical terms. This fact chimes in with the materialistic temper that is the keynote to so much of the New Zealand way of life. In the Dominion's scale of values a very high place is reserved for the achievement of material comfort. The colonial outlook is a still-surviving heritage of the days when pioneers hacked their homes from "the bush" and wrestled with the physical problems of mountains and Maoris, of sheep and shipping. Conditions of life were crude and primitive. Settlers, the women along with the men, had to be hardy and tough. The first overwhelming need, as the European viewed it, was to subdue both nature and the native. Other things would have to wait. Born of the struggle for survival, the habits thus set have outlived their origins and settled into tradition. The New Zealander's mind is wont to grasp at the concrete and the tangible. His appraisal of men and measures is cast in terms of physical accomplishment; and "practical" is the adjective of greatest praise in his vocabulary. Abstractions, theories, ideas—these are of little account or interest unless they can be immediately applied. Utility is the national yardstick, and the test of success fills the place that is vacant of principle.

Many facts are explicable in the light of this formulation. It is apparent that New Zealand has consciously aimed at, and has already largely achieved, a high standard of living. Judged by the indices of material comfort, the country is well off. Its achievement in this sphere can scarcely be disputed. Yet, in its preoccupation with material satisfactions, the Dominion has suffered in other spheres. A nation which ranks high for its social services has contributed virtually nothing in the domain of creative imagination. You may study New Zealand with profit to learn about its social services, but you can find little that has been achieved in the realms of art, of literature, of the spirit. The Dominion may be "a laboratory of social experimentation," but its offerings to the Muses have been beggarly by comparison. Of original creativeness in painting, sculpture, music, architecture, or poetry, there is practically nothing that will live. In prose literature only Katherine Mansfield can claim respect, but her adult life was passed in Britain in reaction against her colonial upbringing. The aesthetic values do not appeal to enough of the New Zealand public. Taste for the finer flowerings of the human genius is insufficiently developed. Beauty is little esteemed, still less deliberately sought. Those two islands contain in city and countryside much natural loveliness side by side with man-made ugliness. Education is too often "practical" and dominated by utilitarianism. It seldom inculcates the values of gracious, humanized living.

The lack of cultural achievement is one of the many results attributable to the fact that New Zealand is so small. A homogeneous population of under two millions, isolated from the world's

great centers, does not afford enough internal diversity to stimulate that intellectual curiosity which is the fountainhead of creative originality. Neither does it insure that serene air of confidence, the sign of maturity and independence, which can inspire the artist with a positive ideal. Nor again does it provide the
economic essential of a constant market and a sufficient clientele.

The smallness of New Zealand deserves a mention of its own.
In part it is due to the geographical restrictions of the islands'
landscape and to the economic limitations of available resources.
But to a much larger extent it is the product of a man-made policy that is, in general, instinctive rather than articulate and on
that account all the more compelling, for in the national psychology of the Dominion the desire to continue small has become a
dogma as sanctified as free trade to late nineteenth-century Englishmen, or neutrality to the Swiss, or the "white Australia policy" to New Zealand's neighbor. Over some six decades New
Zealand has shown itself chary of expansion and has shunned the
discomforts of growing-pains. Being prosperous on the whole, and
flourishing in a material sense, the few inhabitants of the Dominion have preferred to maintain their relatively high living standard by skimming the cream off a rich little country. To the argument that the New Zealand population should grow considerably, the fear that more numbers would entail less prosperity all
round is an ever potent obstacle. It is to the trade-unions, and the
working class in general, that this attitude is normally attributed.
True it is that since the depression of the eighties the labor movement of New Zealand has looked with anything but a kindly eye
on the adult immigrant. It has feared to weaken its bargaining
position in the face of the employers by introducing to the Antipodes that reserve pool of unemployed labor which has characterized the older, industrial, economies.

Let it be added, however, that this resentment against the
newcomer as a competitor, who will take someone else's job and
will work harder just because he is new, has not been confined
only to the trade-unions. When Hitlerite persecution compelled
some of the finest products of Central European culture to start
a new life elsewhere, the New Zealand government, responsive to
the sentiments of its electorate, granted the barest minimum of

admissions. Nor were the members of higher-paid professions any more broad-minded. Foremost among those organized groups which of set purpose made the way hard for the refugee immigrant were the New Zealand branch of the British Medical Association, the New Zealand Institute of Architects, and similar bread-and-butter bodies. Even the experience of war and the imminent threat of invasion did not elicit so marked a change of attitudes as in Australia, whose home territory did actually suffer from enemy attack. When a bipartisan parliamentary committee reported in 1946 on the subject of New Zealand's future immigration, their viewpoint amounted to a willing acceptance of the doctrine that numbers were not to grow appreciably. Since the report was unanimous, it may reasonably be taken to represent a national conviction. Like the women of imperial China who bound their feet, New Zealand deliberately cramps its own natural development.

Smallness, coupled with isolation, supplies one of the principal reasons underlying the exceptionally close attachment of New Zealand to Great Britain. But it is not the only one, for many causes have contributed to this relationship. The trade nexus, for instance, and the Dominion's financial indebtedness are strong, material bonds. Thus, considered as an economic concern, New Zealand has been throughout most of its history a large farm organized to feed Britain and stocked with British implements. All the exporters and importers who thrive on this two-way trade are induced by motives of personal gain to maintain the lucrative connection. Besides its commercial ties, New Zealand has in the past relied upon Britain for its defense. Desiring to remain small, it was compelled to seek a protector. Most fortunately the protector was found in that nation from which the Colony derived originally and to which it was still bound by nonmaterial ties of sentiment. That the New Zealander, even in the second and third generation, continues to refer to Britain as "home" is striking evidence of the feelings that still dominate his outlook. Markets, security, and nostalgia are the triple links holding the South Pacific settlement to its North Atlantic birthplace.

The psychology that supervenes upon these facts and feelings is more complex than might appear. Some of the reasons for the dependence upon Britain, apart from trade and defense, may be analyzed as aspects of colonialism. In their heart of hearts New Zealanders are keenly aware that one and three-quarter million souls cannot alone wield much influence in a world population of over two billions. Only by attaching themselves to something that is bigger and more potent can New Zealanders feel that they possess a significance greater than their size. Now, Britain is by any standard a great country. Grouped together with its dominions and colonial empire, it constitutes one of the paramount forces in world politics and has unquestionably contributed to human civilization a record which challenges that of any other imperial people. By identifying itself with so huge a political agglomeration, New Zealand acquires a sense of sharing in Britain's history-making. Thereby it compensates for its own smallness and the feelings of inferiority that attend upon weakness. The same cause explains not only New Zealand's attachment to Britain but also its overattachment. Just as the new convert must attract attention and allay doubting suspicions by excess of zeal, so must the smallest, weakest, and most distant Dominion be the loudest and most assiduous in its protestations of loyalty. It is no accident that this Dominion has shown fewer signs of independence than either Canada, South Africa, or Australia. In the Boer War and the two world wars, New Zealand supplied its fighting contingent to join the forces of the Empire, often contributing a larger proportion of its manpower than it could really afford. Nor is the mother-country slow to return acknowledgments. Britain treats New Zealand generously and is glad to have one extra-loyal and exemplary Dominion whose conduct can be held up as a model for the larger sisters to imitate.

The psychological dependence on Britain can still be most accurately described by the term "colonialism." The farm that feeds Britain and "buys British" must think British thoughts and copy British ways. The Englishman or the Scot, turned Antipodean, clings to customs of the past, and his grandson holds romantic illusions about a "home" he has not seen. The working life of many a New Zealander has been conducted on one side of the world; his emotional life, on another. At times he has seemed to be attached to a place where he did not live and to live in a

place where he was not attached. Yet the feelings which cement
the colony to the mother-country are ambivalent in their effects.
Because his country is tiny, weak, and remote, the New Zealander
must identify himself with all the achievements of Britain. But
the identification must not be absolutely complete, or the micro-
cosm would be entirely absorbed by the macrocosm. So, in order
further to compensate, New Zealand advances to itself and others
the claim that it "leads the world." That is a claim which has
been popular in the Dominion ever since the nineties. Siegfried
himself noted and described it with some amusement. What appears to me so significant is that the same dogma is still put forward with all seriousness and has been continuously reasserted
over the forty years since the French scholar wrote his master-
piece. The publicity of the government, the press, and a host of
private organizations constantly assures the public that New Zealand leads the world in this, that, and the other. So often is the
point repeated and asserted about so many features of the Dominion's life that it is now earnestly believed by the majority. It is
held as a faith which few call in question.

Let me grant that the dogma can under some circumstances
prove quite useful. It implies a willingness to progress and inno-
vate which can be capitalized by anyone who has a new project
to propose. In his advocacy he can suggest that if his plan is
adopted, New Zealand will be starting a new experiment and
thus will again lead the world. But the same dogma can also be
curiously inverted to support a kind of conservatism[6] which is as
fundamentally characteristic of the Dominion as its supposed pro-
gressiveness. If you propose some change, you may hear the retort that you should let well alone and should not interfere with
that which is already better than what other countries possess.
New Zealand, too, often overlooks the fact that, while it may
have pioneered a certain measure, the outside world of which it
knows so little also adopts similar measures, and other nations, if
not originally first in the field, can and do surpass what was perhaps originated in the South Pacific. Because the Dominion four
decades ago may have been the first to introduce some scheme,

6. Professor Condliffe has given an admirable exposition of this point.

that does not mean that it is still up to date.[7] Here is where the lack of contacts with other countries, and the inability to pool ideas and share experiences, leads New Zealand to rest too satisfied with its own achievements. In its best guise the notion that New Zealand leads the world often promotes a healthy spirit of innovation and experimentalism. Under its worst forms it can degenerate into smugness and complacency, the national delusion of the self-satisfied.

The events of the recent war, however, have realigned the problem of New Zealand's external relations in a new perspective. In the first World War, New Zealand troops fought gallantly in the Middle East and in western Europe, but the Dominion itself was not threatened because Britain and Japan were allies. From 1941 to 1943 invasion of New Zealand by an empire situated within the Pacific was an imminent probability. At the hour of greatest danger the Dominion's best forces, few in number but first rate in quality, were in North Africa. Britain, which had carried on the struggle virtually single-handed until June, 1941, was hard pressed in every theater and could do little that was really effective in the Pacific. So the defense of New Zealand, as of Australia, depended on the United States, and it was to the American forces which won the victories in the battles of the Coral and Bismarck seas and in the campaign of the Solomons that New Zealand owed its salvation. The subsequent course of military affairs has made of the United States the preponderant power in the central and southern Pacific. To this inescapable fact, therefore, New Zealand must reorient its policy and its psychology.

The postwar world finds the Dominion no less in need of protection than it was before, since if it is determined to remain small, it must pay the price of continual vulnerability. The evolution of technique from the stone age to bronze, from bronze to iron, from iron to electricity, and from electricity to our own air-atomic era, places a small people at an even greater disadvantage. Hence New Zealand policy since 1944 has been directed

7. See A. E. C. Hare, *Industrial Relations in New Zealand* (Wellington: Whitcombe & Tombs, 1946), for a convincing account of this theme as it applies to industrial relations.

toward building against a future war all possible bulwarks except large-scale immigration. As its outermost line of defense, it has enthusiastically contributed to the foundation of the United Nations, wherein it has stood out as a vocal champion of the small-state viewpoint and opponent of the big power veto. Simultaneously New Zealand has been extending its diplomatic relations and making closer contact with other countries. In 1946 there were stationed in Wellington the ministers of France, of the United States, and the U.S.S.R.; there were high commissioners of the United Kingdom, Australia, and Canada; and there were consular representatives of many other states. The Canberra Pact, concluded between the Australian and New Zealand governments in January, 1944, symbolized a new era of neighborliness between the Anzac dominions. Toward the mother-country the traditional emotions have persisted without abatement. Despite its inability to give direct aid to New Zealand in 1942, Britain has retained an enormous reserve of good will which is augmented by its continued willingness to purchase the bulk of the Dominion's exports and to supply a wide range of imports. So potent are these links that New Zealand waited until the end of 1947 to adopt the Statute of Westminster and so emancipate its General Assembly from the controls of the Colonial Laws Validity Act of 1865. Although the government announced in 1944 its intention of adopting the Statute, it hesitated for three years to invoke the public opposition which the National party were prepared to offer.

Because of the strongly surviving bond with Britain, New Zealand faces two ways in its relations with the United States. It cannot ignore the implications of American power in the Pacific, and it is now more receptive than ever before to American cultural influences. It is anxious for the friendship of the United States, would be greatly alarmed at a recrudescence of American isolationism, and looks to America to help it maintain its precarious position on the fringe of southeastern Asia. But its accord with the United States cannot be wholehearted when trade relations are on their present basis. While Britain buys so much of the Dominion's produce, and while the Ottawa system and the American tariff discriminate against each other, it is difficult for New Zealand to establish firmer economic ties with its mighty trans-Pacific neighbor. This stumbling block, combined with the pro-British loyalty, served illogically enough to delay New Zealand's participation in the international monetary fund and bank founded at Bretton Woods.[8]

For the future, one may hazard the guess that New Zealand will attempt not only to keep in good repair its life-line to Britain but also to strengthen a second and shorter one to America. Nor is it either unlikely or impossible that its position vis-à-vis the two greatest English-speaking nations will come to approximate more closely to that of Canada. This policy could be entirely practicable; that is, on the assumption that the United States and the United Kingdom themselves co-operate harmoniously. Only if a major rift were to disrupt the concord between these powers, would New Zealand, as well as Australia and Canada, be confronted with the dilemma of a painful choice.

Finally, it is necessary to ask to what extent the conclusions reached in this study of politics in New Zealand hold good for New Zealand only or are capable of receiving a wider reference. Is it safe to generalize from the experience of the Dominion and argue that, if such have been the results of attempting to blend democracy and socialism, then similar consequences can be expected from any repetition of the attempt made anywhere else? Can one, that is to say, hold up New Zealand, according to one's point of view, either as a horrible warning to avoid or as a successful paradise to emulate?

My answer to these questions would be that the trend of events in even a small country has a value for comparative study and certainly should not be ignored. But I would add the caution that the lessons of New Zealand supply merely hypotheses that require further testing in other environments and not definitive short cuts to a speculative millennium. It is true that New Zealand has long experimented and continues to experiment with new devices for fusing politics and economics. But to isolate the

8. Up to the end of 1947 New Zealand had still not ratified the Bretton Woods agreements, even though Britain did so in 1945.

causes and effects within a unified whole as complex as a modern community defies any analytical process yet known to social science. Democracy and socialism, it must not be forgotten, operate in New Zealand within the content of smallness, isolation, cultural homogeneity, and a primarily agrarian economy. All these factors interact both upon one another and upon those factors about which we seek information. Some of the praiseworthy and some of the undesirable features of New Zealand are manifestly connected with these special characteristics of the environment and cannot be accurately regarded as the consequence solely of democracy's mingling with socialism. Legislative measures identical with those of New Zealand would not necessarily give rise to identical results if enacted in another country of larger size, with a more diversified economy and population, and with a different system of administration.

This much, however, can be stated with certainty. There is a fundamental truth in the point observed long ago by Plato that a movement of excess in one direction tends to set up a counter-action in the opposite direction. Nor does one have to subscribe to all the implications of a dialectical theory to admit the obviously valid contention that history does exhibit many an alternation of thesis and antithesis. Thus has it ever been with the ideals that men hold up before them as lamps to light their way. Liberties are good when rightly used; harmful, when abused. Reaction against the ill effects of liberties misapplied can stimulate a countertendency in favor of some other goal such as equality. This in turn can be overdone and call for the requisite correction. It is the task of the social philosopher to formulate in terms of abstract principle the basis on which our governing ideals can interpenetrate each other in the right proportions. No less is it the duty and the art of statesmanship to produce in practice a workable balance. New Zealand is a case in point to show that a regime of privilege and inequality, such as existed up to 1890, can be socially undesirable and that the equalitarianism which has since emerged can itself be pushed too far.

In conclusion one may express the hope that a country still young, still underdeveloped, still awaiting its full growth and maturity, will go boldly forward to what could well be a distinguished future. Let New Zealand continue to build on those foundations that are well and truly laid—on its hatred of privilege, its passion for social justice, and its eradication of poverty. Let it eradicate all remediable flaws—its chronic smallness, restraint upon talent, and pressure to conform—that stunt and stifle its expansion. Rededicated to the cause of mankind's social betterment, let this democracy of the South Pacific take for its guide the words of Delphi's oracle: "Know thyself!"

CHRONOLOGICAL TABLE

CHRONOLOGICAL TABLE

1642 Dutch navigator, Tasman, discovers New Zealand.

1769 Rediscovery by Captain Cook.

1840 Sovereignty over New Zealand conferred on Queen Victoria by Treaty of Waitangi. Settlements inaugurated by New Zealand Company.

1852 British Parliament passes Constitution Act instituting federalism and representative government.

1856 Appointment of first ministries (those of Sewell, Fox, and Stafford) responsible to the New Zealand legislature.

1860 Commencement of Maori wars.

1861 Gold found in Otago. Fox ministry formed.

1862 New ministry under Domett. State telegraph service commenced.

1863 Whitaker-Fox coalition ministry. Control of native affairs transferred from governor to ministers.

1864 Weld ministry established.

1865 Capital of Colony shifted from Auckland to Wellington. Post Office Savings Bank authorized. Second Stafford ministry takes office.

1867 Four seats in House of Representatives assigned to Maoris.

1869 Third Fox ministry formed. Government enters life insurance business.

1870 Vogel initiates policies of public works and assists immigration. Ending of Maori wars. New Zealand University Act passed.

1872 Establishment of Public Trust Office.

1873 Vogel becomes premier.

1875 Abolition of Provinces Act confirmed by results of general election.

1876 New Zealand becomes a unitary state. Atkinson ministry formed. Counties Act and Municipal Corporations Act provide for local government.

1877 National policy of free, compulsory, and secular education in schools adopted. Grey heads Liberal ministry.

1879 Adult male suffrage introduced. Hall forms Conservative government.

1881 Adoption of country quota, giving electoral bonus to rural population.

1882 Frozen meat successfully shipped to Britain.

1884 Stout ministry takes office after general election returns Liberal majority.

1886–90 Emigration from New Zealand due to economic depression.

1887 Conservatives return to power under Atkinson.

1889 Plural voting abolished.

1890 Major maritime strike defeated. Conservatives beaten in general election.

1891 Liberal ministry led by Ballance sponsors social legislation.

1892 Landowners attacked by legislation directed against large estates. Conflicts between House of Representatives and Legislative Council, between ministry and governor. Colonial Office backs ministry's request to appoint more councilors.

1893 Seddon chosen premier after death of Ballance. Franchise granted to women. Liberals win general election.

507

1894 Laws enacted for conciliation and compulsory arbitration of labor disputes and for state loans to settlers.

1896 Liberals retain office after election but with smaller majority.

1898 Old age pensions, on noncontributory basis, enacted despite opposition stone wall.

1899 First New Zealand contingent sent to South African war. Liberals win election.

1902 Liberals re-elected. First Labor candidatures.

1903 State enters business of fire insurance.

1904 Visit of André Siegfried, collecting material for *Democracy in New Zealand*.

1905 Liberal majority confirmed at election.

1906 Death of Seddon after serving thirteen years as premier. Succeeded by Ward.

1907 New Zealand's status changes from Colony to Dominion.

1908 Second ballot system introduced. Liberals favored at polls.

1911 Pensions granted to widows. General election ends Liberal predominance. European population passes one million mark.

1912 Fall of Liberal government after twenty-one years in office. Reform party cabinet takes office under Massey. Report of Hunt Commission on the Public Service. Legislation establishes central personnel agency. Visit of James Bryce, gathering data for *Modern Democracies*.

1913 Serious maritime strikes. Repeal of Second Ballot Act.

1914 New Zealand joins in World War I. Election confirms Reform party in office.

1915 New Zealand soldiers land at Gallipoli on Anzac Day (April 25). Coalition government created.

1919 New Zealand represented at Versailles Conference and signs treaty. Coalition dissolved. General election leaves Reform party in power, weakens Liberals, strengthens Labor.

1920 Mandate over Western Samoa conferred on Dominion by League of Nations.

1921–22 Postwar slump.

1922 General election leaves Reform party precariously in office.

1925 Death of Massey, continuously premier since 1912. Succeeded by Coates, who obtains decisive majority at election. Labor becomes the official opposition.

1926 Family allowances enacted.

1928 Election produces three-party deadlock. United (Liberal) party under Ward takes office with Labor support.

1930–35 Economic depression causes emigration from Dominion.

1931 British Parliament enacts Statute of Westminster. Coalition of United and Reform parties wins general election.

1933 Devaluation of New Zealand pound.

1935 Labor party wins general election and takes office under Savage.

1938 Passage of Social Security Act. Labor re-elected.

1939 New Zealand, first of the Dominions, declares war on Germany.

1940 Fraser becomes prime minister on death of Savage.

1941 New Zealand at war with Japan.

1943   General election confirms Labor government in office but with reduced majority.

1944   Canberra Pact between New Zealand and Australian governments.

1945   End of war against Germany and Japan. New Zealand ratifies United Nations Charter. Nationalization of Bank of New Zealand, linen-flax processing industry, and civil railways. Family allowances granted without means test. Country quota in electoral apportionment abolished.

1946   At general election, in which 95 per cent of electorate votes, Labor and National parties each secures thirty-eight of seventy-six European constituencies. Labor cabinet stays in office with aid of four Maori seats.

1947   Parliament adopts Statute of Westminster.

BIBLIOGRAPHY

BIBLIOGRAPHY

PUBLIC DOCUMENTS

Parliamentary Debates, series beginning in 1854

Appendixes to the *Journal of the House of Representatives*, containing official correspondence with other governments, reports and returns submitted to Parliament, etc. Especially useful are the following:

"Annual Reports of the Public Service Commissioner"

"Annual Reports of the Controller and Auditor General"

"Reports of the Civil Service Commission, 1866"

"Reports of the Civil Service Commission, 1880"

"Report of the (Hunt) Commission on the Public Service, 1912"

"Report of the (Smith) Commission on Native Affairs, 1934"

"Reports of the Representation Commission"

"Reports of the Chief Electoral Officer"

BOOKS

ALPERS, OSCAR. *Cheerful Yesterdays.* Wellington: Whitcombe & Tombs, 1930.

BAGEHOT, WALTER. *The English Constitution.* "World's Classics," No. CCCXXX. London: Oxford University Press, 1928.

BEAGLEHOLE, J. C. *New Zealand: A Short History.* London: Allen & Unwin, 1936.

———. *The Discovery of New Zealand.* Wellington: Whitcombe & Tombs, 1940.

BEAGLEHOLE, J. C.; LIPSON, LESLIE; McGECHAN, R. O.; and WOOD, F. L. W. *New Zealand and the Statute of Westminster.* Wellington: Whitcombe & Tombs, 1944.

BRYCE, JAMES. *Modern Democracies*, Vol. II, chaps. 53–57. New York: Macmillan Co., 1921.

COKER, FRANCIS W. *Recent Political Theory.* New York: Appleton-Century Co., 1924.

COLLIER, J. *Life of Sir George Grey.* Wellington: Whitcombe & Tombs, 1909.

CONDLIFFE, J. B. *New Zealand in the Making.* London: Allen & Unwin; Chicago: University of Chicago Press, 1930.

DRUMMOND, J. *The Life and Work of Richard John Seddon.* Wellington: Whitcombe & Tombs, 1907.

EVATT, H. V. *The King and His Dominion Governors.* London: Oxford University Press, 1936.

FINER, HERMAN. *The British Civil Service.* London: Allen & Unwin, 1937.

GAUS, JOHN M.; WHITE, LEONARD D.; and DIMOCK, MARSHALL E. *The Frontiers of Public Administration.* Chicago: University of Chicago Press, 1936.

GREAVES, H. R. G. *The British Constitution.* London: Allen & Unwin, 1938.

HARE, A. E. C. *Industrial Relations in New Zealand.* Wellington: Whitcombe & Tombs, 1946.

HAYEK, FRIEDRICH A. *The Road to Serfdom.* Chicago: University of Chicago Press, 1944.

JENNINGS, W. IVOR. *Cabinet Government.* London: Cambridge University Press, 1938.

KEY, V. O., JR. *Politics, Parties and Pressure Groups.* New York: Thomas Y. Crowell & Co., 1942.

LASKI, H. J. *The American Presidency.* London: Allen & Unwin, 1940.

———. *Democracy in Crisis.* Chapel Hill: University of North Carolina Press, 1933.

———. *Parliamentary Government in England.* New York: Viking Press, 1938.

———. *Reflections on the Revolution of Our Time.* New York: Viking Press, 1943.

LE ROSSIGNOL, J. E., and STEWART, W. D. *State Socialism in New Zealand.* London: Harrap & Co., 1912.

LOUGHNAN, R. A. *Biography of Sir Joseph Ward.* Sydney, N.S.W.: New Century Press, 1929.

McBAIN, H. L. *The Living Constitution.* New York: Macmillan Co., 1927.

MERRIAM, CHARLES E., and GOSNELL, HAROLD F. *Non-voting: Causes and Methods of Control.* Chicago: University of Chicago Press, 1924.

MÉTIN, ALBERT. *Le Socialisme sans doctrines.* 2d ed. Paris: Félix Alcan, 1910.

MORRELL, W. P. *The Provincial System in New Zealand.* London: Longman's, 1933.

———. *New Zealand.* London: Ernest Benn, Ltd., 1935.

MUIR, RAMSAY. *How Britain Is Governed.* London: Constable & Co., 1933.

NASH, WALTER. *New Zealand: A Working Democracy.* London: J. M. Dent, 1944.

RAPPARD, W. E. *The Crisis of Democracy.* Chicago: University of Chicago Press, 1933.

REEVES, WILLIAM P. *State Experiments in Australia and New Zealand.* 2 vols. London: Allen & Unwin, 1902.

REEVES, W. P., and WRAY, C. J. *The Long White Cloud.* 3d ed. London: Allen & Unwin, 1924.

SAUNDERS, ALFRED. *History of New Zealand.* 2 vols. Wellington: Whitcombe & Tombs, 1896.

SIEGFRIED, ANDRÉ. *Democracy in New Zealand.* Translated by E. V. BURNS and with Introduction by W. D. STEWART. London: Bell & Sons, 1914.

SIMON, E. D. *The Smaller Democracies.* London: Left Book Club [Gollancz], 1939,

SOMERSET, H. C. D. *Littledene.* Wellington: Council for Educational Research. 1938.

STEWART, W. D. *Sir Francis H. D. Bell: His Life and Times.* Wellington: Butterworth & Co., 1937.

———. *William Rolleston.* Wellington: Whitcombe & Tombs, 1941.

SUTCH, W. B. *Poverty and Progress in New Zealand.* Wellington: Co-operative Publishing Co., 1941.

TAWNEY, R. H. *Religion and the Rise of Capitalism.* Rev. ed. London: J. Murray, 1937.

WEBB, LEICESTER C. *Government in New Zealand.* Wellington: Department of Internal Affairs, 1940.

WHITE, LEONARD D. *Introduction to the Study of Public Administration.* 2d ed. New York: Macmillan Co., 1939.

WOOD, F. L. W. *New Zealand in the World.* Wellington: Department of Internal Affairs, 1940.

INDEX

INDEX

Alpers, Oscar, 22–23
Aristotle, 7
Atkinson, Harry Albert, 32, 63–72, 75–78, 80, 82–84, 87, 90, 98–100, 105–7, 109, 112–14, 117, 126, 129, 131, 133–35, 137, 143, 147, 199, 217, 254–55, 274–75, 356, 374
Australia, 1–4, 6, 10–11, 18, 85, 135, 152, 192, 199, 213, 274, 289, 299, 337, 352, 362, 413, 421, 434, 442, 446, 450, 475, 487, 495–97, 499–501

Bagehot, Walter, 22, 73, 280, 310, 350
Balfour, Lord, 4
Ballance, John, 24, 65, 70, 72, 80, 105, 129, 137, 169, 203, 254–56, 261–62, 268, 275, 286–88, 293–98, 301, 356
Beaglehole, J. C., 15, 215
Bell, Francis Dillon (the father), 200
Bell, Francis Henry Dillon (the son), 200, 228–29, 254, 256, 261–62, 266, 269–70, 275, 279, 287–88, 290–93, 295, 306–8, 311, 329, 359–60, 373, 424
Bentham, Jeremy, 174
Beveridge, William, 232
Britain, 2, 4–6, 10–11, 21–23, 72–74, 85–86, 92, 95, 105, 109, 139–40, 144–45, 148, 154, 162, 170, 172, 192, 197, 213, 219–20, 223, 226, 234, 242–43, 246–47, 262–63, 267–69, 274, 280–81, 287–89, 296, 308, 315–16, 320, 324, 326, 333, 338, 352, 354, 357, 363, 370, 377, 401, 403, 412–13, 420–21, 434, 442–43, 446, 450, 456–57, 475–78, 486–87, 494, 496–501
Bryce, James, 195, 243, 363, 365

Cabinet, the: changes in personnel of, 75–81, 255–58; collective responsibility of, 36–37, 85–89, 261–67; composition of, 89–94, 193–258, 271–79; duration in office of, 74–75, 253–55; functions of, 96, 154, 279–84; legislative councilors as members of, 91–94, 269–71; organization of, 378–89; relation of, to House of Representatives, 81–85, 258–60, 262, 328–50; size of, 94–96, 267
Canada, 4, 6, 10–11, 17, 135, 230, 274, 304, 413, 434, 497, 501
Civil service, the: central personnel agency of, 153–54, 374, 418, 428, 434–48, 474–76; classification of, 152–56, 162, 427–29, 448–51; commission of 1866, 150–54; commission of 1880,

156–59; commission of 1912, 371–72, 426–31, 433–35, 454; education of, 430–32, 451–61, 469–70, 486–87; patronage in, 158–59, 161, 303–4, 422–27; in the Police Department, 436–37, 470–71, 473–76; in the Post and Telegraph Department, 435–37, 468–70, 473–74; promotions in, 464–68; in the Railways Department, 436–37, 468–70, 472–74; recruitment to, 153–56, 159–61, 422–27, 430, 450–55, 476–78; reporting in, 463–65; training of, 430–32, 461–63; salaries of, 152–53, 157–59, 161–62, 220, 229, 448–50, 474; size of, 152, 157–58, 161, 368–69, 432, 437
Coates, Joseph Gordon, 221, 244, 254, 256–57, 261, 263, 287–88, 290, 293–96, 307–9, 311, 331, 374, 392
Coker, Francis W., 219
Colonial Office, the, 16–17, 47, 63, 99, 105, 139, 357, 420
Condliffe, J. B., 46, 72, 210, 275–76, 296, 363, 424, 498
Conservative party, the, 23, 32–33, 37–38, 41–43, 57–72, 76–77, 83, 91, 113, 123, 125, 130–31, 135, 141–42, 169, 186, 200–201, 203–9, 211, 216–17, 233, 244, 340–42, 356–58
Controller and auditor-general, the, 326–27, 389, 442–43, 479
Cook, James, 15
Cripps, Stafford, 249

Davidson, J. M., 404
Departments: control of, by the cabinet, 378–89; number of, 143–44, 147, 371–73, 375–76; overhead organization of, 373–75, 395, 409–10; reorganization of, 371–75, 381–420
Dewey, John, 143, 251–52
Dickens, Charles, 38
Dimock, Marshall E., 370, 384, 485
Disraeli, Benjamin, 23, 63, 85, 105, 108–9, 127, 240, 273
Domett, Alfred, 20–21, 50, 54, 79, 90, 95, 99–101, 117
Drummond, J., 201, 212, 234, 298–99, 422
Durham, Lord, 16–17

Education, 99, 128–29, 147, 150–51, 292, 373, 407–10, 430–32, 436–37, 449, 471–73
Electoral system, the: expense of, 38–43,

517